Authority and society in Nantes during the French wars of religion, 1559–98

MANCHESTER
1824

Manchester University Press

STUDIES IN EARLY MODERN
EUROPEAN HISTORY

This series aims to publish
challenging and innovative research in all areas
of early modern continental history.
The editors are committed to encouraging work
that engages with current historiographical
debates, adopts an interdisciplinary
approach, or makes an original contribution
to our understanding of the period.

SERIES EDITORS
Joseph Bergin, William G. Naphy, Penny Roberts
and Paolo Rossi

Authority and society in Nantes during the French wars of religion, 1559–98

ELIZABETH C. TINGLE

Manchester University Press

Manchester and New York

distributed exclusively in the USA by Palgrave

Published by Manchester University Press
Oxford Road, Manchester M13 9NR, UK
and Room 400, 175 Fifth Avenue, New York, NY10010, USA
www.manchesteruniversitypress.co.uk

Distributed exclusively in the USA by
Palgrave, 175 Fifth Avenue, New York,
NY10010, USA

Distributed exclusively in Canada by
UBC Press, University of British Columbia, 2029 West Mall,
Vancouver, BC, Canada V6T 1Z2

British Library Cataloguing-in-Publication Data
A catalogue record is available from the British Library

Library of Congress Cataloging-in-Publication Data applied for

ISBN 0 7190 6726 X *hardback*
EAN 978 0 7190 6726 6

First published 2006

15 14 13 12 11 10 09 08 07 06   10 9 8 7 6 5 4 3 2 1

Typeset in Monotype Perpetua with Albertus
by Northern Phototypesetting Co Ltd, Bolton
Printed in Great Britain
by Bell & Bain Ltd, Glasgow

For Mog, Katie and William

Contents

List of figures and tables

Figures

Tables

Acknowledgements

This book grew out of a chance encounter with a taxation register in the Archives Municipales of Nantes during the early weeks of 1997. The city had a lasting impression on me. Unusually for the west of France, the snow lay thick on the ground, the Loire had half-frozen over and ice floes were making their way downstream, to the Bay of Biscay. It was more like the St Lawrence at Quebec than temperate Brittany. The cold weather did not last, but the question remained of why the taxation register had been drawn up, by whom and for what purpose. This enquiry led me into the wars of religion.

Research for the book would not have been possible without the kind and professional help of the archivists and librarians of Nantes. I owe a special debt of gratitude to the staff of the Archives Municipales of Nantes and of the Archives Départementales of Loire-Atlantique, where the majority of research for the book took place. Thanks must also be given to the librarians of the Médiathèque of Nantes and to the curators of the Musée Dobrée for allowing access to the museum's rare books collection.

Colleagues in the History Division of University College, Northampton, deserve many thanks. The division supported several periods of sabbatical leave, and the School of Social Sciences generously provided research expenses for travel to France. The librarians of University College, Northampton, have provided much support in finding British-based sources. Away from Northampton, the colloquies of the European Reformation Research Group have been invaluable as a source of inspiration and advice. Thanks are also due to the readers and editors of Manchester University Press for their help with this work.

Special thanks must be given to two groups of people, with whom Brittany will always be associated in my mind. Wendy Davies and Grenville Astill first introduced me to Brittany when I was an undergraduate, during fieldwork on the East Brittany Survey. It was during one of the many associated field trips to the Redon region that I met my husband, Mog. He has patiently supported my work and travelled often to southern Brittany, in latter years along with our children Katie and William. Their support has been vital to the completion of this book.

Elizabeth Tingle, Creaton

List of abbreviations

A.B.	*Annales de Bretagne et de pays de l'Ouest*
A.D.L.A.	Archives Départementales de la Loire-Atlantique
A.E.S.C.	*Annales, Économie, Société, Civilisations*
A.M.N.	Archives Municipales de Nantes
B.A.A.B.	*Bulletin archéologique de l'Association Bretonne*
B.N.F.F.	Bibliothèque Nationale de France. Fonds français
B.S.H.P.F.	*Bulletin de la Société de l'Histoire du Protestantisme Français*
B.S.A.H.N.L.I.	*Bulletin de la Société Archéologique et Historique de Nantes et la Loire-Inférieure*
B.S.A.I.V.	*Bulletin de la Société Archéologique d'Ille-et-Vilaine*
F.H.	*French History*
F.H.S.	*French Historical Studies*
J.M.H.	*Journal of Modern History*
Morice	H. Morice, *Mémoires pour servir des preuves à l'histoire ecclésiastique et civile de Bretagne*, 3 vols (1742–46).
Morice & Taillandier	H. Morice and C. Taillandier, *Histoire ecclésiastique et civile de Bretagne*, 3 vols (1756; reprinted 1974)
R.H.	*Revue historique*
S.C.J.	*Sixteenth-Century Journal*
Travers	L'Abbé Travers, *Histoire civile, politique et réligieuse de la ville de Nantes*, 3 vols (written c.1750; Nantes, 1837).

Place of publication is Paris unless otherwise stated.

1

Introduction: authority and society in sixteenth-century Nantes

At 6 o'clock on the evening of 13 April 1598, Henry IV rode through the Saint-Pierre gate into Nantes. There was no formal royal entry. Henry entered not as a guest but as a general, for after ten years of rebellion, Nantes was the final Catholic League city to capitulate to the crown. The king and his bodyguard passed straight into the old ducal château, where the cathedral chapter and the municipality came to pay their respects. Shops were ordered to be closed and the inhabitants warned not to fire their arquebuses.[1] Two weeks later, the king issued the famous edict of toleration for the Protestants of France that allowed them legal rights of worship and coexistence in the state. Nantes would henceforth be associated with the religious freedom of Huguenots and to be remembered as the place where the French wars of religion came to an end.

The aim of this study is to explore the city context of these events, the motives for Nantes' participation in the religious wars and for its revolt against the crown in 1589, and why the Catholic League rebellion lasted longer here than in any other town. This is not a simple narrative of Nantes' experiences of the religious wars. The central focus is on authority, its theoretical construction, its institutional embodiment, its reception and negotiation, and changes within these over time. During the religious wars the understanding and exercise of many different levels of authority came under close scrutiny by contemporaries, and the nature and legitimacy of authority were questioned. This book offers a study of city governance in a period of pressure and change. It combines examination of the changing relationship of the city government and the royal state with analysis of the experience of authority within the urban community.

For historians of the late nineteenth and early twentieth centuries, such as Lucien Romier and H.-J. Mariéjol, the French wars of religion were primarily political in causation and perpetuation. At their heart lay struggles between factions of great aristocratic families, and their conflicts with the crown. The Bourbons, Montmorencies and Guises used religion as a cloak to

disguise their essential purpose, which was to control more closely the king and
the state. Conflict arose after the death of Henry II in 1559 left the monarchy
weakened by the accession of two boy kings and a female regency under
Catherine de' Medici.[2] The wars ended when a party of *politiques* or moderates,
for whom the unity of the state was more important than religious conflict, cast
aside confessional differences and turned to Henry IV to restore peace and
order.[3] Provincial and urban societies such as Nantes had little part to play in
this 'top down', centrist approach to the civil wars.

In the first half of the twentieth century, there was a reaction against the
history of great men and political events, particularly associated with the
Annales school of historians, which was influenced by Marxism and struc-
turalism. They privileged social and economic explanations of religious conflict
and war. Historians such as Henri Hauser and Lucien Febvre interpreted
Protestantism as the ideological refuge of merchants, lawyers and artisans.
Civil conflict was part of their struggle against the social and political dominance of the feudal land-holding nobility and church.[4] From the 1950s onwards
in Anglo-Saxon scholarship, there was a growing interest in the Protestant
movement and politics, with works such as those by Robert Kingdon and
Nicola Sutherland.[5] Out of an intellectual concern with 'history from below',
and a growing interest in the sociological and anthropological methodologies
of Émile Durkheim's followers, historians such as Emmanuel Leroy Ladurie,
Natalie Davis, Richard Gascon and Janine Estèbe turned to socio-cultural
examinations of sixteenth-century society. They interpreted the religious wars
as part of a profound social and cultural crisis affecting all French social
groups.[6] Since the 1980s, a new orthodoxy has emerged, arguing that the wars
were 'a conflict fought primarily over the issue of religion . . . [which] was . . .
the fulcrum upon which the civil wars balanced', with religion defined as a
community of believers rather than a body of beliefs.[7] Above all, in his seminal
work on religious culture, Denis Crouzet has argued for the centrality of religion to the conflicts that took place after 1560, to the exclusion of other
factors.[8]

Penny Roberts has observed that changing perspectives on the nature and
causes of the French civil wars arose from a shift in historians' interests, away
from central government to the provinces and to local experiences of events.[9]
Jean-Marie Constant has identified three issues particularly favoured by
historians writing at the turn of the twentieth and twenty-first centuries: firstly,
the study of social groups and communities, particularly the nobility; secondly,
the history of social relations, networks, forms of sociability and clientage; and
thirdly, city life and government, the relationships between different urban
social groups and their relations with the countryside, nobility and crown.[10]
Above all, the study of cities has provided a fuller understanding of how relig-

ious change and civil conflict affected the lives and experiences of ordinary people. Although only 15 per cent of the French population lived in urban communities in the sixteenth century, towns were 'the centre of social relations, power, wealth, a more supervised and civilised world than the countryside'.[11] They were nodal points of religious and political culture. Their importance in the realm was marked by a constant symbolic interchange between kings and urban elites, through patronage and formal royal entries.[12] P. Benedict's work on Rouen, N. Davis on Lyon, W. Kaiser on Marseille, R. Descimon and B. Diefendorf on Paris for example, have shown that religious change and divisions affected townspeople and led to strife, independent of the actions of the royal government.[13] Similarly, political activity was not confined to the king and noble elites but took place in all communities.[14] Annette Finley-Croswhite has even argued that the French religious wars were in large part an urban conflict and ended when Henry IV reopened 'the dialogue between crown and the towns, enhancing his authority and the power of the crown in the process'.[15]

What has emerged from local urban studies is the interdependence of political, social and religious factors in causing and defining the course of the religious wars: that all communities were affected by a complex interplay of local and 'national' issues and events.[16] Despite this, Stuart Carroll observes that the political history of the French civil wars has been unfashionable. While religion has received much attention, the study of political culture is less advanced, yet their inter-relatedness is clear: 'religious divisions of the sixteenth century permeated all levels of society and introduced an ideological element to politics. During the civil wars, religion and politics, both at court and in the localities, became inter-twined.'[17] A number of doctoral students have begun to rectify this with studies of regional politics, such as the work of R. Souriac on the Comminges region, Tim Watson on Lyon and Philip Conner on Montauban.[18]

This study of Nantes is about the impact of the religious wars on the exercise and understanding of authority in the city, principally that of the municipal government. Five questions have framed the work. Firstly, what impact did religious change in the form of the growth of Protestantism have upon the urban community of Nantes, particularly with regard to conceptions and acceptance of authority within the city, and how were the new problems resolved? The emergence of the new religion led to disorder, which made day-to-day administration more difficult for the urban authorities, while royal religious policy strained the city government's relations with the crown. The resolution of these tensions forms the core of the first half of this work. Secondly, what was the impact of confessional change and conflict upon the religious and cultural life of the majority of Nantes' inhabitants, particularly the practice of Catholicism? Changes within the institutional church and devotional practices were marked

features of the years after 1560. The rebuilding of Catholic authority and identity during the wars of religion had a great impact on urban politics during these
years. Thirdly, under scrutiny is the impact of conflict upon the relationship
between the crown and Nantes' city government. Problems of royal authority
after 1560 led to changes in the constitutional and institutional relationship
between the city and the king, which were responsible for the creation of a
formal municipality in Nantes in 1565 and for the rebellion of the city against
Henry III in 1589. A fourth question is that of the impact of religious and political change upon relations between elites and popular groups within Nantes,
particularly the poor. Finally, the importance of regional identity will be
assessed. Nantes was the largest city of Brittany, until 1532 a separate duchy
within the French kingdom. Nantes' inhabitants were proud of their provincial
identity and privileges. Here, the tensions between provincial particularism and
central power in the later sixteenth century are examined. Comparisons with
other cities of northern France are also made, for it is essential to ask whether
Nantes' experiences were typical, whether there was a separate 'history' of
western and middling-rank urban communities for this period, or the experiences of the wars of religion were common to all.

The main research basis for the study of Nantes is the surviving archive of
the city government. The registers of the deliberations of the city council are
almost complete for the period 1554 to 1598, with the exception of the years
of the Catholic League administration. Records of the city's treasurer, the
bourgeois militia and those concerned with security of the city are also rich if
not complete.[19] Less full are the sources for religion, social and cultural life.
Nantes was badly damaged by Allied bombing in 1943 and 1944, during which
the city's notarial records and the archive of the cathedral and chapter were
largely destroyed. However, Nantes benefited from voluminous works by
historians in the eighteenth and nineteenth centuries, notably the Abbé Travers
and Dom H. Morice, who summarised and reproduced many primary sources
which are now lost. Extensive use has been made of these studies and collections, in what has sometimes amounted to an 'archaeology' of the history of the
religious wars. Surviving evidence has determined the primacy given to municipal government and governance, and to the exercise of authority in the early
modern town.

Structures of authority and models of change:
crown, province and town in sixteenth-century France

Authority can be defined as 'legitimate or institutionalised power characterised
by the voluntary submission of the subject' in which the powerful holds an

acknowledged right to command, and the subject, an acknowledged obligation to obey.[20] Peter Blau argues that authority entails voluntary compliance, not coercion, for its exercise rests on social norms. However, it also rests on 'imperative control' because social norms and group sanctions exert pressure on individuals to obey the superior's directives; 'compliance is voluntary from the perspective of the collectivity of subordinates, but it is compulsory from the perspective of individual members'.[21] Dennis Wrong identifies five forms of authority: coercive, induced, legitimate, competent and personal. Above all, it is the institutionalisation of power that defines legitimate authority.[22]

Michel Foucault has observed that in western societies since the middle ages, royal power has provided the essential forms around which political and legal thought and legitimacy have been elaborated.[23] Long before Foucault's writings, studies of power relations in sixteenth-century France focused on the development of the monarchy over the period and its relationship with the social groups and provincial institutions of the realm, including towns. A broad outline chronology has been developed: the strengthening of royal authority under Francis I and Henry II, its decay during the religious wars when the theoretical and practical powers of the crown were undermined, and its restoration under Henry IV. When in 1519 Claude de Seyssel published *La monarchie de France*, he defined monarchical power as absolute.[24] The king's authority came directly from God and was exercised without institutional restriction, so long as the ruler concerned himself solely with matters of the royal prerogative. The monarch's sovereign rights and functions were the supreme administration of justice, the making of laws and ordinances, the regulation of religion and church life, military affairs and fealty of subjects, for he remained the kingdom's superior seigneur, supported by his vassals.[25] With regard to the government of the French provinces, the monarch was the source of all public authority exercised by others; his officers were part of the royal body and thus subject to him.[26] But in practice, the crown depended for its legitimacy and administration on a wide range of institutions. Authority was widely diffused throughout the realm: 'local government was still not seen as part of the state. It consisted of a number of sources of independent power with which it was possible for the state to form relationships'.[27] The customs, laws and privileges of each territory were recognised, and there was legal and administrative decentralisation.[28] This was necessary, for as Michel Nassiet stresses, France was too large to be administered effectively from the centre.[29]

In addition to limitations imposed by physical size, ideologically and constitutionally there was a contractual basis to the French kingdom. Royal power was exercised less in conformity with abstract principles than in accordance with specific conventions. The law was of paramount importance, for it provided a set of rules by which the king exercised his prerogative, which governed the monarch's relations with his subjects, and which they used with each other. The provinces were bound to the king by law and charter, subject to conditions and special customs which he had to respect.[30] The state was corporate in nature. The estates, parlements, courts of justice, urban governments and parishes were all legal bodies with rights defined in law; the crown used them as administrative and consultative organs, but they did not 'exist primarily for the convenience of government nor did they owe their power to it'.[31] Further, there were limits to the king's authority over his subjects: the religious life of the state; the king's obligation to uphold the law and the rights of his subjects, including customary law; the need to take counsel, and property rights, which made necessary consent for taxation. These limits were best expressed by Seyssel's 'bridles' of religion, justice and police: 'the whole polity was preserved by bonds of law and ties of mutual obligation and respect between ruler and people . . . the state rested upon reverence for law'.[32] Pierre Rebuffi claimed that it was more just for a prince to follow the wishes of all his friends than for him to see them follow the will of a single prince.[33] In Lyon, for example, the king was the source of the town council's authority and guarantor of the city's charter, but the inhabitants considered their community to have its own traditions and privileges which predated the monarchy, which the king was expected to respect.[34]

During the reigns of Francis I and Henry II, theorists began 'to argue in an increasingly aggressive style for the concentration of authority upon the king and atrophying of any institutional checks upon his role'.[35] Philippe Hamon argues that there was a growing movement of sacralisation of royal authority, with kings portrayed as God's exalted.[36] There was a new and absolutist style of legal and political thinking, based on Roman and canon law.[37] Guillaume Budé argued that royal authority 'lacked any limitations except eternal principles binding all men', and Charondas Le Caron, that the king was above the law, was supreme over civil law and had authority to give new laws to the people.[38] As for provincial groups and institutions, Robert Knecht has argued that the Renaissance kings subjected them to a more authoritarian style of government.[39] There was systematisation and expansion of the organs of central government. The financial administration was expanded; reform of justice was attempted in the 1530s, and in 1552 a new tier of courts, the présidiaux, was created. The first half of the century saw the widespread appointment of royal governors to all the provinces of France, which brought them under closer crown supervision. French was increasingly used as the language of administration, and was institutionalised in the ordinance of Villers-Cotterêts of 1539. Royal correspondence with provincial institutions expanded enormously, and there was great extension of royal council judgements and legislation to the regions of France.[40] Quentin Skinner argues that there was some neglect of the legal and representative institutions of the constitution, parlements and estates, as shown by the increasing tax burden, taken without consent, and sale of offices. This diluted the authority and social standing of members of provincial law and fiscal administrations while planting more royal officers in the localities.[41] Denis Richet argues that the most striking feature of sixteenth-century town government was its colonisation by venal royal officers, with their close dependence on central power.[42] Royal officers were socially, financially and politically dependent upon the monarchy. Their service extended beyond their technical functions to serve the prince in a wide range of capacities at the local level, thus extending his authority.[43]

But John Russell Major warns us that the extent of centralisation must not be exaggerated. The bureaucracy of the state remained small, communications were slow, and the forces of coercion were tiny.[44] While the kings might bully provincial institutions into compliance, they had to be seen to uphold the traditional order of the state. William Beik has shown the importance of alliance and cooperation between crown and provincial authorities in Languedoc in their search for status and effective authority.[45] Monarchs promoted local participation even when they sought to increase supervision and control.[46] Hamon argues that there was no conscious policy of centralisation and systematic integration in France. The majority of royal 'gains' in this period were not pre-meditated but were responses to particular crises.[47]

Traditional political accounts saw the advance of royal authority halted in the mid-century by the royal minorities and religious wars that followed the death of Henry II in 1559. Skinner has argued that the newly weakened position of the crown allowed a contemporary backlash against absolute monarchy, citing as evidence a resurgence of interest in the theory that sovereignty resided in the people and not the king alone.[48] This view emerged strongly at the Estates General held in 1560 and 1561. Jean Lange, speaker for the third estate at Orléans in 1560, stated that 'the encroachment of one portion upon the sphere and rights of another was a false profit which would eventually bring about the disruption of the state. The king, like any other member of the realm, should be content with his sphere, for if he sought to increase his grandeur at the expense of the people, there would eventually occur the destruction of king and people alike.'[49]

The loss of authority during the religious wars was seen to have had two main origins. First were the attacks on the legitimacy of monarchical rule by subjects discontent with royal religious policy. For example, the St Bartholomew's day massacres of 1572 prompted the Protestants of the Midi to promote alternative forms of authority in town, regional and military councils. Justification for resistance to the crown came from theorists who expanded ideas of popular sovereignty, such as François Hotman, who argued that the descendants of the Francs Gaullois who created the royal state retained the right to supervise policy through their representatives in the Estates General of the realm, and Théodore de Bèze, who gave emphasis to the role of 'inferior magistrates' in protecting the kingdom from tyrannical kings.[50] After the peace of Monsieur of 1576, Henry III's continued toleration of Protestantism led many Catholics to question his authority.[51] From 1584 and the advent of the Protestant Henry of Navarre as heir to the throne, Catholic militants adopted popular sovereignty as a justification for their revolt against the crown. The Catholic League 'sought to establish the supremacy of the people, vested in the Estates General, to depose a heretic king and to preserve the unity of faith'.[52]

Secondly, there was a quiet reappropriation of local autonomy by institutions which had come under closer royal tutelage in the first half of the century. For provincial and urban governments, the problems of war, disorder and fiscal difficulty prompted their elites to reject the increasing tutelage of French monarchs and reassert the independence they had in the later middle ages. For Robert Descimon, Bernard Chevalier and others, urban governments 'recreated the idea of the medieval commune by defending municipal privileges and ending crown infiltration of municipal administrations'.[53] Some groups demanded a greater role in central government as well. At Pontoise (1561) and Blois (1576) the deputies asked that the Estates General meet every two years.[54] In 1576 the Estates General wanted to appoint twelve deputies from each order to propose legislation.[55] They argued that it was the right of particular groups to enjoy special legal privileges, upheld in customary law, and that the law of any territory should be local, instituted by the people of that region. Legal privileges should be upheld by a king who was a judge and administrator, sworn to protect such laws. Taxation other than customary dues could be collected only with consent. A division of authority and mutual spheres of actions of the component parts of the state would ensure its harmonious existence.[56]

The traditional picture of the downward-spiralling effectiveness of royal authority during the religious wars has been modified by studies of local communities, particularly towns. Despite difficulties of practical government, there were developments in royal sovereign power in the later sixteenth century.[57] The period witnessed a continuing trend towards recognising the authority of the crown over legislation and the direct subjugation of all persons to the monarch through law.[58] James Collins argues that the shifting definition of sovereignty, away from judgement and towards legislation, strengthened the king and weakened the authority of independent jurisdictions such as those of seigneurs.[59] There was emphasis on positive legislation, applicable to all subjects, in the search for a solution to civil and religious strife. Michel de l'Hôpital, for example, stressed the authority of kings to give law to their subjects to control disorder.[60] Further, customary law came under closer royal supervision. The sixteen-century project to codify regional law and to improve the administration of justice brought closer scrutiny by royal officers and increasing crown intervention in its application. [61] The customal of Brittany, codified in the mid-century, was again reformed in the 1580s under the direction of the Rennes jurist Bertrand d'Argentré. Even in the midst of war, the crown attempted to reform the political nation. The effective work of royal commissioners in enforcing the edicts of pacification after 1562 has been shown in work by Penny Roberts and Olivier Christin. [62] The edicts of Moulins of 1566 and the reforms of Henry III in the later 1570s testify to reforming intentions, even if they were of limited success.

A view is also emerging of a closer coalition of crown and local authorities within towns, rather than a widening gap, at least before 1588. Laurent Bourquin argues that the religious wars should not be seen simply as a failure of central authority, for they permitted a search for new solutions for political problems. [63] Royal authority was used to bolster that of local bodies, which was seriously challenged by the religious wars. Barbara Diefendorf has argued that in Paris, religious conflict reduced the effectiveness of the municipal authorities. Popular rebellion provoked by economic problems, aggravated by religious and political unrest, threatened more frequently; turbulent crowds could easily escape the magistrates' control, and the Paris militia was unreliable. Over time, the magistrates emerged, hesitantly but firmly, 'as defenders of constituted authority. They were willing to enforce the king's edicts even when these . . . violated their Catholic beliefs, because they shared an even stronger belief in a legitimate and orderly state.' [64] Michel Cassan has reached similar conclusions for the reign of Charles IX in his work on towns in the Limousin. [65] Finley-Croswhite's study of Amiens has supported this, stating that 'the religious wars created many new opportunities for nobles, elites, townspeople and the king'. [66] Jotham Parsons argues for the resilience of royal authority and a huge reservoir of loyalty and obedience to the crown as the author of legislation and the common good. [67] The decline in royal authority and the fragmentation of the state in the 1580s and 1590s led to a desire for stronger kingship among many of France's provincial elites. In 1576, Jean Bodin rejected his earlier 'constitutionalist' position to argue for strong monarchy as the preserve of order and stability in the state. [68] The experience of war and disorder led ultimately to the victory of Henry IV, who 'restored the efficiency of government so that it was again responsive to the king's will'. [69]

Despite royal claims to a monopoly of authority in the French state, in practice there were other sites of power. Each of these was affected by the religious wars. The authority of religion was a primary force in sixteenth-century society, regulating the behaviour of individuals and legitimising the actions of secular authority. In mid-century France, Catholicism was the common matrix which bound society together. Christian theology and the ritual of the mass promoted a unified social identity of a single community in which man was reconciled to Christ and his neighbour through the eucharist and a belief in redemption.[70] Secular society had religious roots and goals: the right ordering of society and the state derived from religious truth. The advent of a new religious group, Protestantism, had a devastating impact on France, for it 'threatened the very bases on which civil society was built and the accustomed relationship that linked the individual to the collectivity and God'.[71] The presence of heresy in the community threatened judgement, damnation and God's ire in the material world. Confidence in the church itself was shaken; although anti-clericalism was nothing new, the ecclesiastical hierarchy was blamed for the spread of heresy because of abuses within the church. Toleration of heresy in the state undermined the authority of the king. If the monarch failed to exterminate heretics he was unworthy of his office and deserved to lose his crown. Further, once confessional conflict and war had broken out, disorder and disobedience materially affected the exercise of power. The secular authority of judicial officials and town councils was constrained by conflict and disorder. Local elites were limited in their actions by popular pressure, while disturbances could also bring outside intervention into city affairs from kings or magnates, who might ride roughshod over local privileges and be slow to leave.[72]

The personalisation of authority in the sixteenth century meant that bonds between individuals, particularly those of patronage and clientage, were the cement which held together state and society. Regional studies have uncovered the mechanisms of these relations, for example Robert Harding's work on royal governors, Jean-Marie Constant and Stuart Carroll on the Guise family, and above all Sharon Kettering's work.[73] The central elite, aristocrats and royal ministers, were maintained in their loyalty to the crown by gifts, offices, pensions and lands. In the parlements, law courts, estates and city administrations of the realm, royal clients were given favours, gifts and status in return for peaceful, cooperative and well-administered regions and towns. In turn, provincial and municipal elites had their own clients, with whom they worked to further mutual social and political interest. Finley-Croswhite argues that clientage conferred legitimacy on kings, ministers and others exercising government authority, for it 'humanised power by involving human agents in the struggle for consent' and 'often opened the dialogue that brings together ruler and ruled'.[74] In the traditional historiography of the religious wars, the conflicts caused a destitution of the patronage system, which contributed to the reduced authority of the monarchy. Nicolas Henshall blames the minorities of the 1560s for mismanagement of the political elite: the 'balance of faction at court was destroyed, patronage was misdirected and the Crown found itself with too little local influence to give a lead'.[75] Harding also has argued that royal power was weakened in the French provinces because of failure to provide sufficient patronage to the greater magnates and governors of the realm. In turn, their patronage powers and authority were also diminished.[76] Of equal importance for the undermining of royal authority, according to Carroll, was the devolution of patronage further into the hands of local elites, reducing the king's influence and adding to political instability, and these ideas have again been questioned by Finley-Croswhite.[77]

Patriarchy as a defining and all-embracing form of authority has also been of recent interest to historians. For most early modern Europeans, the household was the arena in which authority was exercised on a daily basis. For Bodin, 'the republic itself was but a legitimate association of families under a sovereign authority'.[78] Within the household, 'the patriarchal family was the microcosm of the well-ordered commonwealth' where the husband and father had natural and legal sovereignty over his wife and children.[79] Historians such as Natalie Davis and Martha Howell have argued for an extension of patriarchal authority in the sixteenth century, with an expansion of the legal powers of husbands over wives and children, and of masters over journeymen and servants. In 1556 and 1560 royal edicts were issued banning clandestine marriage and regulating second unions, and the ordinance of Blois of 1579 prescribed the death sentence for rape and seduction – that is, marriage without parental consent – and deprived widows of their marriage portions from their late husbands if they should marry their valets.[80] However, personal relations were again about negotiation. In many families, wives rather than husbands supervised servants, ran independent businesses and had powers of attorney over all affairs in their spouses' absences.[81] Widows acquired rights over legal affairs and property, although they would lose this status upon their remarriage. Neighbourhoods and communities possessed collective authority, and here the relations and disputes of everyday life were played out. The ideals of the community were quietness, charity, honesty and consensus, and communal pressure and gossip were important means of regulating behaviour and deviance. When community failed, because of heresy in its midst, social relations were strained and could break down.

Authority was also inherent in and perpetuated by signs and symbols. Cultural historians influenced by post-structuralist methodologies have stressed the significant relationship between power and language, whether in the form of speech, print, symbols or gestures, as in Ralph Giesey's work on royal ceremonies.[82] Symbols could have a limited audience, in the case of spectacles at court, paintings or medals struck for particular occasions, or they could be more widely disseminated, on coins, on public buildings and through civic and church ceremonials. David Potter argues that changes in understandings of authority can be traced through studies of staged, formal entries of kings into French cities. Early in the sixteenth century, such events focused on the city's achievements, where the bourgeois related the greatness of the town and explained, using biblical references, their expectations of king-ship. By the mid-century, pageantry focused more directly on the achievements of the king, using more classical themes.[83] Bourquin argues that Charles IX's 108 royal entries made during his royal tour of 1564–66, compared with his father's total of about thirty entries, were vital means of restoring the relation-ships between crown and civic elites damaged during the first religious war.[84] Urban authority was on display during civic rituals such as Corpus Christi, where the processions displayed and played out the social and political struc-ture of the city. In Nantes, a great procession travelled from the cathedral along the Grande rue to Saint-Nicolas church, returning via the church of Notre-Dame. The city's ecclesiastical and secular institutions marched behind the holy sacrament in hierarchical order while large numbers of spectators watched this symbolic statement of jurisdictions, powers and forces. Other civic celebra-tions also reinforced community solidarity through a shared experience of rituals and symbols: the Te Deum for royal births and military victories, annual pilgrimages and religious feasts. These reinforced the authority of urban elites by displaying the hierarchy of relationships within the community, encouraged amicable bonds between leading families, underscored the close relationship between secular government and religion, and impressed onlookers with the wealth, pomp and spectacle of the gowns and badges of office.

Finally, all studies of early modern societies show the limitations of authority. There was dissent against legally instituted bodies and decisions. A high level of violence, crime and vagabondage was endemic. Below the royal governors and parlements, France remained 'a lightly policed society in which violence and self-help were habitual'.[85] The constituted authorities could hope only to control a fraction of the trouble and to maintain local peace and order. In times of religious or economic tension, crowds could escalate out of control. Above all, what has emerged is a view that authority was not about imposition but about negotiation and exchange.

Structures of authority in mid-sixteenth-century Nantes

Foucault usefully reminded us that power relations in society are best under-stood by examination of their workings at the local level.[86] The lives of the men and women of sixteenth-century Nantes were ordered and regulated by a wide variety of local and regional political, religious and social institutions and communities. Authority was expressed, received and understood, first and

foremost, through the decisions and actions of royal, provincial and city officers and corporations, and also through a range of shared ideologies and values.

Until 1532, the province of Brittany, in which Nantes lay, was a semi-
autonomous duchy. The marriage of Duchesse Anne with Charles VIII, then
with Louis XII of France in the late fifteenth century brought the province
under royal administration, which was consolidated by the match of her
daughter Claude with Francis I. In 1532, an edict of Union was drawn up, a
contract between the crown and the Breton estates which defined provincial
privileges and imposed limitations on royal authority within the province.
Brittany's dioceses were to be filled only with Bretons.[87] The duchy's laws,
customs and legal system were to be maintained, and Bretons would not have
to leave the province to pursue suits. The fiscal regime was also continued; the
fouage or hearth tax remained the basis of impositions, granted, assessed and
collected by the provincial estates. Military service was not to be performed
outside the province, and no garrisons were to be imposed, apart from companies in each of the four strongholds of the duchy, which were raised from the
regional nobility.[88] Relations between the crown and the province were thus
defined by law, written and customary, and contract.

By the 1550s, four institutions administered the province for the crown.
The first of these was the royal governor, the principal representative of the
king in Brittany. The governor was a powerful aristocrat and military
commander. In the mid-century the commission was held by Jean de Brosse,
duc d'Étampes, who as Comte de Penthièvre was an important seigneur in
northern Brittany, distantly related to the former dukes through his great-
grandmother.[89] Under the royal governor, two lieutenant-generals administered the province, d'Étampes' nephew Sebastien de Luxembourg, Comte de
Martigues, and the Marquis de Bouillé. The county of Nantes also had its own
military governor, in mid-century the Comte de Retz. Governors had broad
commissions, to be personal representatives of the king and the 'guard, tuition
and defence' of their provinces, especially military security.[90] Governors were
also political tutors of the province and its urban communities, through whom
royal commands might be transmitted and remonstrances passed up to the
crown. The governor's authority rested on his relationship with the king, his
personal prestige and military might, his patronage and his ability to channel
royal benevolence into the province. This was a highly personalised form of
authority. The Nantais were careful to cultivate the governor's favours with
gifts. However, the governors and their lieutenants were distant figures in the
1550s. Before 1559 they came infrequently to Nantes and rarely intervened
directly in urban affairs.

The maintenance of Breton law and justice necessitated the creation of a
separate sovereign parlement for the region, something achieved by Henry II

in 1554. The court comprised a first and three other presidents, thirty-two councillors, one procurator, two royal advocates and two secretaries. One-half of the positions were to be held by Bretons, and the other half by 'outsiders' from the rest of France.[91] The parlement was the final court of appeal in Brittany in financial, criminal and temporal ecclesiastical affairs; it registered royal edicts and had the right to remonstrate about law that contravened Breton privileges; it oversaw the judicial system of the province and periodically intervened in regional administration.[92] The Nantais had constant dealings with the parlement, pursuing legal cases and appeals. In the 1550s the parlement met every year in Nantes for the spring session, moving to Rennes for the autumn. In 1557, an *arrêt* granted both sessions to Nantes, which looked set to become the court's permanent seat. However, it was the ultimate absence of a permanent parlement that allowed the city government to operate in relative freedom, unlike the governments of other cities such as Dijon and Bordeaux.

The provincial estates supervised the fiscal system of Brittany and some administration. The estates had two main functions: to agree and levy taxation, and to verify new edicts to be registered in the province. They were the designated custodians of Brittany's privileges, with rights to consent to the creation of offices and the installation of garrisons.[93] The estates were relatively small meetings in the mid-century. They met annually, on 25 September, and comprised representatives of the church – the nine Breton bishops and deputies of the cathedral chapters – the nobility, of whom perhaps thirty gentlemen attended on average, and the deputies from around twenty-five towns.[94] From the mid-century there was a small permanent commission of five or six deputies to administer the estates' affairs when it was not in session, known as the *commission intermédiaire*, and three permanent officers, the *procureur syndic*, legal advisor of the estates, the treasurer, who supervised the receivers of the province's taxes, and the *greffier* or secretary of the estates.[95] The estates' relationship with the crown was dominated by a provincial view of contract enshrined in the edict of Union. But this was not an equal relationship. The king was the dominant partner who called the meetings and determined the main agenda. Henri Sée observed that the estates, by resistance, could delay and obtain small reductions in the taxation demanded by the king but at the end of the day royal authority had to be obeyed. The king violated privileges and periodically taxed without consent.[96] But unmediated royal power created resentment and could, in a situation such as that of the later 1580s, lead to rebellion. So relations were carried out using the framework and language of contract, observing the form if not always the substance of provincial privilege.

The actions of the Breton estates directly affected conditions of life in Nantes. Nantes' relationship with the provincial estates was complicated. The city had fiscal privileges of immunity from the direct taxation of the *fouage*, levied

by the estates on the rural population, but concessions for *octrois* had to sought
from this body, so it had some oversight of urban fiscal affairs.[97] Further, extraordinary taxation fell heavily on the urban populations of Brittany. Landlordly
interest of nobles and churchmen, which dominated the estates, ensured that
extra levies were rarely imposed directly on the rural population. These were
raised as indirect tax, usually as duty paid upon the transport and consumption
of wine. Nantes, a major consumer and exporter of wine, thus paid the heaviest
share of extraordinary taxation, a burden shared by all of its social groups.[98]
There was thus some disgruntlement among the city's bourgeois and mercantile
groups over the fiscal regime operated by the provincial estates, in which the
opinions of the third estate counted for less than those of the first two.

There were close links between the provincial estates and the officer
elites of Nantes, for the chief functionaries of the provincial estates were
lawyers and financiers from the royal courts of the city. The *procureur syndic* of
the estates between 1552 and 1583, Artur Le Fourbeur, was a resident of
Nantes; his deputy, Louis Michel, Sieur de Garnison, was also a Nantais, and
was an advocate in the *présidial* court. The successive *greffiers* or clerks of the
estates between 1558 and 1588, Guillaume Meneust and his kinsman P.
Gaultier, were also city residents, and Meneust was an auditor in the Chambre
des Comptes. Finally, the treasurer until 1578, Jean Avril, and his successor,
Gabriel Hus, were too from Nantes.[99] The archives of the estates were kept in
Nantes cathedral. Periodic tensions between the mercantile and officer elites
of Nantes were sometimes played out at the estates. In 1574 the estates
demanded the suppression of the new municipality as it was contrary to the
rights of the ancient royal officers of the city.[100] The royal officers working for
the estates were also servants of the crown. Identities overlapped and could
conflict, but what is certain is that Nantes was represented at the heart of the
administration of the estates.

Fourthly, the Chambre des Comptes settled at Nantes permanently in
1501. This was the 'sister of parlement', a sovereign court which acted in the
fiscal sphere.[101] The court comprised a president, chief accountants or *maîtres
des comptes*, who tried cases and verified accounts, and correctors, auditors and
secretaries, who formed the bureaucracy of the court. The membership came
from Nantes' wealthy families; in the sixteenth century many sons of
merchants moved directly into the court, which often served as a stepping
stone to the parlement for the newly rich.[102] Its functions were to register and
apply royal fiscal edicts, to supervise the royal domain and all taxes levies in the
province, and to check the accounts of state receivers and of town administrations.[103] The Chambre also supervised loans and judged fiscal disputes.[104]

Governance and authority within Nantes itself were diffuse in the 1550s.
Power was divided between a variety of men and institutions; 'each one's

sphere of responsibility was vague and often the powers of the different groups overlapped'.[105] Until 1565, Nantes lacked an incorporated municipal government. In principle, the city was administered directly by the crown as the successor of the Breton dukes. Nantes' relationship with the king was regulated by its legal privileges. The city had its own fiscal regime, so the population was exempt from direct tax and from *franc fief*. Nantes had the right to defend itself with a citizen militia and was exempt from billeting soldiers. The king's authority was represented directly by two groups of institutions: the royal judicial apparatus and the military governor of the city and its château. In the middle ages, the *prévôté* was the basis of the ducal administration of the city, with a *prévôt*, castle, judicial rights of first instance over the parishes of Sainte-Croix, Saint-Denis, Saint-Léonard, Saint-Nicolas and Saint-Saturnin and the southern suburbs of Nantes, and customs rights of one-fortieth on goods traded in maritime commerce.[106] In the sixteenth century the *prévôt* remained the judge of first instance over civil and criminal cases in the southern parishes of the city.[107] He also had broad powers of police, to regulate the economy and markets, trade and public health, and he conserved the privileges of the university. In addition, two superior tiers of royal justice existed by the 1550s. The *sénéchaussée*, with its seneschal, formed the court of appeal for the county of Nantes. The seneschal also had wide functions within city governance. He presided over general assemblies of the urban community, was the president of the third estate when the estates met in the county of Nantes, and had the right to command the town garrison in the absence of the governor and château captain. In 1552 Henry II created a new tier of courts of *présidial*, to act as intermediaries between lower courts and the parlement. The *présidial* established in Nantes took away some the seneschal's work, and there were numerous disputes of jurisdiction between the two courts. All three tribunals sat in the ancient Palais du Bouffay, the *présidial* and *sénéchaussée* together being commonly called the court of Nantes.[108] Royal officers were more than just judges and accountants, however, for they were used as agents for a range of activities beyond the scope of their posts. For example, in 1567, the royal commissioners representing the crown at the provincial estates comprised the royal governor, his lieutenant-general and six senior royal financial and legal officers of Brittany, including René de Bourgneuf, *maître des requêtes*, three *généraux de finances* of different positions, René de Cambout, *reformateur des eaux-et-forêts*, and Bertrand d'Argentré the seneschal of Rennes.[109] Through the actions and influence of officers in Nantes' society and in city government, the crown was able to extend its influence into fields of activity in which it traditionally had no institutional representation.

The royal officer with the greatest claim to represent the king was the military governor of city and château, appointed by the governor of the county of Nantes. His functions were primarily military, consisting of supervision of the city's defence. Like the inhabitants of most walled towns, the Nantais were hostile to intervention from outside, particularly garrisons, and claimed the right to defend themselves. Fortifications were maintained at public expense, and the main defence force was a citizen watch. The city governor also had certain political prerogatives and functions, many of which had fallen out of use by the 1550s. The appointment of René de Sanzay as military governor after 1555 was to change this. Sanzay considered that his predecessors had abandoned too many of their prerogatives and undertook to restore the traditional functions of his position. Such actions brought him into constant collision with the other authorities of Nantes, particularly the *conseil des bourgeois*.[110]

Since about 1420 the competence of the military governor over city affairs had been shared with a *conseil des bourgeois*, created by Duc Jean V. The *conseil* comprised the principal ducal officers (the military governor, constable, seneschal and *prévôt*), six canons from the chapters of the cathedral and Notre-Dame and twelve bourgeois, including a *procureur des bourgeois*, a lawyer who represented the city's interests.[111] In addition there was a treasurer or *miseur* of the city and a separate *miseur* of the bridges, to collect tolls for the town.[112] A range of lower offices were also in the gift of the *conseil*: sergeants, porters of the city gates, town criers, street cleaners and an horologist, which gave the body some patronage to bestow.[113] Emergencies and affairs touching the whole city were discussed in an *assemblée générale*, a general assembly of all inhabitants although in practice dominated by the principal men of the town.[114] The *conseil* had a general although ill-defined regulatory function over city affairs, in conjunction with the other judicial and military officers. The pages of its registers are filled with reports of prices and regulations of markets; the supervision of taverns; concern with the administration of poor relief and the city's Hôtel-Dieu; the cleaning of streets and provision of wells; public works and bridge, quay and fortifications repairs; the defence of commercial and trading privileges; and the organisation of the watch and guard. There was also some direct negotiation with the crown over military duties and taxes. The *conseil* had the right to levy revenue, *octrois*, on people and goods crossing the river bridges, and on goods sold in the market place. The ability to raise loans on this collateral, for royal taxation or forced borrowing, gave it some voice at court. In practice, however, the *conseil* had little independent authority. It shared its functions with other institutions and rarely inaugurated policies on its own initiative, responding to orders from higher authorities such as provincial estates, governor or crown. In 1565, the *conseil* was strengthened by its transformation into an incorporated municipality, a process that is discussed in Chapter 4 below.

A range of groups other than the crown's agents and the *conseil* claimed both ideological and material authority. The Bishop of Nantes was one of the

richest and influential in Brittany. Within the city, he was a temporal and a
spiritual lord, with seigneurial rights including justice over five parishes around
the cathedral, and his own court of first instance, the *régaires*. The bishop's
religious authority affected city life in myriad ways. He possessed jurisdiction
over canon law cases, such as church attendance, sexual behaviour, marriages
and wills which were pursued in his court of the *officialité*. He and his agents
regulated the spiritual and moral life of the laity through visitations and injunctions. The bishops of the 1530s and 1540s were political appointees of the
Crown and came rarely if ever to Nantes. But in 1554, the appointment of
Antoine de Crequi reinvigorated the diocese; he resided, undertook visitations
and conducted synods to better regulate spiritual affairs. The cathedral chapter,
composed of seven dignitaries, twenty canons, a choir and a choir school, the
Psalette, also had temporal lordship over parishes around Nantes and its own
court of *régaires*. The bishop and chapter were landlords of city and countryside; many of the fifty houses owned by the chapter in Nantes in 1789 were
already in their possession in the sixteenth century, and they also possessed
butcheries, a seigneurial bread oven and a mill in Saint-Clément.[115] The canons
were rectors and tithe holders of many parishes in and around Nantes. For
example, the prebendary given to the reader in theology of the cathedral had
rights of presentation to Sainte-Croix in the city, along with the great tithe
from the parishes of Saint-Donatien and Doulon.[116] The cathedral clergy had a
role to play in city politics, for they were represented in general assemblies of
the inhabitants of the town. When important visitors made solemn entries into
Nantes, they were received at the cathedral and saluted at their residence by the
chapter, with symbolic gifts of bread and wine.[117]

The parish was the institution in which the inhabitants worshipped and
which formed the basis of city administration. There were twelve parishes in
Nantes: ten based within the walls and two in the immediate suburbs. Each
church had a *recteur*, a salaried priest appointed by the canon who held the
benefice, and he was assisted by several curates or *vicaires* and choir priests.[118]
The parish was administered by a vestry or *générale* comprising the *recteur*, two
or three churchwardens (*fabriqueurs*) and a group of local notables, who met
after Sunday mass. The churchwardens were the main executors of the parish,
elected for a yearly term and personally accountable for the management of
property, receipts and expenditure of that year. They managed the temporal
affairs of the parish church, its communal resources and funds, repairs to its
fabric, sermons and parish celebrations, they accepted bequests, supervised
mortuary foundations and allocated burial space. By the mid-sixteenth century
the parish's secular functions were also advanced in Nantes. The parish was the
platform for the publication of all types of information, from the bishop, crown
and local authorities, and also acted as the organising unit of the bourgeois

militia. The vestry organised poor relief collections and distributions, and assessed and allocated taxation when it was to be paid. The parish was also an important place for sociability. J. Hardwick has shown that for middling men, 'the horizons of sociability . . . were parochial and localised'; 80 per cent of baptisms attended by notaries, important occasions for male socialising, were in the home parish or an immediately neighbouring one.[119] Through the parish, authority was widely dispersed in the sixteenth-century city. Parish officers came not from the city's elite, but from middling groups. Participation in parish governance gave a wide range of families some political voice in the day-to-day running of their immediate communities.

At the level of most ordinary people, the household was the basis of order and authority. The inheritance rights of Breton children and women gave them some power within their families, for customary law required strict partibility between siblings of both sexes in non-noble families. Testamentary bequests and gifts between spouses were severely restricted; parents could not limit the financial interests of children as future heirs by assigning wedding gifts as replacement for inheritances. Wives had to consent to the sale or disposal of marital property, because they were co-owners of it, and the husbands of women who died without children had to give back their wives' property to the wives' lineage kin.[120] The household was also the site of much employment, production and exchange: here, servants, journeymen, apprentices and casual employees were subject to the authority of the head of household. The household was also the basis for city defence. The militia of Nantes, responsible for guarding the city gates and walls, was based on the parish, each household being responsible for providing a militiaman. Rotas were drawn up by parish so that ten men might serve in turn each night.[121] Thus, authority, in different guises, was disseminated throughout urban society.

Paul Griffiths has defined authority as an 'ongoing set of negotiations between dominant ideologies, groups or individuals, and those subordinate to them'.[122] Urban society was not 'contained' by the force of an elite; governance depended upon persuasion as well as coercion, for reciprocity lay at the centre of power relations. Authority was negotiated, shared and disseminated throughout many different groups. The central thesis of this study of Nantes is that the authority within urban government and society was founded on a concept of mutual obligation or contract, based in tradition and law. During the civil wars, the ideological basis and the practical exercise of authority within the city were affected by religious discord, political and military strife. The way in which the city coped with these tensions and renegotiated power relations is the focus of this study.

NOTES

1 Travers, III, p. 105.

2 L. Romier, *Les origines politiques des guerres de religion*, 2 vols (1913–14); H.-J. Mariéjol, *La Réforme et la Ligue. L'édit de Nantes (1559–1598)* (1904). See also A. Jouanna, *La France du XVIème siècle* (1996). A detailed survey of the historiography of the French religious wars can be found in M. Holt, 'Putting religion back into the wars of religion', *F.H.S.*, 18 (1993) 524–51.

3 Holt, 'Putting religion back into the wars of religion'.

4 For example, H. Hauser, 'The French Reformation and the French People in the Sixteenth Century', *American Historical Review* 4 (1899) 217–27; H. Hauser, *Études sur la Réforme française* (1909); L. Febvre, 'Une question mal posée. Les origines de la Réforme française et le problème général des causes de la Réforme', *R.H.* 141 (1929) 1–73.

5 R. Kingdon, *Geneva and the Coming of the Wars of Religion in France, 1555–1563* (Geneva, 1956); N. Sutherland, *The Massacre of St Bartholomew and the European Conflict, 1559–1572* (London, 1973) and *The Huguenot Struggle for Recognition* (New Haven, 1980).

6 Detailed in P. Benedict, *Rouen during the Wars of Religion* (Cambridge, 1980), p. ix.

7 M. Holt, *The French Wars of Religion 1562–1629* (Cambridge, 1995), p. 1.

8 D. Crouzet, *Les guerriers de Dieu, La violence au temps des troubles de religion (c.1525–c.1610)*, 2 vols (1990).

9 P. Roberts, *A City in Conflict. Troyes during the French Wars of Religion* (Manchester, 1996), p. 1.

10 J.-M. Constant, *Les français pendant les guerres de religion* (2002), p. 9.

11 Constant, *Les français pendant les guerres de religion*, p. 75.

12 R. Muchembled, *L'invention de la France moderne. Monarchie, culture et société (1500–1660)* (2002), p. 19.

13 Benedict, *Rouen*; N. Z. Davis, *Society and Culture in Early Modern France* (Stanford, CA, 1975); W. Kaiser, *Marseille au temps des troubles 1559–96. Morphologie sociale et luttes de factions* (1992); R. Descimon, *Qui étaient les Seize? Mythes et réalités de la Ligue parisienne (1585–94)* (1983); B. Diefendorf, *Beneath the Cross. Catholics and Huguenots in Sixteenth-Century Paris* (Oxford, 1991).

14 See S. Carroll, *Noble Power during the French Wars of Religion. The Guise Affinity and the Catholic Cause in Normandy* (Cambridge, 1998), p. 4.

15 S. A. Finley-Croswhite, *Henry IV and the Towns. The Pursuit of Legitimacy in French Urban Society, 1589–1610* (Cambridge, 1999), p. 180.

16 Benedict, *Rouen*, p. xiv.

17 Carroll, *Noble Power*, p. 3.

18 R. Souriac, *Décentralisation administrative dans l'Ancienne France. Autonomie commingeoise et pouvoir d'état 1540–1640*, 2 vols (Toulouse, 1992); T. Watson, 'The Lyon City Council c.1525–1575, Politics, Culture, Religion' D.Phil. thesis, University of Oxford, 1999; P. Conner, 'Huguenot Heartland. Montauban during the Wars of Religion', PhD thesis, University of St Andrews, 2000; also see P.-J. Souriac, 'Une société dans la guerre civile. Le Midi toulousain au temps des troubles de religion 1562–1596', Thèse du Doctorat, University of Paris IV-Sorbonne, 2003.

19 A.M.N. series BB 2–22 (registers of the city council); CC (treasury) and EE (militia and security). See bibliography for full details.

20 This is a common sociological definition, based ultimately on J. H. Mills and M. Weber. See D. Wrong, *Power. Its Forms and Uses* (Oxford, 1979), pp. 38, 49.

21 P. Blau, *Exchange and Power in Social Life* (New York, 1964), p. 117. A discussion of collectivism in power relations can also be found in H. Arendt, *On Violence* (New York, 1969).

22 Wrong, *Power*, p. 24; Talcott Parsons, 'Power and the Social System' (1963), reprinted in S. Lukes, ed., *Power* (Oxford, 1986), pp. 103–33.

23 M. Foucault, 'Disciplinary power and subjection', in *Power/Knowledge. Selected Interviews and Other Writings 1972–1977* (London, 1976), reprinted in Lukes, ed., *Power*, pp. 229–41.

24 C. de Seyssel, *La monarchie de France*, ed J. Pujol (1961); discussed in W. Church, *Constitutional Thought in Sixteenth-Century France. A Study in the Evolution of Ideas* (Cambridge, MA, 1941), pp. 23–4.

25 D. Potter, *A History of France 1460–1560* (Basingstoke, 1995), p. 30.

26 Church, *Constitutional Thought*, p. 38.

27 N. Henshall, *The Myth of Abolutism* (London, 1992), p. 10.

28 J. R. Major, 'Renaissance Monarchy. A contribution to the periodisation of history', *Emory University Quarterly*, 13 (1957) 112–24.

29 M. Nassiet, 'Brittany and the French monarchy in the sixteenth century. The evidence of the letters of remission', *F.H.*, 17 (2003) 425.

30 R. Mousnier, *The Institutions of France under the Absolute Monarchy 1598–1789*, 2 vols (Chicago, 1979), I, p. 607; N. Roelker, *One King, One Faith. The Parlement of Paris and the Religious Reformations of the Sixteenth Century* (Berkeley, 1996), p. 59; D. Richet, *De la Réforme à la Révolution. Études sur la France moderne* (1991), p. 349; H. Höpfl and M. Thompson, 'The history of contract as a motif in political thought', *A.H.R*, 84 (1979) 919–44.

31 Henshall, *Myth of Abolutism*, p. 9; Roelker, *One King, One Faith*, p. 67.

32 Church, *Constitutional Thought*, p. 40; see the discussions in Roelker, *One King, One Faith*, pp. 63–4 and M. Braddick and J. Walter eds., *Negotiating Power in Early Modern Society* (Cambridge, 2001), pp. 13–14.

33 Quoted in P. Hamon, 'Une monarchie de la Renaissance', in J. Cornette, ed., *La monarchie entre Renaissance et Révolution 1515–1792* (2000), p. 22.

34 T. Watson, '"When is a Huguenot not a Huguenot?" Lyon 1525–1575', in K. Cameron, M. Greengrass and P. Roberts, eds, *The Adventure of Religious Pluralism in Early Modern France* (Bern, 2000), p. 169.

35 Q. Skinner, *The Foundations of Modern Political Thought*, II: *The Reformation* (Cambridge, 1978), p. 259.

36 Hamon, 'Une monarchie de la Renaissance', pp. 18–19.

37 Potter, *History of France*, p. 35; Skinner, *Foundations of Modern Political Thought*, pp. 260–1.

38 Church, *Constitutional Thought*, pp. 62–4.

39 R. Knecht, *Francis I* (Cambridge, 1982), conclusion.

40 Potter, *History of France*, p. 288.

41 Skinner, *Foundations of Modern Political Thought*, pp. 256–67.

42 Richet, *De la Réforme à la Révolution*, pp. 378–9.

43 Hamon, 'Une monarchie de la Renaissance', pp. 37–9.

44 J. R. Major, *From Renaissance Monarchy to Absolute Monarchy. French Kings, Nobles and Estates* (Baltimore, 1994), pp. 32–3.

45 W. Beik, *Absolutism and Society in Seventeenth-Century France* (Cambridge, 1985).

46 Henshall, *Myth of Abolutism*, p. 11.

47 Hamon, 'Une monarchie de la Renaissance', pp. 45–6.

48 Skinner, *Foundations of Modern Political Thought*, pp. 267–72.

49 Quoted in Church, *Constitutional Thought*, p. 98.

50 François Hotman, *Francogallia* (1573); extracts in Church, *Constitutional Thought*, p. 87; de Bèze is discussed in Skinner, *Foundations of Modern Political Thought*, pp. 316, 330–3.

51 F. Baumgartner, *Radical Reactionaries. The Political Thought of the French Catholic League* (Geneva, 1975), p. 55.

52 Church, *Constitutional Thought*, p. 158.

53 Finley-Croswhite, *Henry IV and the Towns*, pp. 11–12; Descimon, *Qui étaient les Seize?*; B. Chevalier, *Les Bonnes Villes de France du XIVème au XVIème siècle* (1982). A summary of this view can be found in Muchembled, *L'invention de la France moderne*, pp. 108–9.

54 Major, *From Renaissance Monarchy to Absolute Monarchy*, p. 113.

55 M. Wilkinson, *A History of the League or Sainte-Union 1576–1595* (Glasgow, 1929), pp. 12–13.

56 Guy de Coquille, quoted in Church, *Constitutional Thought*, pp. 277–82.

57 Hamon, 'Une monarchie de la Renaissance', p. 12.
58 Church, *Constitutional Thought*, p. 1; Braddick and Walter, eds, *Negotiating Power*, p. 14.
59 J. Collins, *Classes, Estates and Order in Early Modern Brittany* (Cambridge, 1994), p. 114.
60 Church, *Constitutional Thought*, p. 206.
61 Church, *Constitutional Thought*, pp. 102, 109.
62 P. Roberts, 'Religious pluralism in practice. The enforcement of the edicts of pacification', in Cameron et al., eds, *The Adventure of Religious Pluralism*, pp. 31–44; O. Christin, 'From repression to pacification. French royal policy in the face of Protestantism', in P. Benedict, G. Marnef, H. van Nierop and M. Venard, eds, *Reformation, Revolt and Civil War in France and the Netherlands 1555–1585* (Amsterdam, 1999), pp. 201–14.
63 L. Bourquin, *Les nobles, la ville et le roi. L'autorité nobiliaire en Anjou pendant les guerres de religion (1560–1598)* (2001), p. 236.
64 Diefendorf, *Beneath the Cross*, p. 173.
65 M. Cassan, *Le temps des guerres de religion. Le cas du Limousin (vers 1530–vers 1630)* (1996).
66 Finley-Croswhite, *Henry IV and the Towns*, p. 45
67 J. Parsons, 'Governing sixteenth-century France. The monetary reforms of 1577', *F.H.S*, 26 (2003) 3.
68 J. Bodin, *Les six livres de la République*, trans. R. Knolles as *The Six Bookes of a Commonweale* (London, 1606); discussed in Church, *Constitutional Thought*, pp. 247–52.
69 Finley-Croswhite, *Henry IV and the Towns*, p. 5.
70 A discussion of the symbolic function of the eucharist in sixteenth-century French society and politics can be found in C. Elwood, *The Body Broken* (Oxford, 1999), chapter 1.
71 Diefendorf, *Beneath the Cross*, p. 178.
72 Diefendorf, *Beneath the Cross*, pp. 157–8, 173; see also M. McClendon, '"Against God's Word". Government, religion and the crisis of authority in early Reformation Norwich', *S.C.J.*, 25/2 (1994) 353–69, at 360–1.
73 R. Harding, *Anatomy of a Power Elite. The provincial governors of early modern France* (New Haven, 1978); J.-M. Constant, *Les Guises* (1984); Carroll, *Noble Power*; S. Kettering, 'Clientage during the Wars of Religion', *S.C.J.*, 20 (1989) 221–39; S. Kettering, 'Patronage in early modern France', *F.H.S.*, 17 (1992) 839–62; S. Kettering, *Patronage in Sixteenth- and Seventeenth-Century France* (Aldershot, 2002).
74 Finley-Croswhite, *Henry IV and the Towns*, p. 3.
75 Henshall, *Myth of Absolutism*, p. 18.
76 Harding, *Anatomy of a Power Elite*, pp. 46–9.
77 Carroll, *Noble Power*, pp. 146, 250; Finley-Croswhite, *Henry IV and the Towns*, p. 45.
78 Summarised in Church, *Constitutional Thought*, p. 223.
79 J. Farr, *Authority and Sexuality in Early Modern Burgundy 1550–1730* (Oxford, 1995), p. 24.
80 M. Planiol, *Histoire des institutions de la Bretagne*, V: *Le XVIè siècle* (1895; reprinted Mayenne, 1984), p. 333; N. Z. Davis, 'Women in the crafts in sixteenth-century Lyon', in B. A. Hanawalt, ed., *Women and Work in Pre-Industrial Europe* (Bloomington, 1986), pp. 167–97; M. C. Howell, *Women, Production and Patriarchy in Late Medieval Cities* (Chicago, 1986).
81 J. Hardwick, *The Practice of Patriarchy. Gender and the Politics of Household Authority in Early Modern France* (University Park, Pennsylvania, 1998), pp. 88, 129.
82 R. Giesey, 'Models of rulership in French royal ceremonial', in S. Wilentz, ed., *Rites of Power* (Philadelphia, 1985), pp. 41–64.
83 Potter, *History of France*, pp. 43–53.
84 L. Bourquin, 'Les défis des guerres de religion 1559–1610', in Cornette, ed., *La monarchie entre Renaissance et Révolution*, p. 72.
85 Potter, *History of France*, p. 134.
86 M. Foucault, *Discipline and Punish* (Harmondsworth, 1977).
87 B. Pocquet, *Histoire de Bretagne*, V: *1515–1715* (Rennes, 1913; reprinted Mayenne, 1975), pp. 18–19.
88 Planiol, *Histoire des institutions de la Bretagne*, pp. 89, 141–2, 154.

89 A. Croix, *L'âge d'or de la Bretagne 1532–1675* (Rennes, 1993), p. 29.

90 Potter, *History of France*, p. 118. For a detailed analysis of the nature and function of governors see Harding, *Anatomy of a Power Elite*.

91 Planiol, *Histoire des institutions de la Bretagne*, pp. 213–14.

92 Collins, *Classes, Estates and Order*, p. 75.

93 Planiol, *Histoire des institutions de la Bretagne*, p. 76; Major, *From Renaissance Monarchy to Absolute Monarchy*, p. 37.

94 Planiol, *Histoire des institutions de la Bretagne*, pp. 55–61. Attendance was higher in crisis years, for example during disputes over taxation in the reign of Henry III. See below, p. 00.

95 Croix, *L'âge d'or*, p. 19.

96 H. Sée, 'Les états de Bretagne au XVIème siècle', *A.B*, 10 (1894) 381, 383.

97 Sée, 'Les états de Bretagne', p. 199.

98 Collins, *Classes, Estates and Order*, pp. 118–35.

99 Sée, 'Les états de Bretagne', pp. 27–30.

100 Sée, 'Les états de Bretagne', p. 199.

101 M. Wolfe, *The Fiscal System of Renaissance France* (New Haven, 1972), p. 279.

102 Collins, *Classes, Estates and Order*, p. 75.

103 Wolfe, *Fiscal System of Renaissance France*, p. 272.

104 P. Bois ed., *Histoire de Nantes* (Toulouse, 1977), p. 165. See G. Saupin, *Nantes au XVIIème siècle. Vie politique et société urbaine* (Rennes, 1996), pp. 57–8.

105 Benedict, *Rouen*, p. 31.

106 Bois, ed., *Histoire de Nantes*, p. 165; J. Vailhen, 'Le conseil des bourgeois de Nantes', 3 vols, Thèse du Doctorat, University of Rennes, 1965, pp. 74–7.

107 For details on judges and their procedures, see C. Plessix-Buisset, *Le criminel devant ses juges aux XVIème et XVIIème siècles* (1988).

108 Saupin, *Nantes au XVIIème siècle*, p. 53.

109 Sée, 'Les états de Bretagne', pp. 16–19.

110 Saupin, *Nantes au XVIIème siècle*, pp. 16, 141.

111 Vailhen, 'Le conseil des bourgeois', pp. 94ff.

112 Planiol, *Histoire des institutions de la Bretagne*, p. 174.

113 Vailhen, 'Le conseil des bourgeois', pp. 117–19; R. Schneider, *Public Life in Toulouse 1463–1789. From Municipal Republic to Cosmopolitan City* (Ithaca, 1989), p. 62.

114 Hardwick's study of notaries shows that a range of middling-status men did attend these meetings. They were 'not key political players but demonstrated an association with governance and public confidence' by so doing. See Hardwick, *Practice of Patriarchy*, pp. 200–1.

115 G. Durville, *Le chapitre de l'église de Nantes. Aperçu sur son histoire du VIIème siècle au concordat* (Nantes, 1907), p. 36.

116 G. Durville, 'Aperçu sur l'histoire du chapitre de Nantes du XIIème siècle au Concordat', *B.S.H.A.N.L.I*, 47 (1906) 269–324.

117 Durville, *Le chapitre de l'église de Nantes*, 30.

118 The term *recteur* is used in Brittany for the parish priest, whether he was a rector (the owner of his own tithes) or a vicar (a salaried appointee of the rector). The French term *curé* was seldom used.

119 Hardwick, *Practice of Patriarchy*, p. 174.

120 Hardwick, *Practice of Patriarchy*, p. 54.

121 The same was true of Paris; see Diefendorf, *Beneath the Cross*, p. 25.

122 P. Griffiths, A. Fox and S. Hindle, eds, *The Experience of Authority in Early Modern England* (Basingstoke, 1996), pp. 1–2.

2

Setting the scene: the city and its people in the mid-sixteenth century

The origins of Nantes lay in its location at the confluence of the rivers Erdre and Loire. Here, the Loire divides into several channels around a series of islands, which allow the river to be bridged, making the nearest such crossing point to the sea. The Loire is tidal at Nantes and permitted a relatively deep port at La Fosse. Fifty kilometres to the west lay the Bay of Biscay, giving access to Spain and to northern Europe. To the east, upstream, lay the cities of France, Paris, Orléans and ultimately Lyon, although the Loire was notoriously difficult to navigate. Too much water in winter caused floods, while too little flow in summer exposed sandbanks and narrowed shipping channels. The river Erdre ran north into the Breton interior, a wide, picturesque watercourse along whose banks the local nobility, officers and rich merchants built châteaux. Nantes itself was built on the north bank of the Loire, straddling the Erdre, which bisected the city, and was joined by numerous bridges to islands such as La Saulzaie and Gloriette. Early modern Nantes had a watery aspect, which made it the Venice of the west of France (see figure 2.1).

The visitor approaching Nantes from Poitou to the south would reach the Loire at Pirmil. The Loire bridges were the pride of the city: six spans between five islands, bringing a traveller to the city gate of La Poissonnerie. Constructed of wood in the mid-century, the bridges were wide and high, with houses and shops built on them. The crossings required constant repair, so to traverse the Loire was a privilege for which one had to pay. The city council gained much of its revenue from passage tolls and *octrois* from the river bridges. Nantes was a *ville close*, defined from the surrounding countryside by its rampart walls and ditches. Visitors from Paris and the east entered by the cathedral gate, at Saint-Pierre. The road to Rennes and the north led across the Erdre via the gate at Port Communau, and the route to Vannes and the west left through the north-west gate at Sauvetour. There were two further gates leading to the Loire quays, Briand-Maillard and Saint-Nicolas, through which kings and royal governors made their formal entries. Each gate was guarded by

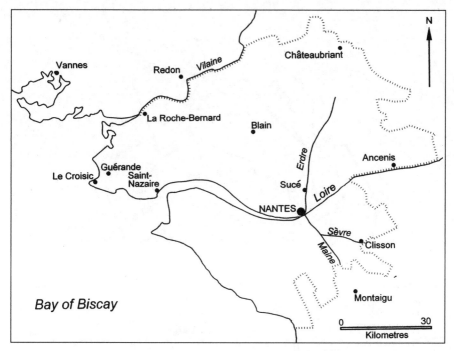

2.1 Map of Nantes and its region

inhabitants on watch duty, a task performed without enthusiasm, so access to
the town was relatively unhindered (see figure 2.2).

Nantes was a city with multiple functions. It was the seat of an ancient
bishopric, a judicial centre with parlement, *présidial* and *sénéchaussée* courts in
the mid-1550s, and the fiscal administration of Brittany was overseen here, in
the Chambre des Comptes. The military and judicial heart of the city lay on its
south side, in the Palais du Bouffay, immediately east of the Porte de la Poissonnerie. This was the ancient ducal castle, converted in the fifteenth century
to law courts and prisons. Here the law courts of Nantes met while in the
square outside the pillory was erected and executions took place. But most
days the Place du Bouffay was given over to a market, shops and stalls.[1] To the
north of the square was the Hôtel des Monnaies, where coin was struck and
currency checked. A few minutes' walk east of Bouffay lay the 'new' fifteenth-
century château of the Breton dukes. The massive *enceinte* of thick, low walls
and towers of grey granite formed a self-contained enclave with its own water
gate onto the Loire. The château was the occasional residence of king or royal
governor; the city captain and garrison were billeted here, with their armoury
and prisons.

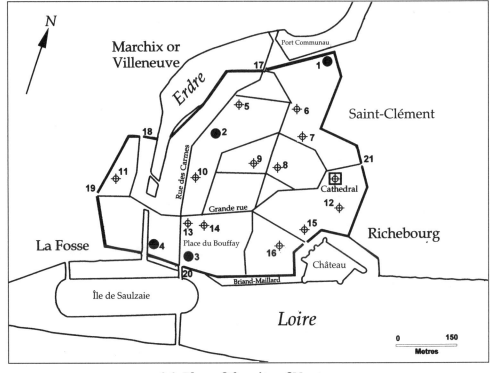

2.2 Plan of the city of Nantes

● **Secular building**
1. Chambre des Comptes
2. *Hôtel de ville*
3. Courts of Nantes
4. Hôtel-Dieu

17. Port Communau gate
18. Sauvetour gate
19. Saint-Nicolas gate
20. Poissonnerie gate
21. Saint-Pierre gate

Based on map by F. Cacaut of 1757.

⊕ **Church/Convent**
5. Saint-Léonard church
6. Franciscan convent
7. Notre-Dame collegiate church
8. Saint-Vincent church
9. Poor Clares convent
10. Carmelite convent
11. Saint-Nicolas church
12. Saint-Laurent church
13. Saint-Saturnin church
14. Sainte-Croix church
15. Sainte-Radegonde church
16. Dominican convent

Beyond the château the city walls turned north and ran uphill to the ancient core of the city, the cathedral quarter, dominated by the white lime-stone basilica of Saint-Pierre. Surrounding the cathedral were the buildings of the chapter, choir school and bishop's palace. In addition to the cathedral, there were three mendicant convents in Nantes and a house of Poor Clares. The Franciscans had a large church in the north of the city, big enough to hold the university. The Dominicans' convent was next to the château. The Carmelites, in the west of the town, had a church noted for religious art. Its treasures included the tomb of the last duke of Brittany, François II, and his wife, Marguerite de Foix, sculpted in 1504 by Michel Colombe.[2] There were also a collegiate church of Notre-Dame, eight further parish churches, and three or four chapels inside the city walls.

North of the cathedral, the rampart turned west and ran along the bank of the Erdre and back down to the Loire. Here was located the Chambre des Comptes and later, from 1578, the new *hôtel de ville*. Outside of the northern ramparts lay the Port Communau, where goods entering Nantes from the north, by road or river, were traded. At the south-western edge of the city were the stone quays of La Fosse, the maritime port, surrounded by merchants' warehouses and *hôtels*. Next to La Fosse was the Port au Vin, where wine from the Loire valley was bought and sold. Across the Erdre mouth and south of Bouffay lay the quay of Briand-Maillard. Trade here was dominated by Loire commerce coming into the city to be sold or exchanged overseas. The western and eastern port zones were separated by the bridges of Nantes, which acted as a barrier to large ships. Goods were moved between them on smaller river craft.

A main street ran north–south from the Port Communau to the Porte de la Poissonnerie (rue des Carmes), and another ran east–west from the Paris road to the Saint-Nicolas gate on to La Fosse (Grande rue). They crossed at the Place des Changes, a major commercial site. There were few open spaces in Nantes. Mostly, the city comprised a dense warren of irregular streets and alleyways, frequently insanitary and malodorous. In August 1572, the *bureau de ville* recorded that 'those who own pigs allow them to wander about the streets and by this means cause infection among the inhabitants', while butchers regularly killed beasts in their shops and threw the blood and offal in the streets.[3] Along the wider roads were the houses of the well-to-do. The rue des Jacobins and La Fosse were lined with granite and limestone *hôtels* of the judicial and mercantile elites such as the Maison de Tourelles of the merchant André Ruiz, where he entertained Charles IX in 1564.[4] However, most buildings were built tightly against each other, two- or three-storeyed, half-timbered, narrow houses, opening out onto communal yards at the back. In the smaller streets and alleyways lived the middling and poor people, in close and cramped quarters. Julie Hardwick has shown that notaries, from the middle strata of Nantes' population, lived in apartments spread over several levels, with rooms linked by communal areas, public stairways and galleries, in which there was little spatial specialisation other than a room for an *étude*.[5] Shared public spaces, courtyards, wells and latrines led to constant contact with the neighbours.

Outside the city lay the suburbs where, Alain Croix estimates, 59 per cent of the city's population lived.[6] To the north-west were the parish of

Saint-Similien and the suburbs Bourgneuf and Marchix. To the east lay Saint-Clément with the Charterhouse and municipal college for boys, and the populous suburbs of Saint-André and Richebourg. To the south and south-west of the ramparts lay suburbs which were part of intra-mural parishes, the Île de Saulzaie in Sainte-Croix, and La Fosse, in Saint-Nicolas. The southern suburbs housed the institutions of the city's poor, the Hôtel-Dieu and from 1570, the Sanitat or pest house, isolated in theory from the population of the walled town.

Society and economy in the second half of the sixteenth century

The streets and quays of Nantes were populated by a rich variety of people. In the mid-century, Nantes was the largest city of the province of Brittany, with a population of about 20,000.[7] Like all early modern towns, Nantes had a sharply pyramidal wealth structure. Detailed taxation rolls from the early 1590s show that a minority of the population owned much of the community's wealth, for the upper 10 per cent of taxpayers – thirty individuals – paid 47 per cent of the assessed tax.[8] There were differences in wealth between parishes.[9] The three small, central parishes of Notre-Dame, Saint-Laurent and Saint-Vincent were relatively wealthy, being favoured by clergy, royal officials and legal professionals. Here, there were small numbers of households, and most had large tax assessments. Taxation was evenly distributed across the population, and both the mean and the median assessments were high. The wealth of this group of parishes is confirmed by Croix's study of their demography, for they were little affected by subsistence crises (see Table 2.1).[10]

A second group of parishes, Sainte-Croix, Saint-Saturnin and La Fosse in Saint-Nicolas, all waterside districts, formed the largest and most populous zones in the city, and were mixed in terms of wealth and social group. Tax assessment was spread over large numbers of households, although about 40 per cent was paid by people in the middle and higher tax bands. These parishes had high mean assessments but low median and modal figures, with 50 per cent of taxpayers assessed at less than 1 *livre*. Finally, a third group of parishes was relatively poor. In Saint-Clément, the eastern suburb, Saint-Léonard and Sainte-Radegonde, 50 per cent or more of households were assessed at 10 *sous* or less. In Saint-Léonard and Sainte-Radegonde, 4.3 per cent and 8.3 per cent respectively of the taxpayers contributed 50 per cent of the total assessment. Mean, median and modal assessments were low.

Despite wealth differences between parishes, residential segregation was limited. There were preferred districts for particular groups of people – lawyers, judicial officers and priests in Saint-Laurent, merchants and immigrants in La Fosse – but everywhere wealthier inhabitants lived along the major streets while their poorer neighbours lived around the corner, in side roads and courtyards.[11] In Saint-Léonard parish, for example, Monsieur d'Argentré, *conseiller en la cour* of Parlement, lived in close proximity to two priests, an auditor of the Chambre des Comptes, a weaver, and the currier François du Gast and his tenant, a poor woman who hawked second-hand clothes.[12] The social geography of Nantes resembled that of Paris; 'fiscal notables' were distributed unevenly across neighbourhoods and there was a 'multi-nuclear pattern of wealth and poverty'.[13]

Table 2.1 Average tax assessment by parish

Parish	Total no. of households	Mean assessment (livres)	Median assessment (livres)	Maximum assessment (livres)
Notre-Dame	93	12.28	8	70
St-Laurent	65	12.67	8	90
St-Vincent	84	8.6	4	45
St-Saturnin	305	7.36	3	60
Ste-Croix	489	6.28	2	70
La Fosse	481	6.45	1.5	86
St-Léonard	161	2.27	0.25	60
Ste-Radegonde	72	3.44	0.5	38
St-Clément	334	2.7	1	20
St-Similien	447	1.69	1	36
St-Nicolas	192	4.78	2	40
St-Denis	168	6.69	3	50

Source: A.M.N. CC 86.

The basic social unit of each parish was the household, the site of individual identity, social position, economic production and legal rights. Nantes had many similarities with other large cities of northern Europe. The taxpaying household head was typically a married man: this was the case in about 75 per cent of all households in 1592–93. Widowers and single men led 17 per cent, and widows 7.6 per cent, although there were differences between parishes. The nuclear family, often with resident servants, predominated. Over the whole city, there was a mean household size of 4.12 members, but it ranged from 3.7 for suburban Saint-Clément to 4.6 for Saint-Saturnin (see Table 2.2). The majority of households were small: 75 per cent of the population lived with five or fewer members while only 2.5 per cent of surveyed households lived with ten or more. There was a direct correlation between mean tax assessment and household size. Wealthier inhabitants, on average, had larger households. In both Saint-Clément and Saint-Saturnin, households assessed at under 3 *livres* of tax had typically between three and five members; only where households were assessed at more than 20 *livres* did their size rise above six people. Yet the households of poorer folk were rarely smaller than two, and their size was due to the absence of servants, resident kin, and spouses, not to individuals living alone.[14] In Saint-Léonard there were at least five households of non-related, co-habiting poor women, including one with four single women who worked cleaning the streets, and one of widows in an attic room who sold candles. Thomas Sokoll shows this to have been a feature of urban pauper households in southern England and questions whether it was a voluntary arrangement or part of the poor relief system of towns.[15]

Table 2.2 Household size and wealth

Parish	Mean household size	Mean tax assessment (livres)	% households with children	% households with male servants	% households with female servants
St-Clément	3.7	2.7	65.7	8.76	11.49
Ste-Croix	4.25	6.28	53	10.25	42.27
St-Saturnin	4.6	7.36	59.4	20.28	58.69

Source: A.M.N. CC 86, EE 30.

The largest dependent group within households was children, who formed 31.5 per cent of the listed population although only 58.3 per cent of households included them, typically in groups of two to three.[16] Again there were differences between parishes. Only 53 per cent of households in Sainte-Croix included children while 65.7 per cent of those of Saint-Clément did so.[17] Male and female servants were also important household members, comprising 15.3 per cent of the surveyed population. Households containing large numbers of children had few servants. In the suburban parish, children no doubt performed the tasks which servants did within the city walls; the wealthier parishes contained more employees.[18] Women servants predominated, for about 34.7 per cent of households employed female domestics, although only 11.5 per cent of Saint-Clément's households did so, as opposed to 58.7 per cent in Saint-Saturnin. Fewer households employed male servants, which included resident journeymen and apprentices – 11.4 per cent of all households, and again fewer in Saint-Clément than in Saint-Saturnin.

Women were a minority of taxpayers in Nantes as in all contemporary cities, constituting about 11 per cent of assessed households in 1593. These were most frequently widows, but there were also wives with absentee husbands and single women.[19] Female heads of household were among the poorer groups in urban society and often were not assessed for taxation. A study of the poor parish of Saint-Léonard illustrates this. Here, 16.8 per cent of households were female-led: there were 12 widows, 5 wives and 16 single women. Of these, ten were exempt because of poverty and one for nobility, and the remaining women were assessed for only 3.5 per cent of the parish's taxes. There is a marked correlation between the wealth of a parish and the number of female taxpayers. The wealthy parishes of Saint-Laurent and Saint-Vincent record 23 and 23.8 per cent of female-led households, respectively, whereas the suburban parishes of Saint-Clément and Saint-Similien record 6 and 7.6 per cent.[20] Within each parish, fewer women than men paid tax, and where they were assessed they headed relatively wealthy households. Economic position and a Christian culture of charity seem to have operated against burdening women, widows and children with taxation. Such groups had relatively few rights within the urban polity; they were also subject to fewer obligations.

A group of urban dwellers with even fewer rights in the polity was the poor. The extent of poverty in sixteenth-century Nantes is hard to calculate, for there are no extant full rolls or computations of paupers. Estimates for other French cities vary. Richard Gascon argues for Lyon that one in five inhabitants was poor or vulnerable to poverty. The structural poor, unable to work and dependent on alms, comprised 5–10 per cent of the urban population, while 'cyclical' poor in need of occasional assistance could reach 20–30 per cent.[21] In Nantes, we can identify four main types of pauper. First, there were the sick, temporary inmates of the city's hospitals. In the Hôtel-Dieu during the second week of December 1554, for example, there were 32 men, 35 women and 14 children being cared for; the numbers rose to 55 men and 35 women at the end of the month.[22] The patients were city folk for whom no alternative existed or, much more commonly, visitors or migrant workers. Barbara Davis has observed for Toulouse that hospital residence was unpopular and city residents avoided it.[23] The list of clothing of those who died, about 50 per cent of admissions, attests to their poverty, particularly for the women, most of whom even lacked shoes.[24]

Second, there were people who were unable to support themselves because of youth or age, sickness or disability and who were considered deserving of parish relief. A poor roll of the suburb of Saint-Similien of 1580 lists fifty-eight households, comprising 185 individuals. Poor households fell into four categories. Families with young children, whether led by married couples, widows or widowers, constituted two-thirds of those in receipt of relief. The other three groups comprised single people, mostly widows or widowers; orphaned children; and aged or infirm married couples.[25] J. Collins has observed the heavy bias towards women recipients; in Sainte-Radegonde during 1580, eleven of seventeen households listed on the relief roll were headed by women, including six widows, six single women and two abandoned wives.[26]

Thirdly, there was a much larger group of poor workers who could support themselves by their labour most of the time, but who became paupers as soon as bread prices rose. In the mid-1570s, a temporarily employed gate porter in Nantes earned 6 *sous* a day; if he bought the cheapest rye loaf at 6 *deniers*, a week's supply for himself alone would cost more than half a day's pay, assuming that he ate only one loaf a day. Shelter, fuel, clothing and other food-stuffs, for him and his family, were also necessary.[27] As soon as prices rose, such people joined the ranks of the hungry.[28]

Thus the largest group of potential paupers were simple labourers or artisans, whose earnings, kin and neighbourhood contacts would suffice for household provision in good times, but who were unable to support their fami-lies when prices or unemployment rose. These people survived in an economy of makeshifts. One feature of the social world of the poor was the complexity of their households.[29] In Saint-Similien in 1580 there were three households of elderly widows and unrelated orphan children: La Gastine sheltered two little orphans, and Olive Bedard and a third widow aged over eighty years, three each.[30] By grouping together, individuals fared morally and materially better than if they shifted for themselves alone. Davis' study of Toulouse has shown that poverty 'was more than the lack of material wealth, it was the absence of familial, friendship, corporate or neighbourly networks that could prevent people falling into dire straits whether or not they were able to work'.[31] Poor people living together created new social networks in order to survive.[32]

Added to the domiciled poor was a fourth group, a large numbers of mobile paupers. The rural poor flooded into the city at Easter and Corpus Christi, as pilgrims and to beg. Peasants flooded into the city when famine struck. There were beggars, frequently children, vagrants, the unemployed and the dispossessed, who wandered from town to town and whom everyone feared as troublemakers, thieves and vectors of disease. City folk were anxious to be rid of them, and they were the object of periodic expulsions.

The men and women, both rich and poor, who lived in Nantes came from many different regions. As in most early modern towns, the population was maintained and augmented through immigration: Croix calculates that 21 per cent of the spouses marrying in Nantes' parishes between 1570 and 1600 were born outside the city.[33] Rural migrants came for seasonal, temporary or perma-nent stays, for work or for poor relief. Analysis of the geographical origins of the patients of the Hôtel-Dieu in December 1554 shows that the majority came from the diocese of Nantes, particularly from the vineyards south of the Loire. Most men patients came from Nantes itself (28 per cent), Nantes diocese (22 per cent), upper Brittany (22 per cent) and the Loire valley (12.5 per cent). The women came from Nantes (43 per cent) or the diocese (40 per cent), with a much smaller proportion from the Vannetais in Brittany (6 per cent) and the Loire valley (8.5 per cent).[35] A few came from further away – from Paris, Picardy and the Auvergne, for example. The movement of people was predominantly masculine; fewer women than men came to Nantes to work, and from shorter distances away. In Saint-Nicolas in the later part of the century, of 139 migrant women who married in the parish church only thirteen had travelled more than 20 kilometres from their birth place, the rest having moved a shorter distance.[36]

Some of Nantes' residents came from considerably further away, however, for there were important 'foreign' colonies associated with the port of La Fosse. A dozen Italian families and a handful of Portuguese families resided in Saint-Nicolas in mid-century, but the largest 'foreign' community comprised Spanish merchants. The first families arrived before 1455; others came in the mid-sixteenth century, with the resumption of trade after the end of Habsburg–Valois hostility, among them the Ruiz, Miranda, Rocca, Marquez, Compludo, Espinoza, Hérédia and Santo-Domingo clans. There were perhaps 130 families in all. All were Basque, from Bilbao, San Sebastián, Burgos and Medina del Campo.[35] Towards 1600 there were around 800–1,000 'foreigners', perhaps 3–4 per cent of the total city population, who were mostly settled in the port parish of Saint-Nicolas, baptising their children in this church.[37]

The families were assimilated quickly, and a large proportion became members of the civic elite.[38] The Rocaz family became receivers for the *fouages* of Vannes and Cornouaille and churchwardens of Saint-Nicolas; Julien de Mirande became a canon of the collegiate church of Notre-Dame.[39] The Spanish intermarried with local families or purchased letters of naturalisation and became French subjects. A good example is the career of André Ruiz.[40] Born in Medina del Campo, he arrived in Nantes before 1537 to train in commerce in the household of a Spanish merchant, possibly Jean de la Presse. Ruiz's activities were initially mercantile: he formed associations with his brothers, who remained in Spain, and Nantais Spanish merchants, to export textiles, books and paper. In time he acted as a commissioner for merchants of Rouen, Lyon and Thiers to export their wares to the Basque ports and Medina del Campo. Subsequently Ruiz became involved in finance. From 1548 he was farmer of the municipal tax on merchandise entering Nantes, the *denier pour livre*; from 1565 he farmed the royal customs tax on goods entering and leaving the port of Nantes (the *prévôté*); then in the latter years of his life he was part of a consortium farming royal tolls in the province of Brittany, the *impôts et billots*. Ruiz purchased a royal office for his son, dowered his daughters for marriages to Spanish and Breton notables and purchased properties in and around Nantes.

The economy of Nantes was mixed, as is shown by the variety of occupations found in the city, from clergy and *parlementaire*, to stevedore and fish hawker. In 1593, the most frequently cited professions were those of royal and municipal officers (14 per cent), legal professionals (12.3 per cent), then traders in clothing (12.5 per cent), dealers in food and drink (9.5 per cent) leather workers, including shoe makers (9.4 per cent) and those in the building and wood trades (9.4 per cent).[41] These figures do not, however, give an accurate picture of the distribution of work among the population. Householders who were defined by their occupations were among the wealthier of their parish communities, although the relationship between economic rank and profession was not a simple one.[42] A recognised occupation was a badge of respectability and of an identified position within society, a mark of social distinction as much as an economic category. Householders who belonged to corporate bodies, with important legal and fiscal privileges and social distinctions within the city and the realm, were careful to state their professions. Thus, in the poor, suburban parish of Saint-Clément only seven householders were labelled with occupations, while in the wealthy intramural parishes of Saint-Denis and Saint-Laurent, where officers and legal groups predominated, 78 per cent and 64.6 per cent of householders respectively stated their professions.[43] The vast majority of Nantais lacked a fixed occupational identity because their income was obtained from a variety of work activities; most but not all of these came from low-income groups.[44] The very wealthy inhabitants of La Fosse gave no occupation; predominantly merchants, they invested in ships, bonds and lands, traded in a range of commodities, organised rural industries, and had diverse sources of income. They preferred to be recognised by their titles of land ownership rather than by their 'trades'.[45] Similarly, craftsmen and labourers earned their livelihoods in a number of ways. Labourers worked on building sites, cleaned the streets, portered and unloaded ships. Women hawked, laundered and ran taverns. Wealth, parish organisations, kinship and household, rather than economic function, remained the main determinants of status and identity for the Nantais.

A wide range of goods was manufactured in Nantes, although we know little about the volume or extent of production. No single industry dominated. Ship building, rope and sail manufacture took place by the Loire. Port activities such as portering and carting were concentrated in waterside parishes. There was a nucleus of leather workers in the Erdre-side parish of Saint-Léonard, where there were tanneries, curriers and harness manufacturers.[46] There was some small-scale cloth manufacture, of linen and canvas, concentrated in the poorer parishes of Saint-Léonard and Sainte-Croix; Gayle Brunelle shows that many female servants in artisan households were employed manufacturing cloth as well as in other tasks, to contribute to household income.[47] Metal traders and arms manufacturers were numerous in the city; as well as locksmiths and blacksmiths, there were arquebus and sword makers, cannoners and powder makers, and metal finishers were concentrated on the port of La Fosse. The majority of trades were not found in specific zones but distributed around the city, for these workers made their livings servicing the resident population: bakers, butchers, tailors, soapmakers, shoemakers and builders were found in all parishes.[48] There was also a large, half-invisible retail sector dominated by women, comprising the small-scale selling of wine in *cabarets*, fish hawking, second-hand clothes dealing and vending used candles.[49] Most men and women in Nantes made and mended things, sold and resold small items, and laboured. Work was seasonal, particularly that associated with maritime commerce. Ships came to the city's quays in the greatest numbers in spring and summer, grew fewer during the autumn and were fewest during the winter months. A working family was dependent upon the labour of all its members to make ends meet. The mixed urban and household economies of Nantes were at least facilitated by the 'free' nature of most production in the city; in the mid-sixteenth century there were only twelve craft guilds in contrast to the situation in larger towns such as Rouen and Paris, where most trades were incorporated.[50] There was an annual 'free' fair in February, where goods could be sold tax-free.[51] Most production was small-scale and domestic; an independent artisan owned his own tools, and he produced and sold his goods in a shop assisted by a skilled journeyman, a young apprentice or his wife and family.[52] The free nature of Nantes' crafts did not, however, open them up to women, who were excluded from formal participation in many types of paid work and production, other than as wife, assistant or widow.

The activity which most dominated city life was water-borne commerce. Nantes was a great redistribution centre, between the east and west of France and between northern Europe and the Iberian world. In the mid-sixteenth century, about 2,000 ships visited the maritime port annually. Most were small and middle-sized craft, of 6–7 tonnes (42 per cent) or 10–30 tonnes (55 per cent), used for coastal navigation and trade, mostly with the west of France. About 3 per cent of the total – perhaps thirty vessels a year – were Atlantic sailing ships of 80–150 tonnes. In addition, there was a vast Loire fleet of perhaps 1,200 boats of small tonnage, for trade up and down the Loire.[53] Contemporaries believed that trade between Nantes and Spain was the mainstay of the city's economy. In 1564 the bourgeois of Nantes wrote to the king that this commerce provided 'not only [the merchants'] well-being and fortune but the livelihood of an infinite number of poor people, who are maintained solely by this trade'.[54] The main Hispanic trade was with the Basque region, principally Bilbao, which served as a distribution centre for Castile through Burgos and the fairs of Medina del Campo.[55] The trade with Bilbao was the object of special trading agreements between the two cities. In 1430 Duke Jean V concluded a treaty with the king of Castile which allowed for the institution at Nantes of a consul to defend the interests of Spaniards trading in the duchy.[56] In the early sixteenth century the city council at Bilbao allowed Nantais representation on its council of commerce. Mutual trading privileges and a moderation of fiscal exactions for textiles and wool followed. By the mid-century the Spanish colonists and their associates in Nantes had created an association for the charging of ships destined for Bilbao, the Compañia de los Señores del Salvo Conduto, along with a devotional confraternity in the Franciscan convent. No merchant of Nantes could trade with Bilbao, in either direction, without being part of this company and submitting to its regulations.[57]

The main export to Spain was textiles: canvas and linen manufactured in the countryside of northern and eastern Brittany, western Normandy, Anjou and Poitou. Nantes' merchants visited or sent factors to regional markets, or treated directly with local producers to buy up pieces for export. Although more irregular, grain was another export to northern Spain, and was purchased from Brittany, Normandy and the Beauce. Other goods included books from Lyon, paper from Thiers and playing cards. In turn, Nantes was a redistribution centre for Spanish goods for much of Brittany and northern France, through the valley of the Loire and its tributaries. Most important were iron and steel from the Basque region, wool, cochineal, confectionery, medicinal oranges and a few fine textiles such as sheets, silks and hose. Nantes was one of seven towns permitted in 1559 to trade in *denrées* (spices and drugs).[58] Further, the city was a staging post for Spanish traders and goods en route to Flanders, Bruges and Antwerp, and the Baltic and North Sea regions.[59] Imports were fewer than exports at Nantes, and there was a trade surplus realised in hard currency.[60] Trade with Spain rose in the mid-century. During the Habsburg–Valois wars, in terms of cargoes leaving Nantes it was perhaps 10 per cent of the total of the port, rising to 22 per cent after the peace of Cateau-Cambrésis.[61]

Traditional histories of Nantes interpret the city as one without a specific hinterland: its regional position at the crossroads of Brittany and Aquitaine, and on the edge of the Loire valley, made it exterior to all of them and dependent upon none.[62] This was not the case. Firstly, many of the estates in the diocese of Nantes were owned by the city's clergy, merchants and legal officials. The rents financed an urban lifestyle while the agricultural produce was consumed or marketed within the town. Secondly, in terms of volume, the main goods moving through the port of Nantes were not those of the Spanish trade but locally produced wine and salt. Jean Tanguy, the historian of the port of Nantes, argues that the wine trade was the rock on which the Nantais economy was based, for it enriched her merchants and attracted a large fleet of boats to her ports.[63] The wine came mostly from the area south of the Loire, the *vignoble nantais*, much of which was owned by the city's elites. Salt came from Guérande and the bay of Bourgneuf. The domestic grain trade was also important. There was a *halle aux blés* near to the *port aux vins* where local cereals and 'imports' from southern Brittany were sold. Finally, Nantes was also a great fish market, principally for Newfoundland cod and North Sea herring. Although few fishing vessels operated from its quays, the northern Breton fisheries used the city as an entrepôt for their wares and to purchase their essential preservative, salt. The main trading partners with Nantes were the cities of the Loire valley and Brittany, via its many coastal ports.[64] The Company of Merchants frequenting the Loire and its tributaries was an important group of Nantes' traders, and the city's merchants sent their representatives to the company's meetings in Orléans.[65] The company's functions were to clear the river of obstacles, to maintain the haulage road at the side of the Loire and its tributaries, and to lobby the royal court against new and heavy tolls on merchandise. The company contributed towards the costs of building stone quays at port Briand-Maillard in Nantes in 1549.[66]

Authority in theory and practice – the functions of urban police

Effective authority in the early modern city was the result of a complex relationship between ideology, institutions and individuals. The stability of urban society and the authority of city government in Nantes were based in large measure on a 'shared commitment to community norms, peace, unity and commonweal' by elites and popular groups.[67] The city was a moral and spiritual union of people which provided the agency for a life of goodness, virtue and probity.[68] There was no legally defined status of citizen in sixteenth-century Nantes, but the inhabitants were entitled to certain rights, according to individual status, wealth, gender, age and membership of a corporation or an estate. Political functions, the holding of public office or the participation in the election of municipal government, theoretically devolved on all householders, although in practice they were the preserve of the wealthy elites. Fiscal immunities granted to the community were enjoyed by all householders, particularly exemption from direct taxation and from *franc fief*. Civic and legal rights, to own property, to make contracts, to pursue legal suits and to join corporations such as craft guilds, devolved upon heads of household. Social rights, to poor relief, to a share in the cultural and religious life of the community, to shop in protected markets with a regulated grain supply and to benefit from the defences of the city, were the prerogative of all recognised residents. However, in theory, the defining attribute of an inhabitant of any social status was not a body of rights, but a set of duties. As the Auvergnat magistrate Jean Combes wrote in 1576, 'a good citizen and one who deserves this title must not refuse any office which his place of residence obliges him to accept . . . otherwise . . . he deserves to be stripped of his title of "citizen" and deprived of all the privileges and commodities appertaining to his town'.[69] These were contributions to state and civic taxation, to poor relief and to urban defence.[70]

The relationship between ideology and institutions in the maintenance of urban stability can be illustrated for Nantes through an examination of the theory and practice of urban police. According to Bernard Chevalier, the term *police* began to be used in the fourteenth century to describe the general organisation of society and its government. In time, it came also to mean the maintenance of order and peace, respect for and preservation of property, and the amelioration of the conditions of life. In his classic work on *police*, N. de la Mare observed that the well-being of men and women was dependent upon three factors: the state of the soul, the health of the body, and fortune. Religion and morality were the most important and underpinned *police*, 'for if religion alone were upheld, all the other functions . . . would be accomplished'.[71] Police comprised maintenance of church organisation, doctrine and the purity of faith and the observation of sacraments and feasts. But *police* was also responsible for the material conservation of mankind and for the procurement of the necessary goods and articles for human welfare. It was thus concerned with 'all the laws which regulate health, foodstuffs, clothing, lodging, public highways, security and tranquility' along with commerce, manufacture and the mechanical arts, which were legitimate means of acquiring 'fortune'.[72] Religious obligations and material concerns combined in the Christian mandate to 'love thy neighbour', to live in fraternal harmony and charity, mediated through good works. E. P. Thompson's notion of a 'moral economy' can be applied to sixteenth-century society. There was a 'consistent traditional view of social norms and obligations, of the proper economic functions of several parties within the community', mediated through the church and the upholding of true religion.[73]

There were important elements of contract in the general notion of *police*. *Police* was the third of Seyssel's constitutional 'bridles' on monarchy. This consisted of safeguarding traditional ordinances, usages, liberties and privileges but also the maintenance of the subjects of all three estates in good accord and contentment. The sovereign was to achieve this by treating the nobility well, limiting sumptuary, encouraging manufacture and trade and limiting taxation.[74] *Police* as a bridle on power also had resonance for urban government.

Municipal authority was checked by 'the authority of custom and in particular by a conception of the good order and harmony which exists between all classes of men in the kingdom'.[75] In towns, each stratum of society had its proper status along with its accompanying rights and obligations. The function of urban government was to maintain these privileges and provide mechanisms for arbitration when an individual's rights were infringed by others. While the creation and enforcement of regulation was the prerogative of elites, under-pinned by paternalism, the upholding of the values of the city was the responsi-bility of all inhabitants. Thus, the impetus for *police* came from above and from below; it was a system of shared values and of dispersed authority where 'power rested on a nice balance between coercion and negotiation held within the tenacious tentacles of custom'.[76]

At its simplest level *police* was also synonymous with urban adminis-tration, particularly religious, moral, social and economic affairs.[77] In Nantes, an edict of December 1564 outlined the police powers which the newly organ-ised municipality appropriated to its own jurisdiction. The content of the edict illustrates contemporary understanding of the term and the municipality's responsibilities for urban police. The municipality was to organise the watch and guard of the city, claiming supervision of the city's defence (article 6); it was to supervise all revenues and expenditures of civil communities, whether parishes, confraternities or guilds (article 9); wholesale and retail commerce, and craft production were to be regulated, and there was a particular concern with the prices of foodstuffs, weights and measures (articles 10 and 11). The city also took responsibility for the organisation of poor relief and correction of blasphemers, vagabonds and beggars (article 17).[78] Thus a Christian, moral responsibility for good order in spiritual and material matters directly under-pinned urban administration and the practical, daily policing of the people. These theoretical and practical notions combined in the activity known as 'police' in sixteenth-century Nantes.

Two of the most important functions of practical urban police, resulting from the ideologies outlined above, were the provisioning of the populace and the care of the poor.[79] These examples are used here to illustrate urban gover-nance in the mid-sixteenth century. In the early modern city, the maintenance of the grain supply was vital, for large parts of the urban population lived largely on bread. Steven Kaplan has argued that subsistence was the 'uncon-tested tenet of public policy during the old regime, founded on the conviction that social stability could be guaranteed only by guaranteeing the food supply . . . Without order, government could not endure and society could not hold together . . . the prerequisite for order was to provide for the subsistence of the people.'[80] The policing of food staples was a political act, which justified the legitimacy of municipal government; the city population 'considered that the fight against high prices and speculation was . . . the social responsibility of the honourable men who governed them'.[81]

Before 1565, the *conseil des bourgeois* of Nantes shared responsibility for provisioning with the other royal officers, the seneschal and *prévôt*. Policing was largely about visible, public supervision and intervention by judicial officers when infractions occurred. It took place at two main points: the marketing of grain, and the production and sale of bread. In periods of 'normal' prices, the provisioning trades were left largely to their own devices, under the public eye of municipal officers. Supervision of grain supply centred on the public markets. The cereals trade seems to have been free, without licensing, and open to all comers. Commerce was mostly in the hands of middling and small-scale merchants operating locally or regionally, and landlords trading in the products of their estates.[82] Merchants were obliged to sell their grain at the market of the Poterne; sales directly from barges and private granaries were forbidden. Grain was offered to city buyers for three days before being opened up for sale to commercial agents. Sales were negotiated and sealed by the public act of measuring the grain sold, carried out by town officials known as grain measurers. Police centred on two features of the trade: the quality of grains sold and their price. Prices were assessed officially and reported upon by two grain-measurers at 1 p.m. on Saturdays, during the height of the market.[83] Visible, public marketing was considered the best guarantee of honesty and fairness.

In periods of shortage, the *conseil des bourgeois* would intervene to improve supplies, usually in the early spring, when prices began to rise steeply. First of all, pressure was put on merchants to supply the city more efficiently while measures were taken to prevent forestalling and the export of grain. Judicial officers would visit granaries to assess their contents. If no grain appeared at the market, dealers were ordered to open their granaries and sell at a fixed price, and bourgeois who possessed more than their needs were ordered to sell the surplus to city residents.[84] In time of dire need, the *conseil* would also commission merchants to search out supplies for the city. The winter and spring of 1562–63 were a period of shortage, following a poor harvest aggravated by war. In January, wheat was imported from Flanders.[85] In February, nine wealthy individuals lent money to purchase grain and Jean Guerin was sent to lower Brittany to buy for the city.[86]

The creation of a new municipality in 1565, together with famine in that year, led to greater regulation of provisioning. This coincided with greater royal intervention in the grain trade in the kingdom at large. An ordinance of Blois of 1559 created a *bureau des blés* at Paris, and it was forbidden to export grain without royal licence, the ban being reinforced by a further edict of 1571 which made the export of cereals the preserve of the monarch himself.[87] This in part was to satisfy public opinion that cereals 'should be consumed in the region in which [they were] grown, especially in times of scarcity' and to prevent export in times of dearth.[88] Many of the years between 1560 and 1580 saw royal embargoes on grain exports from Brittany or only small amounts allowed under special permit for Spanish or Portuguese markets.[89] Domestic commerce in grain remained free in Nantes, but was subject to closer observation in 'normal' times and increased intervention when shortages threatened. In the autumn of 1565 there began a great shortage of grain that lasted into 1567. As early as August, the municipality obtained letters from the royal governor prohibiting exports.[90] Grain dealers and bakers were ordered to provision the city with sufficient stocks to sell to the inhabitants at a fixed price, and threatened with corporal punishment and a fine of 500 *livres* if they disobeyed.[91] By the early spring, granaries were being visited to assess stocks, private sales were forbidden, and inhabitants were given permission to seize grain that was sold illicitly. The municipality undertook a highly public prosecution of the *échevin* Jean Picaud, who was fined 60 *livres* for failing to bring all his grain to market and for having sold 150 *sétiers* of rye to merchants from the upper Loire.[92] On 20 May 1566 it was estimated that the city was provisioned for only two to three days. All grain held by merchants on the port was ordered to be purchased, and anyone who resisted would be arrested. In the same month, the municipality undertook to borrow up to 10,000 *livres* to buy grain in lower Brittany, which would be sold to the public at 'a reasonable price'.[93] But the essence of emergency policing remained increased supervision and regulation of marketing. It was reactive rather than preventative, and it was short-term. The personal presence of mayor, *échevins*, royal judicial officers and sergeants of the courts visiting markets, granaries and ports, and the suspicions of the hungry population, served as the main regulatory mechanisms. There was no attempt to create public granaries or stockpiles as in other cities, such as Amiens.[94] Sanctions were moral as much as judicial.

The second strand of the police of subsistence was the supervision of bread production. This centred on the bakers of the city. Until the late 1560s baking was a free trade, regulated by the urban authorities. It was the preserve of small-scale artisans working in their own shops, which were numerous and widely distributed around the city. The type of bread made and above all its weight were closely policed. Scales had to be displayed at all times in shops and on stalls. All bread had to carry the mark of its baker, and the stamp for marking bread must be registered with the clerk of police, so that a loaf could be traced to its producer.[95] The *conseil* made great show of supervising weights and of punishing infractions.[96] After 1565 the new municipality took over the police of the trade. In September 1565, for example, bakers were visited and their grain stocks estimated; particular attention was given to twenty-four bakers in the populous suburbs of La Fosse, the Marchix and Saint-Clément, the Loire ports and the parish of Saint-Léonard.[97] On 16 February 1570 Widow Bonnyer and Guillaume Guilbaud were both fined 20 *sous* for selling their loaves two ounces short of the official measure; Jean Bellot was fined for selling unmarked bread, and several hawkers, including a cauldron maker and his wife, were warned not to sell loaves, or they would incur a fine of 10 *livres*.[98] The symbolic effect of frequent prosecutions was important; it demonstrated to the labouring people of Nantes that the authorities were acting vigilantly in their interests.[99]

The institutional framework of bakery supervision also increased. In March 1567 the bakers were incorporated into a craft guild. Privileges to trade were granted to a relatively limited number of master bakers in exchange for greater self-regulation and policing of production and sale by the artisans themselves. Only masters received by the guild could make and sell bread in Nantes, except at the Wednesday and Saturday markets and on fair days, and there was to be no hawking of bread at all. The bakers were confirmed in their preferential access to the grain market, having the right to buy at any time, and on market days to purchase before other bakers and merchants.[100] All of this reduced competition and facilitated supervision; elected guild officers had to visit all bakers twice a week. Similarly, the butchers of Nantes were incorporated into a guild in the early 1570s. Other craft corporations remained few in the city. Police authority was thus devolved downwards, to guild officers and masters, who acquired public and legal responsibility for the quality of their goods. However, the police court retained overall supervision of food supply. Guild officers reported to the police, masters were sworn in, and prosecutions were undertaken in this court by both the guilds and the municipality. Guild and police were complementary moral and judicial authorities for the preservation of good standards and fairness in the provisioning of the city.

The control and treatment of the poor was a second, related, preoccupation of police in Nantes, for the maintenance of order and the legitimation of authority in the city. In the sixteenth century relief of the poor was a religious and a civic duty. The poor and the sick were identified with Christ and needed succour and comfort for His sake as a means of meriting salvation.[101] Long before the provisions of the ordinances of Moulins (1566) and Blois (1579) it was an obligation of parishes and communities to relieve their poor members. Town government, therefore, had long had an important role in public assistance, not only from 'a question of conscience but a question of good police, a problem to regulate for the common good'.[102] Police of the poor had also a desire for order at its heart; 'poor relief served the . . . purpose of containing the potential threat to the social order from the ever-swelling ranks of the labouring classes'.[103]

Studies of poverty in the sixteenth-century city have shown that this was a period of change in the perception and treatment of the poor. Three broad themes have been identified. Firstly, the incidence of poverty increased: there were more paupers in 1600 than in 1500, and more mobile or vagrant poor than in the past, although numbers everywhere have been disputed. Population increase, reduced employment opportunities, depressed wages, price inflation across the century, famine, disease, war and civil disturbance reduced the material means of many people, causing the numbers of those who were poor, dislocated and vagrant to rise.[104] Secondly, changes in ideology and motives behind charitable giving have been identified. It has been argued that the sixteenth century witnessed a gradual decline in medieval notions of Christian charity. John Bossy and A. Galpern have argued that previously, charity in practice meant social integration and enlarged sociability and was central to the attainment of salvation.[105] By 1600 this had changed. Paupers, once seen indiscriminately as Christ's poor, were categorised as natives and outsiders. The idea became current that the community owed relief only to its own members, while the vagrant was a danger to the social order and a blasphemer.[106] The poor became less of an asset in the economy of salvation than a material problem in the secular world. Work on the Catholic Reformation offers a contrasting view, however, for Tridentine-inspired reformers put emphasis on good works, where 'the salvation of souls [was] inherently linked to the reduction of hunger and poverty'.[107] Structured charitable giving was still, however, an important part of the growth of charitable works associated with this movement.

A third feature of change was the transfer of responsibility for the organisation of assistance from the church into the hands of secular urban authorities. This arose from an insufficiency of resources, growing anticlericalism, the idea that the clergy were not the most efficient managers of institutions for the laity, and from the influence of humanist writers such as Juan Vives.[108] From the late fifteenth century, the main relief institutions of towns were laicised, their administration being removed from clerics and handed to lay bourgeois, and public funds allocated to their upkeep: Lyon (1478), Amiens (1481) and Paris (1505) exemplified this trend. A series of serious subsistence crises in the second quarter of the sixteenth century led to further concentration of urban public assistance in the hands of municipalities. In Lyon, 1531–34 saw the creation of an *aumône générale*, to distribute aid to a greater number of people, in a more orderly and equitable way than in the past. A central roll would be made of the city's deserving poor who were to be given relief. All charitable giving, including church collections, would be given to a central fund; there were to be no individual handouts, and begging was forbidden.[109] Other cities followed suit: Rouen (1534), Grenoble (1538) and Paris (1544), for example.[110] By these means, distinctions between 'deserving' and 'unde-serving' poor were institutionalised and a much clearer division was created between the supported few and 'the mass of those arbitrarily excluded'.[111]

Before 1565 poor relief in Nantes was a mixed regime of private and public charity. It could be generous, but it was also fragmented.[112] There were handouts at funerals and anniversary obits, often of small amounts to large numbers of people, to maximise the prayers received in return.[113] There were doles from monasteries and cathedral chapters. Confraternities would aid their poorest members. But the main source of public relief in mid-century Nantes was the Hôtel-Dieu, a medieval foundation rebuilt by the bourgeois in 1502–07.[114] In the mid-century, the Hôtel-Dieu admitted between eighty and ninety patients at a time; only the curable sick were admitted, not beggars, invalids or the aged.[115] Nantes also had two smaller hospitals, administered by religious institutions. The hospital of Saint-Clément was run by the cathedral chapter and lay east of the city walls, on the road to Paris. Its function was to shelter pilgrims and to care for the sick inhabitants of the fiefs of the chapter. The hospital of Toussaints, located by the bridge of Nantes, was administered by a confraternity.[116] The half-century before 1560 witnessed increased laicisa-tion of the administration of these hospitals, as in other French cities. From 1504, the *conseil des bourgeois* shared responsibility for administration of revenues of the Hôtel-Dieu with the cathedral chapter, and they jointly elected two lay administrators annually to oversee the hospital's affairs. The subsistence crisis of 1531–32 revealed the inadequacies of the city's relief of the poor, and the *conseil* took steps to bring the Hôtel-Dieu under closer scrutiny. In December 1532 the bourgeois received sole right to elect administrators, and by a royal edict of 1539 administration was formally transferred from the clergy to the *conseil*. Nantes' two smaller hospitals were also taken more closely under the *conseil*'s control. In 1556, the bourgeois chose the hospital of Saint-Clément as the site for their new college, and its patients were moved to the Hôtel-Dieu and Toussaints.[117] The confraternity of Toussaints jealously guarded their independent hospital administration, but they were perennially short of funds; in 1558, the hospital lacked a place to store wine for the poor, and one of its halls needed repair.[118] Appeals for financial aid by its administrators increased the *conseil*'s tutelage of the hospital's affairs.

Despite the emphasis of municipal authorities on hospitals, the most frequent form of assistance was out-relief, doles of bread and money given to paupers in the parishes, usually after mass on Sundays. We know virtually nothing about the administration and allocation of this relief, other than that it was based on parish collections and voluntary donations. Studies of relief in other towns suggest that it was rarely sufficient to survive on, being unable to cover a minimum diet, let alone housing, clothing or other needs. Had the poor relied exclusively on benefits, they would have starved. They had to supplement their benefits with other income, by begging, crime or prostitution but mostly by work.[119]

From the late 1550s, the *conseil* took increasingly systematic measures to police the poor. In 1562, the first civil war brought with it hunger and plague. In November, the *conseil* ordered the expulsion of poor vagabonds begging on the streets, claiming that they came from regions where there was contagion. Extra guards were put on the city gates to prevent paupers from entering.[120] A week later, each parish was ordered to draw up a roll of deserving poor, and to present it to the *conseil*.[121] Alms were sought from those who were able to give but not enough offers were made, so on 28 January 1563, tax rolls were ordered drawn up by the *recteur* and churchwardens of each parish, while the clergy of the county, regular and secular, were asked to contribute alms.[122]

The management of the emergency of 1562–63 was a prelude to the reform of poor relief administration after 1565. There were two fundamental problems in Nantes. Firstly, it was difficult to find administrators for the Hôtel-Dieu. The supervision of the hospital was an onerous charge, for it included the oversight of personnel, purchase of foodstuffs and management of the hospital's funds. The office was also a financial burden, for advance payment of goods was met by the administrators and reimbursed by the *conseil*, which took time.[123] The duties fell on the whole family of the administrator; in December 1560, François Salmon asked for exemption from his election, as he was aged and unmarried, and 'for this charge it was very necessary that a wife went frequently [to the hospital]'.[124] Those with sufficient wealth would buy themselves out of the charge; in 1555, Pierre Maveraie, Yvon Rocaz and Guillaume Poullain each gave to the hospital 10 *livres* of *rentes* on their properties in order to be discharged of the duty.[125] Secondly, there was a perennial shortage of financial resources. In ordinary years, the city's relief was just about enough to prevent paupers from starving to death, but in times of hardship, existing structures were unable to cope. The hospitals each had their own endowments, while fines for police and guild offences went to the Hôtel-Dieu, as did a tax on wood used in ship building and the city's right of revenue from Sunday fishing.[126] Beyond that, relief depended upon parish collections and bequests of various sorts. There was an ongoing attempt to force individuals and religious institutions to pledge regular gifts. Many of the city's wealthy endowed the Hôtel-Dieu with annual *rentes* on property, usually of 10 *livres* in the mid-century, but much of this gift financed obit masses for the patron and did not benefit the poor.[127] From 1545 the confraternities were forced to give regular 'gifts': in November 1556, for example, the shoemakers' guild of St Crispin offered the rents due to the confraternity while the *prévôt* of the confraternity of St John gave 25 *livres* for their part.[128] But revenue proved irregular, for rents and gifts were often defaulted upon.

After 1565, the municipality took to itself the principal responsibility for fund raising, administration and distribution of poor relief. In October 1568, there was a reform of assistance. A *bureau des pauvres* was created, with three governors of the poor elected annually, one from each of the bourgeois, the judicial officers and the cathedral clergy. The *bureau* met weekly, and its function was to oversee and coordinate all of the city's relief institutions and the organisation of parish relief, 'so that alms would be well and duly distributed and the revenues of the hospitals properly administered'.[129] Almsgiving was to be centralised. Within each parish, a receiver was appointed to solicit alms from householders and to encourage the wealthy to pledge regular gifts, and boxes for the poor were set up in each church. Alms in kind, even scraps of food, were to be taken to the hospitals or to the houses of parish paupers. The poor themselves were to be more closely policed. Begging was prohibited. Paupers had to apply for aid to the governors, who decided whether or not to admit to a hospital or grant relief. The names of the assisted of each parish would be listed on a roll, along with their entitlements, and doles were given out on Sundays, from their parish church. In return, the poor would each wear a badge on their clothing.[130] Nantes' reforms had parallels with those of other French cities.

Efforts were made to improve the administration of the Hôtel-Dieu. The new municipality was more robust in its dealings with the lay administrators. Attempts to evade service were less successful than before. For example, in 1578 Jean Collet, porter of the gate of La Poissonnerie, refused his election because of his age and function, and offered 100 *sous* annual rent for the poor; this was refused and the seneschal asked to constrain Collet to take up the charge.[131] The municipality also tried to resolve the cash flow problems of the administrators. In December 1569, André Rouxeau and Jehan Erauld received 1,000 *livres* in advance to provision the poor; it was their task to raise the same amount from the hospital revenues over the year and pass it on to their successors at the end of their term of office.[132] Finally, further attempts were made at hospital rationalisation. In January 1569 the empty leper hospital of Saint-Lazare, in the northern suburb of Haut-Pavés, was closed and its revenues united with those of the Hôtel-Dieu.[133] The municipality tried also to incorporate the hospital of Toussaints, although the opposition of its confraternity prevented this.[134] However, Toussaints was transformed into a sort of subsidiary to the Hôtel-Dieu. Its *procureur* was ordered to accept sick and infirm sent to it by the *bureau des pauvres* and to present its accounts for weekly inspection.[135]

Municipal police regulation of moral, social and economic life in the city, considered to be mutually interdependent, was one of the primary manifestations of authority in Nantes. Policing of the poor and other social policies were major factors in the preservation of order, which was seen by historians as a form of social discipline; 'elites expected certain benefits for their benevolence towards the poor, including orderly behaviour'.[136] Robert Duplessis has argued for sixteenth-century Lille that investigations of the poor, and compilations of detailed lists of paupers and the badges its recipients had to wear, enhanced the municipal authority's knowledge about and control over a large section of the urban population.[137] Charity also imposed obligations on its recipients. Kathryn Norberg has shown for Grenoble that paupers were obliged to become good citizens and good Christians, industrious, moral and sober, and to attend church and confession regularly, in return for alms.[138] Order was thus enhanced in the early modern town.

But as Marten Prak has recently argued for the Netherlands, positive, direct action by municipal authorities, rather than fines and repression, was vital in forging bonds between the city's governors and its labouring population.[139] The public act of organising assistance for the poor and hungry was an important legitimising action of paternalist authority. The measures taken were regulatory and disciplinary but also hampered the sort of popular mobilisation that could be prompted by deprivation. Municipal action in the spheres of provisioning and assistance were not just the gestures of a philanthropic and self-interested elite; they arose from, and strengthened, common values of Christian charity and civic responsibility, creating bonds of common interest between elites and popular groups. The municipal police and assistance mechanisms 'curbed the potentially destabilising influence of either a polarised class structure or intractable material grievances'; also, because the municipality dominated charitable institutions and frequently intervened in the town's economy, so artisans' and labourers' interests were 'shaped by and mediated through the political elite'.[140] It was 'part of a programme to eliminate or diffuse opposition to the established order'; artisans were shown that the constituted authorities were on their side.[141]

Conclusions

Authority was hierarchical and institutionalised in Nantes, but it was also dispersed widely throughout urban society. Governance was not only the preserve of a small ruling oligarchy.[142] At the level of the citizenry, a wide variety of individuals, mostly male taxpayers, had experience of authority and the maintenance of order. Parishes, through their churchwardens and other officers, had long been responsible for the collection of taxes and poor rates and distribution of alms; from 1569, parish officers played an enhanced role in identifying, registering, supervising and relieving the domiciled poor among their community. The day-to-day administration of the city's hospitals was largely in the hands of men of the middling sort, two being appointed annually to supervise resources and the treatment of paupers. Police of the provisioning trades was devolved down to guild masters themselves after 1565. In return for greater control of their trade they gained heavier responsibility for its good order, for which they were accountable to the municipality. Many of these positions were temporary, so a large number of individuals had some experience of governance and the exercise of authority within the community. The result of a wide diffusion of authority among the middling men of Nantes was greater integration of these groups into civic governance. These men and their households had a real stake in the maintenance of order, stability and hierarchy, of masters over servants and workers, parents over their children and husbands over wives.[143] Of course, not all was orderly and regulated. Not all households fulfilled their civic responsibilities; individuals and communities could be violent and disorderly, with quarrels and scores to settle. But a wide participatory public gave large numbers of residents a stake in the common-wealth of the city.

Relations between city, province and crown, and between individuals, were understood in terms of law and contract; there were mutual obligations between different authorities and social groups. There was a strong moral and religious dimension to royal, civic and even household authority, mediated through the theology and culture of the Catholic Church. If the early modern city was to remain peaceful, its residents had to share a basic consensus of values on at least the most fundamental questions of social organisation and religious belief. Such consensus was precisely what was to disappear in the second half of the sixteenth century.[144] The rise of Protestantism challenged the fundamental cultural premises upon which civic culture was based. More importantly, the sectarian and military conflicts unleashed from 1560 both threatened the effective authority of crown and city agents, and called into question the relationship between the two. It is to this process that we now turn.

NOTES

1 G. Saupin, *Nantes au XVIIème siècle. Vie politique et société urbaine* (Rennes, 1996), p. 232.
2 Today the ducal tomb is situated in the cathedral of Nantes.
3 A.M.N. BB 10: Délibérations et assemblées de la municipalité 1572–73, fo. 4.
4 Saupin, *Nantes au XVIIème siècle*, p. 231.
5 J. Hardwick, *The Practice of Patriarchy. Gender and the Politics of Household Authority in Early Modern France* (University Park, Pennsylvania, 1998), p. 78.
6 A. Croix, *Nantes et le pays nantais au XVIème siècle. Étude démographique* (1974), p. 208.
7 P. Bois, ed., *Histoire de Nantes* (Toulouse, 1977), p. 173.
8 A.M.N. EE 30: Recensements des hommes, des armes et des vivres, 1592; A.M.N. CC 86: Impôts 1592–1600. The militia survey covers households within six quarters (four of

Nantes's parishes); the tax assessment roll of 1593, imposed on all inhabitants to pay for the costs of the siege of Blain, covers eleven of the twelve parishes.

9 In Poitiers 5.8 per cent of the population paid 52 per cent of the tax assessed in 1552. See H. Heller, *The Conquest of Poverty. The Calvinist Revolt in Sixteenth-Century France* (Leiden, 1986), p. 185. In Paris in 1572 only 20 per cent of the assessed population paid more than 20 *livres*. See R. Descimon, 'Paris on the eve of St. Bartholomew. Taxation, privilege and social geography', in P. Benedict, ed., *Cities and Social Change in Early Modern France* (London, 1989), p. 85.

10 Croix, *Nantes et le pays nantais*, p. 214.

11 Descimon, 'Paris on the eve of St. Bartholomew', p. 88. See also P. Benedict, *Rouen during the Wars of Religion* (Cambridge, 1981), pp. 26–7.

12 A.M.N. CC 86.

13 Descimon, 'Paris on the eve of St. Bartholomew', pp. 85, 88.

14 See T. Sokoll, *Household and Family Among the Poor. The Case of Two Essex Communities in the Late Eighteenth and Early Nineteenth Centuries* (Bochum, 1993), p. 244. In Lyon 78 per cent of families lived in nuclear households in 1597 and the mean household size was 4.13. See O. Zeller, *Les recensements lyonnais de 1597 et 1637. Démographie historique et géographie sociale* (Lyon, 1983), pp. 87, 96–102.

15 Sokoll, *Household and Family*, p. 250. This observation is also made by M. Holt for Dijon in *The French Wars of Religion 1562–1629* (Cambridge, 1995), pp. 209–10.

16 This data is confirmed by Croix's work on parish registers in *Nantes*, pp. 50–2. The figure is small compared with those for contemporary towns.

17 In Lyon in 1597 there were also few children. The mean number of children in a family was 2.5, and the median 1.7. See Zeller, *Recensements lyonnais*, p. 110.

18 The proportion in Lyon in 1597 was 12.8 per cent. See Zeller, *Recensements lyonnais*, p. 122.

19 For detailed analysis of women in sixteenth-century Nantes see J. Collins, *Classes, Estates and Order in Early Modern Brittany* (Cambridge, 1994), pp. 235ff.

20 This trend is also found in Paris in 1572. See Descimon, 'Paris on the eve of St. Bartholomew', p. 77.

21 R. Gascon, *Grand commerce et vie urbaine au XVIème siècle. Lyon et ses marchands* (environ *1520*–environ *1580*, 2 vols (1971), I, pp. 403–4.

22 Records for the Hôtel-Dieu of Nantes are not extant for the period after 1560 and are patchy before that date. See A.M.N. GG 731: Liste des pauvres à l'hôpital Hôtel-Dieu de Nantes 1554.

23 B. Davis, 'Reconstructing the poor in early sixteenth-century Toulouse', *F.H.*, 7 (1993) 266.

24 M. Le Méné, 'L'hospitalisation à l'Hôtel-Dieu à Nantes (décembre 1537–juillet 1539)', *Université de Nantes. Enquêts et documents*, 4 (1978) 21.

25 A.M.N. GG 743 Rôles des pauvres. Saint-Similien 1580. A diocese-wide survey taken in 1580 is extant only for two of Nantes' parishes, Saint-Similien and Sainte-Radegonde.

26 J. Collins, *Classes, Estates and Order*, p. 235.

27 1 *livre* = 20 *sous*; 1 *sou* = 12 *deniers*.

28 A similar figure was calculated by N. Davis for Lyon in 'Poor relief, humanism and heresy', in *Society and Culture in Early Modern France* (Stanford, CA, 1974), p. 24.

29 Observed for Essex by T. Sokoll in *Household and Family*, pp. 247–8.

30 A.M.N. GG 744: Rôles des pauvres.

31 Davis, 'Reconstructing the poor', p. 26.

32 M. Dinges' work on Bordeaux is summarised in M. Prak, 'The carrot and the stick: social control and poor relief in the Dutch Republic, sixteenth to eighteenth centuries', in H. Schilling, ed., *Institutions, Instruments and Agents of Social Control and Discipline in Early Modern Europe* (Frankfurt am Main, 1999), p. 150.

33 Croix, *Nantes et le pays nantais*, p. 119.

34 Le Méné, 'L'hospitalisation à l'Hôtel-Dieu', pp. 11–21.

35 Croix, *Nantes et le pays nantais*, pp. 148–9, 174.
36 Croix, A., 'Deux notes sur Nantes', *Annales de démographie historique* (1970) 143–4, 147–8.
37 Bois, ed., *Histoire de Nantes*, p. 121.
38 Saupin, *Nantes au XVIIème siècle*, p. 277. This is in contrast to Gascon's findings for Lyon in *Grand commerce et vie urbaine*, I, p. 365.
39 Croix, 'Deux notes sur Nantes', pp. 147–8.
40 For details of the life of Ruiz see H. Lapeyre, *Une famille des marchands. Les Ruiz* (1955), pp. 48ff.
41 A.M.N. CC 86.
42 In parish registers professions were rarely recorded below a certain social level. See Croix, *Nantes et le pays nantais*, p. 60.
43 A.M.N. CC 86.
44 See D. Glass, 'Socio-economic status and occupations in the City of London at the end of the seventeeth century', in P. Clark, ed., *The Early Modern Town* (London, 1976), p. 223.
45 The same has been found at La Rochelle. See K. Robbins, *City on the Ocean Sea. La Rochelle 1530–1650* (Leiden, 1997), pp. 35–7.
46 A.M.N. CC 86.
47 G. Brunelle, 'Contractual kin. Servants and their mistresses in sixteenth-century Nantes', *Journal of Early Modern History*, 2 (1998) 375–6.
48 Similar results are found in Rouen and Paris. See Benedict, *Rouen*, p. 26; Descimon, 'Paris on the eve of St. Bartholomew', p. 91.
49 A.M.N. CC 86.
50 E. Pied, *Les anciens corps d'arts et métiers de Nantes*, 3 vols (Nantes, 1903).
51 J. Vailhen, 'Le conseil des bourgeois de Nantes', Thèse du Doctorat, University of Rennes, 1965, p. 379.
52 See also Benedict, *Rouen*, p. 17.
53 J. Tanguy, *Le commerce du port de Nantes au milieu du XVIème siècle* (1956), pp. 16–17.
54 A.M.N. GG 643: Religion reformée.
55 Tanguy, *Le commerce du port de Nantes*, pp. 20–55.
56 Lapeyre, *Une famille des marchands*, p. 370.
57 P. Jeulin, 'Aperçus sur la contractation de Nantes 1530 environ – 1733', *A.B.*, 40 (1932–33) 288, 494.
58 Lapeyre, *Une famille des marchands*, p. 376, 584–90.
59 Jeulin, 'Aperçus sur la contractation', 294–5.
60 Lapeyre, *Une famille des marchands*, 202.
61 Figures from Tanguy, *Le commerce du port de Nantes*, pp. 59–61.
62 See Bois, ed., *Histoire de Nantes*, pp. 119–20; J. Meyer, 'Le commerce nantais au XVIème siècle. Tentative de mise en situation', in P. Masson and M. Vergé-Franceschi, eds, *La France et la mer au siècle des grandes découvertes* (1993), pp. 91–125.
63 Tanguy, *Le commerce du port de Nantes*, pp. 59–61, 78.
64 Jeulin, 'Aperçus sur la contractation', pp. 317–19.
65 Lapeyre, *Une famille des marchands*, p. 172 and Tanguy, *Le commerce du port de Nantes*, pp. 77–8.
66 P. Jeulin, *L'évolution du port de Nantes. Organisation et trafic depuis les origines* (1929), pp. 172–3.
67 P. Wallace, *Communities and Conflict in Early Modern Colmar, 1575–1730* (Atlantic Highlands, New Jersey, 1995), p. 3.
68 M. Bookchin, *From Urbanization to Cities: Towards a New Politics of Citizenship* (London, 1995), p. 19.
69 R. Descimon, 'Milice bourgeoise et identité citadine à Paris au temps de la Ligue', *A.E.S.C.*, 48 (1993) 888–9.
70 E. Tingle, 'A city at war. Changing definitions of citizenship in Nantes during the later wars of religion 1580–9', *European Review of History – Revue européenne d'histoire*, 7 (2000) 99–108.
71 N. de la Mare, 'Preface', in *Traité de la Police*, 4 vols (1705).

72 De la Mare, *Traité de la Police*, I, pp. 3–5.
73 E. P. Thompson, 'The moral economy of the English crowd in the eighteenth century', *Past & Present*, 50 (1971), reprinted in E. P. Thompson, *Customs in Common* (London, 1991), p. 188.
74 C. de Seyssel, *La monarchie de France*, ed J. Poujol, (1961) I, pp. 11, 119; II, pp. 154–65.
75 Discussion of Seysell in Q. Skinner, *The Foundations of Modern Political Thought*, II: *The Reformation* (Cambridge, 1978), p. 261.
76 A. Randall and A. Charlesworth, 'The moral economy. Riot, markets and social conflict', in A. Randall and A. Charlesworth, eds, *Moral Economy and Popular Protest. Crowds, Conflict and Authority* (Basingstoke, 2000), p. 18.
77 B. Chevalier, *Les bonnes villes de France du XIVème au XVIème siècle* (1982), p. 219; J. Collins, *The State in Early Modern France* (Cambridge, 1995), p. 184.
78 Municipal edict of 15 December 1564, reproduced in C. Mellinet, *La commune et la milice de Nantes*, 3 vols (1836–44), III, pp. 195–9.
79 Randall and Charlesworth, 'Moral economy', p. 20.
80 S. Kaplan, *Provisioning Paris. Merchants and Millers in the Grain and Flour Trade during the Eighteenth Century* (Ithaca, 1984), p. 23. See also R. Abad, *Le grand marché. L'approvisionnement alimentaire de Paris sous l'Ancien Régime* (2002).
81 Chevalier, *Les bonnes villes*, p. 237.
82 Similar conclusions have been drawn for Amiens: see M.-L. Pelus, 'Marchands et échevins d'Amiens dans la seconde moitié du XVIème siècle. Crise de subsistances, commerce et profits en 1586–1587', *Revue du Nord*, 64 (1982) 68; 80 per cent of Nantes's provision came from Brittany itself. Grain supply figures are given in A. Croix, *La Bretagne aux XVIème et XVIIème siècles. La vie – la mort – la foi*, 2 vols (1981), I, p. 415. As in Paris, the grain trade, with its constantly changing loci of surplus and deficit, a need for a vast network of contacts, its unreliability and its low public esteem, caused the commerce of provisioning to be the work of a multitude of petty dealers. See Kaplan, *Provisioning Paris*, p. 82.
83 A.M.N. HH 1: Prix des grains 1565–1648.
84 A.M.N. FF 148: Police. Boulangerie.
85 A.M.N. BB 4: Délibérations et assemblées des Conseils des bourgeois 1555–1564, fo. 407r.
86 A.M.N. BB 4, fo. 410r–v.
87 F.-A. Isambert, ed., *Recueil général des anciennes lois françaises depuis l'an 420 jusqu'à la Révolution de 1789*, XVI (1829), p. 17.
88 Isambert, ed., *Recueil général des anciennes lois*, XVI, p. 238.
89 A.M.N. FF 174: Police. Commerce des blés 1514–1790; A.M.N. FF 176: Police des grains 1570–1753.
90 A.M.N. FF 187 Approvisionnement de la ville – guerres de religion.
91 A.M.N. FF 187.
92 A.M.N. BB 5 Délibérations et assemblées municipales 1565–67, fo. 109r; A.M.N. FF 187.
93 A.M.N. FF 187.
94 Pelus, 'Marchands et échevins d'Amiens', pp. 52–3.
95 A.M.N. FF 148.
96 The importance of public acts for keeping order is discussed in J. Miller, 'Politics and urban provisioning crises. Bakers, police and Parlements in France, 1750–1793', *J.M.H.*, 64 (1992) 256.
97 A.M.N. BB 5, fo. 65r.
98 A.M.N. FF 150: Police. Boulangers 1568–70.
99 Thompson, 'The moral economy', p. 200.
100 A.M.N. FF 148.
101 Chevalier, *Les bonnes villes*, p. 233; A. Galpern, *The Religions of the People in Sixteenth-Century Champagne* (Cambridge MA, 1976), p. 30.
102 Chevalier, *Les bonnes villes*, p. 235.
103 Quoted in Prak, 'The carrot and the stick', pp. 149–50.
104 O. Grell, 'The religious duty of care and the social need for control in early modern

Europe', *The Historical Journal*, 39 (1996) 258.

105 Summarised in J. Farr, *Authority and Sexuality in Early Modern Burgundy 1550–1730* (Oxford, 1995), p. 39.

106 G. Duby, ed., *L'histoire de la France urbaine*, 5 vols (1980–85), III, p. 228.

107 D. Hickey, *Local Hospitals in Ancien Regime France. Rationalization, Resistance, Renewal 1530–1789* (Montreal and Kingston, 1997), p. 8.

108 Hickey, *Local Hospitals*, p. 19.

109 Davis, 'Poor relief, humanism and heresy', pp. 38–45; Chevalier, *Les bonnes villes*, p. 238.

110 Hickey, *Local Hospitals*, pp. 18–19; B. Diefendorf, *Beneath the Cross. Catholics and Huguenots in Sixteenth-Century Paris* (Oxford, 1991), pp. 20–1.

111 Davis, 'Reconstructing the poor', 276.

112 Davis, 'Poor relief, humanism and heresy', p. 37.

113 Galpern, *The Religions of the People*, pp. 38–9.

114 Croix, *La Bretagne*, I, pp. 631–2, 658–9

115 Le Méné, 'L'hospitalisation à l'Hôtel-Dieu', pp. 14–15.

116 A.D.L.A. H 495 Aumônerie de Toussaint 1462–1791.

117 A. Jarnoux, *Les anciennes paroisses de Nantes*, 2 vols (Nantes, 1982), II, p. 41.

118 A.M.N. BB 4, fo. 106v.

119 Prak, 'The carrot and the stick', p. 160.

120 A.M.N. BB 4, fos 394r–395r.

121 A.M.N. BB 4, fo. 400r.

122 A.M.N. BB 4, fos 408v–409r.

123 J. Hardwick, *Practice of Patriarchy*, p. 215.

124 A.M.N. BB 4, fo. 252r.

125 Travers, II, p. 337; A.M.N. BB 4, fos 14v–15r.

126 Croix, *La Bretagne*, I, p. 706; A.M.N. GG 693: Hôtel-Dieu. Administration des revenus 1562–77.

127 See Prak, 'The carrot and the stick', p. 152.

128 A.M.N. BB 4, fos 40v–41r.

129 M. Fardet, 'L'assistance aux pauvres à Nantes à la fin du XVIème siècle (1582–1598)', *Actes du 98ème congrès national des sociétés savantes, Nantes 1972*, Section Philologie et Histoire (1973), p. 392; Croix, *La Bretagne*, I, p. 587.

130 Mellinet, *La commune et la milice*, III, pp. 230–1; R. Duplessis, *Lille and the Dutch Revolt. Urban Stability in an Era of Revolution 1500–1582* (Cambridge, 1991), p. 156.

131 A.M.N. GG 702: Hôtel-Dieu. Administration des revenues.

132 A.M.N. GG 701: Hôtel-Dieu. Administration des revenues.

133 Travers, II, p. 414; L. Maitre, *L'assistance publique dans la Loire-Inférieure avant 1789. Étude sur les leproseries, aumôneries, hôpitaux-généraux et bureau de charité* (Nantes, 1879), pp. 48–9.

134 Travers, II, p. 424.

135 M. Fardet, 'La vie municipale à Nantes sous le gouvernement du duc de Mercoeur. Le rôle militaire joué par cette ville (1582–1598)', Thèse, École des Chartres, Paris, 1965, p. 123.

136 Prak, 'The carrot and the stick', p. 164.

137 Duplessis, *Lille*, p. 156.

138 K. Norberg, *Rich and Poor in Grenoble 1600–1814* (Berkeley, 1985), pp. 27–64.

139 Prak, 'The carrot and the stick', p. 165.

140 Duplessis, *Lille*, pp. 156, 309.

141 R. Duplessis and M. Howell, 'Reconsidering the early modern urban economy. The cases of Leiden and Lille', *Past & Present*, 94 (1982), 61–2, 77.

142 Chevalier, *Les bonnes villes*, p. 14.

143 D. Garrioch, 'The people of Paris and their police in the eighteenth century. Reflections on the introduction of a 'modern' police force', *European History Quarterly*, 24 (1994) 527.

144 Benedict, *Rouen*, p. 45.

3

Challenges to authority: the development of Protestantism in Nantes, 1558–72

'The faith of the people of Brittany has always been so constant and pure that the heresy of the last century, so widespread in all the provinces of the kingdom, was not able to penetrate this one.'[1] Antoine Boschet's seventeenth-century life of the Jesuit missionary Julien Maunoir echoed the popular belief then current in Brittany that the province was little affected by the Calvinism which emerged in France after 1550. But the reality was different. After 1558, up to thirty Protestant churches were founded at different times, especially in eastern and southern Brittany, with important congregations in Vitré, Rennes, and particularly, Nantes. The size of the church here was never large in comparison to cities such as Rouen or Troyes, but the presence of Protestantism had a profound effect upon religious culture and political life. The theory and practice of urban authority and governance were deeply affected, while the relationship between and the city and the crown was strained. In this chapter, the process and significance of the growth of Protestantism in Nantes is assessed, before the repercussions of the movement on political and religious life in the city are discussed.

The coming of Protestantism to Nantes

'The Gospel came to Brittany only in 1558. I have not found the least evidence for its appearance before this date.' Thus wrote Philippe Le Noir, Sieur de Crevain, in his *Histoire ecclésiastique de Bretagne* of 1683.[2] There is certainly only limited evidence for early heresy in the county of Nantes. The sole Breton martyr recorded in Jean Crespin's *Histoire des martyres* was Nicolas Valenton, *receveur* of Nantes, burnt alive for heresy in Paris in the aftermath of the Affair of the Placards of 1534.[3] Whether Valenton acquired his new learning in Nantes or Paris is unknown. Later, ten individuals from the Nantes region were registered in the *Livre des habitants* of Geneva between 1553 and 1558.[4]

More revealing of the penetration of Reformed ideas into the Nantais are the episcopal visitation records of 1554, although only the registers for the deaneries of Retz and Clisson, to the south of Nantes, survive. One of the objectives of the visitation was to look for heresy in the diocese. Three 'signs' were sought: disrespect towards the mass and the sacraments, doubts about the powers of saints, and diffidence about the existence of purgatory.[5] Non-attendance at mass was widespread but was not in itself considered an indicator of heresy. More serious was refusal to take Easter communion or to participate in the annual parish Corpus Christi procession. At Saint-Viaud and Saint-Michel-Chef-Chef none of the local nobles attended Corpus Christi, while at Gestigné the Seigneur du Gast and Dom René Le Roy stayed in the church porch during the consecration of the Host. There were individuals who questioned the teachings of the church. A blacksmith of Haute-Goulaine said of indulgences that 'there was no more forgiveness to be had from the Church than from my anvil'.[6] At Fresnay, the brothers Jean and Pierre Longespee, both clergymen, affirmed that they did not pray to the Virgin Mary and did not participate in Rogation-tide processions, nor did they give money to the church. Pierre did attend mass but left during the elevation of the Host. Finally, it was reported that travelling preachers were welcome in some households. At the château of Plessis-la-Ghaisne in Corsept parish there was a resident minister; before each meal he read aloud from the Gospels while the family and their servants knelt and listened. The household also did not attend mass.

From this evidence it is difficult to assess the influence of Protestantism on the region. Outward behaviour resembling Protestantism was encountered in many rural parishes, but this was more likely to be anticlerical than heretical. The majority of religious offences encountered by the bishop's visitors were not heretical at all: swearing, blasphemy, non-attendance at mass and sexual immorality. Protestantism as a faith was that of a small minority, noticed by the neighbours and revealed to the visitors because of its eccentricity. Two groups were notable for their leanings towards Reform, the lower clergy and the nobility. In sum, there was some unorganised heterodoxy confined to a small but visible number of the rural elites.

In Nantes itself, the situation was similar to that of the countryside, with small numbers of people with heterodox ideas meeting clandestinely in little groups, where they communicated at all. An ordinance of the *conseil des bourgeois* of 1554 forbade all private lessons and was directed against people who met to read together at night.[7] The Nantais knew of the new ideas circulating in the kingdom. John Knox was held prisoner on a galley on the Loire at Nantes in 1548, and in 1555 there was a heresy case before the parlement sitting in Nantes, of an Augustinian friar from Carhaix in Lower Brittany who was accused of unorthodox preaching.[8] Also, in the late 1550s the widowed

Vicomtesse de Rohan, Isabeau de Navarre, retired to the château at Blain near to Nantes. Her three sons, raised in the household of Jeanne d'Albret, Isabeau's niece, became important supporters of the Reformed religion in Brittany. But in the city itself religious dissenters remained hidden from public view during most of the 1550s.

Calvinism came visibly to Nantes in 1558, with the visit of François d'Andelot to the city. The nephew of the Grand Constable Anne de Montmorency and the younger of the Châtillon brothers, d'Andelot had been converted to Protestantism during a period of captivity in Italy in the early 1550s. In 1548, he married Claude de Rieux, daughter of an important Breton noble family, who brought him large estates to the north of Nantes. D'Andelot came to visit the west for three reasons; as an admiral of the fleet, to inspect fortifications and to mobilise ships against the English; to visit his wife's estates; and to bring the Gospel to the region.[9] With him travelled two Parisian preachers. At Nantes, the Gospel was preached in d'Andelot's household, which was opened to all who wanted to hear the message; a few days later d'Andelot left for his *seigneuries* at Bretêche and La Roche-Bernard, where Protestantism was preached openly under his protection. When d'Andelot returned to Paris, the two ministers remained, evangelising in the small towns and *bourgs* of the country north-west of Nantes. At about this time, Reformed churches were 'gathered' in Rennes and Vitré.[10]

A formally constituted church was slow to emerge in Nantes. By February 1560 Protestants were meeting in the city. In a letter to the Queen Mother Catherine de' Medici, the royal governor, the Duc d'Étampes, wrote, 'those of the new law [religion] say that they are permitted to assemble together to say their prayers so long as it is in a private place and without scandal'.[11] But the creation of a church came only in September 1560. Pastor du Gravier of Rennes came to Nantes in this month to solicit aid for two Protestants due to appear before the parlement. While here, he preached at the house of René Pastoureau at La Furetière in the suburban parish of Saint-Donatien, at which about eighty people were present. Le Noir records this as the first public assembly of the faithful in Nantes.[12] Shortly afterwards, in October, the community acquired a pastor, Antoine Bachelard, who 'gathered' a congregation.[13] From this date a formal church with minister, elders, deacons and a consistory existed; it kept baptismal records, held prayer meetings and lobbied the city's governors and judges for legal recognition of its activities.

In October 1560, papers were seized by the seneschal, which listed the organisational districts of this new church and the membership of one of these. The congregation was divided into five cantons, Saint-Pierre, Saint-Nicolas au-delà de l'Erdre (the Fosse port district), Le Pilori, La Poissonnerie and an unknown fifth canton. La Poissonnerie had three elders, at least one deacon and a congregation of around fifty men. The three elders comprised two merchants and an apothecary, a social profile similar to that of the churches of Troyes and other northern French cities.[14] The deacon – a master glazier – collected and distributed alms and visited the sick, proof of organised poor relief among the congregation. In addition there were a number of *avertisseurs*, men who went around the congregation informing members of the time and place of meetings, with one man specially delegated to notify of consistory gatherings.[15] At this date there was no central meeting place; the faithful of La Poissonnerie met several times a week in private houses to pray or sing psalms. René Pastoreau's house was regularly used, as were the home of the bookseller Mathurin Papollin and the inn of the Chapeau Rouge. Prayer meetings were held in different places, to avoid detection.[16] As the venues changed frequently, the *avertisseur* performed an important function in the church.

The Reformed congregation's first struggle was for a recognised place of public worship. In the autumn of 1561, the community gained the support of the provincial estates in petitioning the crown for a site. Their request was inserted into the *cahiers de remontrances* of the estates sent to the king, against the wishes of the clergy but with the support of members of the regional nobility. D'Andelot also lobbied for this cause, writing to d'Étampes, and in November Lieutenant-General Martigues allowed the congregation to use a building called Le Pressoir on the estates of the *conseiller au parlement* Robert du Hardaz, to the south of Nantes.[17] Although it was burnt down later that month, the Reformed community continued to meet at the site throughout the early part of 1562, until the first civil war prevented public worship.

Some authors have suggested that there was a distinctive flavour to Breton Protestantism in the early 1560s. Philip Benedict has written that the structure and experience of the early Reformed churches in Brittany may have been particular to the province. He argues that the origins of organised Calvinism were rural and noble, becoming urban only in its second phase, after 1560. The first institution that linked the provincial congregations together was an assembly of gentlemen, meeting in May 1560.[18] Also, that the church developed and retained a strong regional identification. During 1561 links developed between the churches in Brittany, culminating in the first provincial synod at Châteaubriant in August. Six pastors were present, along with an elder and a deacon from each of the churches of Rennes, Nantes, Vitré, Châteaubriant and La Roche-Bernard. Officers from churches without pastors were also present, from Plöermel, Blain and Nort-sur-Erdre.[19] Breton synods were held annually throughout the 1560s; at the height of Calvinism's fortunes in 1565, there were twenty three Reformed churches in the province, although not all had ministers.[20] In exile in La Rochelle after 1585, Breton Protestants set up their own separate church and consistory.[21]

Who became a Protestant in Nantes? Early twentieth-century historians believed that there was a class basis for the Reformed movement. Lucien Febvre argued that Calvinism was a creed of the bourgeoisie, which sought new forms of religion appropriate to its growing place in the social and political order, while Henri Hauser saw a link between artisans, proletarianisation and Protestantism; journeymen with declining living standards and fewer opportunities of becoming masters were attracted to a creed which emphasised spiritual equality and social justice.[22] More recently, Henry Heller has taken up the standard of economic determinism, arguing that heretical belief, particularly in towns, was 'inextricably mingled with fiscal grievance, economic anxiety and political exasperation'.[23]

In Nantes adherence to the Reformed faith did not coincide with economic group or with material hardship. As in Rouen, there were no clear social lines dividing Catholic and Protestant, although the more proletarianised of the city's workers were less likely to abandon their traditional faith than those with some material independence.[24] Important among Protestantism's earliest converts and chief supporters in Nantes were members of the regional nobility. Traditionally this was explained by opportunism resulting from declining living standards in the mid-century, brought about by inflation, indebtedness and the need for employment after the end of the Italian wars.[25] There was also anti-clericalism, resentment of the legal and fiscal privileges of clerics and envy of their material wealth, from which some nobles wished to benefit. Before 1560, Protestantism seems to have been a 'house church' of some noble families. At the château of Blain, the Vicomtesse de Rohan held Reformed services in her chapel from 1560 and was permitted by the king to live freely as a Calvinist so long as worship was confined to her household.[26] At Bretêche, La Roche-Bernard, Le Croisic and Guérande, Calvinist worship took place under the protection of the seigneur, d'Andelot. Some of the noble families of the northern part of the county of Nantes also turned their chapels into centres of Reformed worship. These conversions were partly from personal conviction, partly a result of the influence of Rohan and Rieux lords. Bernard Varigaud comments of d'Andelot that his name, the high esteem in which he was held, his offices and his patronage attracted nobles from the region.[27]

Urban congregations were soon added to the household churches of nobles. We know more about urban churches than about their rural and noble counterparts in Brittany, because Le Noir's history – the main source for the province – concentrates on the city experience. In Nantes, aristocrats and county nobles were not regular members of the congregation, for they made only seasonal or temporary residence in the city. However, lords gave important patronage and protection to the church, through influence at court and with royal governors – d'Andelot was on the royal privy council from November 1561 – and by their personal prestige. D'Andelot held sermons within his household, making them open to the public, which city authorities dared not forbid.[28] The Vicomte de Rohan was proprietor the inn of the Chapeau Rouge, which was used as a meeting-house.[29] When Protestants were harassed in Nantes, these aristocrats intervened on their behalf. Following the arrest of Protestants in July 1561, Rohan wrote to d'Étampes and to the royal court complaining of the actions of the city authorities. A few days later, Rohan came to Nantes, called the seneschal before him and forbade him to pursue the co-religionists who assembled for prayer meetings in private houses and else-where.[30] He also stood bail for the release of the prisoner de la Guillotière.[31]

The core membership of the Reformed church of Nantes consisted of urban social groups. When the community first emerged into public notice, it was assumed that the congregation was of lowly status; 'mostly poor and simple folk', commented Governor d'Étampes in 1560.[32] The list of male members of the congregation of the canton of La Poissonnerie seized in October 1560 gives some indication of the social composition of the church in Nantes. This can be supplemented and confirmed by names taken from lists of Protestants and names of 'suspected' officers recorded in the registers of the *conseil des bourgeois* between 1560 and 1561.[33] Fifty-eight individuals appear in these sources. They do not represent the full Protestant community in Nantes but they give an indication of the main adherents. As in many French towns, the membership comprised royal officers, merchants and above all artisans.[34] Forty-three of the men listed in these sources had known occupations, shown in Table 3.1.

Firstly, there were several officers from the sovereign courts of parlement and Chambre des Comptes along with judicial officers from the *présidial* and *prévôté* courts. In comparison with the total number of royal and judicial offi-cers in Nantes, however, the group is small, visible rather than numerous. Barbara Diefendorf has found a similar situation in Paris. While some members of the city elites were attracted to the Reformed church, they abandoned it quickly when they found that religious dissent was incompatible with a career in the royal bureaucracy.[35] In Nantes, Michel d'Essefort, one of the 'suspect' *conseillers au parlement* of the city, must have repudiated Protestantism for he went on to participate in municipal government after 1565. Those who held influence and power tended to be prudent, anxious not to compromise their families' positions and open to pressure from the royal government to conform to Catholic cultural norms.[36] Secondly, merchants were important. The merchants of the Protestant community were middle-rank traders of the city, not part of its mercantile elite, as in Rouen's Protestant community.[37] Thirdly, there were prosperous and educated tradesmen: apothecaries, a surgeon and a

Table 3.1 Male members of the Protestant church in Nantes, 1560–62.

Occupation / status	Number
Noble	6
Royal officers	
conseiller au parlement	3
maître des comptes	1
City judicial officers *présidial* and *prévôté*	3
Merchants	4
Grocer	1
Apothecary	2
Barber surgeon	1
Bookseller	1
Innkeeper	2
Teacher	1
Locksmith	2
Metal trades	5
Shoemaker	5
Tailor	2
Stocking-maker	1
Glazier	1
Carpenter	1
Mason	1

Source: *Narration sommaire*, pp. 16–17; Varigaud, *Essai sur l'histoire des églises réformées*, I, appendix 3.

bookseller. Finally, there were artisans from four groups of trades in particular: garment production, shoemaking, metalworking and building – crafts that were prominent in other Reformed communities such as Dijon.[38] David Nicholls has suggested for Normandy that Protestantism appeared in larger workshops, where literature could be circulated by hand and ideas easily spread.[39] In Nantes, the metal trades important in the early Reformed church were based on workshops with two or more artisans, which were large by the city's standards. Absent from the documentary record for Nantes is clerical involvement, either regular or secular. This may be because the sources for adherence are mostly municipal rather than judicial, for the absence of former Catholic clergy among Nantes's Protestants is in contrast to other cities of France. There were also few members of the food and distributive trades, or the river and maritime trades, which were numerous in the city, again, a trend found in other cities.[40] But in most ways, the Protestant community of Nantes was similar to those of other large trading towns. The Reformed church was dominated by middling people, from below the highest-status occupations but 'with the degree of literacy, self-confidence and independence needed to reject the tutelage of the clergy and embrace the idea of the priesthood of all believers'.[41] There was some geographical pattern to Protestantism. The five cantons of the church were all in the southern, waterfront parishes of Sainte-Croix and Saint-Nicolas, the heart of the trading and artisan communities and the most populous parishes of the city.

It is difficult to uncover the reasons why individuals chose to become Protestant. Among the earliest explanations, economic factors were the most important, and Heller has argued that the Reform movement had its origins in material crisis, subsistence problems and epidemic disease.[43] There is no evidence for this in Nantes. Yet the socio-economic structures of the city were important in the growth of heresy. Nantes was a large port town, with a varied population. Benedict observes that the presence of a wide range of artisans made Protestantism more likely to strike roots in a city; 'just as port cities were prone to infection by plague, so too . . . were they prone to infection by heresy'.[43] Nantes' merchants travelled widely, along the Loire valley, to northern Spain, around the Atlantic and Channel coasts, and to the North Sea regions where Protestantism was widespread. Likewise, many journeymen, particularly in trades such as textiles, metalworking and building, travelled from city to city, to seek work and to improve their skills. Yet while travel offered possibilities for contact with heresy, Protestantism was always a minority and dangerous position to adopt in Nantes. Factors other than acquaintance must have been important in conversion to the new faith.[44]

Varigaud, summarising the ideas of the sixteenth-century preacher René Benoist, argued that reading and reflection were essential in becoming Protestant. We know nothing of the role of preaching in spreading Reformed ideas in Nantes.[45] Jean Crespin tells us that Nicolas Valeton came to the Gospel through 'some good people with whom he kept company and by reading the New Testament in French'.[46] The penetration of the vernacular Bible, even into Brittany, the publication of the metrical psalms in French and the example of the new persecuted martyrs drew adherents.[47] Reformers such as Luther and Calvin produced a flood of printed religious tracts in the vernacular, in which they made their arguments accessible to artisans, merchants and other notables; the 'very existence of the printed word, increasing the opportunities for prolonged scrutiny of religious and other writing . . . changed the . . . relationship between church and people' by allowing for individual abstract thought.[48] While printers were rare in Nantes, booksellers came often to the city. Philip Conner argues that entrepreneurial strategies of booksellers could offset the lack of local printers, especially in the sale of lucrative, smuggled heretical literature.[49] Nantes was a large export centre for books to Spain. As early as 1508 the printer Jean Cabiller set up an entrepôt here to relay books to the fair of Medina del Campo. Mathurin Papollin, Protestant, was an agent for Seneton of Lyon, sending books to the same fair, and two Genevan booksellers were arrested for possession of prohibited books in 1561.[50] While the majority of books sent to Nantes were Catholic or secular, the opportunity for passing on illicit literature was also present.

Disappointment with the Catholic Church was important. Anticlericalism did not cause the Reformation, but among certain individuals it made the acceptance of new doctrines easier.[51] Guédas Porcher, barber surgeon, arrested in October 1560, told his interrogators that about ten years previously, following travels to Rome, Venice and Constantinople, he became aware of abuses in the Roman Church which led him to disillusionment with that faith, 'but for the last five years, since he came to Nantes, he has been content to attend prayers and services held as they do in Geneva'.[52]

Trade contacts were influential. The shoemaker Jean Guischard's servants were Protestants, and Jean Bras-de-Fer, locksmith and arms manufacturer, ran a workshop of three to four journeymen, who accompanied him to prayer meetings.[53] Family and neighbourhood also mattered. Heller argues that Calvinism was particularly orientated towards the family and household, for here discipline would be taught and morals supervised on a daily basis, as a form of obedience to God.[54] Almost all known Protestants in Nantes were men, but most of their spouses and servants shared their religious convictions. The wives of Gabriel Corbin and Jean Richard attended a meeting without their husbands in June 1561, for example.[55] James Farr has shown for Dijon that there was a clear geography of Protestant and Catholic militancy based on parish and street.[56] In Nantes, there was a concentration of Protestants in the waterside parishes, but little is known of confessional street geography. It seems, however, that Protestant and Catholic were mixed in the city, with little clear segregation between religions.

Finally, the cultural distinctiveness of Protestantism made it attractive to some. Nicholls argues that Protestantism was particularly appealing to the urban middling sort, for it was a 'new form of urban asceticism', an 'intellectualised form of expiation of the urban sins of avarice and usury', based on individual rebirth in Christ rather than reliance on the intercession of saints and clergy for remission of sins.[57] For most Protestants in Nantes, acceptance of the Reformed religion had a profound effect upon their outward behaviour, their social and cultural lives. Calvinists were noted for their severe morality and austere comportment, because of their actions and behaviour. Membership of a Reformed church meant submission to its strong moral discipline, which was enforced by the consistory, 'to guard against the corruptions and vanities of daily life'.[58] The most common manifestations of Reformed belief were an emphasis upon preaching, a rejection of the cult of saints and religious imagery, and refusal to attend mass or to observe fast regulations.[59] Protestants disapproved of religious festivals and revelry, particularly dancing and singing secular songs. They kept themselves apart and attacked the daily, seasonal religious and social activities of their neighbours. On St John the Baptist's day (24 June) 1561, the household of Jean Guischard, shoemaker, abstained from the traditional dancing and drinking around bonfires. Instead they sang psalms through an open window of their house; then they threw water over the revellers and their fires, reproaching those who took part. They called the dancing women 'whores' and told them 'they would be better off in a brothel than dancing and singing such lewd songs'.[60]

Nantes' Protestant community was similar in composition to other Huguenot churches in France, but the congregation was never large. It was numerous enough to form a visible and distinct section of the city population in the early 1560s, and more significant in numbers than has been estimated, however. In 1683, Le Noir counted around 400 baptisms recorded in the Reformed church register of Nantes between 1560 and 1572. Roger Joxe has taken the annual mean of thirty-four baptisms per year to estimate a Protestant population of 850–950.[61] This figure does not take into account changes in the number of baptisms over the decade. Baptisms declined after 1568; this means that the figures for the early 1560s were perhaps two or three times Joxe's annual mean. Thus, at the height of Protestantism's popularity in Nantes, there may have been about 1500 members of the congregation, or 5–7.5 per cent of the city's population. But compared with those in other northern French cities, the population was small. Troyes' Protestants numbered 8–9 per cent of a city population of about 45,000, Rouen housed 15–20 per cent of a city of comparable size, and Caen, 25–33 per cent.[62] Nantes' size and its status as a national and international port might have encouraged greater numbers.

One reason for the relatively small size of its congregation may be that Nantes was an important judicial centre. Benedict has argued that the presence of an elite of holders of high royal office discouraged the adoption of Protestantism in some cities.[63] Until 1560 the Breton parlement sat for half of each year in Nantes and the Chambre des Comptes for Brittany resided here. Nantes was also the centre of a bishopric with an active cathedral chapter. Secondly, the economic institutions of the city may have worked against large-scale Protestantism. Artisans organised into guilds dominated the Reformed movement in most cities of France. In Nantes there were few craft guilds, with their particular institutional and workshop cultures and solidarities. This may have militated against the adoption of Protestantism by large numbers from one trade, for masters and journeymen were linked less formally here than in cities with incorporated trades. Journeymen were more likely to set up on their own to work after a time and individuals more likely to associate religious activity with their parishes rather than with their crafts. Most importantly of all, there was a strong Catholic culture in Brittany as a whole and Nantes in particular. The Catholicism of the city was reinforced by the its close economic and social links with northern Spain. The trading elites of Nantes, their employees and contacts were unlikely to risk their economic ventures in Iberia by adoption of a prohibited creed.

The Protestant community and the Catholic city: conflict and coexistence

The emergence of Protestantism in Nantes had a profound and immediate impact on attitudes to the authority of city institutions and on practical governance in the town, even though the movement was relatively small compared with those in other cities. After 1559 dissent and disorder periodically rocked the city, which were difficult to pacify, making day-to-day administration more problematic. From its very beginnings, the Huguenot community in Nantes took shape within a city culture that was implacably hostile to the theology and physical existence of Protestantism, and which viewed Calvinism as a threat to the its spiritual and material well-being. Suspicions, tensions and outbreaks of violence between Catholic and Protestant, as in other parts of the French kingdom, marked the years 1559–1562.[64] In May 1560, Nantes had its own day of placards, when posters were fixed to the portcullis of the château and to the residences of the principal judicial officers, making violent threats against Catholic judges who oppressed Protestants.[65] In February 1561 Protestants returning from a sermon threw stones at the windows of one of the city's churches, where mass was being held. This provoked a riot where Protestants were stoned.[66] In April, the exhumation and burning of a man's corpse led to another disturbance.[67] By the summer, Protestants were meeting publicly in the churches and cemeteries of nearby *bourgs* such as Saint-Herblain and Sucé-sur-Erdre, and in houses in the suburbs of Nantes. On 18 July the Reformed congregation held a demonstration of faith. An armed company assembled at La Furetière and then marched in ranks through the Saint-Pierre gate and through the city. Numbers were wildly over-estimated at 600–700 and it was rumoured that the force intended to capture the keys to one of the town's gates.[68] There followed the worst outburst of sectarianism in Nantes, lasting for two weeks as the Catholic population reacted violently to Protestant 'provocation'. The baby son of Claude Roux was forcibly rebaptised as a Catholic in the church of Sainte-Croix because his parents were 'Lutherans, disobedient to the church'.[69] On 1 August there was a riot at the house of Mathurin Papollin, bookseller, by a crowd angered by a prayer meeting being held there, and the building was destroyed.[70] Later in the same year, the Reformed place of worship at Le Pressoir was burnt down. In retaliation, on 28 December, Holy Innocents' day, a sermon in the cathedral was disrupted by armed horsemen and protesters who hurled missiles at the altars.[71]

Historians have explained the antipathy of Catholic and Protestant in socio-cultural and religious terms, as the violent outcome of 'two radically conflicting visions of the world and of the place of the sacred within it'.[72] Protestants found Catholic theology, rituals and symbols to be profane; they sought to discredit them and to rid the world of false beliefs and idols, by challenging Catholic preaching and disrupting rituals and iconoclasm. Such actions shocked and offended Catholics, who lived in a world filled with sacred objects and places. Natalie Davis has argued that to mock and attack priests, churches and images was a polluting act; desecration placed the whole community in danger and was certain to be followed by divine retribution. Catholics were thus obliged to rid the world of the infection of heresy and to restore the divine balance.[73] Denis Crouzet has argued less for a notion of endangered community than for a millenarian vision shared by a wider French society; their belief that they were living in the 'last days' necessitated the purging and purifying of society of God's enemies.[74] In these circumstances, the city authorities had great practical difficulties in maintaining order and effectively exercising their authority.

Further undermining practical governance was the corrosive impact of Protestantism on the ideological props to authority in the city. Contemporary authors emphasised the religious and cultural threat posed by heresy to the influence and institutions of the Roman church. Reform entailed a dismantling of the ecclesiastical hierarchy and its replacement by a new system of church government shared between ministers and lay elders of the congregation. Monasteries, cathedral chapters, colleges and confraternities would be dissolved and their property sold. Reform also meant an end to the financial and judicial privileges of the clergy and their control over issues such as marriage and inheritance.[75] The authority of clerical knowledge and teaching was also threatened. In Antoine du Val's words, Calvin wanted everyone to be a theologian; each person would read and interpret the Holy Scriptures according to his or her own judgement, such that a soap maker would dispute with a doctor of the Church.[76] Heretics seduced with fine words and persuasion, with gifts, promises and money, as Satan tempted Christ with the riches and kingdoms of this world.[77]

Divisions of faith also ruptured community solidarity and shared values. Deviation from religious truth threatened not just the individual heretic but the entire social body. In their early, clandestine phase Calvinist groups were accused of social and moral delinquency.[78] It was suggested that their nocturnal psalm singing was followed by sexual orgies, and that fathers willingly gave up their children to be sacrificed, falsely believing that they would be received in heaven with the holy martyrs.[79] Later on, Protestants' day-to-day behaviour invited hostility because they set themselves apart from their neighbours by their sober dress, high moral conduct and absenteeism from community rites and feasts. The Catholic community placed great value on solidarity and consensus. Sensibilities were shocked when Protestants abstained from and even attacked the activities and symbols on which communal identity and well-being were founded. Religious unity, truth and material prosperity were interdependent. If heresy were allowed to take hold, the wrath of God would fall on society, children, lands and possessions.[80] The outcome would be the destitution of honour and worldly prosperity.

By the later 1550s heresy was equated with sedition, conspiracy and attempts to overthrow the royal government.[81] Contemporaries argued that people who had so little respect for the sacred would have even less regard for secular authority.[82] A fracture in the unity of religion was fraught with peril for the monarchical state.[83] Divine wrath would fall upon a heretical kingdom, and 'each kingdom divided among itself will be brought to desolation and every city or house divided against itself shall not stand'.[84] As Guillaume Du Preau stated, 'there is no kingdom, province, town nor lordship that can remain in peace for long where everyone is free and allowed to follow whichever religion he pleases'.[85] If an example were needed, then Germany was pointed out to show the troubles that religious discord could produce.[86]

In Nantes it was believed that heretics wished to subvert the political order for their own ends. Bishop de Crequi stated that 'there is danger that, having forgotten God, they [Calvinists] forget the duty and obedience they owe to the king and to justice'.[87] The secret nature of Protestant communities was held to be the result of their false doctrine and their plots: 'if they were preaching the pure Gospel, why did they have to hide . . . do we not see them gathering at night as well as by day, in caves and ditches, with all sorts of arms, as if they wished to undertake an assault on a town?'[88] In its early days, Calvinism was considered to be a form of popular revolt.[89] Lieutenant-General Bouillé wrote that heresy gave 'great heart to all the community and put them at liberty to pay no more taxes or rents, because all sorts of libertinism would be released'.[90] Heresy also disrupted patriarchal lines of authority; 'when [heresy] entered and gained a foothold in a house, city or kingdom, it [creates] such division and discord that the husband is not in accord with his own wife, nor the citizens between themselves, nor subjects with their lord'.[91] The result was anarchy: the son wanting to kill his father, and brother turning against brother, to the ruin and division of houses. The wife of a Nantes weaver expressed general fears in 1561 that the Protestants had made threats to kill anyone who was not of their sect.[92]

It was the duty of social and political superiors to prevent this disaster. The main responsibility lay with the king, whose function as executor of God's justice was to rid the kingdom of the infection of Protestantism and thus the danger of sedition. The king was God's elect, and in his coronation oath he swore to uphold the Catholic faith and to extirpate heresy. If the monarch failed to do this he was unworthy of his office, for 'he opened himself to the accusation that he was wilfully permitting a corruption of the social body for which all of his subjects must pay the price.'[93] Heresy undermined royal authority because of the fundamental belief that the right ordering of society derived from religious truth. Urban governments shared some of the responsibility for combating Protestantism; they also had a moral and religious duty to uphold religion. Heresy threatened the authority of city governments as it did that of the crown. It could invoke divine wrath and was a threat to civil order. M. Holt argues for Dijon that the city council held itself responsible for preventing contagion of any sort, including heresy.[94]

What were the solutions to the problems of heresy and disorder? In Nantes, the predominant view of the city's Catholic majority was that heresy should be driven from the kingdom. The Catholic Church led the protest against Protestantism in the diocese to reassert its own spiritual pre-eminence. We know from the records of the episcopal visitation of 1554 that Bishop de Crequi was concerned about the infiltration of Protestantism into his see, although it is not known if anything was done to combat its spread. From 1558 and the first public manifestations of Calvinism, the Catholic Church took a more militant stand. The battle began in earnest in the spring of that year when one of François d'Andelot's ministers preached openly in the parish church of Le Croisic. Bishop de Crequi responded by attending the town's Corpus Christi procession. One household did not participate, and Protestants were rumoured to have gathered there. A crowd led by the bishop stormed the house but the Protestants fled, killing three Catholics in their escape.[95] In Nantes itself, the clergy initiated a number of anti-heresy actions. One Sunday in October 1560, Canon Levesque of the college of Saint-Jean was walking through the city centre when he saw an engraving for sale on a street stall, showing Moses and the Tablets of the Law. He was outraged by the text upon the tablet; 'Make no *image* of that which is in heaven or on earth and do not worship false *images*',[96] and took issue with the vendor over the heretical use of the word 'image' instead of 'idol'. The canon reported the incident to the seneschal, who, fearing a plot, ordered the arrest of all suspected Protestants in the city.[97] In November 1561 the cathedral chapter destroyed the Huguenot place of worship at Le Pressoir. On the orders of Vicar-General de Gand, three choristers, the sacristan and the sub-dean of the cathedral set the building alight using wood from the bishop's estates, nearby. All fled to Vannes the following day.[98]

Among the secular authorities, heresy was disliked equally for its spiritual evils, the threat it posed to military security, the problems it created for the judicial and legal frameworks of urban governance, and the disorder it brought to the city's streets.[99] The presence of a Protestant community first came to public notice in Nantes in a judicial enquiry that followed the conspiracy of Amboise. In March 1560 a group of Protestant noblemen around Jean du Barry, Seigneur de la Renaudie of Perigord, attempted a coup d'etat to end Guise family tutelage of the young king Francis II. The conspiracy was organised in Nantes with the help of a Breton nobleman, La Garaye.[100] After the failure of the plot, some of the conspirators escaped through the county of Nantes. There is no evidence that the conspiracy received any support in the city, but the inhabitants were greatly shaken by the event. The conspirators were accused of wanting to kill the king and his family, to overthrow the monarchy and impose a republic, and to impose their new religion by force of arms.

The conspiracy had important implications for Nantes, in particular the *conseil des bourgeois*. Firstly, a veil of suspicion hung over the city, for the *conseil* was considered to have been partly responsible for allowing plots to be hatched without detection in the town. Secondly, the enquiry which followed revealed a relatively numerous Protestant community in the city, hitherto hidden from official view. The Protestants were actively sought out during the enquiry, arrested and interrogated, although then released. Thereafter, all Protestant activity was viewed as potential plot or sedition. The dangerous nature of Protestantism was confirmed by the actions of the community itself during the years 1560–62. The placards of May 1560 threatened and frightened the royal officers.[101] The demonstration by armed Protestants and subsequent sectarian troubles of July–August and December 1561 created and maintained a climate of tension and alarm.

The fear of sedition and the reality of disorder were worsened by the failure of the crown to support local initiatives against heresy. In the spring and summer of 1560, after Amboise, the royal government moved erratically towards religious moderation. Francis II ordered the release of religious prisoners and allowed them to petition him. In May the edict of Romorantin transferred the prosecution of heresy cases from royal to ecclesiastical tribunals, while punishment of illicit assemblies and seditious acts was translated from parlements to *présidial* courts. Robert Knecht argues that clerical courts were slack and secular tribunals permeated with unreliable, inefficient officials, so that Calvinist communities were henceforth left undisturbed by legal actions against them.[102] In October 1560, following the 'images' affair in Nantes, the *conseil des bourgeois* asked the royal governor to expel suspected heretics. The crown took a dim view of the affair. On the

advice of Lieutenant-General Bouillé, who feared wider disorder within the
city, the king ordered the disarmament of all citizens of the town, Catholic as
well as Protestant. The *conseil* objected, seized the arms of known Protestants,
and called upon the governor 'to search out those evilly disposed towards the
[Catholic] faith and others who have conspired . . . against the king and his
majesty . . . if no firmer justice is to be done, expel them from the city and
county of Nantes'.[103] But the Protestants remained at liberty.

The death of Francis II and the accession of his younger brother Charles
IX in December 1560 led to greater leniency towards Protestantism. The royal
council under the regency of the Queen Mother sought independence for the
crown from noble factions. To achieve this, a policy of religious moderation
was adopted. The King of Navarre was appointed lieutenant-general of the
realm, and moderates were appointed to the royal council, including Gaspard
de Coligny and Michel de l'Hôpital.[104] A colloquy was held at Poissy in
September 1561 to search for a solution to the religious divisions within the
realm, with Théodore de Bèze and other Reformers invited to discussions with
Catholic theologians. The virtual collapse of repression and the hint that the
crown was sympathetic towards Reform emboldened the Calvinists of Nantes
to meet more often and more openly, as in other cities of the kingdom.[105]

The *conseil des bourgeois* was worried by the increasing leniency of the
crown towards heresy. Above all else it was concerned not to allow the Protestant church its own legal position within the city and kingdom. The bourgeois
lobbied the crown against toleration and for greater judicial powers for the city
courts to use against heresy. Large sums of money were spent sending deputies
to the royal court, to represent the city's views. Neither of the bourgeois'
requests was accorded. In January 1561 royal letters confirmed the edict of
Romorantin. All heresy cases were suspended. Bouillé observed the continued
problems within the province in a letter to d'Étampes: 'at this moment all is
well but those of our religion have a marvellous hatred for those of the new law
. . . if it [the edict] does not give you more force than that which you have
already, I think that before long you will be constrained to let them cut each
other's throats, without being able to prevent it.'[106] To acquire more authority
over heresy, the *conseil* asked the parlement at Rennes to publish the January
edict, which in theory endowed the *présidial* court at Nantes with greater
powers to avoid 'emotions and scandals' and ban illicit assemblies.[107] However,
in April another edict ordered that no one was to be disturbed on account of
his religion – which was commonly taken to mean full liberty to choose one's
religious profession – and prisoners of conscience were to be released. It effectively granted Protestants toleration within their own houses. This was not
registered in the parlements but sent directly to local authorities.[108] Urged by
the governor, a 'council' or jury of 12 notables was created in Nantes in May

to prevent assemblies.[109] On 31 July yet another edict was issued prohibiting Protestant assemblies and forbidding sacraments other than Catholic rites. Catholics believed rightly that Calvinists would ignore it. Lieutenant-General Bouillé remarked that while it attempted to maintain peace and union between the two religions, it was ineffective, too mild and unable to halt the disturbances.[110]

The edict of Saint-Germain of 17 January 1562 granted limited legal toleration to French Protestants. The regency government, having witnessed the failure of both repression and compromise, concluded that toleration was a necessary expedient to bring order to the realm while church reform was carried out. Advisers such as l'Hôpital even concluded that coercion on matters of conscience was the very root cause of the troubles in France.[111] As elsewhere in the kingdom, Protestants in Nantes were forbidden to worship inside the walled town, to assemble at night or to raise arms. They were allowed to preach openly and hold services outside the town so long as they did so peacefully, while nobles could organise churches on their own estates. Private prayer meetings were allowed inside towns; pastors, consistories and the holding of synods were recognised and permitted.[112] The bourgeois of Nantes were not persuaded by the government's position and opposed the edict. They 'blamed the breakdown in law and order on tolerance and impunity, leniency not harshness'.[113] The *conseil* registered its opposition to the edict and set up a commission of twelve deputies to coordinate the city's remonstrances at court.[114]

The crown's policy of toleration confused and angered the Catholic bourgeois of Nantes. Royal policy undermined the king's prestige. Legal recognition of Protestantism was a severe breach of the king's prerogative and called his authority into question. Laxity of justice on the part of the king and his officers was widely held responsible for the growth of heresy. Calvinism was a problem that the crown ought to address, through use of its legislative sovereignty and the judicial apparatus, devolved to Nantes' institutions. The *conseil* considered that to deal effectively with heresy, the city needed greater legal powers; 'they [heretics] have shown that they fear neither God nor us . . . and if it does not please the queen and the king of Navarre to execute good strong justice, I am sure that they will undertake more actions if they are allowed suffrance.'[115] Instead, the crown moved slowly and sporadically towards greater toleration, refusing to give the city or courts the legal powers they requested, while also failing to solve the kingdom's problems by pacification.

The failure of the royal government to solve the problem of heresy put the relationship of crown and city under strain. In Nantes, the city's elites had a view of sovereignty and religion 'that stressed the irreducible unity of the kingdom and the link between law and religion that sustained it'.[116] They shared du Val's view that 'as there is nothing more glorious than a Christian prince who defends and guards the Catholic faith against the enemies of truth, so there is nothing more damaging to his nobility and greatness, nothing that gives him greater blame than to endure by too great a negligence or indulgence, that faith waver and perish . . . '[117] Further, the failure of the bourgeois of Nantes to lobby the crown against toleration damaged the *conseil's* reputation as a mediator between the city and the king. Worse still, confidence in the contractual, consultative nature of monarchy was shaken by the government's lack of heed of the city's views. Thirdly, heresy led to rifts within the Nantes elite, which further undermined their authority, especially between the bourgeois of the *conseil* and the royal judicial officers. Du Preau's accusation that judges were responsible for the poor upholding of justice received some sympathy in Nantes, and there were accusations of dissimulation, tepidity, faint-heartedness and negligence in heresy cases.[118] On 22 August 1561 Jean de Luc, *procureur des bourgeois*, was dismissed after the cathedral chapter objected that 'he performed his duties badly and did not attend meetings', but the real reason appears to have been his suspected Huguenot sympathies.[119] In December 1561, several of the city's judicial officers were denounced as 'moral and capital enemies of the inhabitants of Nantes': Robert du Hardaz, Michel d'Essefort, both *conseillers* in parlement; Le Blouays, lieutenant of Nantes, Maître François Garreau, and Antoine de Cornal, *conseiller* of the *présidial* court of Nantes.[120] Finally, heresy led to disorder on the streets of Nantes, with threats to property and the social order. Thus, in a multitude of ways, the exercise of authority by the city's institutions was undermined.

But what is striking about Nantes, distinguishing it from other cities in northern France, is the relatively low number of large-scale incidents and the small amount of bloodshed. Rouen experienced nine serious 'incidents' in 1560–61; Nantes had perhaps four, excluding the plotting of the conspiracy of Amboise.[121] There was aggravation between confessions, but disorder was short-lived, and with the exception of July–August 1561 it did not develop into a bloody culture of retribution. There were no executions of heretics in the city and few sectarian deaths, only two or three before 1562. For most of the period, Nantes was relatively peaceful; violent incidents, while important, were infrequent. The lack of firm instruction on how to proceed and the fact that repression provoked more disorder in the city than laxity, meant in practice that a policy of tacit toleration was adopted by Nantes' governing groups after 1560. There was necessary coexistence, for Catholic and Protestant lived cheek by jowl. Guillemette Bonyveau and her family, who were Catholics, lived as lodgers in a house owned by the Protestant Penmaingeon. Bonyveau informed against Penmaingeon in a judicial enquiry of July 1561, but feared the landlord's violence against her if he should find out. Marie Robouan, a

Catholic, was a servant in the household of the Protestant weaver Michel Pertuis. She observed him receiving Calvinist visitors, with whom he would withdraw to have private conversations. Name-calling and threats were frequent. By the summer of 1561 the locksmith Jean Bras-de-Fer went about the city armed and accompanied by three or four journeymen. He threatened to chastise anyone who told him to attend Mass. One Friday morning, the wife of Vincent Vilaine saw Bras-de-Fer and a small party returning from a suburban prayer meeting; she shouted at them from her upper-storey window, 'what a fine company we have here, returning from their sermon!' Bras-de-Fer aimed his pistol at her and made threats.[122] Much of the conflict between confessions was verbal, as far as we can tell. Robert Scribner has identified several manifestations of toleration in sixteenth-century Germany: neglect to mete out severe penalties for religious deviance, inability to enforce religious unity, toleration of religious minorities whose services proved economically beneficial to a community and 'toleration of practical rationality', all features of daily life among ordinary people of different confessions who lived side by side.[123] All of these appeared in Nantes after 1560.

The nature and tactics of the Nantes Protestant community were important in limiting violence. The Huguenot population was relatively small, but these were highly visible people, with distinctive behaviour. Benedict argues that the disproportionate appeal of Protestants to nobles and middling groups made the population seem bigger than it was to contemporaries.[124] Yet it was never numerous enough to overwhelm the town, while the existing mix of different peoples in the populous waterside parishes perhaps facilitated a certain acceptance of diversity. Secondly, because of its minority status, the Protestant community made increasing resort to legal and judicial resolution of conflict from the middle of 1561 that would become central to its relations with the royal authorities thereafter.[125] In September, after the riot that destroyed his home, the bookseller Papollin appealed to the governor and town authorities for compensation for his losses. D'Étampes ordered the *conseil* to make amends. In November, after lobbying the provincial estates, the Protestants were allowed the use of Le Pressoir for worship.[126] Finally, Protestants were, on the whole, peaceful people, even if armed. There was little if any iconoclasm, nor were there physical attacks on priests. The small and increasingly legalistic Protestant community perhaps reduced conflict by attempting to meet its basic objectives through discussion and conciliation with royal and city authorities.

The nature of town governance in Nantes was also a factor in limiting conflict between confessions, which will be discussed in detail in Chapter 4. Some historians have claimed that town councils were reluctant to prosecute heretics in their midst because of shared values of civic ecumenism or at least a

tacit toleration of heresy. Mark Konnert's study of Châlons-sur-Marne has
shown that confessional hostility was mild here by contemporary standards. He
explains the low levels of conflict and violence in the town by the devotion of
the civic elites to ideals of urban solidarity and integrity, a commitment to a
civic agenda, and shared humanist ideals of education and reform, which over-
rode religious divisions within the city.[127] In Nantes there was no such irenicism
or tolerance. The bourgeois disliked heresy and would have liked its extirpation from the city and realm. As they remonstrated to the king in November
1561, the bourgeois 'never made nor required to be made a church other than
those built and made according to the . . . Roman church'.[128] Failing this, the
conseil sought to limit the legal, public practice of Protestantism. But the
Reformed minority were left alone so long as they were quiet, orderly and
unthreatening in their behaviour. The men of the conseil disliked heresy but they
had an equal distaste for disorder. This was a prime cause of de facto toleration
in many Reformation cities. Scribner has shown for Erfurt that toleration was
never the policy of choice but always one taken to avert a larger disaster.[129]
Especially feared in Nantes was the impact of the presence of open and
provocative Protestant groups on trade with Spain. In the early 1560s, the
bourgeois were in the process of negotiating an important treaty allowing
mutual trading privileges with merchants from Bilbao and other Iberian ports.
Spanish antipathy towards heresy might cause a rupture in these arrangements.[130] Also, Protestant plots and militant manifestations were alarming
enough, but they were rarely as dangerous to lives and property as rampaging
Catholic mobs. To be too repressive was to provoke greater disorder than that
which was being quelled.

   The attitude of the royal governor, the Duc d'Étampes, was also important in maintaining a relative tranquillity in Nantes. He was largely conciliatory
in his treatment of the Protestant community and its claims to public worship.
D'Étampes seems to have shared de l'Hôpital's views that 'conscience is of such
a nature that it cannot be forced but must be . . . persuaded by real and sufficient reasons'.[131] Although a Catholic, d'Étampes was seen by both Catholic
and Protestant commentators as having no particular antipathy towards the
Reformed religion, in contrast with the Guise family.[132] His inclinations seem
to have been for peace, order and a measure of freedom of conscience, and he
himself had close relatives given over to Calvinism: two sisters-in-law and possibly his wife.[133] The governor's religious policies in Brittany combined a close
obedience to royal legislative measures with moderate application on the
ground. Likewise, his lieutenants-general, Martigues and Bouillé, although
antipathetic towards heresy and greatly frustrated by the constraints upon their
powers to act, adhered to royal policy, even where they found it misguided, and
were in constant communication with their superiors. In May 1560, d'Étampes

responded to the anger raised in Nantes by the appearance of Protestant placards by exhorting the population not to take part in illegal assemblies. After the
'images' incident of October of that year, he quickly released those arrested for
heresy and sedition, merely detaining the leaders and ordering the others not
to leave town.[134] At intervals, he urged the citizens of Nantes to live in unison
and friendship, to take no part in sedition and not to assemble contrary to the
edicts of the king.[135] D'Étampes' attempts to secure religious coexistence in
his government were among his responsibilities as the king's vice-regent in
Brittany, and were important in securing his authority and position among all
groups.

An anti-Protestant campaign was thus not pursued with great violence in
Nantes. What comes over from the municipal registers is a tacit and grudging
toleration of Protestantism in practice, provided that individuals were quiet,
private and discreet in their religious affairs. There was no active rooting-out
of Protestants, except following serious 'emotions'. There were no expulsions
from the town and no serious attempt to prevent the public worship at Le
Pressoir, as there were in towns such as Troyes or Toulouse. Nantes resembles
Châlons-sur-Marne, where, Konnert argues, city councillors would have
preferred a totally Catholic city, but order came first.[136] Like that of Tours,
Nantes' urban government was more concerned with consolidating its own
authority within the city than with provoking sectarianism and defying the
religious policy of the crown, as will be seen in Chapter 4. At no point did religion become more important than politics and overseas trade.[137] The problem
for the city authorities was that the disputes which broke out periodically
between the Catholic majority and the Huguenot minority had a corrosive
impact upon the effectiveness of governing institutions. The apparent unwill-
ingness and inability of the crown to resolve the problem of heresy discredited
the king and caused uncertainty, even paralysis, among the city's ruling groups.
Street conflicts were contained, although with some difficulty, but there
remained a climate of distrust and fear about what would happen in the future,
in the city and in the kingdom at large.

War and peace, 1562–72

In March 1562 the massacre of a Huguenot congregation worshipping at Vassy
by the retinue of the Duc de Guise sparked the outbreak of civil war in France,
which had been widely feared. The conflict had no parallel in Brittany. The
province remained peaceful. In the *bourgs* dominated by Protestant lords to the
north of Nantes, Guérande, Blain and La Roche-Bernard, arms were taken up
and defences strengthened, but there was no fighting. In Nantes, defensive

measures were taken to prevent attack. In April the city watch stepped up the watch of the walls and gates, a survey was made of the provisions held in the town, and the water gate at Briand-Maillard was closed, all river craft being forced to berth at the quays of Richebourg or La Fosse, outside the city walls.[138]

How might d'Étampes best maintain the peace of his province? Observations of the war in other regions of northern France would have shown that the main sources of conflict were Calvinist minorities within cities, who might seek to take the town for their own party, and the Protestant nobility of the surrounding countryside, who might raise troops to pursue Huguenot war aims. If these two groups rose in Brittany, war would follow. To keep the peace, d'Étampes ordered that the Nantes Protestants be unmolested and retain the position allowed them by the edict of January. The church continued to meet outside the city walls, partly protected by noble participation.[139] Calvinists were forbidden to enter the city bearing arms, unless they were gentlemen. Attempts by the cathedral chapter to prevent the sale of Reformed literature, and of the *conseil* to prevent preaching, failed.[140]

In July 1562, d'Etampes called a conference at the château of Nantes before his household and invited notables, which took the form of a formal disputation between two Protestant pastors of Nantes, Antoine Bachelard and Philippe de Saint-Hilaire, and the doctor of theology, Jacques du Pré.[141] The guests were chosen from among the religious orders of Nantes, from noble families of the county and from the leading military officers of the governor. In particular, the presence of the d'Avagour brothers and cousins, Seigneur de la Muce-Ponthus and Jean de Rieux, was important. The d'Avagour and Muce-Ponthus families were Protestants and possible clients of François d'Andelot. Rieux may have been a relative of d'Andelot's wife. There were four areas of disputation: the nature and organisation of the church, methods of worship, sources of truth, and the sacraments.[142] Nothing was resolved; the theological divisions between the two parties were too firmly entrenched. But the aim of the colloquy was not to solve religious differences but to try to convince Catholics and Protestants that peace was possible. In particular, the Protestant nobility of the county, clients of Rohan and d'Andelot, may have been under particular pressure to join the Huguenot party. D'Étampes sought to assure both confessions that his role, as Breton overlord, was to ensure coexistence and that he took responsibility for the protection of both groups. While waiting for a national solution, d'Étampes was following Michel de l'Hôpital's and Catherine de' Medici's ideas at Poissy, applying them to the quasi-autonomous Breton context. He hoped to encourage provisional toleration and reconciliation within the duchy's borders, on the basis of patronage and clientage networks, to maintain provincial neutrality from a national problem and to mediate a settlement without involvement in a 'foreign' war.

Until the late summer of 1562 Nantes' Protestants remained largely unmolested and continued to worship.[143] But in August d'Étampes and Martigues left Nantes to fight against rebels in lower Normandy. The absence of the royal governor allowed greater authority to devolve upon the *conseil des bourgeois*. The war also increased the opportunities for action against the Reformed church, while weakening its position within the city. Before leaving the province, d'Étampes judged that it was dangerous to leave the Calvinists in continuation of their assemblies, and he forbade ministers to exercise their cult. In August, royal letters were received in Nantes, expelling ministers from Brittany, on pain of death.[144] In September, the bourgeois attempted to purge the *présidial* court of Protestant sympathisers. They replaced Artus Lefourbeur ('member of the so-called Reformed church and who favours false preachers') with François Tregoust, and they asked that other suspect judges be forbidden to prosecute cases involving Protestants.[145] In November there were still Huguenots in Nantes, for a prayer meeting was reported to have been held at the house of the apothecary Pineau, although many of the community had by now fled to Blain. There are hints of sectarian passions during the war.[146] In the summer of 1562, there were two forced rebaptisms of children who were seized at Le Pressoir and carried to Sainte-Croix church, where the military governor and the captain of the franc-archers garrisoned in the town acted as godparents.[147] There may have been some forced conversions or abjurations.[148] But the *conseil* and other elites did not encourage persecution. Huguenots were grudgingly permitted in the city, allowed freedom of conscience and permitted prayer at home. But they were not to worship in public or to demonstrate their creed. Outwardly, they were to conform to the Catholic norms of the city, its sacraments and its holidays. Individual Protestants were tolerated in the city but public Protestantism was not.

The peace of Amboise of 19 March 1563 ended hostilities and restored the legal right to worship to Protestant groups. Huguenots in Nantes began to assemble again for worship, on the nearby fiefs of Calvinist nobles at La Gâcherie and Barbin.[149] But the war had hardened the attitude of the bourgeois. The period 1562–63 can be seen as a watershed in the treatment of Protestantism in the city. Previous equivocation and vacillation with regard to what to do about heresy in the town disappeared. The new edict of pacification was received with extreme repugnance, and enforcement was initially difficult. The bourgeois were encouraged in their stance by a series of letters and edicts in 1563, which allowed for a narrower interpretation of the edict's clauses. In June the edict of Vincennes forbade trade on Catholic feast days; in December this was confirmed, along with restrictions on sites of worship and limitations on Protestant baptisms and burials, with funerals to take place only at night.[150] In Nantes, Protestants were disarmed.[151] The city authorities aimed to marginalise the Reformed community and to thrust it outside the city, physically, institutionally and legally. This policy was ultimately successful; the Protestant 'problem' was largely solved by 1570.

The edicts of toleration, particularly that of Amboise of 1563, were of fundamental importance in defining the position of the Protestants within the civic community of Nantes and in determining the methods of Catholic actions against them. The edicts gave the new confession legitimacy and a public legal status; specific rights were to be upheld in law and the royal judicial framework used for their enforcement.[152] Indeed, Protestants were dependent upon the law to give legitimacy for their faith, for they lacked the numerical strength to achieve a settlement by force.[153] But the legal, institutional status of the Reformed church also made it more visible and imposed strict limitations upon it. The congregation could be supervised by royal officers. More importantly, the Reformed community was brought into the sphere of law. The contest against heresy henceforth took the form of legal battles, against contraventions of the edicts and contestation of Protestants' privileges.[154]

What is known of the Huguenot church in Nantes between 1563 and 1572 centres on its fight to exercise the legal rights granted by the edict of Amboise, through the creation of a public site of worship in the suburbs of Nantes, as shown by Penny Roberts.[155] In early 1564 the congregation petitioned the provincial estates and the crown, and renewed their requests to d'Étampes for a site of worship. They asked for the use of a house on La Fosse, outside the city walls. This was opposed by the clergy and the *conseil*, for the property lay within the fief of the bishop. Further, it was argued, Protestantism was odious to the King of Spain, and trade with the region would be jeopardised by a Protestant church on the port.[156] D'Étampes proposed sites in the suburbs of Saint-Clément, Richebourg and the Marchix, all of which were opposed. Finally, the royal governor allowed Protestants to meet in a house at Beauregard, in the Marchix. The congregation continued to be relatively healthy. A new pastor, François Oyseau, came in the early 1560s and the city was represented at annual provincial synods, although none of these were held in Nantes.[157]

But the position and numbers of Protestants slowly declined after 1563. Persecution and intimidation continued sporadically. During Corpus Christi 1564 five notables of the Reformed community were fined and imprisoned for refusing to decorate their houses with tapestries for the annual procession of the Host. In October, Charles IX ordered their release and reimbursement; letters were registered in the Rennes parlement stating that Protestants did not have to decorate their houses and that if adornment were required by the church authorities it should be done by the parish, at its own expense.[158] Also in 1564, Protestant merchants were refused entry into the city's company of merchants which frequented the Loire and its tributaries, and the rules of the society were changed to exclude non-Catholics.[159]

Two changes in the political institutions of Nantes also led to greater restrictions on Protestants. In 1565, the creation of a fully fledged, incorporated municipality enhanced the authority of the city government and gave it greater jurisdictional powers to use against the Reformed community, as discussed in detail in Chapter 4. The death of d'Étampes and his replacement as royal governor by Martigues in 1565 also hardened anti-Protestant positions in the city. In June he signalled his new powers with an ordinance that forbade Protestants to open schools, to sing psalms, or to baptise in ways other than those prescribed by the edicts.[160] Early in 1566 the Reformed church was forced to relocate to the fief of the Seigneur de la Muce at La Gâcherie. Worship was still relatively vibrant: thirty-five marriages were celebrated and the church had two pastors.[161]

The second and third religious wars saw further erosion of the Reformed community's position in Nantes. Shortly after the first hostilities at Meaux in September 1567 the Protestants of Nantes took refuge in Blain, where many remained until 1571. It appears that public worship was proscribed in the city, although records for the period are poor. The pacification edict of Saint-Germain of August 1570 again restored the legal position of Calvinists in France. They were allowed freedom of conscience throughout the realm and rights of public worship in places where it had taken place before the war; Protestants were to be admitted to all universities, schools and hospitals; they were to have their own cemeteries; they were to enjoy judicial privileges to protect them against prejudicial judgements by the parlements, and all confiscated offices and property were to be returned.[162] In Nantes, there was great hostility to the edict. The municipality designated two deputies to lobby against its application in the city's jurisdiction.[163] Yet once it was registered, the municipality upheld the edict and its members swore to do so before royal commissions who visited the city in July 1572.[164] Concern for order and obedience to the crown remained the prime concerns of the municipality, despite its antipathy to heresy. Pastor Oyseau returned to reconstitute his flock and restart its worship. But the Protestant community was reduced to a small, subjugated and legally powerless minority, almost marginal to municipal life.[165] It was forced to worship at La Gâcherie; there were no marriages and only six or seven baptisms in over a year.[166]

The St Bartholomew day massacres have mythic status in the official histories of Nantes. In a letter of 26 August 1572, the royal governor Montpensier informed the municipality of the assassination of Admiral Coligny and the deaths of the Huguenot leadership in Paris; he assured them of the king's intention to treat likewise with Protestants in other towns and urged the Nantais to

follow the Parisian example.[167] In a general assembly of 8 September the bourgeois decided not to contravene the edict of pacification and their recent oaths
before royal commissioners to uphold it, and ordered the citizenry not to
commit excesses against Huguenots.[168] By this time the Protestant community
posed little threat, and was no more than an occasional irritant to the city's
authorities. The war that followed the St Bartholomew's day massacres affected
Nantes very little, but once more the Calvinists fled to Blain. By 1573 the
Reformed churches of southern Brittany were depopulated, although congregations continued in Nantes, Châteaubriant, Blain, La Roche-Bernard, Vieillevigne and Piriac. The church of Nantes was small and often met in secret, but
it continued to worship under Pastor Oyseau until the edict of Nemours
expelled Huguenots from the city in 1585.[169] Religious tensions within the city
diminished in these decades, despite warfare in the wider kingdom.[170]

Conclusions

The advent of Protestantism in Nantes had a profound effect upon the understanding and exercise of authority in the city. At its height, 5 to 7 per cent of
Nantes' population were Protestant, and there were tensions within the urban
community. However, Nantes did not experience violence and bloodshed on
the scale of Paris, Rouen or Troyes in northern France, let alone Marseille or
Toulouse in the south, but neither was there a modus vivendi between
Catholics and Protestants of the sort observed in small towns such as Châlons-
sur-Marne. There was a de facto coexistence at street level between confessions, except at particular flash points and during open warfare in the kingdom
at large. This arose partly from a perceived difference between public and
private Protestantism, and partly because this position was forced upon a
magistracy unable either to repress heresy or to contain disorder when
sectarian passions broke out. Calvinist demonstrations of faith, from disdaining
popular celebrations to carrying arms in the city, did provoke popular, Catholic
reactions from a majority population fearful of sedition and the wrath of God.
But 'emotions' were short-lived, and there were few judicial or executive
actions against Protestants in the city.

The presence of a Huguenot community had a profound effect upon city
governance. Morally and spiritually, heresy threatened to bring divine anger
upon the community. In material terms, the presence of two religions sparked
urban conflict and disorder in the lightly policed early modern community,
which was difficult to quell. Order on the streets of Nantes was made even
more difficult to uphold because the religious issue created a rift between the
crown and city government over the best means of resolving the crisis of

heresy. The city administration of Nantes was heavily dependent upon crown authority to legitimise and support its actions. When sedition and heresy appeared publicly in Nantes following the conspiracy of Amboise, the municipal elites looked to the royal government for guidance and assistance. They considered that the best means of dealing with the problem of Protestantism was by repression and that local judicial institutions should be given greater powers to act. In contrast, the royal government pursued a policy of conciliation, moderation and toleration, but this failed to solve the problem. By choosing this route, the crown jeopardised its legitimacy; the contract which bound king to subjects required that he eliminate heresy and uphold the Catholic Church. Secondly, the crown's policy in practice was one of vacillation and indecision. Edicts issued across the years 1560–61 granted freedom of conscience but condemned public manifestations of Protestantism. How were these to be applied? Royal governors and city governments were genuinely unsure how to act and were without advice. The result was indecision, irresolute governance and regular outbursts of sectarian passions which went unpunished. The crown's influence over magnates and cities declined, and France tumbled into civil war as Protestants and Catholics attempted to resolve the religious issue through force of arms.

In Nantes, warfare remained far away although the city raised taxes and augmented its defences. The post-war period saw a greater return to order as the conflicting groups in the city moved away from physical conflict to a greater use of law and justice to resolve their disputes. Traditional authority reasserted itself. The Protestant community of Nantes had begun to use legal means to address their needs and grievances before 1562. With the edict of Amboise of March 1563, the royal courts became the forum for dispute settlement, reinforced by the arbitration of the king, as Roberts has shown. Rights defined by edict limited the freedom of action of Protestants. As the authority of the *conseil des bourgeois* improved with regard to the crown and other authorities, as we shall see in Chapter 4, the policy of toleration changed. Attacks were made on the legal and institutional position of Protestants within Nantes, and the community was increasingly marginalised. Protestants were pushed out of public institutions, merchants associations and judicial and fiscal offices in the state. Private Protestantism, of individual and household, was tolerated but public Protestantism declined. The second and third civil wars further reduced the position of the Huguenots in Nantes. When the community returned from exile to the city in 1571, they had a pastor but numbers had declined and they were forced to worship outside the city, on sympathetic noble fiefs. From this time onwards, Protestantism within the city walls posed almost no threat to the authority of the city's governors or its Catholic majority. It is to the political repercussions of Protestantism in Nantes that we now turn.

NOTES

1 A. Boschet, *Le Parfait Missionaire ou la vie du Révérend Père Julien Maunoir* (1697), p. iv.

2 P. Le Noir, *Histoire ecclésiastique de Bretagne depuis la Réformation jusqu'à l'Édit de Nantes*, ed. B. Varigaud (Nantes, 1851), p. 5. For an assessment of Le Noir's *Histoire* see P. Benedict, 'La chouette de Minerve au crépuscule. Philippe Le Noir de Crevain, pasteur sous Louis XIV, historien des églises réformées du XVIème siècle', *B.S.H.P.F.*, 146 (2000) 335–66.

3 J. Crespin, *Histoire des Martyrs Persecutez et mis à mort pour la verité de l'Évangile*, 3 vols, ed. D. Beniot (Toulouse, 1885–89), I, pp. 303–4.

4 P.-F. Geisendorf, ed., *Livre des habitants de Genève*, 2 vols (Geneva, 1957).

5 D. Nicholls, 'The nature of popular heresy in France', *The Historical Journal*, 26 (1983) 271–3.

6 All examples from the 1554 visitation are from A. Bourdeaut, 'Le clergé paroissial dans le diocèse de Nantes avant le Concile de Trente. Les infiltrations protestantes', *B.S.A.H.N.L.I.*, 24 (1940) 96–8.

7 A.M.N. BB 4: Délibérations et assemblées du conseil des bourgeois, 1555–62, fo. 209v; also in J. Vailhen, 'Le conseil des bourgeois de Nantes', Thèse du Doctorat, University of Rennes, 1965, p. 278.

8 Bourdeaut, 'Le clergé paroissial', p. 98.

9 R. Joxe, *Les protestants du comté de Nantes XVIème–XVIIème siècles* (Marseille, 1982), pp. 40–1.

10 B. Varigaud, *Essai sur l'histoire des églises réformées de Bretagne (1535–1808)*, 3 vols (1870–71), I, pp. 10–14, 22.

11 Varigaud, *Essai sur l'histoire des églises réformées*, I, pp. 36–7.

12 Le Noir, *Histoire ecclésiastique*, p. 53.

13 Travers, II, p. 354.

14 P. Roberts, *A City in Conflict. Troyes during the French Wars of Religion* (Manchester, 1996), p. 63.

15 Joxe, *Les protestants du comté de Nantes*, p. 68. *Narration sommaire de ce qui est advenu en la ville de Nantes par ceulx que l'on a prétendu conspirateurs contre la majesté du roy (1560)*, ed. E. Gautier (Nantes, 1860), pp. 10–11.

16 Varigaud, *Essai sur l'histoire des églises réformées*, I, p. 71.

17 Le Noir, *Histoire ecclésiastique*, p. 75.

18 Benedict, 'La chouette de Minerve au crépuscule', 356.

19 Varigaud, *Essai sur l'histoire des églises réformées*, I, p. 76.

20 J.-Y, Carluer, 'Deux synodes provinciaux bretons au XVIème siècle', *B.S.H.P.F.*, 135 (1989) 334.

21 Benedict, 'La chouette de Minerve au crépuscule', 356.

22 On the early historiography of Protestantism, see D. Nicholls, 'The social history of the French Reformation. Ideology, confession and culture', *Social History*, 9 (1984) 25–43, and D. Nicholls, 'Looking for the origins of the French Reformation', in C. Allmand, ed., *Power, Culture and Religion in France c.1350–c.1550* (Woodbridge, 1989), pp. 131–44.

23 H. Heller, *The Conquest of Poverty. The Calvinist Revolt in Sixteenth-Century France* (Leiden, 1986), p. 179.

24 P. Benedict, *Rouen during the Wars of Religion* (Cambridge, 1981), pp. 238–9.

25 See J. Salmon, 'Religion and economic motivation. Some French insights into an old controversy', *Journal of Religious History*, 2 (1963) 196–8; Benedict, *Rouen*, 237–8; J. R. Major, 'Noble income, inflation and the wars of religion in France', *A.H.R.*, 69 (1964) 631–45 summarises the traditional view and refutes it for the Albret–Navarre family.

26 Morice & Taillandier, II, p. 279.

27 Varigaud, *Essai sur l'histoire des églises réformées*, I, p. 11.

28 Travers, II, p. 354.

29 Le Noir, *Histoire ecclésiastique*, p. 74.

30 Morice & Taillandier, II, pp. 282–3.

31 A.M.N. BB 4, fo. 287r.

32 *Narration sommaire*, p. 16.
33 Joxe, *Les protestants du comté de Nantes*, p. 68. *Narration sommaire*, pp. 10–11.
34 See Roberts, *A City in Conflict*, p. 77.
35 B. Diefendorf, 'Prologue to a massacre. Popular unrest in Paris 1557–1572', *A.H.R.*, 90 (1985) 1,071.
36 M. Greengrass, *The French Reformation* (Oxford, 1987), p. 58.
37 Benedict, *Rouen*, pp. 78–81.
38 J. Farr, 'Popular religious solidarity in sixteenth-century Dijon', *F.H.S.*, 14 (1985) 202–3.
39 D. Nicholls, 'Social change and early Protestantism in France. Normandy 1520–1562', *European Studies Review*, 10 (1980) 290, 296.
40 Similar to La Rochelle's early community. See K. Robbins, *City on the Ocean Sea. La Rochelle 1530–1650* (Leiden,1997), pp. 146–8.
41 Benedict, *Rouen*, p. 92; N. Z. Davis, *Society and Culture in Early Modern France* (Stanford CA, 1975), pp. 2–4. In Dijon the new faith attracted affluent artisans, who paid higher taxes than others in the city; militants were likely to come from wealthier segments of their occupational groups, whether Protestant or Catholic. See Farr, 'Popular religious solidarity', pp. 204–5.
42 Heller, *The Conquest of Poverty*, pp. 57–8.
43 Benedict, *Rouen*, p. 49.
44 A similar conclusion is reached by B. Diefendorf for Paris in *Beneath the Cross. Catholics and Huguenots in Sixteenth-Century Paris* (Oxford, 1991), p. 118.
45 T. Watson, 'Preaching, printing, psalm singing. The making and unmaking of the Reformed church in Lyon, 1550–1572', in R. Mentzer and A. Spicer, eds, *Society and Culture in the Huguenot World* (Cambridge, 2002), p. 12.
46 Crespin, *Histoire des Martyrs*, I, p. 303.
47 Varigaud, *Essai sur l'histoire des églises réformées*, I, p. 2.
48 Heller, *The Conquest of Poverty*, p. 125; Nicholls, 'The nature of popular heresy', 265.
49 P. Conner, 'Huguenot Heartland. Montauban during the Wars of Religion', PhD thesis, University of St Andrews, 2000, pp. 224–5.
50 Joxe, *Les protestants du comté de Nantes*, pp. 26–7, 70, 74.
51 Heller, *The Conquest of Poverty*, pp. 53–4.
52 *Narration sommaire*, p. 14.
53 Joxe, *Les protestants du comté de Nantes*, p. 339.
54 Heller, *The Conquest of Poverty*, p. 202.
55 Morice, III, p. 1281
56 Farr, 'Popular religious solidarity', pp. 207–10.
57 Nicholls, 'Looking for the origins of the French Reformation', p. 143.
58 Diefendorf, *Beneath the Cross*, p. 122.
59 W. Naphy, 'Catholic perceptions of early French Protestantism. The heresy trial of Baudichon de la Maisonneuve in Lyon, 1534', *F.H.*, 9 (1995) 460–3.
60 Joxe, *Les protestants du comté de Nantes*, p. 339.
61 Joxe, *Les protestants du comté de Nantes*, p. 81.
62 Roberts, *A City in Conflict*, p. 77; M. Lamet, 'French Protestants in a position of strength. The early years of the Reformation in Caen, 1558–1568', *S.C.J.*, 9 (1978) 37–8.
63 Benedict, *Rouen*, p. 49.
64 As identified by N. Z. Davis, 'Rites of violence', in *Society and Culture in Early Modern France*, pp. 152–88.
65 Joxe, *Les protestants du comté de Nantes*, pp. 53–4; letter from Captain Sanzay to d'Étampes, 9 May 1560, in Morice, III, pp. 1,244–5.
66 B. Pocquet, *Histoire de Bretagne*, V: 1515–1715 (Rennes, 1913, reprinted Mayenne, 1975), p. 57; letter from d'Étampes to the Queen Mother in Varigaud, *Essai sur l'histoire des églises réformées*, I, pp. 36–7.
67 A.M.N. BB 4, fo. 280r.

68 Report of the seneschal, 18–22 July 1561, in Morice & Taillandier, II, pp. 1,276ff. See also letters of July 1561 to Martigues, in *Lettres de Catherine de Médicis*, ed. H. de la Ferrière and B. de Puchesse, 11 vols (1880–1943), I, p. 217 .

69 A.M.N. GG 416: Parish registers of Sainte-Croix, 21 July 1561.

70 A.M.N. GG 642: Religion réformée.

71 *Proces verbal* of *prévôt* of Nantes, 24 December 1561, in Morice & Taillandier, II, p. 1,299.

72 Benedict, *Rouen*, pp. 59, 64–7.

73 Davis, 'Rites of violence', pp. 152–88.

74 D. Crouzet, *Les guerriers de Dieu. La violence au temps des troubles de religion (c.1525–c.1610)*, 2 vols (1990).

75 Heller, *The Conquest of Poverty*, pp. 136–7.

76 A. Du Val, *Mirouer des Calvinistes et armure des Chrestiens, pour rembarrser les Luthériens et nouveaux Évangelistes de Genève: Renouvellé et augmenté de la plus part, à tel signe* (1562), pp. 9, 43.

77 Du Val, *Mirouer des Calvinistes*, p. 70.

78 L. Racaut, *Hatred in Print. Catholic Propaganda and Protestant Identity during the French Wars of Religion* (Aldershot, 2002), pp. 33–5, 53–4.

79 Du Val, *Mirouer des Calvinistes*, pp. 9–10.

80 G. Du Preau, *Harangue sur les causes de la guerre entreprise contre les rebelles, & séditieux, qui enforme d'hostilité ont pris les armes contre le Roy en son Royaume: & mesme des causes d'où proviennent toutes autres calamitez & misères qui journellement nous surviennent* (1562), p. 25.

81 Racaut, *Hatred in Print*, pp. 68–9.

82 M. Greengrass, 'France', in B. Scribner, R. Porter and M. Teich, eds, *The Reformation in National Context* (Cambridge, 1994), p. 57.

83 W. Church, *Constitutional Thought in Sixteenth-Century France. A Study in the Evolution of Ideas* (Cambridge, MA, 1941), pp. 78–9.

84 Matthew 12:25.

85 Du Preau, *Harangue*, p. iv.

86 Du Val, *Mirouer des Calvinistes*, p. 29.

87 Letter from Antoine de Crequi to the Cardinal of Lorraine, 27th October 1560, in Joxe, *Les protestants du comté de Nantes*, p. 70.

88 Du Val, *Mirouer des Calvinistes*, p. 9.

89 T. Watson, '"When is a Huguenot not a Huguenot"? Lyon 1525–1575', in K. Cameron, M. Greengrass and P. Roberts, eds, *The Adventure of Religious Pluralism in Early Modern France* (Bern, 2000), p. 162.

90 Letter from Bouillé to d'Étampes, 7 December 1560, in C. Mellinet, *La commune et la milice de Nantes*, 3 vols (Nantes, 1836–44), III, p. 164; Morice, III, p. 1262.

91 Du Val, *Mirouer des Calvinistes*, pp. 28–9; Racaut, *Hatred in Print*, pp. 81–3, 86.

92 Morice, III, p. 1,277.

93 B. Diefendorf, 'The failure of peace before Nantes', in R. Goodbar, ed., *The Edict of Nantes. Five Essays and a New Translation* (Bloomington, MN, 1998), p. 2; B. Diefendorf, 'Simon Vigor. A radical preacher in sixteenth-century Paris', *S.C.J.*, 18 (1987) 408.

94 M. Holt, 'Wine, community and Reformation in sixteenth-century Burgundy', *Past & Present*, 138 (1993) 66–7.

95 Crespin, *Histoire des Martyrs*, II, pp. 585–6.

96 My emphasis.

97 *Narration sommaire*, pp. 7–8.

98 Le Noir, *Histoire ecclésiastique*, p. 340; letter from lieutenant of Nantes to d'Étampes, 24 December 1561, in Morice, II, p. 1,297.

99 Farr, 'Popular religious solidarity', p. 194.

100 Joxe, *Les protestants du comté de Nantes*, p. 57; L. Cimber and F. Danjou, eds, 'L'Histoire du Tumulte d'Amboise (1560)', *Archives curieuses de l'histoire de la France* (1835), IV, pp. 25–32.

101 Letter from Sanzay to d'Étampes, 9 May 1560 in Morice, III, p. 1244.

102 R. Knecht, *The French Civil Wars* (London, 2000), p. 69.

103 A.M.N. BB 4 fos 253r–254r; A.M.N. EE 193: Guerres civiles et religieuses 1560–61.
104 Knecht, *French Civil Wars*, p. 72.
105 Benedict, *Rouen*, pp. 53, 239.
106 Letter from Bouillé to d'Étampes, 20 January 1561, in Morice, III, pp. 1,266–7; Varigaud, *Essai sur l'histoire des églises réformées*, I, p. 86.
107 A.M.N. GG 642.
108 A.M.N. GG 642; N. Roelker, *One King, One Faith. The Parlement of Paris and the Religious Reformations of the Sixteenth Century* (Berkeley, 1996), p. 252.
109 A.M.N. BB 4 fo. 285v; Travers, II, p. 357.
110 Letter from Bouillé to d'Étampes, in Morice, III, p. 1,287; Varigaud, *Essai sur l'histoire des églises réformées*, I, p. 75.
111 A. Tallon, 'Gallicanism and religious pluralism in France in the sixteenth century', in Cameron et al., eds, *The Adventure of Religious Pluralism*, p. 28; L. Petris, 'Faith and religious policy in Michel de l'Hospital's civic evangelism', in Cameron et al., eds, *The Adventure of Religious Pluralism*, pp. 137–8.
112 A. Stegmann, ed., *Édits des guerres de religion* (1979).
113 R. Bonney, 'The obstacles to pluralism in early modern France', in Cameron et al., *The Adventure of Religious Pluralism*, p. 217.
114 A.M.N. BB 4 fo. 323v.
115 Letter from Bouillé to d'Étampes in Mellinet, *La commune et la milice*, III, pp. 162–3.
116 M. Greengrass, 'Epilogue. The adventure of religious pluralism in early modern France', in Cameron et al., eds, *The Adventure of Religious Pluralism*, p. 311.
117 Du Val, *Mirouer des Calvinistes*, pp. 25–6.
118 Du Preau, *Harangue*, pp. 16–17.
119 A.M.N. GG 642.
120 A.M.N. GG 642; Varigaud, *Essai sur l'histoire des églises réformées*, I, p. 74.
121 Benedict, *Rouen*, p. 58.
122 Details from the seneschal's enquiry following the July incident, published in Morice, III, p. 1285.
123 B. Scribner, 'Preconditions of tolerance and intolerance in sixteenth-century Germany', in O. Grell and B. Scribner, eds, *Tolerance and Intolerance in the European Reformation* (Cambridge, 1996), p. 31.
124 P. Benedict, 'The dynamics of Protestant militancy. France 1555–1563', in P. Benedict, G. Marnef, H. van Nierop and M. Venard, eds, *Reformation, Revolt and Civil War in France and the Netherlands 1555–1585* (Amsterdam, 1999), p. 37.
125 See P. Roberts, 'Huguenot petitioning during the wars of religion', in Mentzer and Spicer, eds, *Huguenot World*, pp. 62–77.
126 Le Noir, *Histoire ecclésiastique*, p. 75.
127 M. Konnert, 'Urban values versus religious passions. Châlons-sur-Marne during the wars of religion', *S.C.J.*, 20 (1989) 387, 403.
128 A.M.N. BB 4 f0. 298v.
129 Scribner, 'Preconditions of tolerance', pp. 35–7.
130 Joxe, *Les protestants du comté de Nantes*, p. 56.
131 Michel de l'Hôpital's speech to the Assembly of Clergy, 1 September 1561, quoted in J. Lecler, *Histoire de la tolérance au siècle de la Réforme* (1955; reprinted 1995), p. 459.
132 Crespin, *Histoire de Martyrs*, III, p. 335; Le Noir, *Histoire ecclésiastique*, p. 83; Morice & Taillandier, II, p. 287.
133 Joxe, *Les protestants du comté de Nantes*, pp. 35–6.
134 Joxe, *Les protestants du comté de Nantes*, p. 69.
135 For example, letter of 19 May 1561 to the *conseil des bourgeois*, quoted in Travers, II, p. 357.
136 Konnert, 'Urban values'.
137 D. Nicholls, 'Protestants, Catholics and magistrates in Tours, 1562–72. The making of a Catholic city during the religious wars', *F.H.*, 8 (1994) 32–3.

138 A.M.N. BB 4 fos 333r–334v.

139 Crespin, *Histoire de Martyrs*, III, p. 335.

140 Le Noir, *Histoire ecclésiastique*, p. 93.

141 J. Du Pré, *Conférences avec les ministres de Nantes en Bretaigne, Cabannes et Bourgonniere, faicte par maistre Jacques du Pré, docteur en théologie à Paris et Predicateur ordinaire de l'Église Cathédrale de S. Pierre de Nantes en juillet 1562* (1564).

142 Varigaud, *Essai sur l'histoire des églises réformées*. I, pp. 100–1.

143 Crespin, *Histoire de Martyrs*, III, p. 335.

144 Le Noir, *Histoire ecclésiastique*, p. 85.

145 A.M.N. GG 642; Varigaud, *Essai sur l'histoire des églises réformées*, I, p. 108.

146 See for example a letter from Catherine de' Medici to d'Étampes, 4 August 1562, concerning a riot at Nantes, in *Lettres de Catherine de Médicis*, I, p. 369.

147 A.M.N. GG 417: Parish registers of Sainte-Croix, 18 August 1562.

148 Travers, II, p. 375; Varigaud, *Essai sur l'histoire des églises réformées*, I, p. 107.

149 Varigaud, *Essai sur l'histoire des églises réformées*, I, p. 125.

150 D. Potter, ed., *The French Wars of Religion. Selected Documents* (Basingstoke, 1997), pp. 82–4.

151 Varigaud, *Essai sur l'histoire des églises réformées*, I, p. 130

152 P. Roberts, 'Religious pluralism in practice. The enforcement of the edicts of pacification', in Cameron et al., eds, *The Adventure of Religious Pluralism*, pp. 31–44. See also O. Christin, 'From repression to pacification. French royal policy in the face of Protestantism', in Benedict et al., eds, *Reformation, Revolt and Civil War*, pp. 209–12.

153 Roberts, 'Huguenot petitioning', pp. 76–7.

154 Nicholls, 'Protestants, Catholics and magistrates in Tours', p. 23.

155 P. Roberts, 'The most crucial battle of the wars of religion? The conflict over sites for Reformed worship in sixteenth-century France', *Archiv für Reformationgeschichte*, 89 (1998) 247–66.

156 A.M.N. GG 643: Religion réformée; Varigaud, *Essai sur l'histoire des églises réformées*, I, p. 134; Joxe, *Les protestants du comté de Nantes*, p. 81.

157 See Carluer, 'Deux synodes provinciaux bretons', pp. 329–51.

158 A.M.N. GG 643: Letters from Charles IX, May–August 1564; A.M.N. GG 644 Religion réformée. Governor's edict, June 1565; Varigaud, *Essai sur l'histoire des églises réformées*, I, p. 137.

159 Joxe, *Les protestants du comté de Nantes*, pp. 158–9.

160 Varigaud, *Essai sur l'histoire des églises réformées*, I, p. 142.

161 Le Noir, *Histoire ecclésiastique*, pp. 135–6.

162 Potter, *French Wars of Religion*, pp. 118–21.

163 Le Noir, *Histoire ecclésiastique*, p. 169.

164 Travers, II, pp. 439–40.

165 Benedict, 'La chouette de Minerve au crépuscule', p. 355.

166 A.M.N. GG 642: Religion réformée. Declarations of the municipality and letters to Governor Montpensier, August 1570; Le Noir, *Histoire ecclésiastique*, p. 169.

167 Le Noir, *Histoire ecclésiastique*, pp. 354–5.

168 Varigaud, *Essai sur l'histoire des églises réformées*, I, p. 192.

169 P. Benedict, 'Les vicissitudes des églises réformées de France jusqu'en 1598', *B.S.H.P.F.*, 144 (1998) 62.

170 P. Benedict, 'Un roi, une loi, deux fois: parameters for the history of Catholic-Reformed co-existence in France, 1555–1695', in Grell and Scribner, eds, *Tolerance and Intolerance*, pp. 84–6.

4

City governance in crisis: crown, *conseil* and municipality in the early religious wars, 1559–74

In the work of Bernard Chevalier, the relationship between cities and the royal state in sixteenth-century France is characterised by rise and fall. He argues that during the reigns of Francis I and Henry II royal authority over cities increased. Military affairs were put in the hands of specialists, crown supervision of justice and police was extended with the creation of more officers, and the kings eroded urban fiscal resources. Towns were no longer seen as the indispensable supports of the state as in the later Middle Ages, but as obstacles to its efficient administration, in need of closer tutelage and reform. But the death of Henry II and the outbreak of civil war in the early 1560s reversed this trend, and royal authority was weakened.[1] Religious and military conflict encouraged provincial and urban particularism.[2] Historians of Brittany have argued that this was particularly true of Nantes. To regain its former status as capital of the duchy, and to augment its position with regard to Rennes, Nantes became increasingly hostile to royal religious, military and fiscal policies. Fernand Braudel's argument, that there was a marked return to the age of medieval independence, culminating in the rebellion of the Catholic League after 1588, had particular resonance for the city that held out longest against Henry IV, until 1598.[3]

In Nantes, this model of political change is not so clearly defined. In the previous chapter it was argued that the years 1560–62 witnessed a decline in royal authority, for disorder, uncertainty and fear caused by the presence of Protestantism in the urban community were worsened by the crown's lack of firm counsel and its increasing toleration of heresy culminating in the edict of January 1562. The authorities in Nantes simply did not know how to act and watched helplessly as France was engulfed in civil war. But the outcome of war was a new decisiveness by the crown and the city's elites to assert their authority separately, but also in concert to restore order to religious and secular affairs. The 1560s and early 1570s were a period of new initiatives in crown–city relations, for the more efficient administration of the kingdom, a result of the crisis of the early civil wars. This process of declining confidence, followed by the repositioning of authority within the city of Nantes, is the subject of this chapter.

Royal authority in Nantes before 1560

There is clear evidence for closer royal tutelage of Nantes in the mid-sixteenth century. In the 1550s the royal judicial apparatus of the city was enlarged and its administrative scope expanded. The main cause was the need to regularise the judicial organisation of Brittany after its formal union with France in 1532. Brittany retained its distinctive legal code, and the end of the ducal chancery created a need for a sovereign law court of appeal for Breton cases, as experiments with *grands jours* using Parisian magistrates had proved unsuccessful. In 1552, five *présidial* courts were created for the province, one to be seated in Nantes, to receive appeals from the *prévôtal* and *sénéchaussée* courts of the county. In 1553, a parlement was formed. Initially it was to have two terms, the autumn in Rennes and the spring in Nantes. After much lobbying and great cost – 100,000 *livres* to the royal treasury and 50,000 *livres* compensation to Rennes – Henry II granted the permanency of the court to Nantes in June 1557.[4] A second cause of administrative expansion in Nantes was the need to regularise the management of royal prerogative interests inherited from the duchy, military affairs, fiscal resources and the royal demesne. 'French' institutions were imported into Brittany. In 1555, a seat of the admiralty and a *maîtrise* of the *eaux-et-forêts* were created in Nantes. In January 1560, Francis II created a 'corps, college and community' of a mayor and ten *échevins* for the city of Nantes, although this was not executed immediately.[5] A formally constituted municipality would ensure efficient urban administration and closer police surveillance of the economic and social life of the city, making the bourgeois directly responsible to the crown. The number of royal officers, servants and thus to some extent clients of the crown increased. The expansion in personnel was linked to a third motive of the crown, to augment its revenue and to find new means of exploiting the resources of subjects.

While judicial and administrative structures expanded, day-to-day government depended upon the efficiency and co-operation of the men who held office. In practice, the exercise of royal authority in Nantes was limited by fierce disputes between the king's formal representative in the city, Captain Sanzay, and the civilian elites represented by the *conseil des bourgeois*. In 1555, Constable Montmorency, governor of Nantes, named René de Sanzay as his lieutenant. Sanzay considered that his predecessors had abandoned too many of their prerogatives, and he resolved to restore the traditional competencies of the post. He claimed rights to call and preside over general assemblies of the city, to have jurisdiction over all military and security affairs, and to have certain police functions over the ports of Nantes.[6] The *conseil* considered these issues to be its own preserve; from the beginning of his office, Captain Sanzay and the bourgeois clashed.

The main cause of dispute was the organisation of *guet et garde*, watch and guard duty on the city's walls and gates. The bourgeois claimed that the privileges of the city allowed them to organise their own defence. Each household had a duty, in turn, to provide a man for night watch and daytime guard duty at the city's gates. Those failing to serve were fined 5 *deniers*.[7] Captain Sanzay complained that the inhabitants did not meet their obligations. Soon after his arrival in 1555, Sanzay arrested several men whom he accused of not fulfilling their guard duty and imprisoned them in the château. Others who defaulted he fined 10 *deniers*, double the customary rate. When the *prévôtal* judge objected, he too was arrested. The *conseil des bourgeois* made vigorous representation to the Breton parlement and to the crown; the bourgeois were not responsible for castle guard duty, only that of the city walls, and individuals were not constrained to serve in person but could find a substitute or pay the fine. After all, some were too old and others went away on business. The dispute rumbled on. In 1556–57, Sanzay arrested several merchants of La Fosse for failure to perform guard duty and again fined other defaulters, admitting no exemptions from service.[8] In August 1557, fear of Spanish and English raids led Sanzay and the bourgeois to co-operate in a survey of men fit to bear arms, and there was an attempt to create a properly constituted militia with parish officers and ensigns.[9] But these measures were unpopular and temporary. By 1558, Sanzay was again writing to governor d'Étampes to complain about the bourgeois' lack of co-operation, and by the time peace broke out in spring 1559, the watch was again badly organised and largely evaded.[10]

In 1556, a second dispute arose between Captain Sanzay and the *conseil des bourgeois* when the captain claimed the right to visit and inspect any ship entering the port of Nantes, for which he charged a fee of 8–10 *livres*. The bourgeois accepted his claim to search ships, but strongly objected to the tax and the delay to departures that inspections caused.[11] Worse was to come. In November 1558 Sanzay named one of the château archers, Jean Seguin, as permanent porter of the gate of Port Communau, ordering the *conseil* to receive Seguin's oath and to pay his wages. The *procureur des bourgeois* refused, on the grounds that this contravened the privileges of the city.[12] The appointment of porters was an important gift of patronage in the hands of the bourgeois. In March 1559 Sanzay again appointed a porter, this time to the gate of Saint-Nicolas, against the *conseil's* wishes.[13]

Thus, in the king's name, Captain Sanzay attempted to extend the authority of the military governor over security, police and even economic affairs. The *conseil des bourgeois* was anxious to check Sanzay's pretensions. The captain was only partially successful. The king, rather than extending royal prerogative by supporting the actions of his agent in Nantes, did not seek consistently to augment his authority at the city's expense. The dispute over watch duty was resolved in the city's favour. In 1557, the *conseil* protested to the crown about the illegality of Sanzay's claims to fine and imprison defaulters, stating that he was causing disgruntled merchants to leave the city. Sanzay was offered a monthly sum to cover fines for which the bourgeois were responsible, but he had no authority to fine the inhabitants.[14] In the case of the city gates, however, Sanzay's rights to appoint guards were confirmed. The military emergencies of 1558–59 led the crown and Governor d'Étampes to support the replacement of civilian porters with men at arms. Fiscal problems also led the king to support Sanzay's actions in visiting and taxing shipping. There was no money to pay the garrison in Nantes, so the fines levied on merchants would contribute to this expense.[15] The crown had no conscious policy of extension of its authority through Captain Sanzay's actions, however. It saw its role as the adjudication of disputes between rival institutions within Nantes, leaving the administration of the city in local hands. Military and fiscal emergencies led the crown to seize opportunities for short-term benefit. There was no long-term plan to extend royal power.

Henry Heller has argued that the 1550s saw growing disaffection between urban populations and the king or his representatives; in Tours, Poitiers and La Rochelle there was opposition to tax and political disaffection by all social groups, even notables.[16] There were tax disputes in Nantes also, with remonstration from the city to the crown over the rapaciousness of its demands. In 1551, Henry II threatened to reimpose the customs tax known as the *imposition foraine* on Brittany, for which exemption had been granted by the dukes. The repurchase costs, negotiated by the provincial estates, were 132,000 *livres*, of which Nantes paid 19,200 *livres*. In 1557 a forced loan of 50,000 *livres* on the province cost Nantes 20,000 *livres*, with another 10,000 *livres* charged in 1559.[17] But despite these frictions, disaffection was not noticeable in Nantes. Royal political tutelage was relatively light. Governor d'Étampes was largely absent and his interventions in urban government were not always successful. In 1558, he wrote to the bourgeois asking for 250–300 of their best-armed men to serve in his infantry. A representative of the *conseil* was sent to protest at how few armed men there were in Nantes, and that deprivation of the city, which was a frontier town, would encourage enemies to harass the region.[18] Royal intervention in city affairs was largely responsive to local demands. The king gave the lead but worked through local officers and agents, bolstering institutions and arbitrating between them. Government operated inside a framework of contract, which king and city recognised.[19] The relationship between centre and periphery was one not of aggressive aggrandisement of central power but of governance by negotiation and compromise, supporting Nancy Roelker's arguments that 'a delicate equilibrium between the various elements of the constitution were seen as the norm in the mid-century'.[20] Authority was diffuse, sometimes conflicting, but it worked because power was shared among a range of different groups. This mode of urban government, devolved to local elites but supervised by the crown, worked well when all parties had fundamentally the same objectives, of ensuring order and respecting privilege. The emergence of a new group, Protestants, affected the moral and practical relationship of checks and balances in such a way as to challenge the theoretical basis and the practical operation of mid-sixteenth-century authority and governance.

The growth of Protestantism and the origins of the first religious war, 1559–62

The death of Henry II in July 1559 and the accession of the fifteen–year-old Francis II led rapidly to strains in the complex institutions and personal ties that constituted provincial urban government. The tutelage of the crown by the new queen's relatives, the Duc de Guise and the Cardinal of Lorraine, antagonised many of the kingdom's political groups for they were disliked as usurpers of the rights of the princes of the blood to guide the monarch in his youth. Even more unpopular were the military and fiscal policies of the new regime. The recent Habsburg–Valois wars left the crown 40 million *livres* in debt, so financial retrenchment was essential.[21] The army was disbanded, pensions suppressed, alienations of royal demesne lands revoked, and interest payments on debts suspended. Further, the Guises were widely suspected of partisanship, of granting the limited royal patronage to their own clients, and of using the crown to further their own dynastic interests. The death of Francis II and the accession of the boy king Charles IX in 1560 further undermined royal authority. The regency was assumed by the Queen Mother, Catherine de' Medici. Robert Knecht points out that despite her abilities, female regents had less authority than males, while the rapid changes made at the centre of government, with the retirement of the Guises from court and the promotion of the Châtillon and Bourbon families, added to political tensions within the nobility and thus in provincial administration.[22]

But above all else, provincial and urban government was challenged by the growth of militant Protestantism, as we have seen, even if it was relatively limited in scale. After the death of Henry II the movement grew rapidly and became politicised as political alliances and confessional allegiances among the nobility became intertwined.[23] At the same time the new Guise administration intensified repression of heresy with more draconian legislation in the autumn of 1559.[24] Religious persecution fuelled social and political dissatisfaction and stimulated manifestations of faith by Protestants. In response, Catholics began to react against increasingly open displays of Protestantism, while fears of plots and sedition grew. The threat to royal government, and the need to restore law and order to the kingdom, led the regency government to adopt a policy of religious moderation, which is discussed above in Chapter 3. But hopes of easing religious violence were misplaced. Protestants took advantage of the more liberal regime and the appointment of sympathisers to the privy council to demonstrate their faith openly. Catholics, horrified at the spread of heresy in their communities, reacted with violence. Noble factional dispute grew and assumed a more overtly confessional form. In April 1562, political tensions escalated into civil war.

The first serious political troubles of the wars of religion began in Nantes in February 1560. A group of Protestant noblemen led by Jean du Barry, Sieur de la Renaudie, and a Breton called La Garaye met in the city to plan a coup against the chief counsellors of the young king.[25] The conspirators wanted to replace the Guise faction with their own counsellors, call the Estates General of the realm, restore good governance and end the persecution of Protestants. The attack on the royal court was to take place at Easter, at Amboise. The plotters met in Nantes because it was far from the main centres of royal government yet easily connected to Amboise by the river Loire. The parlement was in session in the city, which was full of lawyers and plaintiffs, and an important marriage was taking place in the retinue of François d'Andelot. One hundred and fifty gentlemen could thus assemble in the city without being noticed.[26] But the 'tumult' at Amboise failed, and its conspirators were betrayed, were executed or fled.

In Nantes itself, the presence of Protestantism in the city was first acknowledged with the discovery of the conspiracy. In the immediate aftermath, it was feared that marauding Protestant noblemen would attack Nantes as they fled the realm. On 1 March Francis II ordered Constable Montmorency to strengthen the château guard of Nantes and the coast guard of southern Brittany; on 11 March, the king wrote to the seneschal warning of possible risings, and extra guards were placed on the city gates.[27] Further, a judicial enquiry was set up in Nantes to investigate the plot. The enquiry by the Breton parlement revealed an underground Protestant community in Nantes, although it played no role in the coup. But Amboise raised fears that Protestantism was seditious and that the secret community in the town might hatch plots to overthrow the political and social order. A new climate of disquiet disturbed the streets and institutions of Nantes. Also, as Protestants became more public and militant in their expressions of faith, disorder began to erupt in the city's streets. From May 1560, there were periods of religious disturbance and unrest. The disturbances created a permanent climate of insecurity and a heightened level of disorder among the population. Urban government became much more difficult in these circumstances. Although exonerated, *the conseil des bourgeois* was criticised for its lack of supervision and intelligence of urban affairs. No further steps were taken to transfer political powers from the royal judicial officers to the bourgeois through the formal creation of the municipality. Also, the crown, 'irritated by the disputes at Nantes', was persuaded by the provincial estates and nobles to transfer the parlement to Rennes a year later.[28]

What could the provincial and city authorities do to solve the religious problems and restore order to the city? During 1560, the problem of heresy was treated largely as a security issue. The crown considered that the Amboise plot hatched in Nantes was a result, partly at least, of poor police in the city. In previous reigns this might have led to a garrison being sent to the city to reinforce order and punish the inhabitants. In the political and fiscal context of 1560 this was not pursued, but royal scrutiny of city affairs did increase. The Duc de Guise considered sending commissioners to Nantes, in theory to augment Captain Sanzay's authority but in practice to replace the authority of Montmorency's client with men of his own.[29] Jean de Brosse, Duc d'Étampes, the Breton governor, was already active in Brittany before the royal instruction of July 1560 ordered governors and their lieutenants to reside in their provinces and to exercise their authority in person.[30] During 1560 d'Étampes's policy was to treat religious disorders and tensions as a security problem, to be eradicated through enhanced internal vigilance. But discovery of an organised Protestant church in October of that year revealed that the threat to the city's safety came from within its walls as much as from without. Night watch and guard duty were reinforced, three of the city gates were closed, limiting access into the town, and militia captains were appointed to organise the defence of the parishes. To the dismay of the *conseil*, the crown ordered the disarming of the population to prevent hidden Calvinists from surprising the city. They sent remonstrances to court, for they were loyal servants of the crown who should be left in possession of their weapons for the king's service, while suspected Protestants should be expelled from the city.[31] By 7 December Lieutenant-General Bouillé reported to d'Étampes that the king had rescinded the order and the arms that had been confiscated were returned to the inhabitants. The *conseil* promised that weapons would be used only for royal service, at the governor's command, for which twenty of the principal inhabitants promised their lives and goods.[32]

The period 1559–62 was one of difficulty for the Duc d'Étampes. Robert Harding has argued that the return of royal governors to the provinces from 1559 was a force for the reduction of royal authority in the kingdom. Governors, their companies and escorts militarised the provinces in a way that had not been seen for many years, and the power that this gave them in the localities was a threat to crown authority.[33] It is difficult to apply this model to d'Étampes's administration. D'Étampes was a leading Breton aristocrat; he held large estates in the north of the province and was related to the former ducal family through his great-grandmother. His wife had been a mistress of Francis I and once had great influence at court. He had wide prestige and patronage powers in the province, through offices in his household and military companies; one of the two lieutenants-general of Brittany was his nephew the Comte de Martigues. But after 1559, factional and fiscal problems at the centre of royal government reduced his ability to govern effectively. D'Étampes was not part of the Guise clientele and suffered from the curtailment of royal patronage in the reign of Francis II. Governance was also rendered difficult by different factions at court lobbying for their own interests.[34] For example, François d'Andelot was a constant champion of Nantes' Protestants against the judicial actions of local officers, as was Henry de Rohan, another leading Breton aristocrat. It was difficult to act against the complaints of such men.[35] In 1560, d'Étampes wrote to the king and Queen Mother, asking them to send him letters indicating that they favoured him, to show to local nobles and town governors so that they would better serve the governor and the royal cause.[36]

In Nantes, d'Étampes seems to have lacked a major clientele in either the *conseil des bourgeois* or the courts of justice, although more research is needed on this subject. The Bishop of Nantes of the late 1550s and early 1560s, Antoine de Crequi, may have been an ally of the governor, for his family came from the same region in Picardy as Madame d'Étampes.[37] The Nantais had affection for the Penthièvre lords as descendants of the old dukes. There was great joy in the city when Madame de Martigues gave birth to a daughter in 1562. But Captain Sanzay, the military governor of the city, was a client of Constable Montmorency, whose orders sometimes ran counter to those of d'Étampes. The courts of Nantes also obstructed d'Étampes's wishes from time to time. Harding comments that from 1560 the correspondence of royal governors was full of complaints about the partisanship of parlements and inferior courts, the biased adjudication of crimes and the use of their administrative powers to opposed the governors.[38] In February 1561 d'Étampes failed to get the parlement to publish orders forbidding inter-confessional disputes; the magistrates argued that the king had not issued letters to that effect and the governor could not do so on his own authority.[39] In 1562 he wrote to the royal council that 'your judges cannot definitively judge because of their partialities . . . and your edicts await verification in the parlements where judgements are long and expensive . . . At Laon, your *maître des requêtes* de Cucé administers justice . . . Could you command him to come to me [in Nantes] to do the same.'[40]

But the chief cause of difficulty in restoring order and security was the religious policy of the crown. In Nantes, the majority of the royal officers and bourgeois remained Catholic, strengthened by the Spanish origins, marriage alliances and trading partners of many of the city's elites; few sympathised with the Reform or had relatives who were converts. In the view of the bourgeois, the cause of trouble was the existence of a community of Protestants and the failure of the crown to do anything about it. The authorities became increasingly aware that security measures alone would not solve problems of disorder when this was a symptom of a wider ill. The king's inability to solve the religious problem through its chosen route of toleration and compromise showed the mistaken nature of this policy.

From the spring of 1560, the general assemblies of the inhabitants of Nantes, which included clergy, judicial officers and bourgeois, remonstrated against the new sect. From the summer of 1561, when Nantes experienced its greatest disturbance, objections to royal policy increased. In August, Bouillé echoed city complaints about the edict of July in a letter to d'Étampes. The edict ordered those of diverse opinions to live together in accord – 'this is far from remedying the danger which could come to this kingdom if the situation is allowed to continue for long' – and Bouillé doubted that those 'who did not fear God, the king or justice . . . would be persuaded by remonstration and gentleness'.[41] In November the *procureur des bourgeois* reported that the king's edicts were being observed in the city, but that the inhabitants complained about the continuing illicit assemblies; they had appealed to the judicial officers of the town to enforce the law against conventicles, offering armed force by the bourgeois for its enforcement if necessary.[42] Representation did not prevent the legal toleration of Protestants in January 1562. When news came to Nantes of the registration of the edict in the Breton parlement in March, the cathedral chapter and bourgeois together elected twelve inhabitants to lobby the king against the new law.[43] Government religious policy soured relations between city and crown. Legal recognition of Protestantism was a severe breach of the king's prerogative; the fact that toleration did not work, pacifying neither Protestant or Catholic, nor inducing them to live in harmony, called into question the effectiveness of the crown and highlighted its weaknesses on the ground. Bouillé's predictions to d'Étampes in January 1562 were to prove correct: 'if [the Queen Mother] does not give you greater forces than you have at present, I think that before long you will be constrained to let [the different religious groups] cut each other's throats and we will not be able to solve the problem'.[44]

Objections to royal religious policy were compounded by the practical difficulties of its execution. The unpopularity of the king's edicts was exacerbated in Nantes by genuine confusion over royal intentions. The provisions of the edicts could be interpreted liberally or literally. The edict of Romorantin of May 1560 affirmed prohibition of illicit assemblies and declared those who participated in them to be enemies of the crown; but crimes of heresy were to be tried by lesser jurisdictions, outside that of the parlement.[45] The edict of July 1561 caused even more confusion; the Nantais interpreted it as a ban on conventicles whereas the crown intended it to counsel peace and amnesty.[46] Interpretations were left to royal governors and judicial officers. After two weeks of civil disorder, in August Seneschal Le Maire wrote to d'Étampes asking for advice. 'I am in great confusion with regard to the intentions of the king as to how we should proceed in these matters . . . I only wish to do the best that I can.'[47]

The confusion over royal wishes, and the problems of practical administration that this created, illustrate the mutual dependence of city and crown for local governance. For *conseil* and city judges, a clear royal lead was important in determining their own actions and in reinforcing local powers. Royal equivocation, vagaries and inconsistencies in the application of religious policy undermined both royal and local authority. Disorder escalated in Nantes in 1561 because no single agency could quell it alone. Without royal sanction, the *conseil des bourgeois* would not undertake unilateral action against heresy, despite widespread and popular antipathy towards Protestantism. There were a number of reasons for this. The inclinations of Governor d'Étampes, crucial in containing the actions of the Nantes elites, were for peace, order and a measure of freedom of conscience, as discussed in Chapter 3.[48] Despite difficulties with city institutions, d'Étampes was the king's vice-regent in Brittany, and if he persisted he had ultimately to be obeyed. Secondly, the *conseil des bourgeois* was a weak institution before 1562, with little autonomous authority in the city in political or judicial affairs. Although Francis II had issued an edict creating an incorporated municipality, this remained a dead letter until 1565. Decision-making and executive authority were shared by a number of different, overlapping and competing groups, Captain Sanzay, the seneschal and the *prévôt* as well as the *conseil*. The main function of the *conseil des bourgeois* was to represent and regulate the economic and social policy of the city, its markets, traders, prices, poor relief, bridges, roads and tolls. But even contravention of these regulations had to be prosecuted by other royal officers, for the *conseil* lacked its own police jurisdiction. Further, the lack of authority limited its influence with the royal governor and the crown. The *conseil* could rarely initiate policy, for it was a subordinate body in the city. This lack of independent power was important in limiting the prosecution of an anti-Protestant campaign in Nantes.

Any action taken against heresy in Nantes was frustrated by the fragmented and competing nature of urban justice. Within the royal courts, there was a reluctance to convict, perhaps out of confusion over royal wishes, sometimes out of sympathy with the Reformed community, and often because of apathy and the slow process of the law. For example, the cathedral chapter's campaign against Protestantism was rarely successful because its jurisdiction over heresy was contested. In 1558, when Bishop de Crequi arrested several heretics at Le Croisic and brought them for trial at Nantes, they appealed to the parlement and were eventually released by this court.[49] In July 1561 Vicar-General de Gand arrested two Genevan booksellers and seized a consignment of literature, for prosecution at the bishop's court of the *régaires*. One of the prisoners appealed to the parlement; to de Gand's fury, the higher court revoked the case and entrusted it to the *conseillers* Michel d'Essefort and Robert du Hardaz, suspected Protestants.[50]

The issue of heresy was relegated time and again to second place in disputes between competing parties in Nantes, particularly Captain Sanzay and the bourgeois. Sanzay was the officer directly responsible to the crown for public order, but even with sedition and disputes breaking out in the spring of 1560, the bourgeois did not allow him any further authority over the city. Despite the placard incident in May, Sanzay wrote to d'Étampes, the inhabitants would not obey the ordinances of watch duty, to which the bourgeois themselves had agreed.[51] In the aftermath of the disturbances in the cathedral in December 1561, the *conseil* and Sanzay agreed on an augmentation of the guard of the city gates, a ban on the assembly of Protestants and the expulsion of vagabonds. But this rare example of harmony was blighted in the same assembly by a dispute between bourgeois and royal judicial officers: a motion of no confidence was passed for the judge of the *présidial* court and his sergeants, who were accused of sympathy with heretics and of failing to enquire properly into the recent riot. The bourgeois stated that henceforth they would use only the court of the *prévôté*. The meeting fell to recriminations and denials between different sections of the city's elite.[52]

A further reason for lack of direct action against heresy was bourgeois distaste for disorder and tumult. The bourgeois maintained a rhetoric of Catholic unity, for this was their preference, and they dared not offend the majority population. But in periods of calm, there was no repression of Protestants lest it provoke greater disorder. Even in the climate of disarray in royal provincial government, religious disorder brought unwelcome crown attention and greater interference in urban affairs, usually to the detriment of the city's fiscal and military privileges.[53] After the disturbances of October 1560, the seneschal moved quickly to prevent sedition and to calm the population. He appealed to the Breton parlement to sanction emergency measures at the city gates and the provision of armaments, and asked for four *conseillers* of the court to aid the ordinary judicial officers of the city in keeping order.[54] He hoped to avert the intervention of Bouillé, who had appealed to the king for two companies of gendarmes to guard the city defences.[55] The bourgeois would not disturb Protestants if they would live quietly and 'fell back on a policy of containment which they hoped would keep things more or less under control'.[56] We find in Nantes none of the literary humanist toleration of hetero-doxy that Tim Watson has described for Lyon.[57] But a policy of civic unity was pursued in that Protestants were left alone except in times of unrest and great efforts were made to dampen conflicts before larger upheavals broke out.

The attitudes and actions of the *conseil des bourgeois* reveal a great deal about the nature of authority in Nantes in the mid-sixteenth century. Preroga-tive action against heresy lay with the king, and without his sanction the civic and military authorities were reluctant to act. Urban authorities were anxious to obey. This was difficult, for royal religious policy was contradictory and confusing, as well as intensely disliked. That the crown failed to act effectively against heresy was resented and puzzled the city elites. But the *conseil* still acted within constitutional norms, using judicial mechanisms to resolve the city's problems. Rather than taking matters into their own hands, which would have been difficult anyway given their lack of executive power, the bourgeois fell back on a policy of lobbying royal government and of containment within the city. There was no desire for greater autonomy from the crown in Nantes. The problems of order and authority of the period 1560–62 showed only too clearly the mutual dependence of king and city notables for effective governance at the local level.

The first civil war, April 1562–March 1563

The decline in effective royal authority throughout France was an important cause of war in 1562. In April the Prince de Condé seized Orléans, and Protes-tants took a number of other towns such as Lyon, Blois, Tours and Angers, upriver from Nantes. Eastern Brittany remained peaceful, however. The Protestant fiefs near to Nantes were fortified, principally that of the Rohans at Blain, while soldiers were raised to fight for the Huguenots in Poitou. In Nantes, measures were taken to prevent surprise attacks. On 31 March a secu-rity council was formed comprising Captain Sanzay, the judicial officers and twelve elected representatives including a cleric; it was to meet twice daily.[58] In April, the night watch was extended, from 5.00 p.m. to 5.00 a.m., and the fine for non-attendance raised to 20 *sous*.[59] The gate leading to the quay at Briand-Maillard was sealed and all river craft had to alight at Richebourg or

La Fosse. The Saturday markets held inside the city were moved to the suburbs, to prevent entry into the city by conspirators disguised as traders. The *conseil* undertook a survey of provisions and ordered all householders to purchase supplies for three months.[60] The bourgeois asked that Reformed services should cease in the town, but were refused by d'Étampes.[61] Nantes remained tranquil under the close tutelage of the governor, who was resident in the château and sought to assure Protestants and Catholics that he supported peaceful coexistence.

In August, d'Étampes and Martigues were ordered to gather forces and fight against rebels in Normandy. The absence of the governor's restraining hand had two results for Nantes. Firstly, confessional positions hardened and the city authorities took the opportunity to rid themselves of the threat posed by the Protestant community in their midst. In August, Sanzay received orders from the crown and Montmorency to expel ministers and other suspects from the city.[62] There may have been some religious violence, for the seneschal reported to d'Étampes that some Protestants had abjured and were attending mass.[63] In September it was ordered that all judicial officers who supported Protestantism and who had left town would not be allowed to return.[64] Finally, many of Nantes' Protestants took refuge in Blain.

Secondly, there was an increase in military authority over the city and its population, which the bourgeois were unable to resist. Security threats multiplied in the late summer; an armed English ship berthed in the Loire and there were rumours of war bands in every direction.[65] The king sent Captain de la Tour to Nantes, with orders that the city should raise and support a defensive force of 100 horse and 200 foot soldiers.[66] D'Étampes also asked the bourgeois to raise 400 men from among the better-off inhabitants, armed with arquebuses or halberds; those not able to serve in person could contribute 7 *livres* 10 *sous* per month, the wealthier households individually and the poor in groups.[67] In August, Sanzay successfully extended the bourgeois militia. A roll was drawn up of all men fit to bear arms, and each was ordered to provide himself with a weapon or leave town. Each parish had to appoint a captain, subalterns and an ensign and there were to be regular exercises of arms.[68] Members of the clergy and judiciary and the principal bourgeois were ordered to perform guard duty in person. Barriers were erected in the main streets of the suburbs, and artillery was placed on the city walls, which were ordered to be repaired.[69]

The civilian elites resented the growth in authority of the military officers. In August the seneschal complained to d'Étampes that the troops commanded by de la Tour were unnecessary and that the city would not pay for them, for the inhabitants were capable of organising their own defence. To this end, the bourgeois elected their own security council of twenty-five inhabitants presided over by the seneschal.[68] When Captain Sanzay purchased a cannon on his own authority, the *conseil* agreed to lend him the money to pay for it, but only for two months, during which time the piece was to held in the house of André Ruiz, as collateral for the loan.[71] By December Sanzay was complaining to d'Étampes that the château had no provisions, the garrison went unpaid and the inhabitants would not obey his orders.[72] The *conseil* was powerless to refuse the orders of military commanders but it could obstruct and delay their execution.

Fiscal exactions multiplied. As early as April 1562, the bourgeois were ordered to supply the château with wheat and wine, and Martigues demanded an emergency loan of 1,000 *écus*.[73] In June a fortifications tax of 11,500 *livres* was demanded, then in July a levy for 250 foot and 50 horse soldiers.[74] In August came a royal demand for 6,000 *livres* for a *solde de la gendarmerie*, with further demands for subventions from d'Étampes in December, alongside a royal *aide* of 15,371 *livres*.[75] Simultaneously there were orders to provision and pay troops sent to Nantes. All categories of the urban population had to contribute, including the clergy. The heaviest immediate burden fell on the wealthy bourgeois. The *conseil* was forced to borrow the monies demanded by king and governor for immediate payment, to be repaid from city revenues in future years. In July, for example, it was proposed that 100 of the wealthier inhabitants should each make an advance of 50 *écus*, to be reimbursed from a levy on all the inhabitants; the rest was borrowed at interest from merchants and financiers.[76] By the end of the war, the *conseil* claimed debts of more than 40,000 *livres*.[77]

The war had two results for the city's civilian elites. First, their confessional stance hardened. Wavering members of the administration and royal courts were forced to confirm their Catholic allegiance or leave office. Protestants were not allowed the freedoms that they had had before 1562. Secondly, the war revealed the weakness of civilian authority with regard to military officers, including the unpopular Captain Sanzay. The bourgeois came out of the war with a determination to reforge and increase their authority over the city. It was also clear that the latter step would require royal support for its effectiveness.

Pacification, 1563–1567

On 31 December 1562 a Te Deum and general procession were celebrated at Nantes for the royal victory over Protestant forces at Dreux.[78] On 19 March 1563, the edict of Amboise was issued, concluding peace between the warring parties in France. The provisions of the pacification allowed for the continuation of public Protestant worship on seigneurial fiefs with rights of superior

justice and in the suburbs of one town in each *sénéchaussée*. The Nantes authorities were reluctant to receive the edict, for in their view its provisions for
toleration undermined the Catholic faith and the dominant position they had
been able to assert over the Huguenot minority during the war.[79] The clergy
and *conseil* sent remonstrations to the royal court protesting at its implementation. But by the late summer the edict was registered, reluctantly, in Brittany,
and generally was enforced. D'Étampes worked hard to demilitarise the
province; in September he was able to inform the king that the inhabitants of
Nantes and Rennes were no longer armed and that there was little disturbance
in the area, except at the coasts, which were troubled by the English.[80]

From 1563, there was a clear and sustained effort by the crown and its
agents in Brittany to restore order and royal authority by a return to law as the
primary means of settling disputes between parties, away from sectarian and
military conflicts.[81] This can be seen best in the application of the provisions of
the edict of Amboise within Nantes. In the post-war period, provision of a site
for Reformed worship was the chief cause of friction between crown, city
authorities and the Protestant community, as Penny Roberts's work has shown.
The experience of war, although actual fighting remained distant from Nantes,
created intense confessional polarity. Popular Catholicism took on a more
participatory and public dimension, while at the same time the religious
agenda of the city's elites became more clearly defined. After 1563, Catholics
sought exemption from the provision of a site of Reformed worship for two
reasons: military security, Nantes being a frontier town, and the bad effects
that the presence of Huguenots would have on the trade with Spain. Eventually, a compromise was reached on a house in the Marchix, but Catholics
continued to oppose the choice and seek the relocation of *prêches* to another
town in the region.[82]

What is clear about this dispute is that the crown was successful in moving
the Protestant issue into the realm of law. Roberts argues that Huguenots put
great stress on their adherence to law, and as proof of their loyalty to the crown
they were careful to observe the provisions of the edict of Amboise, commit-
ting themselves to accept royal adjudication of disputes as final.[83] Further, the
edicts of toleration, especially that of Amboise, encouraged Protestants to
resort to law. The edicts defined the position of Protestants within the civic
community by granting the new confession public legal status, rights upheld in
law, and a judicial framework for their enforcement.[84] But the institutional
status of the Reformed church also made it vulnerable. While Protestants were
granted certain rights and privileges, they also had strict limitations imposed
upon them, which too were enforceable in law. For example, there were conditions imposed on Protestant rites of baptism and burial, and the Protestants
were to observe Catholic cultural practices such as not working on feast days.[85]

In 1564 Protestants who refused to hang tapestries on their houses for the Corpus Christi procession in Nantes were arrested and fined, although Charles IX ordered their release and exemption from the practice.[86] In June 1565 the new royal governor Martigues reissued an ordinance confirming these limitations. The ordinance also banned Protestant schools and forbade the public singing of psalms by the reformed congregation.[87] Also, the drawing of the Protestant community into the sphere of law brought it into an arena familiar to its opponents, where they had many friends and skills. Accepting that they could not eliminate heresy from Nantes, the bourgeois's objectives became to enforce the most restrictive interpretation possible of Amboise.[88] The return to law was successful between 1563 and 1567. While violence flared occasionally between Catholic and Protestant, there was a great reduction of religious conflict in the city. Both the bourgeois of Nantes and the Protestant community chose to take their disputes to the courts and to royal adjudication. There was thus a restoration of traditional governance in Nantes.

Royal authority was also reinforced through symbolism and the physical presence of royal representatives in the province. Between 1564 and 1565, Charles IX and his mother undertook a royal progress around the realm of France. Formal entries into the major cities, adjudication of religious and political disputes and the display of royal majesty were to bolster affection, loyalty and deference for the monarch. In October 1565, Charles IX came to Nantes. He made his entry through the gate of Saint-Nicolas, was given the keys to the city and stayed in the château for three days.[89] The king's visit was an important means of displaying his personal authority, which was rarely seen in the west.[90] Royal authority was further bolstered in Brittany by the personal discharge of the royal governor's duties, by d'Étampes and then Martigues, who were resident for much of the middle period of the decade. The lords of Penthièvre proved loyal servants of the crown.[91] Nantes was careful to court Martigues. Shortly after his installation as governor in 1565, he made his formal entry into the city, where the bourgeois organised a splendid reception.[92] Royal commissioners also visited Nantes in the autumn of 1564.[93]

The crown undertook to bolster royal authority more widely through a national programme of judicial and administrative reform. Mark Greengrass argues that the civil war 'created a demand for reform of the French polity from those of both religious persuasions'.[94] This meant finding practical means of ending local disorder by fixing rules of governance and providing for the good administration of cities and localities on a day-to-day basis. State reforms had already been discussed at the Estates General of Orléans and Pontoise in 1560–61, and Chancellor l'Hôpital had used the resulting *cahiers* to prepare reforming ordinances in 1562.[95] The peace edict of Amboise had also contained measures of general police. Greater regulation of justice and administration was to follow in 1564 and 1566. The edict of Crémieu augmented royal super-vision of municipal government; in towns with bishoprics, parlements or *présidial* courts, the king was enabled to intervene in municipal elections by choosing the mayor and *échevins* from lists drawn up by the town councils.[96] In February 1566 there was a declaration that there should be no general assem-blies in towns without the presence of a *conseiller* of parlement, seneschal or other leading judicial officer.[97] The edict of Moulins of the same year was a great reforming statute of eighty-six articles whose main objective was the reform of royal justice. It regulated court procedures, appointments of judges and officials and the workings of urban police. Whether in the longer term the royal administration would have been strengthened by these reforms we cannot say, for war in 1567 prevented their implementation.

Concerns of the royal government over effective authority coincided with those of the civilian elites of Nantes. The greatest lesson of the war for the city's authorities was the weakness of their political position and the fragility of urban privileges in relation to military officers. Their experiences illustrated the necessity of royal involvement in urban government, to support the actions of civilian jurisdiction and administration. The post-war period saw crown and *conseil* work together to strengthen the political and administrative powers of the bourgeois.

As part of the new emphasis on urban governance, and in time for the royal visit, the bourgeois in Nantes finally achieved the implementation of an incorporated municipality in 1564–65.[98] The *conseil des bourgeois* had lobbied for the establishment of the corporation created by Francis II since the edict was issued in 1560. The problems of urban police in the period of religious unrest after 1559, and the contravention of military and fiscal liberties during the first civil war, added to the bourgeois's resolve to govern their own affairs. In 1564, Charles IX laid aside all local objections and issued letters confirming the creation of a municipality. The inhabitants were permitted to elect annually a mayor and ten *échevins*, and to install a *procureur des bourgeois*, *miseur* (treasurer) and clerk. These men would operate an executive *bureau de ville*, while general assemblies of the town were to represent all the corps of the city. The function of the general assembly was to decide upon policies that would be executed by the mayor and *échevins*.[99] Attendance at assemblies was open to all heads of household; in practice, the bourgeois elite and officers debated while others present looked on.[100] On 28 November the inhabitants assembled at the Franciscan convent and elected Geoffrey Drouot as the first mayor, along with ten *échevins*.[101] The increase in local authority of the bourgeois was the best means of preserving order in the city, while effective urban government better supported royal authority and prestige. Urban police powers were granted to the new municipality, along with right of jurisdiction over weights, measures,

ovens, mills and abuses committed in every craft.[102] The mayor and *échevins*
took responsibility for watch and guard; they were to supervise the accounts of
all communities including parishes and confraternities, they were to police the
sales of merchandise and the price of foodstuffs, and they were to organise the
relief of the poor.[103]

To allow for better regulation of trade, in April 1564 Charles IX created
a consulate for merchants in Nantes, with a judge and two consuls elected
annually. This was part of a wider programme of creating consulates for
merchants, and followed the regulations passed in November 1563 for erecting
the consulate in Paris. The municipality was to organise the election of consuls.
Guy Saupin argues that the two institutions, town council and consulate, were
part of the same reforming package for Nantes. The reorganisation of the city's
government was seen by other ruling and privileged groups as a victory for
mercantile pressure on the crown; in the face of hostile pressure, the two
bodies remained closely allied during the sixteenth century.[104] Olivier Christin
argues that increasing royal interference in towns allowed royal power to position itself as a guarantor of the common good 'against feuds and factions, an
arbiter above parties and particularisms'.[105]

The incorporation of municipal government led immediately to a recon-
stitution of the militia under the supervision of the *bureau de ville*. The first
civil war of 1562–63 revealed the inadequacy of Nantes' defence. The militia
lacked formal organisation at parish level, service was performed with great
reluctance outside emergency situations, and guard duty was a cause of dispute
between *conseil des bourgeois* and Captain Sanzay.[106] During the first civil war
greater efforts were made at organisation. A list was made of all householders
liable for service, and they were ordered to arm themselves with arquebus,
pike or halberd. Each parish was to appoint a captain, *cinquantaniers* and
dizainiers, with a tambour and ensign.[107] The companies were to meet regularly
to exercise arms. However, when peace returned, the militia largely
disbanded.

The new municipality formally appropriated to itself responsibility for
the defence of the city in a decree of 15 December 1564. A structure of
captains, *cinquantaniers* and *dizainiers* responsible for ten to twelve households
was resurrected for each parish or group of parishes; in all, seven companies
seem to have been created in this period. Each company was to draw up rolls
of men aged fourteen and over who were capable of guard duty, and all new
residents were to be alerted to their obligations. Officers were to visit households regularly and to make particular note of the comings and goings at inns,
and quarrels and disturbances in neighbourhoods were to be reported to militia
officers.[108] The newly constituted militia paraded with its ensigns at the formal
entry into Nantes of Governor Martigues in 1565. There continued to be

problems of persuading men to serve, especially in peacetime. In 1571, for example, militia captains complained to the *bureau de ville* that of 100 men ordered to serve, a tenth did not appear. The worst offenders were the rich bourgeois, while those men who did appear were of poor quality, or youths, badly equipped and ridiculous to those who saw them.[109] Peacetime exemptions granted by the governor compounded the problem: in November 1571 Montpensier issued letters of privilege for mayor, *échevins*, judges and consuls, *procureurs*, clerks and treasurers because of their involvement in the affairs of the city and the king.[110]

But the structure and organisation of the militia remained permanent from 1565. The captains and subaltern officers were in place as important new agents of municipal police in the parishes of Nantes. Militia service also extended the exercise of municipal authority down into middling groups of society. The captains of the militia were urban notables, wealthy merchants or officers from the royal courts, who were already members of municipal circles. In theory, captains were elected by their companies, supervised by the municipality, and approved by the governor. In practice, there seems to have been co-option or appointment to this rank. Below, the lieutenants, *cinquantainiers* and *dizainiers*, came from middling groups in the parish. In 1569 in Sainte-Croix parish, eight districts were commanded by notaries. Of a list of 144 men fit to serve in the parish, one-third at least were artisans, middling merchants and notaries. This was a bourgeois force.[111] From this date, the captains of the companies attended general assemblies in their militia capacity and often presented problems of order and security to *bureaux* and assemblies. The second and third wars saw an increase in militia authority over internal security, with household visits, the checking of newcomers and organisation of fortifications work as well as guard duty. While the militia was not a disciplined force and was frequently an unreliable force, it did allow for the extension of the authority of the municipality over the inhabitants of Nantes on a day-to-day basis.

The new municipality was not wrung from the crown out of royal weakness. Its creation was part of a policy of co-operation between king and local elites to provide for more effective order and police. Royal and urban authority would be enhanced simultaneously, and the new institution tied city and crown together more closely.[112] Previously, royal decisions were communicated through a range of different royal officers. Now there would be clearer lines of communication between central government and the city, through the mayor and *échevins*. The crown expected better order in administrative, fiscal and even military affairs at city level. Also, the bourgeois would be more loyal to the crown, whence their authority ultimately came. P. Hoffman argues that this was part of a royal strategy of confirming local privileges in order to yoke provinces to the crown.[113]

The attempt to enhance royal supervision of urban affairs by strengthening local police authority can be seen in the resolution of two disputes that
arose in Nantes in the mid-1560s. The most vigorous challenge to the jurisdiction of the new municipality came from the ancient *prévôté* of Nantes. The *prévôt*
objected to the usurpation of his authority over police and economic matters in
the city. The suppression of the *prévôté* by the edict of Moulins gave a temporary resolution to the problem. However, in 1568, short of funds and seeking
to compromise with local pressures and interests, the crown allowed Jacques
Charette to repurchase the office.[114] Charette claimed rights of police over the
city and over the contracts of merchants, against which the municipality
appealed to the crown. In 1570 Charles IX finally augmented the jurisdiction
of mayor and consulate at the expense of the *prévôt*.[115] A second dispute,
between the Chambre des Comptes and the municipality, was resolved in
favour of the sovereign court, however. In 1566, a dispute arose over the
receipts collected by Jean Avril, treasurer of the estates of Brittany. The king
granted the Chambre des Comptes permission to audit the accounts of the
provincial estates and of the Nantes municipality, particularly its receipts of
octrois, since 1551. The mayor objected and delayed but in 1567 was forced to
open the city archives to Bernard de Girard, a royal commissioner despatched
for this purpose. The crown was clearly established as the arbiter of local
conflicts and reinforced its authority by adjudicating disputes between the
city's institutions.[116]

    Ties between crown and city were further strengthened by closer
patronage and clientage ties between the court and the bourgeois. Royal clientage is difficult to uncover in Nantes in this period, but there are hints that the
government made some efforts to expand its client base among the civic elites.
For example, the Spanish merchant André Ruiz was certainly a client of the
crown. Ruiz was a wealthy merchant and financier; from 1565 he was granted
the farm of the royal *prévôté* or customs tax in Nantes.[117] He lent 30,000 *livres*
to Henry II in 1551 and 4,500 *livres* to Charles IX in 1571. Ruiz was a 'friend'
or client of the Italian courtier Albert de Gondi, the Comte de Retz, an ally of
the Queen Mother; Ruiz's son André frequently stayed in Gondi's household
at court and accompanied him to Germany to collect the wife of Charles IX.
The godparents of Ruiz's grandson Louis, born in 1572, were Madame
d'Assérac and the royal governor of Brittany, the Duc de Montpensier. When
Charles IX came to Nantes in 1565, the only private house that he visited was
that of André Ruiz.

    The relationship between royal officers, the municipality and the crown
also augmented royal authority. Philippe Hamon argues that the expansion of
royal officers in the cities of mid-sixteenth-century France bolstered royal
power, for the men who filled the posts were tied to the crown for their own

authority and social prestige.[118] There were certainly links between the seneschal, the *prévôt* and the crown. The king and the royal governor treated directly with, and addressed letters to, these judges in the 1550s and 1560s. There is evidence for patronage of other royal officers as well. In the later 1560s a dispute broke out between the Chambre des Comptes of Nantes and the royal government over reform of the usage of the court. Most of the magistrates resisted the changes, except for the first president, Marc de Fortia, who supported the king and the commissioners sent to oversee the reforms.[119] So the presence and augmentation of royal officers in Nantes in the mid-century furthered the indirect influence of the crown.

The relationship between royal officers and the new municipality of Nantes was at first cool, and occasionally hostile, as we have seen. However, royal officers were always represented on the general assembly of the city and on all commissions set up by the town, for example those created to deal with security issues and the relief of the poor. Gradually, officers also began to serve on the *bureau de ville*, as *échevins* and especially as mayors. Saupin has analysed the social composition of the new *mairie*. Between 1565 and 1597 there were 23 mayors elected, divided almost equally between wealthy merchants (11) and royal officers, mostly in the judicial courts of the city (12), with some holding both positions. Of 100 *échevins* elected over the same period, two-thirds were from the mercantile elite and the rest were officers of the royal and episcopal courts.[120] Royal officers were expected to work for the king's general interests as well as fulfil their official functions, facilitating royal influence in urban affairs.

The *conseil des bourgeois* and the municipality also sent deputies to court, a vital means of communicating with the royal government. By 1555, there was a regular postal service between Nantes, Paris and the court, for Jean Cornichon held the position of post master, providing horses and riders for the journey.[121] But letters were not sufficient for important business; personal attendance at court was essential. Watson has discussed in detail the methods of representation and topics of concern for the city councillors of Lyon in the mid-century.[122] For Nantes as in Lyon, there is evidence from the municipal registers and sporadic surviving correspondence that deputies were regularly sent to court and that they were men closely associated with the town council, substantial bourgeois and, after 1565, sometimes former mayors or *échevins*. In the fourteen months between May 1561 and July 1562, eight deputations sent from Nantes were mentioned in the registers of the *conseil*, and others may have gone unrecorded.[123] The reasons for the journeys were seldom given in detail; 'for the affairs of the town' usually sufficed. Between 1563 and 1566 religious affairs and fiscal matters were the object of several visits to court by Julien Daulfy.[124] The Nantais were also eager for news of the wider kingdom. In the later 1560s, Antoine Gravoil and René Martin wrote to the municipality from court about religious troubles in Languedoc, the Company of Merchants frequenting the Loire, taxes, administration and war.[125] Even if deputies were not successful with their petitions – there is no evidence for the results of these missions – they opened a window into the world of the court for Nantes' municipality and governing groups.

Finally, Philip Benedict argues that one important reason for reasonably good relations between cities and the crown in the 1560s was the relatively light fiscal burden imposed during the reign of Charles IX. The war year 1562–63 was expensive for Nantes, but afterwards there was little peacetime taxation. By 1565, the city debt had reduced to 34,600 *livres* plus expenses for the formal entries of king and governor of 10,500 *livres*.[126] The methods of taxation used in the city were also important in maintaining urban peace and order. Extraordinary tax was normally raised quickly, by borrowing. The city's creditors were mostly its wealthy bourgeois and its financial and judicial offi-cers, who lent in groups: a loan of 10,000 *livres* raised in 1565 was made by at least eight individuals. Loans were then repaid from the receipts of *octrois* on goods entering the city. After the first civil war, the city's creditors had every expectation of repayment at interest, for the receipts of *octrois* were good and there were few new taxes to be paid. In 1566 the crown allowed the city to raise extra *octrois* on merchandise to amortise its debts and to levy 10,000 *livres* on the inhabitants over two years.[127] Taxation for the ordinary inhabitant was largely indirect. While this pushed up the prices of commodities on the market in the long term, it did mean that there were few occasions when direct assess-ment and collection took place and hence when disorder might break out.

The second and third religious wars, 1567–70

Royal efforts to pacify the kingdom and rebuild royal authority were dashed in the autumn of 1567, when a new round of military hostilities began. In September, the Prince de Condé led a conspiracy to capture the king. Protes-tant and Catholic armies mobilised for a conflict that was to last for three years, with only a short respite in the spring of 1568. As in the first war, Nantes remained far from the main conflicts. Despite this, the city was once more forced to adopt elaborate security arrangements and was subject to heavy mili-tary and fiscal exactions by royal commanders. But the new municipality provided more efficient organisation and leadership in police and security measures than had been the case in 1562. The city was better policed and defended, and its privileges were upheld more robustly. While Chevalier and others may see in this process the emergence of the medieval *bonne ville*, the assertion of communal rights seized back from a weak crown, this does not explain the attitude of the Nantais. While royal authority was fissured by the military crisis, its administration in Nantes held firm. At the local level, day-to-day order and respect for royal authority were maintained.

In October 1567 news of the political and military crisis reached Nantes. Almost immediately, the Protestant community was forced out of the city and its members' goods were seized; beds and linen were taken to provision soldiers of the expanded château garrison, for example.[128] Internal security was increased. During 1568 the bourgeois militia began household visits under the orders of Martigues and Bouillé, to investigate the people living in their parishes, determining what quality of person each one was, what religion he or she professed and what arms he or she had.[129] In late August 1568 Captain Biré of La Fosse listed twenty-two 'strangers' in his quarter: eleven visiting priests and monks, two Flemish merchants with passports from Sanzay, a grain merchant from upriver and three refugees from Challans in Poitou. The remaining five, all men, passed without comment and were probably merchants.[130] In October there was a scare in Saint-Similien when a group of visitors from La Rochelle appeared in the parish, but they were only refugees from the Protestant regimes of La Rochelle and the Île de Ré.[131]

The municipality rapidly organised defence measures for Nantes in the hopes of avoiding tutelage by Captain Sanzay or other royal commanders. On 12 October 1567 a general assembly ordered watch and guard to be performed without exception. The guard of the city gates would be supervised by three leading inhabitants, a cleric, a judicial officer and a bourgeois, according to a rota, to check visitors to the town, and chains were installed to pull across city streets in case of invasion.[132] In addition, the municipality undertook to raise 100 dragoons at its own expense to defend the city. Royal letters were sent to Captain Sanzay ordering the raising of 200 infantry to garrison Nantes, again at the city's expense.[133] But the war remained far away. The militia captains complained that the watch had been on duty continually, yet had still paid 4,000 *livres* to keep a garrison. A deputation was sent to the royal governor asking that the city be discharged of the soldiers.[134] Martigues consented on condition that the inhabitants undertook to provide sufficient guard.

As the war continued, however, it became increasingly difficult to refuse the demands of military commanders for the quartering and supply of troops. The municipality was still determined that they should negotiate terms and organise the city's defences rather than allow Sanzay to exert his authority at their expense. In May 1568, the king ordered the city to quarter 100 musketeers under Captain de la Vascherie, for there was no money with which to pay the company. When the municipality claimed penury, Bouillé forced the inhabitants to lend the necessary victuals.[135] Of great concern to military commanders was the safety of the bridges across the Loire. A company of twenty men and their captain were deployed to secure the bridgehead on the south bank at Pirmil, again at the city's expense.[136] Late in 1568 Calvinist troops were reported at Thouars and Fontenay on the borders of Brittany. Martigues brought 400 troops to Nantes and quartered them in the château and at the Saint-Nicolas gate; 200 more followed in February 1569, and then 500 of them were sent with artillery to besiege the Protestant strongholds of Tiffauges and Montaigu.[137] Bread, wine and herring – it was Lent – were supplied for the troops.

On the governor's command, the fortifications of Nantes were strengthened in 1568. In February a survey of necessary work was carried out; all houses built against the walls were ordered to be demolished and the ditches around the city were to be cleaned out.[138] The king ordered a new fortification to be built, a defensive earthwork around the Marchix, opposite the Port Communau on the river Erdre. The municipality dragged its feet, unwilling to organise or fund a project forced upon it by military officers. In the autumn fears of a possible siege spurred greater action, however. Protestant raiding parties entered the county, and in November three priests were killed at Bignon, 3 leagues from Nantes.[139] Pierre Hudes, master architect of Nantes, was ordered to organise work on the walls.[140] All inhabitants were ordered to assist in bridge and fortification work; the militia drew up daily rotas of duty and was employed on these tasks under its captains and officers.[141] The municipality also purchased cannon and employed artillerymen from Le Croisic.[142]

With greater military exactions came increased fiscal demands. To cover the costs of the Nantes garrison, as well as extraordinary demands from Martigues, in March 1568 the general assembly decided to raise 10,000–15,000 livres. 5,000 livres was to be levied on the inhabitants, including clerics, and the rest borrowed at interest from the clergy and wealthy bourgeois.[143] By September the costs of war were estimated at 20,000 livres, with a further 7,000–8,000 livres necessary for fortifications work.[144] The inhabitants would have to be taxed again, and the mayor and échevins ordered rolls to be drawn up.

Fiscal exactions were exacerbated by disruption to commerce. The war of 1568 brought to a halt the manufacture and exchange in textiles in the region. Roads and rivers were unsafe for passage, while Rochelais and English pirates attacked shipping: in February the Colin Tanchet was taken on its return from Bilbao, and in September 1569 three ships were seized just 25 leagues from the Spanish coast.[145]

In 1569 the crown secured a victory against the Protestants and the fighting ended. War had again showed the limits of royal authority. The crown had not been able to enforce a lasting pacification, while conflict brought large-scale disorder to the kingdom. The war again revealed the limitations of urban

authority. Military governors had to be obeyed, their companies accommo-
dated, and the war paid for by the city. Yet the new municipality of Nantes,
despite conflicts with commanders, was able to organise internal security and
military commitments on better terms than in the past. It was able to keep
some of the commanders' rapacious demands at bay, and peace was maintained
within the city walls. There were no recorded disturbances in Nantes during
the later 1560s.

Peace and war, 1570–74

The edict of Saint-Germain of August 1570 ended hostilities in northern
France. With an end to military conflict the municipality worked hard to
augment its authority over city life still further and took a lead in negotiating
with the crown over religious, military and fiscal policies. The new edict of
toleration of 1570 restored to Protestants freedom of conscience and rights to
public worship in the suburbs of two towns in each *gouvernement*. Confiscated
property and offices were to be returned to Protestants, who were to be
admitted to all universities, schools and hospitals and who were granted special
hearings in the parlements. For the first time, royal officers were obliged to
swear an oath to uphold the edict, with severe penalties for infractions and
obstruction.[146] As with all previous edicts, the Catholics of Nantes opposed its
registration. On 4 August 1570 a general assembly met to elect a delegation to
lobby the king for exemption from the edict 'because of the importance of the
town . . . which is maritime and on the borders of the kingdom, and because
of the great abhorrence and enmity that those of the so-called Reformed religion create everywhere'.[147] In August there may have been some street tensions
in Nantes, for Bouillé published an order prohibiting Catholics and Protestants
from attacking each other, although most of the city's Huguenots were still at
Blain at this time.[148] In November, the clergy, supported by the general
assembly, sent Bishop du Bec to court to request exemption for the diocese
from the edict's provisions.[149] The complaints of city institutions had little
effect; Protestants, now few in number, resumed worship at La Gâcherie
in 1571.

Despite tensions over the resumption of public Protestant worship, there
was no serious outbreak of religious violence after 1570. This was testimony
to the increased ability of the corporation to keep order, and to the diminished
presence of the Protestant community. Further, the municipality was
committed to obedience to the crown, as the best bulwark against the erosion
of its powers by other agents, and as a prop to its prestige and authority in the
city. In July 1572 two royal commissioners , President du Gast of the Breton

parlement and President Bourvellière of Paris, arrived in Nantes charged with
the execution of the edict of 1570. In a formal assembly, mayor, *échevins*, judges
and officers swore oaths to uphold the edict.[150] Partly at least, as a result of this,
there was no St Bartholomew's day incident in Nantes. The pursuit of an
overtly royalist policy, even in the face of orders from the royal governor,
would be a marked feature of city politics for the next sixteen years. The crown
was the best guarantor of city liberties and the municipality's authority even in
a period of increasing fragmentation of power in the kingdom at large.

Loyalty to the crown paid off with regard to military obligations in peacetime, which were reduced in Nantes. In the summer of 1570 two companies of
gendarmes were billeted in the suburbs of the city. After a request from
Captain Sanzay, Lieutenant-General Bouillé ordered that they should be moved
into the city and provisioned by the inhabitants. The judicial officers objected,
the court of Nantes refused to allow the troops access or to furnish them with
supplies, and the municipality sent remonstrances to the king asking to be
discharged of this duty. Finally, Bouillé conceded. The city offered a one-off
payment of 500 *livres* to the garrison, and in April the two companies were
finally removed, although the inhabitants were obliged to furnish thirty men
every day to help guard the city.[151]

There was one royal policy which was to cause much friction in the city
in the following decades, however: that of taxation. By 1571, the cost of
troops, defences and taxes during three civil wars had left Nantes' municipality
seriously indebted, fortifications and repairs alone costing 47,000–50,000
livres.[152] Further, city infrastructure needed to be replaced. In the winter of
1570–71 a great flood of the Loire damaged the wooden bridges, which needed
to be replaced with stone, at an estimated cost of 10,000 *livres*.[153] Nantes' trade
had reduced since 1567, through war, pillage and piracy at sea, while relations
with Spain were currently poor, all leading to a reduction in income. To raise
the sums necessary to pay debts and construction costs, duties were increased
on all goods entering Nantes. The king also had pressing financial needs.
Despite Nantes' immunity from direct taxation, special levies multiplied. In
1570, 11,000 *livres* were demanded for a 'solde de 50,000 hommes de pied'.[154]
In March 1571 Charles IX asked for 66,666 *livres* from the county of Nantes,
the city itself to provide 50,000 *livres*, to pay off the *reîtres* and Swiss troops used
in the last war. The city objected because of its debts, offering 26,000 *livres*.[155]
In the same year the estates of Brittany were asked for 300,000 *livres*, a sum
reduced eventually to 120,000 *livres*, of which Nantes owed 25,800. This
amount was eventually conceded and raised in the traditional manner. Eleven
wealthy bourgeois each lent 100 *écus* at 8.33 per cent interest, to be repaid
from revenues on higher *octrois* on merchandise.[156] Finally, the sale of offices
began to affect Nantes. In April 1572 the Chambre des Comptes was enlarged

by twenty new offices, and two sessions were created each year, with different staff working *à l'alternatif*.[156] The officers of the Chambre were dismayed as their prestige and functions were diluted, while the municipality resented the expansion of officers with fiscal and military privileges within the city. Taxation and venality would become the most serious causes of rift between king and municipality in the following reign.

Conclusions

The civil wars in France, although mostly distant from Nantes before 1574, had a profound effect upon urban governance and on the relationship between the city and the crown. In the mid-sixteenth century the French royal state enhanced its authority over urban and provincial institutions. In Nantes, the 1550s saw the reorganisation of justice and the creation of large numbers of royal officers in the city, with the *présidial* and the parlement of Brittany. Further, the royal military governor of Nantes, Captain Sanzay, worked tirelessly to extend his authority over urban affairs, military, political and even economic. But the growth of royal control must not be exaggerated. The king and his direct representative in Brittany, the royal governor, the Duc d'Étampes, remained far from the region. Clientage was under-developed. The presence of growing numbers of men and institutions that claimed a share in urban governance led to disputes, which reduced their effectiveness. Royal authority was asserted largely through the creation of officers, the arbitration of disputes between them and attempts to raise taxation for the Habsburg–Valois war. Authority was devolved to the military, legal and fiscal officers and to the *conseil des bourgeois*, who governed the city together, with relatively little royal interference in daily affairs.

The religious tensions and outbreak of civil war in 1560–62 led to a crisis of effective authority in Nantes, of royal government and of city institutions, which is attributed at least in part to a weakness of royal authority following the accessions of two young kings and a regency government under Charles IX. The difficulties of these years showed clearly the dependence of city government upon the crown, to lay down policy and to provide legitimation for its enforcement. Both of these factors were weak between 1560 and 1563, leaving a vacuum of authority at city level. But they also revealed something of the crown's understanding of the constitution of France, where local communities largely resolved their own affairs with only occasional intervention by the king. The practical result was insecurity, disorder, violence and, from 1562, war. The first civil war had an immediate and important impact upon conceptions and exercise of authority. The crown had two principal policies to bolster its authority in the post-war period. The first was to move conflict resolution away from violence and back into the arena of law and justice. The edict of Amboise of 1563, enforced carefully by the royal government and its commissioners, and the reforming edict of Moulins of 1566 show that the crown attempted to augment its authority through effective exercise of the traditional prerogatives of law and, above all, justice. A second objective was to improve police in the cities of the kingdom to prevent disorder on the streets. For the *conseil des bourgeois* and city administration of Nantes, conflict and war had shown how vulnerable the town was to disorder and, during military operations, to military commanders who trammelled urban privileges. The *conseil des bourgeois* sought urgently to augment its own powers to prevent such events from happening again.

A coincidence of royal and municipal interests thus led to the creation of a municipality in 1565, with its own police authority over defence, social policy and economic affairs. Almost immediately, police was reinforced and extended with the creation of a permanent bourgeois militia, reform of poor relief and closer supervision of provisioning and economic production, as seen in Chapter 2. The crown supported the municipality's authority by providing sovereign legitimacy for its actions, for now the bourgeois were directly responsible to, and agents of, the king. The crown further asserted authority by arbitrating disputes between rival urban institutions. In return for this devolution of authority, or at least a rearrangement of responsibilities between Nantes' institutions, the city was better policed and able to defend itself more effectively against outside forces. Royal and civic authority were augmented by these actions. The wars of 1567–70 again disturbed the relationship of city and crown, and made practical city governance difficult. But after 1566, there was little disorder in Nantes. The city also remained firmly loyal to the crown to the end of Charles IX's reign. But after 1574 the crown began to undermine its own position in Nantes through too frequent intervention in fiscal affairs. Henry III contravened the contractual relation which contemporaries considered regulated relations between centre and province, leading them to question the just extent of royal power. This process will be examined in the next chapter.

NOTES

1 B. Chevalier, *Les bonnes villes de France du XIVème au XVIème siècle* (1982).

2 P. Deyon, *L'état face au pouvoir local* (1996), p. 58.

3 Summarised in S. A. Finley-Croswhite, *Henry IV and the Towns. The Pursuit of Legitimacy in French Urban Society, 1589–1610* (Cambridge, 1999), p. 4.

4 Travers, II, p. 344; J. Vailhen, 'Le conseil des bourgeois de Nantes', 3 vols, Thèse du Doctorat, University of Rennes, 1965, I, pp. 443–8.

5 C. Mellinet, *La commune et la milice de Nantes*, 3 vols (Nantes, 1836–44), III, pp. 153–4.

6 G. Saupin, *Nantes au XVIIème siècle. Vie politique et société urbaine* (Rennes, 1996), p. 16.

7 A.M.N. BB 4 Délibérations et assemblées des conseils des bourgeois 1555–1564, fo. 5r.

8 Mellinet, *La commune et la milice*, III pp. 137–46.

9 Travers, II, p. 345.

10 A.M.N. BB 4, fo. 94r.

11 A.M.N. BB 4, fo. 164v.

12 A.M.N. BB 4, fo. 138r.

13 A.M.N. BB 4, fo. 160r–v.

14 Mellinet, *La commune et la milice*, III, pp. 145–7.

15 Vailhen, 'Le conseil des bourgeois', II, pp. 382–3, 387.

16 H. Heller, *The Conquest of Poverty. The Calvinist Revolt in Sixteenth-Century France* (Leiden, 1986), p. 177.

17 Details in Vailhen, 'Le conseil des bourgeois', I, pp. 160–9.

18 A.M.N. BB 4, fo. 112v.

19 J. Collins, *Classes, Estates and Order in Early Modern Brittany* (Cambridge, 1994), pp. 1, 15.

20 N. Roelker, *One King, One Faith. The Parlement of Paris and the Religious Reformations of the Sixteenth Century* (Berkeley, 1996), p. 60.

21 R. Knecht, *The French Civil Wars* (London, 2000), pp. 64–5.

22 For detailed discussion of this period see R. Knecht in *The French Wars of Religion* (London, 2nd ed. 1996); *Catherine de' Medici* (London, 1998); and *French Civil Wars*.

23 B. Diefendorf, 'The failure of peace before Nantes', in R. Goodbar, ed., *The Edict of Nantes. Five Essays and a New Translation* (Bloomington, MN, 1998), p. 3.

24 See M. Holt, *The French Wars of Religion 1562–1629* (Cambridge, 1995), pp. 47–8.

25 J. Crespin, *Histoire des Martyrs Persecutez et mis à mort pour la verité de l'Évangile*, 3 vols, ed. D. Beniot (Toulouse, 1885–89), III, p. 66; H. de Gassion, *Original des Troubles de ce Temps* (Nantes, 1592); 'L'Histoire du tumulte d'Amboise advenu au mois de mars 1560. Ensemble un avertissement et une complainte au peuple françois' (1560), in F.-J. Verger ed., *Archives curieuses de la ville de Nantes et des départements de l'Ouest,* 5 vols (Nantes, 1837–41), IV, pp. 25–6.

26 Travers, II, p. 354; B. Varigaud, *Essai sur l'histoire des églises réformées de Bretagne (1535–1808)*, 3 vols (1870–71), I, p. 3.

27 A.M.N. BB 4, fos 219v, 221r.

28 Avis de la Dame de Montjean 1560 in Morice, III, p. 1,255; Mellinet, *La commune et la milice*, III, p. 171. The parlement was translated to Rennes by an edict of Fontainebleau in March 1561. See Vailhen, 'Le conseil des bourgeois', I, p. 448.

29 Travers, II, p. 357.

30 F.-A. Isambert, ed., *Recueil général des anciennes lois françaises depuis l'an 420 jusqu'à la Révolution de 1789*, vol. XIV (1829), p. 36.

31 A.M.N. BB 4, fos 251v–254r; Travers, II, p. 356.

32 Letter from Bouillé to d'Étampes, 7 December 1560, in Morice, III, p. 1,262.

33 R. Harding, *Anatomy of a Power Elite. The Provincial Governors of Early Modern France* (New Haven, 1978), p. 38.

34 See Harding, *Anatomy of a Power Elite*, p. 43.

35 For example in August 1561. See letter from Henri de Rohan to d'Étampes, 26 August 1561, in Morice, III, pp. 1,289–90.

36 Discussed in Harding, *Anatomy of a Power Elite*, p. 49.

37 D. Potter, *War and Government in the French Provinces, Picardy 1470–1560* (Cambridge, 1993), p. 135.

38 Harding, *Anatomy of a Power Elite*, p. 193.

39 Letter from d'Étampes to the Queen Mother, February 1560 in Varigaud, *Essai sur l'histoire des églises réformées*. I, p. 37.

40 Quoted in Harding, *Anatomy of a Power Elite*, p. 193.

41 Letter from Bouillé to d'Étampes, 11 August 1561, in Morice, III, pp. 1,288–9.

42 A.M.N. BB, fo. 4 296r.

43 A.M.N. BB, fo. 4 323v; Travers, II, p. 371.

44 Letter from Bouillé to d'Étampes, 20 January 1562, in Morice, III, pp. 1,266–7.
45 Isambert, ed., *Recueil général*, XIV, pp. 31–2.
46 Letter from Bouillé to d'Étampes, 22 August 1561, in Morice, III, p. 1,287.
47 Letter from Le Maire to d'Étampes, 31 July 1561, in Morice, III, p. 1,275.
48 Morice & Taillandier, II, p. 287.
49 R. Joxe, *Les protestants du comté de Nantes XVIème–XVIIème siècles* (Marseille, 1982), p. 46.
50 Varigaud, *Essai sur l'histoire des églises réformées*, I, p. 97.
51 Letter from Sanzay to d'Étampes, 9 May 1560, in Morice, III, pp. 1,251–2.
52 A.M.N. BB 4, fo. 302v; Travers, II, p. 362.
53 See D. Nicholls, 'The nature of popular heresy in France', *The Historical Journal*, 26 (1983), 263.
54 A.M.N. EE 29: Guet et garde 1348–1612.
55 Varigaud, *Essai sur l'histoire des églises réformées*, I, p. 62.
56 T. Watson, '"When is a Huguenot not a Huguenot"? Lyon 1525–1575', in K. Cameron, M. Greengrass and P. Roberts, eds, *The Adventure of Religious Pluralism in Early Modern France* (Bern, 2000), p. 170.
57 T. Watson, 'Friends at court. The correspondence of the Lyon city council c. 1525–1575', *F.H.*, 13 (1999) 280–302.
58 A.M.N. BB 4, fo. 326v.
59 A.M.N. BB 4, fo. 330r–v.
60 Travers, II, p. 373.
61 A.M.N. BB 4, fos 364r–365v.
62 Morice & Taillandier, II, p. 290.
63 Letter from Le Maire to d'Étampes, 10 August 1562, in Morice, III, p. 1,316.
64 A.M.N. BB 4, fo. 385r.
65 Letter from Le Maire to d'Étampes, 10 August 1562, in Morice, III, p. 1,316.
66 Travers, II, p. 372.
67 A.M.N. BB 4, fos 330r–v.
68 Mellinet, *La commune et la milice*, III pp. 184–5.
69 A.M.N. BB 4, fo. 385r.
70 Mellinet, *La commune et la milice*, III, p. 186.
71 A.M.N. BB 4, fo. 382v.
72 Travers, II, p. 379.
73 A.M.N. AA 42: L'entrée de Monsieur de Martigues 1565.
74 A.M.N. BB 4, fos 359r–v, 367v, 370r.
75 A.M.N. BB 4, fos 384v, 385r; Vailhen, 'Le conseil des bourgeois', II, p. 160.
76 A.M.N. BB 4, fos 371v, 372r, 389v.
77 A.M.N. BB 4, fo. 404v.
78 Travers, II, p. 379.
79 P. Roberts, 'The most crucial battle of the wars of religion? The conflict over sites for Reformed worship in sixteenth-century France', *Archiv für Reformationgeschichte*, 89 (1998) 248.
80 Letter from d'Étampes to Charles IX, 10 September 1563, in Morice, III, p. 1,337.
81 O. Christin, 'From repression to pacification. French royal policy in the face of Protestantism', in P. Benedict, G. Marnef, H. van Nierop and M. Venard, eds, *Reformation, Revolt and Civil War in France and the Netherlands 1555–1585* (Amsterdam, 1999), p. 209.
82 A.M.N. GG 643: Religion réformée; Roberts, 'The most crucial battle'.
83 Roberts, 'The most crucial battle', p. 252.
84 See O. Christin, *Le paix de religion. L'autonomisation de la raison politique au XVIème siècle* (1997), pp. 149, 162–5; P. Roberts, 'Religious pluralism in practice. The enforcement of the edicts of pacification', in Cameron et al., eds, *The Adventure of Religious Pluralism*, pp. 31–44.
85 See P. Roberts, *A City in Conflict. Troyes during the French Wars of Religion* (Manchester, 1996), p. 129.

86 A.M.N. GG 644: Réligion reformée; Varigaud, *Essai sur l'histoire des églises réformées*, I, pp. 137, 141.
87 A.M.N. BB 5: Délibérations et assemblées de la municipalité 1565–67, fos 54v–55r.
88 D. Nicholls, 'Protestants, Catholics and magistrates in Tours, 1562–72. The making of a Catholic city during the religious wars', *F.H*, 8 (1994) 23.
89 A. Jouan, Recueil et discours du Voyage du Roy Charles IX en Bretagne par un de ses serviteurs, 1566. ed. in Marquis d'Aubais, *Pièces fugitives pour servir à l'Histoire de France*, I (1759), p. 33.
90 Finley-Croswhite, *Henry IV and the Towns*, p. 47.
91 P. Benedict has drawn similar conclusions for Rouen and Normandy. See *Rouen during the Wars of Religion* (Cambridge, 1981), p. 116.
92 A.M.N. AA 42.
93 Mellinet, *La commune et la milice*, III, p. 152.
94 M. Greengrass, *France in the Age of Henri IV* (London, 2nd ed., 1995), p. 22.
95 See discussion in A. Stegmann, 'Transformations administratives et opinion publique en France (1560–1580)', *Francia*, 9 (1980) 596, 606.
96 Deyon, *L'état face au pouvoir local*, p. 57.
97 Isambert, ed., *Recueil général*, p. 184.
98 M. Cassan has discussed a similar policy of Charles IX which created urban governments in seigneurial towns in the Limousin. See *Le temps des guerres de religion. Le cas du Limousin (vers 1530–vers 1630)* (1996), chapter 8.
99 Mellinet, *La commune et la milice*, III, pp. 153–4.
100 A. Croix, *L'âge d'or de la Bretagne 1532–1675* (Rennes, 1993), pp. 85–6.
101 A.M.N. BB 5, fos 1r–3r.
102 Municipal articles of police, December 1564 in Mellinet, *La commune et la milice*, III pp. 195–9.
103 Travers, II, p. 385; see also Vailhen, 'Le conseil des bourgeois', II, p. 77 and Saupin, *Nantes au XVIIème siècle*, pp. 65, 83.
104 Saupin, *Nantes au XVIIème siècle*, pp. 47–8; P. Jeulin, *L'évolution du port de Nantes. Organisation et trafic depuis les origines* (1929), p. 119.
105 Christin, 'From repression to pacification', p. 212.
106 C. Laronze, *Essai sur le régime municipale en Bretagne pendant les guerres de religion* (1890), p. 172.
107 Mellinet, *La commune et la milice*, III, pp. 185–6.
108 A.M.N. EE 29; F.-J. Verger, ed., *Archives curieuses de la ville de Nantes et des départements de l'Ouest*, 5 vols (Nantes, 1837–41), I, p. 192; Mellinet, *La commune et la milice*, III, p. 202.
109 Mellinet, *La commune et la milice*, III p. 242; G. Saupin, *Nantes au temps de l'édit* (La Crèche, 1998), pp. 61–1. Militias in Paris and Lyon had similar functions. See R. Descimon, 'Milice bourgeoise et identité citadine à Paris au temps de la Ligue', *A.E.S.C.*, 48 (1993) 885–906; O. Zeller, *Les recensements lyonnais de 1597 et 1637. Démographie historique et géographie sociale* (Lyon, 1983), pp. 66–9.
110 Travers, II, p. 432; A.M.N. BB 9: Délibérations et assemblées de la municipalité 1571–72, fo. 214r–v.
111 A.M.N. EE 31: Rôles des compagnies de la milice bourgeoise 1570; analysis of membership in J. Hardwick, *The Practice of Patriarchy. Gender and the Politics of Household Authority in Early Modern France* (University Park, Pennsylvania, 1998), pp. 203–5.
112 Similar conclusions are reached by K. Robbins, *City on the Ocean Sea. La Rochelle 1530–1650* (Leiden, 1997), p. 62.
113 P. Hoffman, 'Early modern France, 1450–1700', in P. Hoffman and K. Norberg, eds, *Fiscal Crises, Liberty and Representative Government 1450–1789* (Stanford, 1994), p. 241.
114 Croix, *L'âge d'or*, p. 37.
115 A.M.N. AA 3: Lettres patents: letter of Charles IX, 29 August 1570; Travers, II, p. 413; Isambert, ed., *Recueil général*, XIV, pp. 208–9; 'Privilèges de la ville de Nantes', *Archives de*

Bretagne, 1 (1883), 98.

116 A discussion of this process in Dauphiné can be found in D. Hickey, *The Coming of French Absolutism: The Struggle for Tax Reform in the Province of Dauphiné 1540–1640* (Toronto, 1986), p. 32.

117 Details of Ruiz's life are taken from H. Lapeyre, *Une famille des marchands. Les Ruiz* (1955), especially pp. 53–5.

118 P. Hamon, 'Une monarchie de la Renaissance', in J. Cornette, ed., *La monarchie entre Renaissance et Révolution 1515–1792* (2000), pp. 37–9.

119 M. de Carné, *Les états de Bretagne et l'administration de ce province jusqu'en 1789*, 2 vols (1868), I, p. 139.

120 Saupin, *Nantes au temps de l'édit,* pp. 50–1.

121 Travers, II, p. 355.

122 Watson, 'Friends at court'.

123 A.M.N. BB 4.

124 A.M.N. AA 63: Deputés en cour.

125 A.M.N. AA 66: Deputés en cour.

126 Travers, II, p. 383.

127 A.M.N. AA 5: lettres patents. Letters patent of Charles IX, 8 November 1565.

128 Roberts, *A City in Conflict*, p. 131.

129 See A.M.N. EE 30: Recensements des hommes, des armes et des vivres.

130 A.M.N. EE 31: Rôles des compagnies de la milice bourgeoise 1570.

131 A.M.N. EE 31.

132 Travers, II, pp. 399–400; Mellinet, *La commune et la milice*, III, p. 216.

133 A.M.N. BB 6: Délibérations et assemblées de la municipalité 1567–8, fo. 20r.

134 A.M.N. BB 7: Délibérations et assemblées de la municipalité 1568, fos 1r–3r.

135 A.M.N. BB 6:, fo. 25v; Travers, II, p. 404.

136 A.M.N. BB 6:, fo. 26v.

137 A.M.N. FF 55: Police de Nantes 1569; Travers, II, p. 416.

138 A.M.N. EE 196: Guerres civiles et religieuses 1568–86.

139 Travers, II, p. 413.

140 A.M.N. BB 6, fos 32v–33r.

141 A.M.N. EE 196; A.M.N. EE 194: Guerres civiles et religieuses 1567–90.

142 A.M.N. EE 195: Guerres civiles et religieuses 1567–77.

143 A.M.N. BB 7, fos 29r–31r.

144 A.M.N. BB 7, fos 49r–50r.

145 Lapeyre, *Une famille des marchands*, p. 54.

146 Knecht, *French Civil Wars*, p. 155; Roberts, *A City in Conflict*, p. 133; Roelker, *One King, One Faith*, p. 316.

147 A.M.N. GG 644.

148 A.M.N. GG 644; Travers, II, p. 421.

149 Travers, II, pp. 431–2.

150 Travers, II, p. 440.

151 Travers, II, pp. 423, 427; A.M.N. BB 8 6 Délibérations et assemblées de la municipalité 1570–71, fo. 77v.

152 A.M.N. BB 8, fo. 253v.

153 'Privilèges de la ville de Nantes', p. 101.

154 A.M.N. BB 8, fo. 253v.

155 A.M.N. BB 8, fos 220v–225v; Travers, II, pp. 426–7.

156 Travers, II, p. 428; A.M.N. BB 9 6: Délibérations et assemblées de la municipalité 1570–71, fos 30r, 35v.

157 Travers, II, p. 435.

5

Taxation, war and rebellion:
Nantes and Henry III, 1574–89

In the city of Nantes, a marked feature of the reign of Charles IX after 1563 was the conscious attempt by the crown to resolve conflict and restore order through the use of legislation, judicial enforcement and the careful deployment of royal officers and agents. The creation of a municipality in the city was part of this policy. Relations between the new municipality and the crown were self-consciously traditional; the king governed at least nominally through the use of law, recognising contract and privilege, and royal authority was emphasised through arbitration between competing local parties. Religious policy, taxation and war created tensions within this polity but the new town council was determinedly loyal to the king.

The reign of Henry III began with much celebration. In September 1574, a Te Deum was sung in the cathedral of Nantes to celebrate the king's return from Poland, and bonfires were lit at the city's main crossroads.[1] The arrival of the new king was eagerly anticipated in Brittany. He was the first adult to succeed to the French throne since 1559. Catholics looked to the victor of Moncontour and Jarnac to solve the kingdom's religious problems.[2] But despite the early promise, Henry's reign has not been treated kindly by historians, although his biographer Philippe Chevallier has attempted to rehabilitate his character.[3] Within a decade, the king 'was almost universally condemned as an inept ruler, more interested in his own pleasures than his subjects' well-being'.[4] Nicola Sutherland has argued that this was a reign of fecklessness and failure that ended in the rebellion of the Catholic League and the king's assassination.[5] Above all, Henry's reign has been seen as one of the destitution of royal authority and a slide to anarchy in the French provinces. Mark Greengrass has stressed Henry's attempts to reform the French kingdom, with the Ordonnances of Blois of 1579, reforming edicts of the early 1580s and the proposals of the Assembly of Notables at Saint-Germain-en-Laye in 1583–84. But these ultimately failed because the king was unable to impose either a religious settlement or peace on the kingdom, or to find sufficient revenue to allow for taxation reform.[6] The battles and sieges of the early civil wars turned into raids, reprisals and pillages by war bands, which preyed on the countryside. Provinces and towns asserted their autonomy in the face of a weakened crown, reappropriating powers of justice and tax lost under the early Valois. Pierre Deyon argues that the result was 'provincial particularism and the project of a monarchy limited and controlled by the nobility', with calls 'to restore to the provinces of the kingdom . . . their ancient rights, pre-eminences, franchises and liberties, such as they were under King Clovis.'[7] The cities of France were seen to reject the tutelage of the monarchy, recreating the medieval commune by defending urban privileges and ending crown infiltration of municipal administration.[8]

The view from Nantes is less bleak for the decade 1574–84. The municipality continued to augment its authority at the expense of other city jurisdictions, in close consultation with the crown. There were serious disputes between the king and the city in this decade over taxation and the creation of royal offices, but crown authority and its power to act were not challenged. But the war which broke out on the southern marches of Brittany in the mid-1580s caused the king's authority to be eroded in the province. Governors took over royal fiscal and administrative authority while Nantes' municipality was forced, through military and economic emergency, to govern on its own, with less resort to the crown for advice. In the final years of the 1580s a crisis over the royal succession, combined with war and material hardship, led the Nantais to blame the crown for their ills. Loyal until early 1589, the Nantais finally decided to follow the royal governor, the Duc de Mercoeur, into rebellion against Henry III and into the Catholic League. But this outcome was by no means inevitable, nor even a long time in gestation. In this chapter, it is asked how a loyal city was moved to rebellion by 1589.

The consolidation of municipal authority, 1574–84

To celebrate the accession of Henry III in September 1574, a bonfire was lit on the Place des Changes in Nantes. In a demonstration of civic unity, representatives of the four secular ruling groups of Nantes were to light the fire together: the military governor, Sanzay, the first president of the Chambre des Comptes, the seneschal and the mayor. At the last moment, however, the seneschal refused to participate, for he would not be preceded by the deputy mayor.[9] In many ways, this scene typifies urban government in the 1570s, riven with rivalries between competing groups. The first decade of the reign of Henry III saw the municipality work further with the crown to augment its own authority over that of other institutions. The nature of municipal administration changed little. Local institutions governed on their own authority as well as that of the king, bolstered by royal support and arbitration.

Consolidation of municipal authority proceeded well. In 1575, the municipality purchased a property called Maison Bizart in the rue Verdun, and in 1578 it moved out of the court of Nantes into this building, which became the *hôtel de ville*. The creation of a separate establishment was of immense symbolic significance, testimony to the municipality's independence from the other royal jurisdictions of the city. Here, the *bureau de ville* could meet in privacy, archives and munitions could be stored and police authority could be exercised. The new town hall was a symbol of the civil authority of the corporation; 'it created a dedicated space to the dignity of urban government, especially the mayor, as well as the standing of the town'.[10]

Civic culture more generally, however, was not promoted during the 1570s and 1580s as much as in other French cities. Processions, festivals and governors' entries saw the mayor and *échevins* parade in official robes, and there was an annual mass and procession following the election of a new mayor in December of each year. But unlike Toulouse or Lyon, Nantes had no official histories or epic poems commissioned to eulogise the city's glorious past.[11] The one area of civic culture in which the municipality had a direct interest was that of education. Even here, the municipality showed parsimony bordering on miserliness as the determining factor in its policy, rather than civic pride. For example, in 1582, Archdeacon Le Gallo died, leaving his extensive library to be sold for the benefit for the poor of the Hôtel-Dieu. Le Gallo's executors offered the library to the municipality, to provide for the glory of the city and the university. The municipality moved instead to find a private buyer. After much prevarication, in 1588 the general assembly voted to acquire the library for 1,200 *écus*.[12]

The city's colleges were similarly treated as fiscal liabilities rather than as cultural assets. The college of Saint-Jean was founded by a rich bourgeois, Guillaume de Launay, in 1471.[13] By the mid-1570s the buildings were in a ruinous state and the neighbours were using its grounds as a rubbish dump. In January 1576, the college's governors asked a general assembly of the city that repairs be carried out. They had found a master who was willing to come from Rennes to take over the direction of the college if the buildings were attended to. A survey of necessary work was undertaken, but repairs were considered too costly and the municipality abandoned the project.[14] In September the governors tried again. They argued that the state of the college was a disgrace to the city administration, which should restore or abandon the building.[15] For a while afterwards, a priest of Saint-Saturnin held school here for twenty boys, but by 1582 the college was almost abandoned. Salvation came not from the municipality, but from Canon Avignon of the cathedral, who offered the town his benefice to endow the college in order 'to assure the future prosperity of literary studies'.[16] By 1587 the college had revived and was full of pupils, and the principal asked the municipality for an increase in the number of his masters.

The municipality's own college of Saint-Clément, founded in 1556, fared only a little better. The college was a great success in the city; its scholars were numerous and it was considered as a prop to the university.[17] Its masters were learned and respected, and had increased in number from four to six. But the relationship between college and municipality was tense. In 1578, the masters left the college over lack of funds.[18] In 1587, the *prévôt*, representing the principal, appeared before a general assembly of the town and claimed that the college was in danger of 'ruin and decay' because of lack of means. The principal was in a state of collapse; he had shut himself away and could not get out of bed without assistance. The principal asked for reimbursement of large debts contracted for repairs, for maintenance of the college during the years of high costs occasioned by famine and war, and for the salaries of his masters, threatening to leave his post. The mayor rejected the principal's claims. But the *procureur syndic* argued that 'it was necessary to maintain and conserve the college as a nursery for the learning of virtue', so the assembly granted 1,000 *livres* and appointed a committee to investigate the necessity of maintaining a staff of six masters.[19] Learning was important, but financial considerations were of prime concern.

While there was little active promotion of a distinct civic culture in Nantes in the 1570s and 1580s, there was a serious effort to augment municipal authority at the expense of other jurisdictions. The first decade of Henry III's reign saw a slow, often difficult, but ultimately successful appropriation of judicial, administrative and military authority, from the military governor, *prévôt* and seneschal. Although these were royal officers, the shift was not an appropriation of crown power by the municipal government. Rather, it was the redistribution of authority between old and new royal jurisdictions, for all were ultimately dependent upon the authority and sanction of the crown.

The 1570s saw continued disputes between the municipality and the royal judges of Nantes over issues of police and precedence. The seneschal and the mayor and *échevins* contested precedence in formal processions. The judges of Nantes also disputed the presidency of the general assemblies of the city. After appeals to the crown, the privy council finally supported the claims of the royal officers; the seneschal or his deputy, the *alloué*, or the longest-serving counsellor of the royal court, should precede the mayor and *échevins* in all urban general assemblies. Jurisdiction over urban police also continued to be disputed, but here the crown arbitrated in favour of the municipality. Charles IX granted police authority to the new municipality in 1564–65. The temporary abolition of the *prévôté* between 1566 and 1568 allowed the bourgeois to consolidate their authority over police affairs. Each week, one *échevin* in turn was appointed to supervise police, and the mayor held a tribunal in the court house. But the seneschal sought to reappropriate police authority to the royal courts. In May 1572 the city grain measurers stopped reporting the price of grain to the *bureau de ville*; the seneschal had forbidden them to do so under penalty of imprisonment and a fine of 100 *livres*.[20] In 1575, the seneschal obtained royal letters transferring municipal police to the royal court of Nantes; rulings of the municipality would henceforth be enforced by the seneschal and *prévôt*, who refused to transfer the tribunal to the new *hôtel de ville* when it opened in 1578. The municipality refused to comply. The crown was lobbied and the military governor of the county, Maréchal de Retz, was asked to intercede. Finally, in 1581 a new *bureau de police* was instituted, to meet every Thursday at the *hôtel de ville*. The *prévôt* was to join the *bureau de ville* on the tribunal bench.[21]

Finally, the long-standing conflict over city security between the municipality and the military governor, Captain Sanzay, was also resolved in the city's favour. As military governor, Sanzay was concerned mainly to assure the safety of the royal château and to supervise the security of the city itself. The municipality claimed that his safety measures for the château were incompetent, and his interventions in city security illegal, for they contravened the rights and privileges of the bourgeois. The accession of Henry III coincided with a dispute which arose between the château garrison and the inhabitants of Nantes. In May 1574 the municipality wrote to the Queen Mother asking that the château should not be left in the hands of 'alien' troops, and the bourgeois militia refused to allow the garrison to escort the city's artillery to Montaigu for the siege of the fortress. In the same month, a row occurred when Sanzay's lieutenant, Captain Gassion, struck one of the militia captains in the face.[22] To calm the situation, the royal governor, the Duke de Montpensier, agreed that the castle guard could be performed by twenty inhabitants of the city, rather than the garrison, under Sanzay's command.

The following March, Captain Sanzay's military authority was eroded still further. During a security scare over Huguenot incursions into southern Brittany, the municipality proposed to wall up the postern gate of the château, to his fury. Further, the city asked Captain Giraud and his company to garrison the château, with the reinforcement of fifty of the bourgeois militia. Lieutenant-General Bouillé acceded to this request, on condition that the city provisioned the garrison with wheat and wine, although he would not allow the transfer of the city keys from Sanzay's keeping to the municipality.[23] The visit of Maréchal de Retz to Nantes in April 1579 was used as an opportunity to disgrace Captain Sanzay. In a solemn assembly, the municipality presented

articles of complaint to the Maréchal. They stated that Sanzay's military administration was high-handed, ineffective and corrupt. The bourgeois objected to
his appointment of two lieutenants to the château command, and one in particular – Sanzay's son – they particularly distrusted. Secondly, Sanzay encroached
on the privileges of the city. He retained two keys to the tower of Saint-
Laurent, which the bourgeois claimed were theirs, he appointed porters to the
city gates against the municipality's wishes, and he let out the towers of the city
walls to shopkeepers who set up homes inside them, prejudicing the security
of the town. Thirdly, Sanzay made excessive demands of the bourgeois for
watch and guard duty; although the city had its own militia and could guard the
city itself, the inhabitants were being milked for fines. That said, the bourgeois
also complained about exemptions from military service given to privileged
groups. The rich would not participate, the clergy claimed exemption although
they owned a quarter of the houses in the city, and the number of judicial officers claiming exception had grown so much in recent years that there were
only a few merchants and artisans left to serve.[24] Sanzay and Gassion were
ordered to go to Paris to justify their positions to the king. In 1580 Sanzay
finally left Nantes. Captain Gassion was appointed to a joint governorship of
the château with a new officer, Captain du Cambout, each serving six months
à l'alternatif.[25] Relations between the château commanders and the municipal
government were less troubled from that time on.

The authority of the municipal government was furthered by the growth
in function of the bourgeois militia in the 1570s. Throughout the decade the
militia captains and their subalterns consolidated their role as executors of
municipal government. The close links between militia and the municipality
were formalised in 1578 when the corporation purchased the honorary consta-
bleship from François Dillon, Sieur de la Chartebouche, for 154 écus. The
mayor became constable and thus overall commander.[26] The captains acquired
an important voice within general assemblies and security committees
appointed in times of military emergency: that created by the Duc de
Mercoeur for a few weeks in 1583 included eight militia captains and their
subaltern officers.[27] The companies were formally responsible for the security
of Nantes and for the administration of police regulations that had a bearing
upon public safety. After the organisation of watch and guard, the main role of
the militia was surveillance of the city's quarters and households. From the
later 1570s, household visits became a regular and permanent feature of the
militia's work. In 1577, Lieutenant-General la Hunaudaye ordered that visits
should take place every eight days.[28] In the summer of 1580, with warfare,
plague and food shortages, captains were ordered to visit households three
times a week, under penalty of a fine of 10 écus. Further, the captains were
authorised by the general assembly to open all letters and messages coming

from suspect regions, regardless of the addresses.[29] The militia also enforced police regulations. Periodically, they expelled vagabonds, prostitutes and 'gens sans aveu' from the city. By the late 1580s the militia captains were the eyes and ears of the municipality. In May 1588, when a new porter was appointed for the gate of Briand-Maillard, an investigation was made of his background. The *recteur* of Sainte-Croix attested to his Catholic faith while the militia officers and sergeant verified his good character and his attendance at guard duty. Finally, his militia captain, Arthur Desmellières, instituted the new porter in his post.[30]

The increased importance of the militia captains in the execution of security and police regulations was not always matched by the reliability and effectiveness of the ordinary militia ranks, however. Despite constant regulation and increasing fines, the municipality could not improve the ordinary inhabitant's commitment to service outside periods of military emergency. During security alerts, all sections of the city's population could be coerced or persuaded to serve their guard duty. In March 1575, for example, Huguenot troops raided the county of Nantes south of the Loire. Each day three commissioners, one from each of the clergy, judicial officers and bourgeois, would supervise the guard of the city gates, and all householders took their turn of duty.[31] The same diligence was repeated for a few weeks of heightened alert in almost every year of the decade, culminating in early 1580 when raids from Montaigu caused the general assembly to order a guard of twelve men on each gate, day and night.[32] But during peacetime the great majority of inhabitants, privileged and poor, regarded militia service with disdain, serving only with the greatest reluctance. The militia itself was thus not a reliable defence or security force. Poor levels of service brought the municipality into conflict with the military commanders of the city and were one reason why the city failed to gain the level of autonomy in defence matters that it would have liked. In times of real emergency, professional military assistance was also necessary. In March 1575, when a Calvinist assault was feared, the municipality employed Captain Giraud and his company to garrison the city.[33] One of the first acts of the Duc de Mercoeur as royal governor was to summon the mayor to discuss the notoriously poor state of the city's guard. The mayor was ordered to call a general assembly and to place before it the governor's proposal that all those given a personal dispensation from service should designate a replacement, while a paid force of 150 inhabitants should be instituted for the watch. Mercoeur threatened to place a garrison in the city if his orders were ignored. The general assembly dutifully reissued orders for militia service, but their effectiveness is open to doubt.[34]

While the authority of the municipality expanded over the 1570s and early 1580s, there was a serious attempt in this period to restrict participation in urban government to a smaller, more tightly controlled elite. Studies of sixteenth-century cities have shown increasing oligarchy in municipal government, partnered with a growing distance between civic elites and popular groups.[35] In France, this trend has received emphasis in the work of Bernard Chevalier, with his hypothesis that the growing body of royal officers, with positions in judicial and financial administration, was increasingly removed from municipal government. It distanced itself from its processes, exempting itself from its charges and becoming 'removed from a commonality of which it shared neither dialect, culture or devotions'.[36]

In 1573 and 1577, the municipality requested the king for a reduction in the number of *échevins* from ten to six. Royal letters conceded this reduction in 1581 on the grounds that insufficient men could be found to fill the posts. Further, the king ordered that mayors should be elected for two years instead of one, because of the small number of people capable of holding municipal office in the city, although this injunction was rejected and the general assembly voted to continue with annual elections.[37] In 1583, there were further attempts to reduce participation in urban government. In May, at a meeting of former mayors and *échevins*, the mayor proposed that general assemblies should be replaced by an ordinary council, 'to avoid the confusion that has been widespread at past assemblies, where there has been an infinite number of people, particularly artisans inexperienced in public affairs, who have hindered the business'.[38] The proposed council would execute important city business and elect new mayors and would be composed only of former and current mayors and *échevins*. The proposal was rejected. In December of the same year, the *procureur syndic* proposed selection of mayors by an electoral college of representatives of the three orders of the city. It was also proposed to restrict the candidates to men who had been deputy mayors.[39] Again, the proposals were rejected by the other groups on the general assembly of the city. However, in December the *bureau de ville* proposed drawing up a list of candidates for mayor by itself, without the usual presence of former mayors. The former mayors protested and the general assembly ruled against the proposal.[40] Later, in 1586, there was another attempt to exclude popular groups from assemblies. At the election of the new mayor in December, the *procureur syndic* proposed that mayoral elections and general assemblies should henceforth comprise only 'invited people' of the clergy and royal office holders, to prevent noisy artisans from disrupting the meeting'.[41] Despite attempts to limit participation in this decade, proposed alterations to the city's constitution made little headway, for any change threatened the prestige and privileges of some group or other. There remained in Nantes 'a participatory and elective culture based upon incorporated privileges' and a relatively diverse and integrative participatory public. Of course not all men had equal weight in these political processes.

Men could aspire only to the type of office and public voice for which they were eligible, and the main criterion for influence remained wealth.

So over the decade 1574–84 the domestic authority of the municipal government increased, although progress was slow and irregular and was marked by disputes between competing jurisdictions. Police authority was finally settled on the *bureau de ville*; the militia was increasingly tied to the municipal government, and its duties extended, and the pretensions of Captain Sanzay to exercise rights over urban administration and defence were overthrown when he left his post in 1580. But the augmentation of municipal authority concerned only domestic urban affairs, police of the economy, social regulation and defence of the city walls. While there was some acquisition of legal powers from the royal courts of *prévôt* and seneschal over these matters, the municipality did not seek to acquire legal or judicial authority beyond these spheres. The crown's role was crucial in the reshaping of urban authority. Municipal authority was possible only with royal arbitration and sanction. The extension of municipal authority within Nantes should be seen as a readjustment of prerogatives between royal tribunals rather than an encroachment on the crown's powers. But in spite of the enormous importance of the crown in underpinning urban government, the period also saw a series of bitter disputes with the king that damaged relations between the court and the province.

The municipality and the crown: disputes over the just limits of royal authority, 1574–84

J. H. M. Salmon has argued that the trend to royal control of municipal government, witnessed in the 1550s and 1560s, weakened after the fall of Chancellor L'Hôpital in 1568. While the crown continued to participate in town affairs through the military governors, the *hôtel de ville* was less directly tutored by the royal council.[42] In Nantes, despite the role of the crown in supporting municipal authority, there is some evidence for this process in the 1570s. The crown continued to cultivate clients, following the practice of the middle years of Charles IX. The Bishop of Nantes, Philippe du Bec, was a devoted royal servant and had influence in city affairs, by participation in general assemblies and because he was frequently sought for advice. Du Bec divided his time between Nantes and the royal court. From September 1582 to Easter 1583 he was a member of the privy council, and he preached twice before the king in 1584.[43] The royal officers were also crown servants, and their numbers expanded in this period, but there is little clear evidence that they were directly tied to the king or his council members by clientage. Indeed Donna Bohanan has argued that the monarchy failed to maintain adequate control of clientage because of a lack of financial resources in this period, a factor which contributed to the decline of its authority.[44]

However, the municipality remained careful to be informed of affairs at court. For the first time, surviving correspondence shows the city's employment of permanent agents, legal officers who resided permanently in Paris or at the court and who were close to the centre of government. They represented the city and passed on information from the court to the municipality. There may have been such agents employed in previous reigns, but no evidence for them survives. Correspondence with one L'Enfant-Dieu in 1574–75 shows that he had taken on the affairs of Nantes in Paris, for a fee of 200 *livres* a year.[45] Between 1576 and 1587, Monsieur Denis, *sécretaire du roi*, was retained for his services, which were vaguely defined but involved communicating important events to Nantes' council. His surviving letters informed the mayor and *échevins* about the Estates General held at Blois (where the city also had deputies and observers), changes to the king's council, the creation of the order of Saint-Esprit, activities of the Protestants and of the Guise family, the League, and a range of affairs directly concerning the city such as munitions, the fortifications of Villeneuve and the mint at Nantes.[46] Deputies from Nantes also travelled frequently to court, as before. In 1574, Rolland Charpentier and Michel de la Garnison went to Chartres, to find that the king was at Lyon. In 1581, de la Garnison again attended court to discuss the reconstruction of Nantes' bridges and the demolition of the enemy fortress of Montaigu. He found the king indisposed to business, for he was busy with the details of the marriage of the Duc de Joyeuse.[47] The personal nature of politics and the paucity of communications meant the necessary employment of partisan agents and observers at the centre of government, to lobby the great and influential and to send back news to Nantes, even if they were not always successful.

The royal governor, the Duc de Montpensier, was rarely in Brittany in the 1570s, for he was occupied with war and diplomacy in Poitou and the south-west. Relations between governor and city were cordial but not close. The municipality sent gifts of wine and other delicacies on several occasions between 1574 and 1577; from time to time, Montpensier replied to the Nantais to assure them of his protection.[48] He was entertained well and his household expenses were paid when he attended the Breton estates in Nantes in 1579.[49] In contrast, relations between the municipality and Montpensier's lieutenant-general in Brittany, René de Tournamine, Sieur de la Hunaudaye, were poor. In July 1580, one of la Hunaudaye's sergeants maltreated an *échevin* on guard duty at the gate of Sauvetout; the bourgeois refused entry to the city to his troops on the grounds that a number of the force were Huguenots, and accused the lieutenant-general himself of conniving with Calvinists. In

May 1581, formal complaints about la Hunaudaie were sent to the king, Montpensier and the Maréchal de Retz, and Bishop du Bec was asked to meet with him to represent the bourgeois' views. La Hunaudaye was accused of building up an arsenal in the city, of requisitioning food and of unblocking the postern gates of the château, all without consulting the municipality.[50] Although la Hunaudaye left Nantes shortly afterwards, complaints from the municipality continued into 1582, accusing him of partisan behaviour towards the enemy at Montaigu because of his alliances with the Protestant families of Rohan and Laval.[51]

But to contemporaries, the distance of the royal court and governor and disputes with local military commanders did not signify a reduction in royal authority. What is noticeable about the reign of Henry III in Nantes is that the king was perceived not as losing authority, but as trying to extend it at the expense of provincial and city privileges. There arose in the 1570s a province-wide dispute between king, the Breton estates and the major towns over the just limits of royal authority. The three battlegrounds were religious policy, taxation and the sale of offices.

By the mid-1570s, the Protestant 'problem' in Nantes had been largely resolved. A Huguenot community continued in the city throughout the decade, with a church on the nearby fief of the Seigneur de la Muce. But the group was small in number, discrete and peaceable. The city authorities were keen to ensure that the Huguenots remained like this, if they had to remain at all, and were deeply antipathetic to royal policy which supported Protestant interests. For this reason, the peace of Monsieur and the edict of Beaulieu of May 1576 provoked anger amongst Nantes' Catholics as it did throughout France. Forced to come to terms with his rebellious brother the Duc d'Anjou and his Huguenot allies, Henry III was constrained to grant extensive concessions to Protestants. The edict permitted greater freedom of religion and legal recognition than had any previous settlement, with rights to worship in major towns and fully bi-confessional chambers for lawsuits in the parlements.[52] Catholics regarded the peace as a betrayal. In some regions, defensive leagues were formed to protest against the edict and to defend the church. The most important of these was founded by the commander of the Picard town of Péronne, Jacques d'Humières, in protest against the granting of his town to the Protestant Prince de Condé. Defiance of the king and his edict grew, culminating in the proceedings of the Estates General held at Blois in December 1576. But Henry diffused the tension and restored his authority by assuming leadership of the League. He also used the mandate of the Estates to make war on the Huguenots, in order to rescind the peace of Monsieur. The new edict of Poitiers of September 1577 was more moderate and restored the provisions for Protestant worship to those of the edicts of the 1560s.[53]

The Breton parlement did not register the edict of Beaulieu until August 1576. Complaints were made by the Nantes clergy and the municipality. But the Nantais also opposed warfare. Men from the city were among the Breton delegation to the Estates General at Blois. The third estate of Brittany voted for uniformity in religion but no war, among five *gouvernements* to do so; the governor, Montpensier, also advocated peace with temporary toleration, for order and tranquillity to be restored to the realm.[54] The League of Péronne had little impact on Nantes, which was suspicious of an association which was 'too aristocratic and did not consider their interests'.[55] In January 1577 articles of Henry III's League were signed in a formal assembly by Bishop du Bec, Mayor Loriot and Lieutenant-General la Hunaudaye.[56] The signatories promised to employ all their powers to maintain the exercise of the Roman Catholic religion, but also to leave undisturbed the consciences of those of the new religion who wished to live in peace and obedience to the king. They swore obedience, honour and humble service to King Henry, and promised to employ their goods and lives for the maintenance of his estate and the conservation of his authority, including financial and military support. This was a clear declaration of loyalty to the king. Later that year, the new edict of Poitiers received little attention. The university complained in October, as did the *procureur syndic* of the municipality in November.[57] But grudging compliance was the order of the day.

There was little anti-Protestant agitation on the ground after 1574, largely because local Protestants were few and subdued. There was a small disturbance in September 1578, stirred by the presence of several armed Calvinist leaders in Nantes; they were ordered to leave the town because 'the people will not suffer them and can no longer be contained'.[58] A proposal to raise the seigneurie of La Muce Ponthus to a superior jurisdiction caused consternation in the city. La Muce's fief at La Gâcherie, a league from the city, was used for Protestant worship. The elevation of the fief to one of high justice would extend the rights of local Protestants. In August 1581, the bishop, canons, mayor and *échevins* went to the parlement to present their opposition to the case. The municipality sent remonstrances to the royal council, protesting that a strong presence of armed Protestant nobles at La Gâcherie would prejudice the security of the city. Complaints were also made about the Sieur de Vieillevigne, a Huguenot, who was fortifying his house, which lay close to Nantes.[59] Despite complaints, letters of erection were registered for La Muce. The institutions of Nantes thus strove to limit Protestantism's position in the city, but in practice tacit toleration was maintained. Even after the proscription of Protestantism in 1585, when most left Nantes for La Rochelle, a few people stayed. As late as September 1588 a general assembly forbade all Huguenots from association and from speaking together more than two at a time in the streets, suggesting that at least a small, perhaps mercantile and foreign, presence remained.[60] Royal toleration was not popular but the upholding of the edicts guaranteed order and security in the city, for most of the time. Despite a visceral dislike of heresy and crown policy, the municipality and royal judges were obedient. Royal toleration did not erode the king's authority in Nantes any more than it had in the past because it ensured order. Order was the key to the exercise of effective local authority.

The grudging acceptance of the crown's religious policy did not extend to the needs of the royal treasury. J. J. Clamagerau argued that for France as a whole in the period 1576–88, taxation doubled.[61] In Brittany, the period 1574–80 saw a major fiscal dispute with serious constitutional overtones. Arguments moved from the issue of rapaciousness to that of prerogative, the king's right to tax in the province and the just limits of the authority of the crown. Resentment of taxation was intensified by the relative tranquillity of the region in this period.[62] The final years of the reign of Charles IX had seen taxation rise in the province. In addition to the annual grant of *fouage* and customs taxes, the estates of Brittany paid at least 300,000 *livres* to the crown between 1571 and 1574.[63] In March 1574 a further 90,000 *livres* was demanded of the province, although this sum was later reduced.[64] Taxation increased further in 1575. It is difficult to recreate accurately the amounts demanded, but it seems that 30,000 *livres* was imposed on the province and mostly on Nantes, for munitions to supply Montpensier's forces at Lusignan. A levy of 40,000 *livres* was imposed on bell towers, and 60,000 *livres* was levied to outfit ships for the relief of Belle-Isle, of which Nantes paid 10,000 *livres*; there were costs demanded by passing armies and for the garrison of troops in Nantes' château.[65] Then in December, Brittany was asked for 52,000 *livres* from walled towns for a *solde des gens de guerre*, with Nantes to pay 15,000 *livres*, which was levied on all inhabitants without privilege.[66] The burden in the city fell mostly on the bourgeois; they were forced to make loans to the municipality to pay tax costs quickly, and were obliged to take out crown *rentes* as well. There were complaints that the better-off citizens had to sell their family properties to pay taxation.[67]

Nantes' dispute with the crown over taxation was part of a wider provincial conflict with Henry III, mediated through the Breton estates. Despite periodic conflicts of interests within the estates of Brittany between the third and the other two estates, the heavy taxation of the mid-1570s created a sense of grievance among all sections of the provincial elite. The king's tax demand of 1574 met with refusal. The three orders listed the enormous expenses which they had met since the start of the wars, to furnish troops for the king and to defend the coasts. They refused further subventions because 'Brittany had always been Catholic, devoted to the king, and no faction had troubled the fidelity of its subjects'.[68] Nantes' representatives to the Breton estates in

September 1574 added their complaints to the remonstrances sent to the king. Raising extra taxes was impossible because of the poverty of the country:

> the clergy have furnished so many tithes that no more can be expected from them; the nobility are exhausted from equipping themselves for war, so the sum demanded by the king can only be raised from merchants, whose commerce is reduced to nothing by the misery of the times, from judicial officers who have not even been paid their wages, and from the towns, who cannot even find *miseurs* to take charge of the upkeep of their streets and walls.[69]

Of greater significance than the volume of taxation was the method by which it was levied. The king began to flout the customary practices of the provincial estates. In 1571 Charles IX had begun forcing taxation upon Brittany by calling mini-estates outside ordinary sessions, a policy that Daniel Hickey has also found in Dauphiné.[70] In theory, these smaller bodies could be coerced into a more compliant attitude towards royal tax demands.[71] Mini-estates were called down to 1574, to the chagrin of the larger body. In 1574, however, the mini-estates refused 90,000 *livres* of taxation. As this precedent suggested that a similar convention in 1575 would be even more recalcitrant, Henry III simply ordered the collection of war taxes without the province's consent. The regular meeting of the estates in September saw strong protest, and the *procureurs* of estates and towns were ordered not to levy any future tax without the body's consent.[72] James Collins has found that after limited participation by nobles at Breton estates before 1576, noble participation in particular began to augment thereafter.[73] It was reported in Paris that 'the nobles and people of Brittany, Normandy, Burgundy and the Auvergne are in league, one with another, and have decided to pay no more imposts, aides, subsidies, loans, taxes, increases and charges over and above what was levied in the reign of Louis XII'.[74]

The central complaint of the estates and the Breton towns was that Henry III had broken his contract with the province. They claimed that he sought to extend royal authority at the expense of local institutions and against the privileges accorded by the contract of Union of 1532. In September 1575, the estates proposed that the king be requested to 'maintain the ancient privileges of the province by virtue of which no extraordinary imposition should be levied without the consent of the estates'[75] In 1576, further remonstrances demanded that the king 'consider their remonstrances and order that pacts and agreements made upon the marriage of the late Duchesse Anne, Queen of France, be observed and inviolate, and there will be no more raising of monies without the consent of the estates'.[76] Nantes played an important role in this dispute. Early in 1576 the city urged the king to remember 'the great losses, fatigues, irritations and extraordinary molestations that they have suffered in their persons and goods because of the wars and troubles of this kingdom' and argued that 'all the goods, riches and faculties of your poor subjects have been exhausted and now there is nothing left either inside nor outside the town'.[77] Custom and contract were central to this dispute. Nantes was exempt from direct tax, as a privileged city. As with provincial levies, if the estates did not assent to taxation it was not legally valid.

The dispute continued through the period 1576–79. The king demanded taxation from the Breton estates and from Nantes, separately, treating with and threatening each in turn. City and province maintained a united defiance before the king's commissions. In 1576 and 1577, the estates refused to vote the king *impôts et billots*, because he had not formally asked for them; the duties would be levied, but for the estates' profit.[78] In March 1577, the crown demanded a subvention of 37,000 *livres* from the diocese of Nantes. The *bureau de ville* refused, because the imposition was contrary to the deliberations and authority of the estates.[79] Estates called to deliberate the tax agreed that it was contrary to the liberties of the province. The municipality agreed to the imposition only after it had been reduced and Henry III threatened to send four garrisons to the city. A new tax, the *traite domainiale*, a customs tax on wine, grain and salt, led to a further revolt by the estates. Not wishing to concede, Henry forbade exports of grain, wine, woad and linen. The municipality of Nantes threatened rebellion. The king conceded and cancelled the tax.[80] In 1578 came more refusals from the estates. The king again forced levies and loans directly in Brittany, including a new tax on cloth; the estates again asked him to heed the ancient rights and laws of the duchy, including consent to taxation.[81] Even the clergy paid only half of its assessed share of taxation in this year, because of disillusionment with the crown.[82]

As part of the reforming mood and measures of 1579, signalled by the great ordinance of Blois, the dispute with Brittany was settled by Henry's acknowledgement of the consultative and repartitional powers of the provincial estates. In an edict of June 1579, Henry promised to restore the contract between the province and the crown. In future, loans would be voluntary. A proposed cloth tax, *petit sceau*, was revoked. If any letters or edicts presented to the parlement or elsewhere prejudiced the privileges of the province, the estates or their *procureur* would be able to oppose them, and henceforth no tax was to be levied on the province without the estates' consent.[83] Taxation continued to mount, although it mostly took place in a constitutional framework. In 1581, there was a levy of 37,533 *écus* based on royal authority alone; the estates protested and demanded that the sum be taken away from the *fouages* granted to the king.[84] Extraordinary estates were called in 1582–83. In 1582, a 'free gift' of 70,000 *écus*, for five years, was granted to Henry on condition that he take account of the remonstrances presented in the estates' *cahiers*, and stop all extraordinary levies on the province.[85]

A third irritant in city–crown relations, also mediated through the provincial estates, was venality, or the sale of offices in the royal judicial and financial administrations. In Nantes, as elsewhere in France, the reign of Henry III saw a great expansion in the creation and sale of offices. The Chambre des Comptes was augmented in 1572 and 1576.[86] The bureaucracy of the *eaux-et-forêts* was expanded, and treasurers were created for the collection of extraordinary taxation. Venality also reached down to the middling sort. Extra notaries were created in the mid-1570s, and in 1581, Henry attempted, unsuccessfully, to extend masterships to the trades of all towns. The carpenters of Nantes drew up statutes in this year, although they were never implemented, and in 1586 the canvas weavers formed a corporation, perhaps taking advantage of the royal initiative.[87] There was a general complaint that 'never before had offices been put up in such large numbers'.[88] Even the château governor was affected. In 1580, one governor was replaced by two, each working a semester during the year. The *bureau de ville* remonstrated to the king about the multiplication of governors, 'which causes harm to the office', and requested a return to the traditional usage.[89] The king suspended the second semester without suppressing it.

Venality provoked considerable resentment. The creation of offices was seen as eroding the traditional political order and the privileges of regional and social groups. It was claimed that offices sold to the low-born damaged the social structure of the country and diluted the wealth and prestige of existing officers in the sovereign courts.[90] The proliferation of posts prevented the efficient execution of justice and led to financial corruption.[91] Remonstrances of the Breton estates of 1578 complained that 'since money has occupied the seats of justice and the magistracy has become venal . . . virtue has been crushed under the foot of . . . corruption and a million pernicious and insupportable offices have been created in justice and finance for those who only aspire to . . . offices for reasons of avarice'; the parlement and the Chambre des Comptes should be reduced to the offices with which they began, and all other offices created since Louis XII should be suppressed.[92] In Nantes, there were frequent complaints that ever-increasing numbers of royal officers eroded the taxpaying population and those eligible for militia service.

In reality, there was little to be done the check this exercise of royal prerogative. The ordinance of Blois promised reform of the kingdom, but this was not implemented.[93] Henry promised reform of the administration of Brittany in the edict for the estates of June 1579. He promised to allow several new fiscal offices to be extinguished upon the deaths of the holders, unless the estates wished to repurchase them, to appoint only worthy men to offices, to avoid fraud and abuses, and not to appoint commissioners for extraordinary taxation without the consent of the estates.[94] In practice, venality became a further levy upon the province, which affected Nantes more than other communities. The estates undertook to buy out offices created by the king, so long as they could raise the sums themselves. In 1577, 200,000 *livres* was offered for the discharge of certain edicts and subventions, raised on increased wine duty. In 1579, the costs of three new *généraux des finances* and of reforming the legal customal of Brittany were again raised on wine.[95] Further offices were repurchased in 1580 and 1582. Again Nantes, as a major consumer and trader of wine, paid a large proportion of these costs.

A fourth cause of friction between city and crown was a project for the construction of a new fortified suburb in Nantes, Villeneuve, in the Marchix. Since the war of 1567–68, royal military officers had proposed the fortification of the northern suburbs, situated on a small cliff above the river Erdre, because their seizure by enemy forces would threaten the city below. In 1571, Charles IX authorised the municipality to raise 5,000 *livres* a year on *octrois* on merchandise for fortifications work, and in 1574, a royal engineer laid out the outline of the defences.[96] Houses and land were compulsorily appropriated and demolished for the fortifications, but the work soon slowed, stopping altogether by 1579. From the outset, the bourgeois were hostile to the project, stating that 'this city has too few resources to provide funds for such a structure and there are too few people to populate a new town'.[97] The city refused to reimburse the owners of the confiscated properties for the value of their possessions, amounting to 33,000 *livres*, because it was the king who owed the money.[98] The municipality tried every available means to represent its case to the crown. The Breton estates were asked to request the king that the ditches be filled in and the work abandoned. In 1579, the Maréchal de Retz and his brother, the archbishop of Paris, were asked to represent the city's views to Montpensier and the king.[99] But these efforts were unsuccessful. The new royal governor of Brittany from 1582, the Duc de Mercoeur, favoured continuation of the project. In 1582, Henry III wrote to the municipality, informing the Nantais of his displeasure that 5,000 *livres* was raised annually for fortifications, but not a *sou* had been employed upon the Villeneuve for the past five years. Finally, in 1584 work restarted, and it continued intermittently for the next few years.

Mack Holt comments that the frequent wars and peace settlements of the 1570s weakened Henry's authority in France; it was questioned and repudiated throughout the kingdom because he could neither sustain war nor peace for any period.[100] In Nantes there is no evidence for the rejection of royal authority before the late 1580s. The examples of crown–city relations discussed here, religious policy, taxation, venality and fortifications, show that the authority of the crown did not undergo any demise in the period 1574–84. There is some evidence that the crown was in a weaker bargaining position than it had been in the 1550s and 1560s. There were particular problems with levying taxation in Brittany, and Benedict argues that more than any of his predecessors, Henry III gave in to pleas for tax reduction.[101] One sign of this is a change in the nature of taxation. There was a trend towards indirect taxes and *rentes* and away from direct impositions, for the former were less visible, were more widely paid and did not require the same level of consent as the latter. This meant, however, that within Brittany the main burden of taxation fell on towns, especially Nantes.[102]

But the erosion of royal authority can be overstated. To contemporaries in Nantes, the main cause of dispute with the crown was its over-assertion of authority, the overstepping of traditional limits of power, at the expense of the legal privileges of town and province. Contemporaries all over France saw the monarchy under Henry III as attempting to advance into areas where its prerogative was at best ambiguous and at worse illegal. At the Estates General of Blois of 1576, there was an attempt to check this expansion. There were calls to make the estates a regular part of government and to restrict the sovereignty of the king through supervision of royal councils and legislation.[103] Central to the relationship between crown, city and province was the concept of contract, a bilateral action where the breaking of the agreement by one party was the cause of injury to the other.[104] Relations with Brittany were governed by the contract of Union of 1532; the Breton people had transferred authority to the King of France, but they retained a portion of it, to be exercised by their provincial estates, particularly the assent to and levying of taxation. The dispute with the crown was over just limits of power on both sides, not about the reduction of royal authority or the assertion of provincial or municipal autonomy. It was about returning constitutional relations to their traditional order, where the rights and privileges of each group were respected.

Despite disputes over the fisc, venality and fortifications, Nantes remained loyal to Henry. The crown was the source of municipal authority. The king arbitrated authoritatively in internal city disputes and passed edicts for the better ordering of urban government. What is clear about the reign of Henry III down to 1584 is the enduring respect for royal authority in Nantes. As Barbara Diefendorf has argued for Paris, so it is evident for Nantes that the city magistrates emerged as defenders of constituted authority.[105] A diminution in monarchical authority would lead to the undermining of the authority of the civic elites and the order upon which their powers were based. In Nantes there is little evidence for the promotion of municipal authority at the expense of the monarchy, for as Philip Conner remarks for Montauban, 'profound aspirations and long-term survival were [only understood] through the context of loyalty to the crown'.[106] When in January 1579 President Barjot, *maître des requêtes* and royal commissioner, visited Nantes, the city assured him of its loyalty, shown in its support of the king's party during the previous war.[107] Provincial and city particularlism was agitated by royal encroachment upon fiscal and legal privileges but relations were still conducted through the proper channels of representation and remonstrance.[108]

Military conflict and the Duc de Mercoeur, 1580–88

The decline and ultimate fall of royal authority in Nantes in the second half of the 1580s was a result not of taxation or venality, but of war. Military conflict brought armies and governors to Nantes, who usurped royal authority and trammelled the city's privileges. This occurred simultaneously with a crisis of the royal succession and fears for the future of Catholicism in France. The result was ultimately the rejection of Henry III's authority in Nantes.

For most of the 1570s, Nantes was distant from the main arenas of warfare in France. Troops moved through the county, requiring food, arms, shelter and money, but they rarely stayed for any length of time. There were occasional raids by Calvinist troops into the southern hinterland of Nantes, between the Poitevin marches of Brittany and the Loire. River traffic and trade were disrupted from time to time. Of greatest concern during this period was the war at sea. Nantes' shipping, particularly with Spain, was affected by piracy out of La Rochelle. In 1575, for example, Rochelais corsairs blocked the mouth of the Loire, and merchandise, particularly salt, rose steeply in price. The royal fleet of galleys offered little help; rather it was a further cause for complaint. In the mid-decade the fleet was accused of piracy, along with the Rochelais. In late 1579, galleys were berthed in the Loire at Nantes. The sailors were such a nuisance that the municipality asked the fleet's captains to prevent their men from entering the city bearing arms.[109]

In 1580 war moved closer to Nantes when a Huguenot force seized the fortress of Montaigu, 40 kilometres to the south. The Nantais feared a Protestant attack, and there were depredations by soldiery on the countryside south of the Loire. Royal commanders moved into the region to secure Nantes' defence. This was a mixed blessing. Defence against the Huguenot forces was vital, but a garrison within the city was insupportable. In the spring of 1580, Maréchal de Retz asked the city to raise a garrison of 150 men, but the *bureau de ville* declined; the militia was deemed sufficient for defence and there was no need for troops in the town.[110] As harvest approached, however, fifty arquebusiers were raised, to prevent pillaging in the countryside by the soldiers at Montaigu. In July la Hunaudaye brought the troop of the *arrière-ban* to Nantes, but it was refused entry as it was suspected of Calvinist sympathies, and the militia put on extra guards to prevent surprise attacks.[111] Finally, in August, la

Hunaudaye informed the municipality that the king intended to lay siege to Montaigu and would need men, munitions and money for this operation. Captain Cambout of the château also asked for 100 men to guard Nantes itself. The municipality offered the king as much money as it could raise, but refused to provide men; bread and wine would be furnished for the besieging force until late in the year and a company of soldiers was lodged in the suburb of Richebourg to protect the town from attack.[112] Late in 1580, Montaigu fell to the royalists and relative peace was restored. The siege cost the Nantais financially, for they had to furnish provisions and money for soldiers, but the privileges of the city had been upheld.

The years 1581–83 saw a tense peace, punctuated by raids and piracy from Poitou which put the city on repeated security alerts. The most significant event in these years was the appointment of a new royal governor to Brittany in September 1582. Philippe Emmanuel de Lorraine, the Duc de Mercoeur, was an aristocrat of great distinction. He was brother-in-law to Henry III, for Mercoeur's half-sister Louise de Vaudémont was queen. Although a member of the Guise family, he was also close to the crown. By his marriage in 1575 to Marie de Luxembourg, daugher of the Comte de Martigues, former governor of Brittany, Mercoeur was Seigneur de Penthièvre and one of the senior lords of the province. Through his wife, the new governor could also claim descent from the ducal house.[113] The Duc and Duchesse de Mercoeur were greatly welcomed in the province, and on 1 September 1583 the duke formally entered Nantes.[114] The clergy, the corporation and the militia assisted in the entry, an honour reserved only for members of the royal family. It was widely hoped that Mercoeur's appointment would be of great advantage to the province and city.

The governorship of Mercoeur witnessed a much closer interest in and supervision of municipal affairs in Nantes than had been the case in the recent past. Stuart Carroll's work on the Guise affinity in Normandy has shown that during the later religious wars, the family developed clientage networks in urban centres, with legal officials and with wealthy bourgeois, to extend their power bases and financial credit, in contrast with their policy in the 1560s.[115] Mercoeur pursued a similar policy in Nantes. Captain Gassion, commander of the château, was already a *fidèle* of the Mercoeurs, for he was raised in the Luxembourg–Martigues household.[116] Mercoeur cultivated clients in the city administration such as the Poullain family of leading merchants; the Gazet and Cousin families, who included royal officers; Pierre André, from a merchant family which was beginning to purchase offices (from 1588 he was advocate-general); and Michel Loriot, son of the mayor of 1577.[117] The duke also pursued policies that brought him popularity. He achieved the suspension of export embargoes on grain from Brittany; he confirmed the privileges of

Nantes which forbade the billeting of soldiers in the homes of city residents; and his aid was solicited by the Nantais to help secure the return of the Breton parlement from Rennes. Mercoeur also joined religious confraternities such as that of the Passion in the church of Sainte-Croix. Like other Guise governors he represented himself as the defender of municipal and provincial privileges.[118]

But Mercoeur also brought the war against Protestants to the county of Nantes. In 1584 he fought against the Prince de Condé in Poitou. In 1585, he gathered 5,000 men and borrowed money from the municipality to fight in the Breton marches, promising to purge the region of Protestantism.[119] In 1586, Mercoeur occupied the Protestant stronghold of Blain. The proximity of war to Nantes augmented Mercoeur's authority in the city. Robert Harding has argued that at the heart of alliances between governors and towns was the twin threat of external military attack and internal insurrection from religious dissidents. The governor's authority was directly proportional to the level of disorder and peril.[120] The city council provided funds for the governor's forces because of its need for military protection. During the middle years of the decade, this was a symbiotic relationship. Mercoeur upheld the city's privileges and autonomy in domestic affairs, for he needed the elite's financial support.

The relationship between Mercoeur and the municipal government underwent a rapid change in the summer and autumn of 1588. A severe military crisis brought the city more closely under the tutelage of the royal governor; as a result, the freedom of action of the municipality was constrained and Nantes' legal privileges were threatened. In June 1588 Montaigu fell once more to the Huguenots while the forces of Henry of Navarre began raiding along the Poitou–Breton border and the south Breton coast. Nantes was forced to pay Captain Sorinière to recruit soldiers to deploy in the countryside, in order to protect the harvest.[121] By the end of July threats of Protestant invasion from across the Loire were so great that Nantes appealed to Mercoeur to come to its aid. The governor and his army arrived several days later and the municipality promised to furnish them with supplies; bread, wine or money would be delivered to the soldiers up to 10 leagues from Nantes, but in return Mercoeur was asked to prevent his troops from living off the countryside.[122]

In August, Mercoeur attacked Montaigu. In retaliation, Huguenot forces under Navarre attacked the ports of Beauvoir, Saint-Nazaire and Bouin, with a descent on Nantes greatly feared. The inhabitants of La Fosse were counselled to move their goods into the walled town, for their protection.[123] The Duc de Guise sent three regiments to assist Mercoeur. The troops were to be provisioned by the municipality. In October the city was obliged to raise an immediate forced loan of grain, wine and money to feed soldiers quartered around the city, and all public works were stopped.[124] In November an order came for 50,000 loaves for troops before Montaigu and 150,000 loaves for Mercoeur's men.[125] The *bureau de ville* sent gifts of 200 *écus* each to the Duc de Mercoeur and Nevers, to encourage them to treat the city favourably. But when Mayor Harouys met with Nevers near to Montaigu, the duke simply demanded a provision of 20,000 loaves a day; without this he would allow his troops to ravage the countryside up to the gates of Nantes.[126] The municipality borrowed yet more money to furnish military supplies until the end of the year. Worst still, the mayor was unable to prevent troops from entering the walled town. Despite pleas to Mercoeur, Captain Saint-Paul's regiment was briefly quartered on the Nantais before passing on to Montaigu. The troop returned early in 1589, this time being billeted in the suburbs of Saint-Clément and Richebourg.[127] Finally, on 10 December, Nevers entered Montaigu and began its demolition. Nantes had to pay the artisans who dismantled the strongholds, although the city did try to reclaim some of the costs from the royal treasury.[128]

The war on the borders of Brittany had two important results for Nantes. Firstly, the economy of the city was gravely affected. Trade was disrupted on land and at sea; the countryside was ravaged by troops of both armies, causing food shortages and high prices. People and livestock were seized and ransomed. At a time of reduced prosperity, the wealthy inhabitants of Nantes were subject to a series of forced loans. Between 1585 and late 1588, the municipality tried to borrow at least 25,000 *écus* at interest.[129] The inhabitants were unwilling and increasingly unable to pay. In November 1587, for example, the general assembly voted to raise 10,000 *écus*; if citizens refused to lend, the seneschal was asked to constrain them to pay so that the safety of the town would not be compromised.[130] Most individuals stated that they would not lend more money to the city until that which had been borrowed in the past was repaid. In the summer of 1588, 10,000 *livres* was needed for military costs, and again the wealthy inhabitants were ordered to furnish loans. Only 2,175 *écus* could be collected, and the *miseur* reported that individuals simply would not pay.[131]

The second result of war after 1585 was the destitution of royal authority in Nantes. This was caused by a combination of economic and military hardship and the appropriation of certain regalian rights by commanders on the ground. With armies to maintain, Mercoeur and others appropriated to themselves the right to collect taxes in the countryside and subsidies from Nantes in the form of loans of food and money, although always in the name of royal authority. The king himself found increasing difficulties in raising taxes in the west. In September 1588, an impost of 30,000 *livres* on the bishopric of Nantes was met with a resolution by the municipality asking for a twenty-year discharge from all levies, because of 'the great oppressions that it had suffered and still suffers daily by the ravages, piracies and billeting of soldiers, both enemy and other'.[132] Further, the royal governor interfered more directly in urban politics.

Protestants were expelled from Nantes, and the city's privileges were suspended when he wished to quarter a regiment on the inhabitants. The basis of Mercoeur's authority after 1585 remained, technically, the crown, but in reality it was his army. Refusals to comply with his orders could result in military reprisals against the city. In the context of war, Mercoeur was both protector and oppressor of Nantes. But the blame for war and economic misery was laid at King Henry's door. Misery and growing political disillusionment were important in the growth of the Catholic League movement in Nantes after 1585.

The rise of the Catholic League, 1584–89

The death of the Duc d'Anjou, the king's brother and heir, in June 1584 precipitated a political crisis that would ultimately cost Henry III his life. Anjou's death had grave implications for the constitution of France, for the Salic law made the Protestant Henry of Navarre the new heir-apparent. There was a real possibility of a Protestant regime in France and the abolition of Catholicism, as in England under Elizabeth I. Within a short time, the Catholic League of Péronne was resurrected in northern France, with the aim of preventing the throne from falling into the hands of a heretic.[133] The League of 1584 was a more determined and widespread movement than before, and it rapidly constrained the free exercise of royal authority. The association took shape in a series of complicated negotiations between aristocratic groups led by the Duc de Guise between September 1584 and May 1585, with manifestos published at Rheims and Péronne. The king was criticised for permitting religious toleration, for court extravagance and for the promotion of favourites to office and wealth, and there were calls for the reforms of taxation and venality, as laid out in the ordinance of 1579.[134] More sinisterly, in December 1584, the League and the king of Spain drew up a treaty at Joinville to bar a heretic from the throne, to promote the candidacy of the Cardinal de Bourbon as heir and to eliminate heresy from France and the Netherlands. Philip II promised a monthly subsidy to the League to aid this work, and Guise agreed to the publication of the decrees of the Council of Trent in France, which had hitherto been resisted as contrary to Gallican liberties. By the summer of 1585 the authority of the king was sufficiently undermined by League opposition in northern France that he was forced to accept its tutelage. On 7 July, the treaty of Nemours revoked all acts of pacification and thus legal and military safeguards for Protestantism. Surety towns were handed to Leaguers, and their troops paid off. On 18 July a further edict banned Protestant worship, excluded Huguenots from royal office and ordered pastors to leave France. In September, Navarre and Condé were excommunicated by the Pope and barred from inheriting the throne.[135]

Nantes had been little involved in the League of 1576, but it has always been assumed that the second League gained early and strong adherents here. In practice, neither Mercoeur nor Nantes' elites were closely involved in the Catholic League in its early years. Although a distant cousin of the Guise brothers, Mercoeur was not a signatory to either of the treaties of Joinville or Nemours. He maintained amicable relations with the League, however, and was granted two surety towns, Dinan and Concarneau in Brittany, by the treaty of Nemours.[136] It is also clear that the duke shared the Guises' antipathy to heresy. He attempted to drive Protestantism out of his governorship and took war to the borders of Brittany and Poitou. But Mercoeur was also careful to maintain obedience to his brother-in-law King Henry. He remained in the west during the mid-1580s, distant from Guise operations, and was in frequent contact with his half-sister, the queen. In Nantes itself, in common with many provincial French cities, the League gained little support during its early years.[137] In November 1587, canons Touzelin and La Benaste requested, on behalf of the Duc and Duchesse de Mercoeur, that the city hold a requiem service for the Duc de Joyeuse, Admiral of Brittany and brother-in-law of the couple. Joyeuse was the object of much opprobrium by the Catholic League. The municipality declined, not because of its support for the League but because of the precedent that this might set for other non-royal events, and the cost.[138] Most towns desired to remain neutral, to avoid taxation and the quartering of troops. The parlement of Rennes registered the edict of 18 July 1585 proscribing Protestantism but appealed to the governor to ensure that Brittany continued loyal to the king and that royal edicts were upheld.[139]

In 1588 the Catholic League moved to active opposition of the king. In May, in Paris, the radical group known as the Sixteen took over the administration of the city in a coup known as the Day of the Barricades. King Henry fled to Normandy; with few financial resources and without active military support he was again forced to capitulate to the League, drawing up terms in the edict of Union of July. The treaty of Nemours was reaffirmed, the Cardinal of Bourbon was recognised as his heir, the royal favourite d'Epernon was disgraced, and the military campaign against Protestants was to be stepped up. The leaders of the League were handed yet more cities and military posts. The Duc de Guise was made lieutenant-general of the realm, and the Estates General were called to Blois, where they met in October. The majority of deputies there were League partisans. They called for the reform of the state through an overhaul of the judicial system, reduction of taxes, abolition of venality and regular meetings of the Estates General. But the Estates ended in disaster. Henry struck at his enemies with the assassinations of the Duc de

Guise the Cardinal de Guise. He was now seen as a tyrant, and revolt against him followed in many of the provinces and cities of France.[140]

There is evidence of League sympathisers in Nantes from the autumn of 1587. In September the general assembly met to discuss 'seditions and associations'; an increased militia guard was to be deployed 'to prevent the possible formation of an association of Catholics and also assemblies which have begun to take place . . . with the pretext of the defence of the [Catholic] religion'.[141] The associations seem to have had a popular base; Vicar-General Descourants, several cathedral canons, the seneschal, the mayor and other justices were ordered to summon the *recteurs* and churchwardens of each parish to enquire into illicit meetings and the proper observance of royal edicts. But it seems that in Nantes, as Penny Roberts has observed for Troyes, the League was promoted only by a few individuals and was easily contained.[142] The municipality remained faithful to the king and hostile to disorder.

On 19 May 1588 the *bureau de ville* received letters from the king with news of the Day of the Barricades in Paris. Henry hoped that there would be no repercussions of this in Nantes. The *bureau de ville* sent replies protesting fidelity to the crown.[143] Later in the month, further letters came from the king in Chartres. He stated his good intentions for the rights of his subjects and his zeal for the Catholic faith. Again, the general assembly responded by assuring the king of its 'perfect and inviolable attachment to his service'.[144] Further letters accompanied by royal commissioners followed.

The issuing of the edict of Union of July 1588 led to the first public manifestation of the League in Nantes. On 14 July, fifty inhabitants assembled at the *hôtel de ville*, led by Vicar-General Descourants, the *théologal* Christi, Canon Benaste, the *recteur* of Saint-Similien and two militia captains. Christi told the assembled crowd that 'while the good Catholics of Nantes pray every day that divine providence grant their most Christian king a fortunate and long life, they know that he is mortal . . . and could be dead within three months without heirs, and they fear that the heretic will usurp the throne of France'.[145] The remedy was individual and collective; each person should work to appease the wrath of God by penitence and an amendment of lifestyle, while all good Catholics should unite in amity and concord in the Holy League. This message was not sedition, Christi argued, for these demands conformed to the provisions of the edict of July. The Leaguers asked that a general assembly be convened to vote on adherence to the Holy Union. After discussions, the bishop and mayor declined the suggestion. The terms of the edict of Union allowed the neutrals and royalists to compromise with League demands and effect reconciliation between rival political groups. In a general assembly of 29 July, Bishop du Bec opened the session by praising the zealous upholding of the Catholic religion by many in Nantes, but added that there was no prince or lord in this kingdom more Catholic and religious than the king himself.[146] The bishop and the mayor read out letters from Henry, and it was resolved that the people 'would live and die together in the Catholic, Roman and apostolic faith, following the orders of the king'.[147] A further assembly was called to administer the oath of Union, as ordered by the treaty and the king. On 14 August the seneschal Jullien Charette led the oath-taking at the *hôtel de ville*. Supporters of the League were notably absent; there were no clerics, nor were officers of the Chambre des Comptes or *présidial* present.[148] There was little agitation during the autumn. The deprivations of war and economic hardship brought unanimity to municipal government and an attempt by the majority to steer city politics along neutral-royalist lines.

The assassination of the Guise brothers at Christmas 1588 precipitated Leaguer action throughout France. On 7 January 1589, the Sorbonne released French subjects from obedience to Henry III and justified the taking up of arms against him. Towns throughout Catholic France rose in rebellion against the crown. In Nantes, however, the municipality continued to steer a neutral course between king and League. Tension was evident. In January, militia security was increased. In early February, rumours were reported to the *bureau de ville* that 'the inhabitants [say] that there are *politiques* at Nantes and by this means, hope to incite the people to sedition'.[149] The mayor exhorted the Nantais to live together in peace and union, in obedience to and under the authority of the king. At the same time, the mayor assured Mercoeur that the municipality desired to maintain unanimity under the good government of the duke and swore to seek out and punish conspirators rumoured to be plotting against the governor.[150] Meanwhile, there was municipal opposition to military preparations being undertaken by Mercoeur. The governor's demand for a tax for non-performance of militia duty on all inhabitants was refused, as were requests for soldiers to assist at the siege of Clisson, and fortifications work on city defences.[151]

The Duke of Mercoeur himself wavered between loyalty to his brother-in-law the king and to his clan, the Guises. Until early 1589 he was at least outwardly obedient to Henry. In January Henry wrote to him proclaiming his peaceful intentions.[152] But on 2 March Mercoeur arrested a royal commissioner, President Faucon de Ris of the Breton parlement, and held him at Ancenis. On 13 March, Rennes declared for the League, although it was won back by royalists a few weeks later. In Nantes, disquieted by these events, more soldiers were quartered in the suburbs.[153] On the night of 6–7 April, the Duchesse de Mercoeur led a coup against the royalist partisans in the city, aided by Captain Gassion and the officers of the bourgeois militia. Eighty leading citizens, including the mayor, were arrested and a League administration took power.[154] Mercoeur's rebellion persuaded the Nantais to follow.

Conclusions

The League capture of Nantes in April 1589 was fuelled by a number of factors of discontent. There is no doubt that the misery of war and economic dislocation suffered by the city after 1585 was an important cause of disaffection. There were severe harvest failures in 1586 and 1587. The countryside was pillaged and trade all but ceased. Frequent military taxation ruined the finances of the wealthy, who were forced to lend money and goods to the municipality. Material insecurity and distress, shared by all members of the urban population, underpinned the religious and political problems that blighted the mid-1580s.

Discontent with the monarchy grew after 1584. As we have seen, relations between the crown and Brittany were strained in the 1570s over issues of taxation, venality and contractual governance. After 1584, these issues again disturbed relations between king, province and city. Henry III had failed to implement the reforms of the ordinance of Blois (1579), the Assembly of Notables (1583) and other meetings intended to balance the budget and gradually eliminate venality of office.[155] Royal taxation remained high, rising sharply from 1587. The ravaged countryside and indebted city would not support these demands. In September 1588 a general assembly petitioned the king to discharge the county from taxes for a number of years and to pay off loans contracted by the municipality for the Duc de Mercoeur, by levying a tax on the whole of Brittany.[156] The contract with Brittany was again violated as the king disregarded the privileges of the estates in his desperate search for revenue. Henry resumed the practice of calling mini-estates to sanction extraordinary taxation. In March 1587, Nantes' deputies were called to Ploërmel to vote for taxes. The deputies protested that the king had no right to levy extraordinary taxation in the province because he had been granted 70,000 écus a year by the estates to stop such practices. Further, they declared, 'the people have been vexed and ruined by armed forces and by the edict concerning coinage'; it was at present impossible to provide the king with money.[157] In all, taxation was too high and contravened the rights of his subjects.

Secondly, venality increased to new levels. In September 1587, the king created two presidents, twelve maîtres, twelve auditeurs and other officials to augment the Chambre des Comptes, though these were finally reduced to two of each post after payment of 30,000 écus to the royal treasury.[158] The salaries of existing office holders went unpaid, as did interest to the holders of rentes, while revenues were diverted to pay for war. Venality was not only costly but was also perceived as iniquitous. Harding has shown that a particular theme of preaching in Nantes at this time was the corruption of the judicial system by magistrates who needed to recoup the costs of their offices from the proceeds of extortion and bribery; officers were corrupt and justice deliberately slow, to increase profits.[159] The widespread dissatisfaction with royal administration can be seen in the preparations for the Estates General of 1588 in Nantes. In the autumn Antoine Brenezay, royal advocate, and Robert Poulain, former mayor, were elected as part of the Breton delegation to Blois. A *cahier de doléances* was prepared in the city. A box for suggestions was placed in the Carmelite church; fifty-eight proposals and four smaller pieces were deposited.[160] The four main requests were that the Catholic religion be preserved, that the king attend urgently to the reform of justice, that there should be a reduction in the taxation of the province and that municipal privileges be upheld.[161]

Above all, the religious context of the Catholic League determined its success. The religious background of the League was complex in Nantes. By 1585, the Protestant community of the city was small and powerless. Nor was there a radical, eschatological Catholic movement as described by Denis Crouzet for Paris.[162] But there were real religious concerns, as we will see in Chapter 6. The period after 1585 saw a growing fear and hatred of heresy. This was not a sectarian movement directed against local Huguenots, most of who left Nantes after the edict of 18 July 1585. Rather, it was directed outwards, beyond the city walls. The fear of a Protestant succession was very real, and Navarre's declarations of Catholic toleration were simply not believed. The city housed Irish refugees from Elizabethan persecution, including an exiled bishop who received alms from the municipality in 1586.[163] Further, the war against the Protestants of Poitou and their attacks on the hinterland and shipping of Nantes associated heresy with conflict and ruin in the minds of the Nantais. There was also a deep concern for the state of the Catholic Church. Religious activism increased in the 1580s, arising partly from Tridentine-inspired piety and partly in response to famine, disease and hardship.[164] Tridentinism and penitentialism fed into a genuine desire for reform of the church, in particular concerning appointments to benefices and the residence of clerics.[165] The cathedral clergy and public preachers were keen advocates of spiritual reform. The *théologal* Christi was the most active mouthpiece of the League in 1588–89; during Lent 1589 he was joined by the late Cardinal de Guise's preceptor, the Parisian Benedictine Jacques Le Bossu. The two preachers promoted the League as a mission akin to a crusade, to keep France from falling into the hands of the faithless and, to promote individual moral regeneration and institutional reform.[166]

Religious concerns provided explanation and remedy for the political, economic and social ills of the times. In the intellectual and cultural world of Nantes' elites and popular groups, secular ills were understood in spiritual terms. Explanation of calamity lay with God's displeasure with individual sin and vices in the kingdom at large. The solution was the assuagement of the divine by a new morality and piety in personal and public affairs.[167] The misery that afflicted Nantes was also the result of God's ire with the sins of the king, above all, his toleration of heresy.[168] By 1589, preachers in Nantes were urging officers and nobles to separate themselves from the corruption that radiated from the royal court and join in the holy struggle to purify and reform both secular and religious institutions. Harding argues that the king had lost the support of the joint oligarchy of magistrates and merchants who ruled the city, and had done so in circumstances where a religious cause united them with the lower social orders.[169] Elites and popular groups could identify with the programme of the League: the defence of the monarchy against heresy, an end to the crown's policy of toleration and the restoration of all French subjects to the Catholicism and reform of the church itself.[170]

In the end, the decision to join the League rebellion seems to have come quickly. The two deciding factors were political. Firstly, the Duc de Mercoeur had troops quartered in the château and suburbs of Nantes, making a stand against him difficult. That said, the municipality had successfully pursued a policy of neutrality between League and crown between December and April, while Mercoeur's own rebellion and Rennes' declaration for the League did not precipitate an immediate response in Nantes. The events that seem to have driven the elites into rebellion were the truce between Henry III and Henry of Navarre and the declaration of Navarre as successor to the throne. The alliance ran counter to the religious convictions of the people of the city. Worse still, Protestant enemies at the gates of the city, who daily raided the countryside and threatened the security of Nantes, were now the allies of the king. It seemed as though the Protestants would at last be able to walk through the city gates as the victors. Madame de Mercoeur made much of the security risk to Nantes, justifying rebellion by stating that the city was menaced by Navarre's troops and by the king's forces, for since the murders of December the king would stop at nothing to achieve his aims.[171]

On 8 April, the *bureau de ville* was suspended and superseded by a broadly based Council of the Union. Despite the arrests, a substantial proportion of the municipality supported the rebellion, as will be seen in Chapter 7. The League was a movement of defence of the city by its patricians as the best means of preserving the integrity of the town and their own position within it. The security of the city was paramount. Finally, revolt in common with other cities in a League was seen as the best way of putting pressure on the royal government to reform the church and administration and to restore the traditional political order in the state.

NOTES
1 Travers, II, pp. 449–50.
2 K. Cameron, 'Satire, dramatic stereotyping and the demonising of Henri III', in A.

Pettegree, P. Nelles and P. Conner, eds, *The Sixteenth-Century Religious Book* (Aldershot, 2001), pp. 157–8.

3 P. Chevallier, *Henri III, roi shakespearien* (1985).

4 B. Diefendorf, 'The failure of peace before Nantes', in R. Goodbar, ed., *The Edict of Nantes. Five Essays and a New Translation* (Bloomington, MN, 1998), p. 7.

5 Summarised in D. Richet, 'Introduction', in R. Sauzet, ed., *Henri III et son temps* (1992), pp. 13–14.

6 M. Greengrass, *France in the Age of Henry IV* (2nd ed., London, 1995), pp. 22–7.

7 P. Deyon, *L'état face au pouvoir local* (1996), p. 53.

8 B. Chevalier, *Les bonnes villes de France du XIVème au XVIème siècle* (1982), pp. 111, 308.

9 Travers, II, pp. 449–50.

10 A. Wall, *Power and Protest in England 1525–1640* (London, 2000), p. 70.

11 T. Watson, '"When is a Huguenot not a Huguenot"? Lyon 1525–1575', in K. Cameron, M. Greengrass and P. Roberts, eds, *The Adventure of Religious Pluralism in Early Modern France* (Bern, 2000), pp. 161–76; R. Schneider, *Public Life in Toulouse 1463–1789. From Municipal Republic to Cosmopolitan City* (Ithaca and London, 1989), introduction.

12 Travers, III, p. 10.

13 L. Maitre, *L'instruction publique dans les villes et les campagnes du pays nantais avant 1789* (Nantes, 1882), p. 153.

14 A.M.N. BB 13: Délibérations et assemblées de la municipalité 1575–77, 94r, fos 229r–v.

15 A.M.N. BB 16: Délibérations et assemblées de la municipalité 1580–81, fo. 37r.

16 C. Laronze, *Essai sur le régime municipale en Bretagne pendant les guerres de religion* (1890), pp. 136–8.

17 Maitre, *L'instruction publique*.

18 Laronze, *Essai sur le régime municipale*, p. 139.

19 A.M.N. BB 20: Délibérations et assemblées de la municipalité 1586–88, fos 78r–80v; M. Fardet, 'La vie municipale à Nantes sous le gouvernement du duc de Mercoeur. Le rôle militaire joué par cette ville (1582–1598)', Thèse, École des Chartres, Paris, 1965, p. 44.

20 A.M.N. BB 9: Délibérations et assemblées de la municipalité 1571–72, fo. 344r–v.

21 G. Saupin, *Nantes au XVIIème siècle. Vie politique et société urbaine* (Rennes, 1996), p. 20.

22 C. Mellinet, *La commune et la milice de Nantes*, 3 vols (Nantes, 1836–844), III, p. 273.

23 Travers, II, pp. 453–7.

24 Travers, II, pp. 480–1.

25 Morice & Taillandier, II, p. 348.

26 Travers, II, p. 473; Mellinet, *La commune et la milice*, III, p. 293.

27 Laronze, *Essai sur le régime municipale*, p. 28.

28 Travers, II, p. 469.

29 A.M.N. BB 15: Délibérations et assemblées de la municipalité 1579–80 (Partially transcribed in 17 Z 2), fo. 271r–v.

30 Fardet, 'La vie municipale à Nantes', pp. 148–9.

31 Travers, II, p. 453.

32 A.M.N. EE 202: Guerres civiles et réligieuses 1580; Travers, II, pp. 494–5.

33 Travers, II, pp. 455–7.

34 Fardet, 'La vie municipale à Nantes', pp. 43–4.

35 For a discussion of the relevant historiography see C. Friedrichs, *Urban Politics in Early Modern Europe* (London, 2000).

36 Chevalier, *Les bonnes villes*, pp. 148–9.

37 A.M.N. AA 3: Letters patent of Henry III August 1581; Laronze, *Essai sur le régime municipale*, p. 27; Fardet, 'La vie municipale à Nantes', p. 17.

38 A.M.N. BB 19: Délibérations et assemblées de la municipalité 1582–85, 166v; Fardet, 'La vie municipale à Nantes', p. 39.

39 Fardet, 'La vie municipale à Nantes', p. 13.

40 A.M.N. BB 19, fos 107r–v, 109–12v.

41 A.M.N. BB 20, fo. 53r; Fardet, 'La vie municipale à Nantes', p. 15.
42 J. Salmon, *Society in Crisis. France in the Sixteenth Century* (London, 1976; pbk 1979), p. 247.
43 Travers, II, pp. 559–60.
44 D. Bohanan, *Crown and Nobility in Early Modern France* (Basingstoke, 2001), p. 41. See also, on loss of royal authority and problems with clientage in the Limousin, M. Cassan, *Le temps des guerres de religion. Le cas du Limousin (vers 1530–vers 1630)* (1996), pp. 214ff.
45 A.M.N. AA 67: Deputés en cour.
46 A.M.N. AA 64: Deputés en cour. Correspondance avec M. Denis 1576–87.
47 A.M.N. AA 68: Deputés en cour.
48 A.M.N. AA 45: Entrées de Monsieur de Montpensier 1571–79.
49 A.M.N. CC 126: Compte de Pierre Langlois 1578–80.
50 A.M.N. EE 198: Companies levées par la ville, letter from Montpensier to Nantes, 15 November 1581; Mellinet, *La commune et la milice*, III, p. 301.
51 P. Le Noir, *Histoire ecclésiastique de Bretagne depuis la Réformation jusqu'à l'Édit de Nantes*, ed. B. Varigaud (Nantes, 1851), p. 356.
52 M. Holt, 'Attitudes of the French nobility at the Estates-General of 1576', *S.C.J.*, 18 (1987) 489; M. Greengrass, 'Pluralism and equality. The peace of Monsieur, May 1576', in Cameron et al., eds, *The Adventure of Religious Pluralism*, pp. 55–6; M. Holt, *The French Wars of Religion 1562–1629* (Cambridge, 1995), pp. 105–6.
53 Details in R. Knecht, *The French Civil Wars* (London, 2000), pp. 195–206.
54 Duc de Montpensier's speech to the Estates General at Blois 1576, quoted in Holt, *French Wars of Religion*, p. 108.
55 F. Baumgartner, *Radical Reactionaries. The Political Thought of the French Catholic League* (Geneva, 1975), p. 35.
56 A.M.N. EE 210: Ligue 1577–90.
57 Travers, II, p. 471.
58 Mellinet, *La commune et la milice*, III, p. 295.
59 B. Varigaud, *Essai sur l'histoire des églises réformées de Bretagne (1535–1808)*, 3 vols (1870–71), I, pp. 240–1.
60 A.M.N. BB 21: Délibérations et assemblées de la municipalité 1588–89, fo. 9r; Fardet, 'La vie municipale à Nantes', p. 185.
61 Quoted in P. Benedict, *Rouen during the Wars of Religion* (Cambridge, 1981), pp. 156–7.
62 Benedict, *Rouen*, p. 161.
63 A.M.N. CC 75: Impôts divers.
64 A.M.N. CC 74: Impôts divers.
65 A.M.N. CC 75.
66 A.M.N. CC 75.
67 A.M.N. CC 77: Impôts divers.
68 M. de Carné, *Les états de Bretagne et l'administration de ce province jusqu'en 1789*, 2 vols (1868), I, p. 145.
69 M. Planiol, *Histoire des institutions de la Bretagne*, Tome V: *Le XVIème siècle* (1895; reprinted Mayenne, 1984), p. 90.
70 D. Hickey, *The Coming of French Absolutism. The Struggle for Tax Reforms in the Province of Dauphiné 1540–1640* (Toronto, 1986), pp. 43–4.
71 Planiol, *Histoire des institutions de la Bretagne*, p. 105.
72 J. R. Major, *The Monarchy, the Estates and the Aristocracy in Renaissance France* (London, 1988), p. 705.
73 J. Collins, 'Sully et la Bretagne', *Dix-septième siècle*, 44 (1992) 90.
74 Greengrass, *France in the Age of Henri IV*, p. 23.
75 A.M.N. AA 77: Remonstrances au Roi 1515–1621.
76 Mellinet, *La commune et la milice*, III, p. 287.
77 A.M.N. CC 75.
78 Planiol, *Histoire des institutions de la Bretagne*, p. 91.

79 Travers, II, pp. 468–9.
80 H. Lapeyre, *Une famille des marchands. Les Ruiz* (1955), p. 376.
81 A.M.N. AA 77.
82 J. R. Major, *From Renaissance Monarchy to Absolute Monarchy. French Kings, Nobles and Estates* (Baltimore, 1994), p. 117.
83 Édit sur les remonstrances des estats, in Morice, III, pp. 1,446–51.
84 Planiol, *Histoire des institutions de la Bretagne*, p. 91.
85 Morice & Taillandier, II, p. 348.
86 Planiol, *Histoire des institutions de la Bretagne*, p. 104; Travers, II, p. 463.
87 A history of Nantes's guilds and associated primary sources are in E. Pied, *Les anciens corps d'arts et métiers de Nantes*, 3 vols (Nantes, 1903).
88 Benedict, *Rouen*, p. 160.
89 Morice & Taillandier, II, p. 348.
90 Benedict, *Rouen*, pp. 160–1.
91 Greengrass, *France in the Age of Henri IV*, p. 23.
92 A.M.N. AA 77.
93 Travers, II, p. 463.
94 Morice, III, pp. 1,446–51.
95 Planiol, *Histoire des institutions de la Bretagne*, p. 105.
96 A.M.N. AA 6: Lettres du roi 1516–74; Travers, II, p. 451.
97 A.M.N. EE 150: Fortifications. Villeneuve 1576–98; Fardet, 'La vie municipale à Nantes', p. 113.
98 Travers, II, p. 467.
99 Travers, II, pp. 481, 485.
100 Holt, *French Wars of Religion*, p. 111.
101 Benedict, *Rouen*, p. 159.
102 J. Collins, *Classes, Estates and Order in Early Modern Brittany* (Cambridge, 1994), p. 160.
103 Salmon, *Society in Crisis*, pp. 220–1.
104 W. Church, *Constitutional Thought in Sixteenth-Century France. A Study in the Evolution of Ideas* (Cambridge, MA, 1941), p. 233.
105 B. Diefendorf, *Beneath the Cross. Catholics and Huguenots in Sixteenth-Century Paris* (Oxford, 1991), p. 174.
106 P. Conner, 'Huguenot Heartland. Montauban during the Wars of Religion', PhD thesis, University of St Andrews, 2000, p. 176.
107 A.M.N. BB 14: Délibérations et assemblées de la municipalité 1577–79, fo. 349r–v.
108 Observed in Dauphiné by Hickey, *The Coming of French Absolutism*, p. 33.
109 Travers, II, p. 488.
110 Travers, II, p. 499.
111 Travers, II, p. 506.
112 A.M.N. EE 197: Guerres civiles et religieuses.
113 P. Biré, *Alliances Généalogicques de la Maison de Lorraine illustrées des faites et gestes des princes d'icelles* (Nantes, 1593); F. Joüon des Longrais, 'Le duc de Mercoeur, d'après des documents inédits', *B.A.A.B.,* 13 (1895) 214–93.
114 A.M.N. AA 46: Entrée du duc de Mercoeur 1577–83.
115 S. Carroll, 'The Guise affinity and popular protest during the wars of religion', *F.H.*, 9 (1995) 137; see also his detailed study *Noble Power during the Wars of Religion. The Guise Affinity and the Catholic Cause in Normandy* (Cambridge, 1998).
116 Morice & Taillandier, II, p. 365.
117 G. Saupin, *Nantes au temps de l'édit* (La Crèche, 1998), pp. 171–4.
118 Carroll, 'The Guise affinity', 137.
119 A.M.N. BB 18: Délibérations et assemblées de la municipalité 1581–82, fo. 72v.
120 R. Harding, *Anatomy of a Power Elite. The Provincial Governors of Early Modern France* (New Haven, 1978), p. 88.

121	Travers, II, p. 576.
122	Travers, II, p. 578.
123	Lapeyre, *Une famille des marchands*, p. 428.
124	A.M.N. BB 21, fos 45v, 48r.
125	A.M.N. BB 21, fos 91v–93v.
126	A.M.N. BB 21, fo. 102r–v.
127	Fardet, 'La vie municipale à Nantes', pp. 205, 210.
128	Fardet, 'La vie municipale à Nantes', p. 209.
129	Fardet, 'La vie municipale à Nantes', pp. 200–2.
130	Travers, II, p. 569.
131	Fardet, 'La vie municipale à Nantes', pp. 201–2.
132	A.M.N. BB 21, fo. 321r–v.
133	Holt, *French Wars of Religion*, pp. 121–2.
134	Knecht, *French Civil Wars*, pp. 222ff.
135	Holt, *French Wars of Religion*, pp. 122–6.
136	Joüon des Longrais, 'Le duc de Mercoeur', p. 244.
137	Amiens was sceptical about the League and remained aloof; Troyes was undecided, and
	Marseille retained a royalist majority on its consulate until 1588. See Carroll, 'The Guise
	affinity', 147; W. Kaiser, *Marseille au temps des troubles 1559–96. Morphologie sociale et luttes
	de factions* (1992), p. 278; P. Roberts, *A City in Conflict. Troyes during the French Wars of Reli-
	gion* (Manchester, 1996), p. 167.
138	A.M.N. BB 20, fos 248v, 250r.
139	Fardet, 'La vie municipale à Nantes', p. 176.
140	Details of the events of 1588 are taken from Holt, *French Wars of Religion*, pp. 129–30.
141	A.M.N. BB 20, fo. 213r; Travers, II, p. 568.
142	Roberts, *A City in Conflict*, p. 167.
143	A.M.N. BB 20, fo. 263r.
144	Travers, II, pp. 571–2.
145	A.M.N. BB 20, fos 411v-412r; Fardet, 'La vie municipale à Nantes', pp. 178–9.
146	A.M.N. BB 20, fo. 430v.
147	A.M.N. BB 20, fo. 430v.
148	A.M.N. BB 20, fos 444v–445r.
149	A.M.N. BB 21, fo. 202r.
150	A.M.N. BB 21, fos 177v–178v.
151	L. Grégoire, *La Ligue en Bretagne* (Paris and Nantes, 1856), p. 34.
152	B. Pocquet, *Histoire de Bretagne*, V: *1515–1715* (Rennes, 1913; reprinted Mayenne 1975),
	p. 90.
153	Grégoire, *La Ligue*, pp. 34–5.
154	Remonstrances aux habitants de Nantes Par un des Citoyens dicelle: Par où se void les prac-
	tiques et menées dont a usé le duc de Mercoeur pour usurper le Duché de Bretaigne
	(Rennes, 1590) published in *Revue de Bretagne et du Vendée*, 27 (1883) 470–80.
155	Salmon, 'The Paris Sixteen', 1584–1594. The social analysis of a revolutionary movement',
	J.M.H., 46 (1972) 544–5; R. Bonney, *The King's Debts. Finance and Politics in France
	1589–1661* (Oxford, 1981), pp. 24–6.
156	Travers, III, p. 5.
157	A.M.N. BB 20, fos 103v, 108r–124v.
158	Travers, II, p. 567.
159	R. Harding, 'Revolution and reform in the Holy League. Angers, Rennes, Nantes', *J.M.H.*,
	53 (1981) 403, 414.
160	Travers, III, pp. 4–5.
161	Laronze, *Essai sur le régime municipale*, p. 162.
162	See the seminal work by D. Crouzet, *Les guerriers de Dieu. La violence au temps des troubles de
	religion (c.1525–c.1610)*, 2 vols (1990).

163 A.M.N. CC 127: Comptes des miseurs de la ville 1586–90, fos 77v–78r.
164 Kaiser, *Marseille*, p. 280.
165 Harding, 'Revolution and reform', p. 403.
166 M. Holt, 'Putting religion back into the wars of religion', *F.H.S*, 18 (1993) 537–8.
167 Lapeyre, *Une famille des marchands*, p. 431.
168 Baumgartner, *Radical Reactionaries*, p. 32.
169 Harding, 'Revolution and reform', p. 414.
170 Salmon, 'The Paris Sixteen', p. 240; Harding, 'Revolution and reform', p. 410.
171 Morice & Taillandier, II, p. 365.

6

The authority of tradition: Catholicism in Nantes, 1560–89

In 1600, with the religious wars over and Brittany once more at peace, a young Bohemian traveller visited Nantes. He admired the fortifications and convents of the city and observed that the Breton towns were 'more rigorous that any others in their observance of the Catholic faith, such that . . . everyone, even the sick, is forbidden, and indeed refuses, to eat meat on fast days'.[1] Yet in the 1550s and 1560s there arose a Protestant movement which attracted up to one in twelve of Nantes' population. The presence of Protestantism and, even more, the sectarian and military conflicts which followed did not only affect politics and government. The Catholic Church and faith were also profoundly shaken. The spiritual and moral authority of the clergy was challenged, along with Catholicism's cultural dominance in urban life, for 'reformed religion presented a challenge . . . to traditional devotions and the community solidarity inherent within them'.[2]

   In Nantes the experience of war rapidly hardened confessional allegiances, which then underpinned political processes for the next thirty years. Simultaneously, indigenous evangelicalism and Tridentine influence caused Catholic practice to evolve, with greater emphasis on pedagogy, participation and penitentialism. The result was a revived religiosity during the civil war, which in turn had a profound impact upon the social and political culture of cities. The Holy League of the later 1580s grew out of renewed Catholic culture and polity. Threats to the religious and material fabric of Nantes by the actions of Henry III were important causes of the city's revolt against the crown. The forging of Catholic confessional identity in this era of religious and military strife, its relationship with indigenous spiritual revival and Tridentine reform, and its impact upon the political culture of Nantes are the subjects of this chapter.

Authority in decline? Mid-century changes
in religious practice in Nantes

By the mid-sixteenth century, Catholic spirituality was undergoing change. Historians such as A. Galpern have argued that belief and participation in traditional rituals declined in this period. In a study of the Champagne region, he argues for a decrease in religiosity in the 1540s and 1550s, shown by changing styles of religious art, which became less emotionally intense, changes in poor relief, with the rise of centralised municipal institutions, a drive against beggars and indiscriminate almsgiving, and declining confraternity membership. Men and women became less interested in public, collective religion and less devoted to the Virgin and saints. Instead, he argues, there was an internalisation of piety, which became more personal and private. Individuals preferred to worship in separate chapels, to use their own pews and to retreat into private reading or meditation. A minority even rejected established religion and became Protestants. It has also been suggested that there was increasing alienation of certain social groups from collective piety, in particular a distancing of elites from popular groups, a product of increasing hierarchy in towns, growing oligarchy in city government and differentiation in guilds between masters and journeymen. Aspirant and exclusivist social groups did not want to share their religious space.[3] At the other end of the social scale, the poor and new migrants to cities could also be excluded from parish life and communal devotion. Natalie Davis argues for Lyon that although big city parishes were increasing in size by the mid-century, the church took virtually no steps to increase its personnel or pastoral provision for such groups.[4] Philip Hoffman agrees that the urban church made little effort to integrate newcomers. Rituals tied to the local landscape did not permit easy assimilation of outsiders, while priests rarely spoke the dialects of rural migrants for preaching or confession.[5] The mass of the labouring poor simply fell through the pastoral net.

There have been challenges to these views. Bernard Chevalier has argued against declining religiosity in French cities in this period; religious culture was communal because it was shared by bourgeois and the *menu peuple*, and traditional piety maintained its strength into the 1550s because it was not seriously challenged before this decade.[6] Andrew Pettegree and others have argued that France's Catholic culture had earlier defenders against Protestant critics than elsewhere in Europe, who rapidly developed vernacular preaching and printing to defend doctrine and condemn heresy.[7] David Nicholls has even suggested that France may have preceded other states in attempting reforms in some dioceses. Calls for renewal of the church at the 'national' level, although widespread, were rarely carried out, but at city level some bishops did attempt reforms, even if results were mixed.[8] As for the increased separation of elites and popular groups, this view too has its critics. William Christian Jnr argues that differences between rich and poor were solely of style. Noblemen kept private chapels and venerated saints of distant places, and the wealthy had more time to spend on their devotions, but their beliefs and rituals were shared with the poor.[9]

In Nantes, the evidence for the 1550s is ambiguous but suggests changing practices rather than widespread disillusionment with tradition. There was a fall in the number of large-scale building projects in the sixteenth century. The previous century had seen many of the city's churches expanded. The cathedral was rebuilt after 1434; Saint-Saturnin was enlarged after 1487, as was Notre-Dame, and Saint-Nicolas was reconstructed almost entirely from 1449 to 1478. Chapels were built on the port of La Fosse, on the Île de Saulzaie and in the suburb of Saint-André. With the exception of the construction of a chapel to St Catherine on La Fosse, there were no building projects on this scale in the mid-sixteenth century. But the reason was not lack of motive. The churches and chapels of Nantes were new and did not need to be rebuilt. Also, there was little available urban space for new religious building in the city. Patrons embellished churches where they could. Four chapels were added to the Franciscan church in the first half of the century, while an aisle and at least two new chapels were added to Notre-Dame.[10] Gifts of liturgical furnishings were also widespread.

Analysis of foundations of masses for the dead in this period sheds more light on the question of change over time. There are problems in recon-structing religious beliefs and practices in sixteenth-century Nantes, for the city's notarial records and diocesan archives were badly damaged during the Second World War. However, from among surviving parish, college and conventual records, 220 foundations of masses have been located, which allow some observations to be made on obit foundations.[11] The donors were mainly middling and wealthy patrons, most commonly priests and merchants. As in many French communities, foundations flourished after 1450, with the high-water mark reached in the 1480s. Thereafter foundations fell back slightly but maintained their levels until the 1560s. While there was a decline in the decade of the 1530s, it was of no greater order than that of the first decade of the century. Thereafter, in the 1540s, foundations increased and were sustained into the next decade. It was only with the advent of the wars of religion that the overall popularity of this traditional devotion declined (see Figure 6.1).

On the surface at least, foundations appear to have been popular in Nantes after they declined in other northern French cities. Further, there was change over time in the type of foundation created. The most popular type during the period 1450–1550 was the weekly mass, usually on a specified day, most popu-larly Friday (the day of Christ's Passion) or Saturday (associated with the

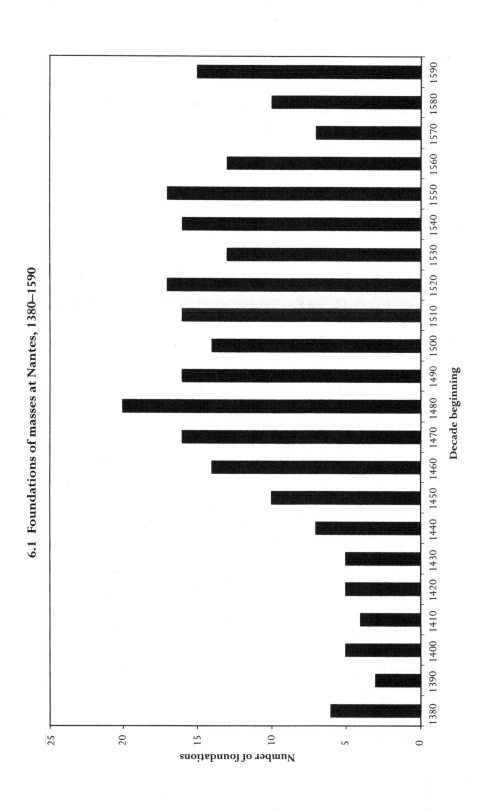

6.1 Foundations of masses at Nantes, 1380–1590

Virgin). But from the late fifteenth century there was an increase in the foundation of anniversary masses – said on the anniversary of the founder's death – and annual masses – a date chosen by the founder for devotional purposes. While weekly foundations were the most popular up to 1530, thereafter they were overtaken by anniversaries and annuals, which represented nearly two-thirds of foundations in the mid-century. The location of foundations also changed in this period. Before the 1530s foundations in parish churches were the most numerous in the city, with the mendicant churches receiving a handful each year between them. But from the 1530s onwards foundations in parish and mendicant churches fell, as lay benefactions declined. At the same time, however, the foundations of secular clergy increased, particularly among the lower members, the chaplains and parish clergy. These men chose annuals and anniversaries rather than weekly masses because they could not afford lavish endowments. They also preferred the clerical environment of the collegiate church of Notre-Dame. These men took great care over their choice of devotions, as we will see below. In Lyon, Hoffman has found similar results. There was a decline in funerals and votive masses from the late 1530s, but the fall in bequests was steeper in the parish churches than among the clergy.[12]

The causes of change in lay piety have been much debated. Declining economic fortunes in the second quarter of the sixteenth century may account for a fall in endowments. Plague and poor harvests blighted the 1530s, while war with Spain interrupted trade intermittently in the 1540s and 1550s. However, Hoffman argues that in Lyon religious provisions in wills fell off long before economic problems hit the city, which began there in earnest in the 1560s.[13] Other causes have to be sought. A prime cause of disenchantment with the church was anti-clericalism. Complaints abounded throughout France about pluralism, absenteeism, excessive financial demands, legal immunity and the shortcomings of parish priests.[14] The *cahiers* of the third estate at the Estates General of Orléans and Pontoise of 1560 and 1561 show a widespread desire among lay elites for reform of the French church, whose wealth, privileges and immunities were resented.[15] Demands were made for good-quality bishops, of appropriate age, sound doctrine and morals, ordained and resident, who would undertake visitations and maintain their dioceses. Parish priests were to be educated in seminaries and paid a decent living. They should be resident, of good morals and learning and aged over thirty. The function of the secular clergy was to instruct and console, to teach scripture through free religious instruction, to make pastoral visits and to aid the sick and dying.[16]

Dissatisfaction in Nantes centred largely on priestly inattention to duty through neglect and absence. The bishops of the mid-century did not set a good example to their subordinates. Those of the fifteenth and early sixteenth centuries had been of good quality, frequently resident, diligent and reforming in their administration of the diocese. Thirty sets of synod rulings were published before 1488, ordering clerical residence, participation in sacraments and the keeping of parish registers in an attempt to improve spiritual and sexual morality. Annual visitations were ordered in 1508, although not always observed.[17] François Hamon (1511–32), the last bishop before the union of Brittany and France, fulfilled his duties conscientiously. He visited his diocese, revised the breviary, missal and ritual and gave generously to the poor.[18] From 1532 to 1554, however, the appointees of Francis I and Henry II were largely absent from Nantes. Louis d'Acigné (1532–42) did not visit his see until his eighth year as bishop and spent only two months there. Jean de Lorraine (1543–50) and Charles de Bourbon (1550–54) came not at all. These statesmen bishops used the revenues and dignities of the see to further their individual and dynastic interests. They took no religious initiatives and gave no spiritual direction to their flock.

Lay concerns, however, focused more on parish priests. The laity expected to have constant access to sacraments from a resident priest attached to their own parish church. Few of the churches of Nantes had an officiating rector. Nine out of twelve parishes were in the gift of cathedral canons and were often held by them; for example, Gilles de Gand, vicar-general in the 1550s, held the parishes of Saint-Nicolas and Saint-Similien in plurality.[19] To attend to the needs of the parish, a vicar (recteur) was appointed and paid a stipend, and was assisted by a number of curates (vicaires). As long as the recteur was diligent, the parishioners were at least outwardly satisfied. One of the important trends in sixteenth-century parish life in Nantes was the readiness of the laity to take clerical matters into their own hands if their expectations were not met, with the support of the conseil de bourgeois. In the late 1540s the parishioners of Saint-Jean took their priest to the prévôtal court for absenteeism and failure to administer the sacraments.[20] In 1562, the parishioners of Saint-Nicolas obtained a sentence against their recteur, Gilles Hamon, ordering him to preach sermons, which he failed to do. The following year the parish seized the revenues of the benefice on account of his non-residence, appointing a former curate in his place.[21]

Yet there is little evidence for complaints about the standards of the urban clergy. The canons of the cathedral and the college of Notre-Dame were frequently university-trained and erudite. Parish priests were adequately educated while chaplains and adult choristers were trained in singing and Latin. The two choir schools of Nantes, at the cathedral and Notre-Dame, gave instruction to their choristers in music, religion and Latin grammar. The majority of these boys became priests.[22] In 1567, Jullien Bonnyer, baker, and Marguerite Du Boys, his wife, founded a perpetual weekly mass in Nantes cathedral to provide their son, a choirboy in the Psallette, with a permanent income of 10 *livres* per year, to start him off in his clerical career.[23] Parishioners and clergy worked closely together. The laity intervened to ensure conscientious performance of services but they also paid supplements to vicars, hired curates and provided extra masses in churches. Hostility towards priests was unusual, being caused by particular circumstances, and was not an endemic feature of parish life. A number of foundations in parish churches were made to augment the incomes of the poorly paid choir priests. In a foundation of 1549 in Sainte-Croix, a donor founded two weekly masses; the chaplaincy was to rotate between the choir priests, and the rights of presentation were to be held by the churchwardens.[24] The career of René Allaire, curate of Saint-Vincent, provides another useful, if later, example. In the 1580s, Allaire served the Samson foundation in the parish church; in 1593 he was given the Navarre chaplaincy as well. The following year, Allaire was appointed to a third chaplaincy, the newly founded mass of Madame de Martigues, whereupon he resigned the Samson chantry to the *recteur*.[25]

Another possible cause of change was a decline in confidence in an elaborate intercessory framework for achieving salvation, often associated with the influence of Reformed ideas. Certainly, devotional practice in the city may have been affected by humanism. Like many other towns in France, in the 1550s the *conseil des bourgeois* founded a college for boys. The master was a renowned humanist teacher brought in from Lisieux, Pierre Bintin. Humanism had a religious programme of enhanced piety and reform of church life, which was to be stripped of superstitious accoutrements, centred directly on Christ and his holy sacrament, and purified of cults and elaborate ritual including veneration of saints, images and relics.[26] Here, perhaps, lies the reason for the decline of elaborate mortuary provision in Nantes. By the mid-sixteenth century, John Bossy argues, that there was a shift from communal religion to individual, interiorised faith.[27] While it was once thought that changes in French Catholicism were largely Tridentine in influence and largely seventeenth-century in date, in cities such as Nantes these trends in piety were already evident in the sixteenth century. Religious simplicity and asceticism predated Tridentine reform. Austere piety had been the hallmark of the ultra-devout since the fifteenth century, inspired by the life of Christ himself and the teachings of the mendicant orders. In the 1470s, Guillaume de Launay, founder of the college of St John, was buried in the churchyard rather than the church of Saint-Saturnin, as a mark of humility. Further, humanism and reformism put increased emphasis on activism, on good works and charity and also on the outward comportment of individuals. The lived experience of faith was to be shown through morality and personal discipline. An austere piety based on faith, good works and outward behaviour was thus emerging in Nantes at the same time as the growth of Protestantism in the city and the beginning of the religious wars.

The early wars of religion and their impact on
Catholicism in Nantes

In the seven years after 1555 there arose, with great rapidity, a Protestant movement in France that came to number approximately 1,000 churches. The new beliefs gained adherents in most urban communities, including those of the west of France. The impact of the Reformed movement on the Catholic Church and on the practices of the laity would ultimately be profound.[28] Philip Benedict summarises the seventeenth-century French clerical view: heresy provided a providential warning for the church to reform its own ills. The clergy had to improve the standard of their faith and morals, and the ordinary Catholic had to be fortified against heresy through better religious teaching and enhanced piety. Although the church was at first ill-prepared to meet these challenges, the saints and reformers of the Tridentine movement worked towards these goals.[29] Denis Crouzet has argued that the second half of the sixteenth century was a period of fundamental change in spirituality, caused directly by the trauma of heresy and war.[30] The outcome of these processes was a counter-reform movement within France that gathered pace after 1598.

In the short term, however, according to Benedict and others, the early years of confessional conflict saw only a limited response by the church hierarchy to the challenge of Protestantism. There was a contemporary view that the crisis over heresy had emerged because of ecclesiastical abuses, but institutional or liturgical reform was not seriously attempted. In Rouen, for example, the clergy's reaction to Protestantism was 'limited and strictly defensive . . . largely one of inertia'; the cathedral chapter did little beyond staging processions and sending an occasional delegate to court to protest against religious toleration, and there is no evidence for any actions taken by parish priests.[31] Penny Roberts' study of Troyes similarly shows that the initial response of the city clergy to the Reformed church was reactionary, comprising vitriolic sermons which stirred up enmity between the faiths, and the creation of a confraternity of the Holy Sacrament. Little was done to instruct Catholics in the doctrines of their faith or to encourage a greater degree of piety.[32] A concern for teaching, reform of lifestyle and pious practice did not emerge until the later 1580s. Benedict explains this inertia in Rouen in three ways. First, studies of sixteenth-century clergy show that they lacked zeal; many clerics were poorly educated and absenteeism was widespread. Second, many of the better-educated clergy, influenced by humanist intellectual currents, were sympathetic to the ideas of Protestantism. Third, vested interest disinclined the city's clergy to create new institutions to combat Protestantism or to give rival bodies enhanced authority so to do.[33] Alain Tallon has added that well into the 1550s, repression was deemed to be sufficient response to heresy because until late in that decade it seemed to be working.[34]

Nantes, like other dioceses, witnessed few structural reforms in the 1550s and 1560s. But clerical life was not entirely forlorn. Among some priestly groups there was a resurgence of piety in the 1550s. This was encouraged by the appointment of a new bishop in 1554, Antoine de Crequi. De Crequi was resident, and he participated actively in diocesan administration and in the direction of spiritual affairs. The bishop was eager to revive episcopal authority. His first act was a general visitation of the diocese in 1554, personally visiting the parishes of the city. Secondly, a synod was held in 1556, and statutes were issued to regulate the behaviour of clergy and laity. Residence was ordered for those having cure of souls, except for cathedral canons; parish incumbents were forbidden from becoming curates in other churches and were ordered to set up little schools for the instruction of children. For lay people, the bishop emphasised morality: parents were forbidden to sleep with their children in the same bed; marriages and churchings were to take place in the woman's parish church; and weddings could be celebrated only after the issue of three sets of banns, again in the parish.[35] Thirdly, he reformed the ritual and breviary of Nantes. Finally, de Crequi preached in person in the cathedral and encouraged the foundation of sermons there for Advent and Lent.[36] The bishop's authority was reinforced by his vicar-general, the Dominican Gilles de Gand. He was a spiritual man and an active administrator who preached in the parish of Saint-Nicolas, where he was rector. De Gand was to be important in the campaign against Protestantism after 1560.[37]

A study of the chaplains of the collegiate church of Notre-Dame shows that they led a more vigorous spiritual life in the 1550s. In the fifteenth and early sixteenth centuries, Notre-Dame had attracted large numbers of requiem foundations. To service these, stipendiary chaplains were employed, often appointed from among priests who served as choristers in the college. A number of foundations required several chaplains to provide elaborate liturgical music. For example, the weekly sung mass created by Jean Coué and his wife in the early fifteenth century required six chaplains and two choirboys. Thus the society of Coué was created. Two further societies were formed, in 1515 – that of Saint-Thomas, founded by Thomas Regis, and 1551 – that of Saint-Claude, for the Compludo chapel. In the 1550s these societies of priests attracted new patronage. In 1552 a weekly mass founded by the Caron brothers was to be serviced by the society of Saint-Thomas.[38] A foundation of twelve annual masses by Jehan Pageaud and his wife in 1556 requested that they be performed by the society of Coué.

The popularity of the societies of Notre-Dame coincided with a notable piety among their members, which was traditional and ritualistic in

expression. For the 1550s and early 1560s, a cluster of wills and mass foundations survive from the chaplains of the college, who seemed to have formed a
close-knit group at this time. Record linkage has made possible the construction of devotional profiles for six individuals, at least at for the latter periods of
their lives.[39] Gilles Jumel, doctor of theology, was a chaplain of Saint-Thomas
and Saint-Claude in this decade. He was a member of two confraternities, those
of the Holy Sacrament at Sainte-Croix and Saints Anthony and Sebastian at
Saint-Saturnin. His will of 1561 was particularly elaborate with regard to
funerary provision. His body was to be accompanied by the poor of the city and
buried with 100 masses, followed by 100 a week later. He donated vestments
and liturgical books to the church of Guénroc; the rest of his money he gave to
the sisters of Sainte-Claire, the Hôtel-Dieu of Nantes and the poor present at
his burial. Even his books were to be sold to profit the poor.[40] André Le Gallois,
chorister of Notre-Dame, was the master of the society of Saint-Thomas by
1550 and a chaplain of Saint-Claude. In 1558 and 1559, he set up three foundations, an anniversary mass for the day of his death, an annual mass and twelve
monthly masses per year. Le Gallois's foundations were to be served by his
brethren, the societies of Saint-Thomas, Saint-Claude and Coué.[41] Later, in
1561, his executors founded a joint mass for Le Gallois and the priest Jean Le
Breton, for whom Le Gallois had acted as executor. A high mass with 'Gloria'
was to be sung at the altar of Saint-Thomas by the society of chaplains there.[42]
Le Gallois's will is also highly detailed. He dedicated his soul to a great number
of patrons, the Holy Trinity, the Blessed Virgin Mary, Saints Michael, Gabriel,
John, Andrew, Peter and Paul, and his guardian angel. One hundred masses
were to accompany his burial; there were to be 100 more the following week
in Notre-Dame and fifty in the church at Rouvier, his baptismal church. A trin-
tall, a sequence of thirty masses normally said or sung on consecutive days, was
to be celebrated for him at Saint-Denis in Nantes, and he left money for the
poor here and at Rouvier.[43] The wills and foundations of four other chaplains
survive for this decade. While lay foundations were declining, these men made
elaborate provision for post-obit intercession and donations to the poor. They
took particular care in their choice of devotions. François Le Roy's annual
mass, founded in 1558, was to take place on the day after Corpus Christi in
front of the great crucifix of Notre-Dame, and Gilles Jumel's annual mass was
to fall on St Giles' day.[44] The movement of spiritual revival associated with
Nantes' collegiate church is echoed elsewhere in the 1550s. In Lyon, for
example, there was a movement to ensure that clergy attended services,
dressed modestly and behaving in a manner appropriate to their ordination.[45]

When the Protestant movement emerged as an organised force in
Nantes, the city's clerical elite did not sit idly by. Although the Huguenot
community was never large, and its threat seemed greater than that which it

actually posed, heresy in the midst of the city and in the kingdom at large caused a strong reaction among the churchmen of Nantes. They waged a vigorous if traditional campaign against heresy in the face of royal toleration.[46] The main weapons used were those martialled elsewhere: repression through use of the law and the judicial process, the use of ritual and religious aids, propaganda through sermons in defence of the old ways, and vilification and violence against the Reformed church. The tensions wrought by Protestantism also led to greater co-operation between church and urban authorities in many cities. In Lyon by the mid-1560s the cathedral clergy were participating in city government and had more influence in urban affairs.[47] In Nantes, a feature of the period 1560–72 was the close alliance between church and bourgeois against heresy. In 1558, following the visit of François d'Andelot and his Reformed ministers to Nantes, Bishop de Crequi warned the *conseil* about men bearing arms whom he suspected of heresy, and asked that officers of the law be more active in searching out culprits. At this time, the *conseil* took little action, however; it forbade the carrying of arms and exhorted officers to do their duty, but no more.[48] After 1560, Gilles de Gand was a frequent partici- pant in general assemblies of the city where heresy was discussed and was active in pursuing Protestants. When a council of security was created in April, at the beginning of the civil war, a canon of the cathedral was included in its daily meeting.[49] After the first war, the vexed issue of the provision of a site for Reformed worship saw further joint action against toleration. In August 1563 the *conseil* met in the cathedral to plan representation at court against a proposed site in the suburb of Richebourg.[50] Episcopal ownership of property and jurisdictional rights prevented sites being used at La Fosse, the Motte Saint-Nicolas and Beauregard.[51] Once the municipality of Nantes was formally inaugurated in 1565, the cathedral chapter had the right to be present at all general assemblies to discuss city affairs. Finally, after the second and third wars, in November 1570, following registration of the edict of Saint-Germain at Rennes, the Nantes clergy sent Bishop du Bec to court to request the prohi- bition of Reformed worship in the diocese, the journey being paid for by the municipality.[52]

Part of the church's greater political influence at the local level arose from newly gained fiscal responsibilities in the state and the city. At the Estates General of 1560 and 1561, the third estate argued that the financial needs of the monarchy should be met from ecclesiastical revenues. The king was given permission to confiscate part of the temporal goods of the clergy. To save itself, the church negotiated at Poissy a payment of 17,000,000 *livres* over a period of several years to pay the mortgage on the royal domain and other debts. There- after clerical taxation was a constant feature of the French fiscal state.[53] The tax immunities of the clergy at city level were also eroded during the religious wars. For Poitiers, for example, Henry Heller has shown that clerical exemptions from contributing to public works and defence were overridden.[54] This was also true of Nantes. In April 1562, Lieutenant-General Martigues demanded a loan of 1,000 *écus* from the city to pay military expenses; the two chapters offered to lend the city 300 *livres* each, and Notre-Dame offered its jewels and plate as collateral for further loans.[55] In June, the *conseil* had to raise 11,500 *livres* for repairs to fortifications. Some of the bourgeois suggested that the clergy contribute one-third of this but it was agreed to tax all property-holders in the city, including clerics.[56] By early 1563 de Gand claimed that the city's clergy had paid 4,000 *livres* in loans and taxes.[57] Further, in 1567 and with the outbreak of the second war, the clergy were ordered to perform guard duty at the city gates along with judicial and municipal officers, and were subject to the billeting of soldiers.[58] Military obligations continued into 1572. The fiscal and military contributions coincided with increasing clerical participation in city affairs. The clergy conceded some of their fiscal and legal immunities in return for greater influence in municipal government.

The public deployment of Catholic ritual was a marked feature of the reaction against Protestantism in all French communities. Street processions accompanied by statues and relics of saints or the holy sacrament became more frequent from the later 1550s, as iconoclasm and attacks on doctrine by Protestants increased.[59] Processions had several functions: as an ornate public spectacle of reverence for a person or doctrine challenged by Protestants, to purify a community polluted by heresy, and as a 'public reaffirmation of elements of the faith that had been called into question by Calvinism'.[60] In 1558 the preaching campaign of François d'Andelot's ministers in the Nantes diocese caused Bishop de Crequi to visit Le Croisic, where he led a procession of the holy sacrament to cleanse the town, provoking a riot later in the day.[61] In December 1562 three processions took place in Nantes, on the 6th, 13th and then 31st of the month, led by Vicar-General de Gand, where again the holy sacrament was carried through the streets.[62] The outbreak of the second war in 1567 saw further devotional activity. On 15 November the university organised a procession from the cathedral to Saint-Nicolas, to give thanks for a recent royal victory and to ask God for the future success of the king's armies; on 30 November the bishop led a procession of the holy sacrament. Military victories, in March and October 1569, were celebrated with processions, Te Deums and bonfires.[63]

The clerical response to Protestantism in French urban communities has too often been seen in terms of failure, as a tardy, insufficient response to threats to its moral and spiritual authority. For Nantes, this is too negative a view. From 1555, Bishop de Crequi warned of the dangers of heresy. But Protestantism was not visible in the city until 1558, while an organised movement did not emerge until after the conspiracy of Amboise of March 1560. Although this may appear complacent with hindsight, there was no immediate threat to contemporaries before this time. Secondly, while the clergy lost their battles against the royal policy of toleration, they did help to win the struggle against heresy in the city. The Reformed church declined after 1563; by 1570 Calvinists were few in number and were forced to worship well outside the walls. Protestantism had been beaten back.[64] Further, the campaign against heresy enhanced the prestige and authority of the clergy in Nantes and increased their visibility in the city as a defence against peril. Also, the church's use of its corporate status to represent its views at city and crown level, and its willingness to make fiscal contributions to the city in times of need, enhanced its political influence in municipal government. By 1570 the clergy were in a stronger position of religious and secular authority in Nantes than they had been before 1560.

The religious tensions and military crises of 1560–70 had an equally important impact on the religion of the laity. Protestant attacks on Catholic sacred places and objects, and particularly the experience of war after 1562, stimulated popular Catholic responses of outrage and reaffirmation of faith.[65] The result was a clear confessional hardening among Nantes' Catholics in this decade, among all social groups. By 1570, there was a distinct political and religious Catholic identity and spirituality different from that of 1550, although many of its outward forms remained the same. Religious conflict led to greater emphasis on public participation in ritual activity in the city, processions, pilgrimages and, above all, sacramental observance. Christopher Elwood has shown the importance of the eucharist to Catholic identity and social cohesion in the early 1560s.[66] Rituals became more self-conscious and external actions increasingly important, as 'a defence and illustration of both institutional resilience and enduring truth'; Catholics manifested their loyalty to their faith by taking to the streets in defence of their community's religious traditions.[67]

A widely observed feature of popular devotion during the early years of the civil wars was that associated with the holy sacrament. According to Hoffman, this was partly a reaction to Protestant criticism of the central Catholic doctrine of the real presence and partly the expression of a different view of human nature and divine grace. All over France confraternities of the Holy Sacrament were established in a 'sort of urban mission, symbolically defending Catholic doctrine'.[68] The holy sacrament had long been a popular object of devotion in Nantes, with a confraternity founded in Sainte-Croix in 1462. The confraternity had two purposes: to increase divine service and to augment zeal for the eucharist. The feast day was the octave of Corpus Christi and was celebrated with a procession and requiem mass for deceased members.

By 1554, the confraternity had 200 members and was maintaining brethren who had fallen into poverty.[69] In the 1560s, the confraternity expanded and its leadership attracted men of a higher social status. Previously, the master and provosts were typically priests and chaplains from parishes in and around the city; by the 1570s Guillaume Tual, master chaplain of the cathedral, was in charge. New bequests were founded in its favour. In 1566, Guillaume Garnier, priest, founded a weekly mass in the suburban chapel of Champ-Fleuri, to be said by one of the priestly members of the fraternity. He also founded an annual memorial in the parish church of Sainte-Croix, with Psalm 129, 'De profundis', the anthem 'Libera' and prayers to be said by the fraternity during their annual feast day procession around the city's churches.[70] The religious wars saw the wider expansion of holy sacrament devotions as well. On 6 December 1562, during a general procession from the cathedral, the host was carried and then displayed for adoration for a week thereafter, for the first time in Nantes.[71] During the second war of 1567–68, the host was paraded around the city on several occasions, and in April 1568 Bishop du Bec preached an important sermon on the eucharist and transubstantiation.[72] For this reason, Corpus Christi came to have a special significance for the public expression of confessional allegiance. Protestants considered this to be the most sacrilegious feast of all.[73] At Corpus Christi 1564, several Protestants were arrested in Nantes for failing to hang tapestries on their houses, in spite of the provisions of the edict of Amboise. The seneschal claimed that street decoration was required by all citizens, to honour God and to prevent disorder between confessions. The dispute continued into the Corpus Christi season of 1565.[74] Religious conflict made necessary the symbolic display of confessional allegiance. Participation in public rituals was a statement of belonging to the Catholic community, a form of works signifying faith.

Parish devotions also increased in the 1560s, reflecting a longer-term trend in lay Catholicism. Barbara Diefendorf argues that the emphasis on parish worship, to keep lay folk under the eye of their priest and confessor, was part of a larger campaign for greater public order and morality waged in tandem by the Catholic clergy and royal magistrates from the mid-century.[75] As confessional conflict increased in Nantes, there was an indigenous, popular and lay-initiated movement to participate publicly in parish rituals, as an outward sign of religious allegiance. In particular, increasing attention was paid to baptism. Concern with baptismal practice had a long history in the diocese. From the early fifteenth century baptism was used as an occasion to enforce conformity with the church's teachings on morality, out of which arose formal registration. The public recording of baptisms allowed for greater scrutiny of parents' and godparents' moral affairs and the prevention of spiritual consanguinity.[76] The first injunction to keep registers occurred in the Nantes diocese in 1406; three

city parishes have extant baptismal registers that date from before 1500, and
four more predate 1550. The parish of Saint-Similien even kept a separate
register for illegitimate children in the later decades of the century.[77]

From the 1550s, there was a renewed emphasis on baptism. Bishop de
Crequi produced a new usage for the ceremony in his breviary of 1555–6.[78] In
the summers of 1561 and 1562, there were forced rebaptisms in the parish
church of Sainte-Croix of children seized from the Protestant congregation. In
July 1562, at the 'conference' between the Catholic doctors du Pré and Benoist
and two ministers of the Reformed church of Nantes, the two sacraments of
eucharist and baptism were discussed.[79] Later that month, a magnificent
baptism was held in the cathedral for Marie de Luxembourg, the daughter of
Lieutenant-Governor Martigues. Du Pré preached a sermon on the nature,
justification, necessity and result of the baptism of infants using examples from
the Old and New Testaments, and the baby was baptised publicly in the presence of large numbers of local nobles and civic elites. In June 1565, Martigues,
then royal governor, issued ordinances prohibiting the Reformed community
to carry out, among other practices, baptisms in public.[80] Finally, registration
of baptisms in Nantes' parish churches seems to have increased in periods of
confessional anguish, although there were differences between parishes (see
figure 6.2). The registers of the parish of Saint-Denis, a small and wealthy
parish, show peaks of recording in the 1560s, 1570s and late 1580s and early
1590s. The latter at least was a miserable time and not one of demographic
increase. In the parish of Saint-Nicolas, which was popular and extensive, there
are similar although less defined trends. Of course, there may have been other
causes, and baptismal registration is notoriously problematic to use for stat-
istical purposes. Changing sexual practices in the midst of war, an influx of
refugees to the city and changing registration practices of priests may have
altered the recording of baptisms at different times. But participation in the
Catholic ritual of baptism seems to have been an important expression of allegiance among the city's population. As the wars continued and prohibitions
were made against non-Catholics holding offices, it became even more important for parents to register the baptism of their children as proof of confessional
identity. Further work is needed on this hypothesis.

Finally, there was an expansion in religious instruction in the 1560s, particularly in theology and dogma, to teach the dangers of heresy and to defend
Catholic doctrine against the criticisms levelled against it by Calvinists.[81]
Diefendorf has identified changes in the content of Parisian sermons in the
1560s. Three themes dominated. First was the nature of the eucharist: Calvinist
critiques led clergy to teach the doctrine of the real presence and the symbolism
and meaning of the mass. Second was the importance of traditional authority
and thus the role of the Catholic Church in understanding doctrine. Third was

6.2 Evolution of baptisms at Nantes, 1550–1600

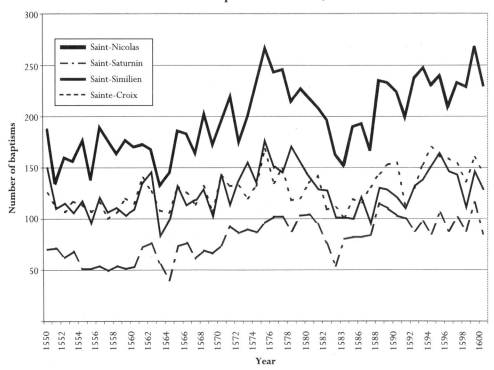

Source: Annual baptism totals listed in Croix, *Nantes et le pays nantais*, pp. 299–315.

the teaching that heresy represented 'a rupture of the body of Christ . . . a cancer . . . to be rooted out'; salvation and safety were in danger if heresy were tolerated.[82] The 1560s saw a similar expansion in preaching and religious education in Nantes, following on from the foundations laid in the 1550s. Preachers invited to the city for the Advent and Lenten sermon cycles were men from Paris with clearly orthodox views and credentials. Jacques du Pré preached at the baptism of Marie de Luxembourg in July 1562; the Parisian preacher René Benoist was present in Nantes in the same month and returned as Lenten preacher in 1565. In 1566 the position of reader in theology (*théologal*) was created at the cathedral. The holder was to preach on Sundays and major feasts, and teach two or three classes of theology at the university during the week.[83] The first incumbent was Jacques du Pré, who was followed in the 1570s by Jean Christi, student of the famous Parisian preacher Simon Vigor.

Similarly, Catholic vernacular literature expanded in the 1560s. Despite the absence of printers in Nantes, there was an active book trade, as discussed in Chapter 3, to sell at the fair of Medina del Campo and in towns such as Salamanca. The registers of the merchant André Ruiz show that between 1557 and 1564 he sent 1,072 cartons of books through the port of Nantes; 919 came from Lyon and 103 from Paris. Books also came from Tours, and 126 cartons were shipped on from Antwerp in 1574.[84] Most of these books were works of theology, liturgy and canon law. Some stayed in the city, and there were around five booksellers in the early 1560s.[85] Andrew Pettegree, Luc Racaut and others show the important role played by Catholic printing in 'shaping the successful defence of French Catholic identity in the face of the Huguenot onslaught'.[86] Coming from the lower clergy, this was a largely unofficial campaign of renewal that preceded and was independent of the reforms of Trent. There was an explosion of vernacular works. For example, René Benoist published a vernacular book of hours, devotional treatises, sermons and a French Bible in the 1560s.[87] In the 1570s and 1580s the *théologal* Jean Christi edited the sermons of Simon Vigor and amassed his own library, as did Archdeacon Pierre Le Gallo.[88] Le Gallo had a correspondent in Paris through whom he purchased works.[89] Philip Conner remarks for the Midi that the national and international market was so good that there was little need for indigenous printing.[90] The same was true for Nantes.

The forging of a new, hardened public Catholic identity during the 1560s had an important impact upon the city's political culture. Firstly, for the city's elites, it was no longer enough just to be a Catholic. Public expression of faith was a necessary political as well as social activity. Those who would not conform were pushed out of the political process, or at least marginalised as far as possible. For example, when in the late 1560s the king tried to force the Chambre des Comptes of Nantes to accept a Protestant president, the Sieur du Verger, the city objected and, along with the Breton estates, maintained its opposition down to 1575.[91] Secondly, the *conseil des bourgeois* and then the municipality took upon themselves a greater role in the police of religion. As well as punishing vice and blasphemy, the municipality sought to maintain Catholicism by distancing heresy from the city, at least as far as was compatible with obedience to the crown. Catholicism came to condition not only political morality, but also allegiance and policy in Nantes, creating a religio-political culture that was new in the city.

The later wars and the Counter-Reformation: prelude to the Catholic League?

In the historiography of Catholic piety in sixteenth-century France the watershed for change is traditionally placed in the 1580s. From 1584, the threat of the accession of the Protestant Henry of Navarre to the French throne created a wave of Catholic reaction, of opposition to the crown and of penitential piety to plead with God to avert the coming disaster. Crouzet's arguments that the Catholic League was composed of 'godly warriors' motivated by faith have found support in a number of studies, of Rouen, Toulouse and, above all, Paris.[92] Its defining characteristic was ostentatious piety, with features that were to become hallmarks of Tridentine practice.[93] A study of piety in Nantes however shows that religious revival predated the mid-1580s, although it did increase in expression in the latter years of this decade. The Catholic League movement came relatively late to the city, and its religious dimensions arose from pre-existing concerns.

From the middle years of the 1570s there were changes in expression of piety, associated with the activities of Bishop Philippe du Bec. Du Bec was from the Norman family of Du Bec-Crespin, with wide contacts at court and within the nobility of France, Catholic and Huguenot. His sister Françoise was the mother of the Calvinist adviser of Henry of Navarre, Philippe Duplessis-Mornay, and relations between siblings were good.[94] Despite family connections with Protestantism, du Bec was a devoted Catholic, attending the final session of the Council of Trent in 1562–63.[95] He became Bishop of Nantes in 1566, transferring from the see of Vannes. From the outset, he brought a reforming spirit into the diocese. He refused to be installed into his see with traditional pomp; to imitate the simplicity of Christ he made his formal entry into the city on foot.[96] Du Bec preached often in the cathedral and was concerned to improve both the quality of priests and the morality of the laity. In 1576, a visitation was held throughout the diocese with two main objects. Firstly, episcopal authority was to be asserted over local churches; curates were ordered to obtain the bishop's permission as well as that of the parish priest to administer the sacraments; incumbents were to hold masses on weekdays as well as on Sundays, and they were to attend two episcopal synods per year. Secondly, the morality of the laity was to be better policed. The names were taken of those who lived together unmarried or had illegitimate children, taverns were ordered to be closed during Mass and threshing in churchyards was forbidden.[97] In particular, du Bec was concerned with marriage. There was an episcopal campaign in the 1570s to register marriages.[98] Six out of twelve of Nantes parishes began registration between 1574 and 1589 as a record of participation in the sacrament of the church and of legitimate union.

The mid-1570s also saw the increased politicisation of the upper clergy in Nantes. During the 1560s, the vicar-general and the cathedral chapter played active roles in the city's fight against Protestantism. From about 1576 there was a shift in focus, away from city politics and towards more 'national' concerns. Nantes' upper clergy stood increasingly in opposition to royal policy, not only at the local level but in the kingdom at large. In February 1575, the two Nantes chapters and the deputies of the diocesan clergy met to name representatives to lobby Pope Gregory XIII and King Henry III against the Protestant churches. Toleration was condemned as 'against and pernicious for the state and the church'.[99] In November 1576, Bishop du Bec was at the Estates General of Blois, where he supported the anti-Calvinist deliberations of the first estate. Yet du Bec was quick to concede to demands to join Henry III's League. It may have been the bishop who brought the royalist league manifesto to Nantes, where an 'Association made between the Princes, Lords, Gentlemen and others, the clerical estate and the third estate, subjects and inhabitants of the duchy' was signed by the bishop, Lieutenant-General La Hunaudaye and Mayor Michel Loriot on 12 January 1577. The signatories promised 'the conservation of our religion and the service of His Majesty', and the edict of toleration of Beaulieu was to be upheld.[100]

But the spirit of co-operation with the crown did not last. From this time increasing disaffection with royal religious policy appeared. In November 1577, the university opposed the publication of the treaty of Bergerac and in 1581, the cathedral chapter rejected the edict of Fleix.[101] Divisions appeared within the upper clergy, in particular between the bishop, a royalist, and the cathedral chapter, which contained more radical Catholics. After 1585, the chapter became increasingly involved in the Catholic League movement of opposition to the crown. Jean Christi initiated an effort to have the city declare for the League in July 1588 and again in February 1589.[102] Cathedral canons were prominent in the League revolt of April of that year.[103]

The early 1580s witnessed a second resurgence of public piety. Military and security crises and a series of severe epidemics and famines led to 'dramatic manifestations of religious fervour [that] were part of a deeper culture of concern during these troubled years'.[104] Plague broke out in Nantes in 1581–83, and there were serious food shortages in 1580, 1584 and 1586. Religious activity increased enormously in these periods of stress, to seek divine aid and to avert God's wrath manifest in this series of disasters.[105] Penitence and prayers increased. The plague stimulated numerous processions from the city's parishes to the traditional site of Saint-Sebastien d'Aigne.[106] New devotions appeared, a result of Tridentine influences from outside the city, such as the *oratoire*, the display of the holy sacrament and relics on the altars of each of the city's churches for a week at a time, with a special procession to carry the host to the next church.[107] The piety of the 1580s was thus a fusion of traditional responses to dearth and disease and new practices advocated by Tridentine reformers.

Preaching continued to be important in the shaping of piety and public opinion. The Lent preachers of the 1580s were famous sermonisers from outside the city, and were important messengers of Parisian ideas. The Franciscan Feu-Ardent in 1584, Julien Cormerais and Fr Nicolas Bernard,

Edmond Bourgoing, prior of the Paris Dominicans, and the Benedictine Jacques Le Bossu of Saint-Denis in Paris all came to Nantes in the 1580s.[108]

There was revived interest in the monastic orders. The Carthusians were revitalised. Pierre Quintin, *recteur* of Saint-Léonard, left 103 *livres* of *rentes* to add two new coenobites to the existing twelve; in 1586, Widow Perrin added another two, making a total of sixteen.[109]

In contrast, at least among Nantes elites, traditional devotional forms declined. Until the 1560s, foundations of masses had continued, even if patronage had shifted from the laity to the clergy. In the 1570s and 1580s, foundations fell rapidly. This decline, to 50 per cent of the level of the 1550s, cannot be explained by war and economic problems alone. The 1570s were a relatively prosperous decade compared with the 1560s and 1580s; further, foundations took off again in the 1590s, when economic conditions were at the century's worst. Confraternity membership also seems to have declined, although detailed sources on membership are lacking. In 1577, the fraternity of Saint-Jean-de-l'Hôpital was suppressed, its numbers having fallen away in favour of the Holy Sacrament confraternity.[110] These changes had parallels in other French cities. In Troyes, membership of confraternities, also fell, particularly that of guilds dedicated to patron saints. Older confraternities also lost much of their male membership and became predominantly female.[111] In the Lyonnais there was a decline in pious bequests in wills: 85 per cent of wills made 1521–55 left bequests for masses or charitable donations; after 1556 this fell to 66–67 per cent.[112] In Nantes, where new confraternities were founded they were notably more austere and devotional. In 1588 the silk and woollen cloth merchants founded a confraternity to Saints James and Christopher in the Carmelite church. Many of its functions were traditional ones: dedication to saints who were protectors of travellers, a weekly mass and an annual procession on 26 July. But emphasis was more on devotion than on festivity. The yearly feast was dominated by religious services, high mass, vespers and matins; the following day saw a vigil for the dead and requiem services. There was also devotion to the holy sacrament, for on the Sunday after Corpus Christi the brothers held a solemn procession around the Carmelite convent.[113]

There was also a more marked form of Christocentrism, continuing from earlier decades, focused on devotion to the body of Christ. The few wills and foundations that we have from the 1570s and 1580s show the importance of the eucharist, at least to devout members of the elite. Pierre Le Gallo, archdeacon of Nantes, stated in his will of 1582 that 'it has pleased God . . . to maintain me in his Catholic and apostolic church, always armed with its holy sacraments, and with the help of his blessed angels to fortify and defend, preserve and guarantee me against the temptations and assaults of the enemy'.[114] Antoine de Gravoil founded a weekly mass in Sainte-Croix in 1589 'to induce faithful

Christians to adore with honour and remembrance His precious body which he left on this [earth] in the holy sacrament of the eucharist, so that we might remember his painful passion, for our consolation and the nourishment of our souls, until the last day'.[115] There was a flowering of other cults associated with the body of Christ, the Holy Name and the Five Wounds. For foundations of annual masses, the seasons of Easter and Corpus Christi and the feasts of the Virgin were particularly popular.

A second feature of the Christocentrism of the 1570s and 1580s was a desire to emulate the life of Christ through good works and activism in the community. There was a shift in investment away from mortuary foundations to good works for the poor. The influence of Bishop du Bec was again important. Charity was a constant theme of his preaching from the later 1560s. The bishop played a role in the reform of the city's poor relief in October 1568 when a *bureau des pauvres* was created. Three governors of the poor were elected annually, one from each of the bourgeois, judicial officers and cathedral clergy, to oversee and co-ordinate all of the city's relief institutions.[116] In 1569 du Bec publicised the new regime from the pulpit and with it the essential activity of good works. 'Sell what you have and give alms and you will store up treasure in heaven that will never be exhausted and will never fail . . . Invest alms in the pauper and he will pray for you . . . as water extinguishes fire so almsgiving extinguishes sin.'[117] Good works offered salvation to all social groups and anyone could participate. In 1580 women were authorised for the first time by the municipality to make the Lenten alms collections in the city's parishes.[118] In the context of the economic problems of the 1580s, charity was important in preserving the social as well as the religious fabric of the city, for Christ's poor were visible on every street.

The 1570s and particularly the 1580s saw increased emphasis on public morality and discipline, and on the appropriate use of sacred space and time. The Abbé Travers noted that it was a long-standing custom at Nantes to let free a white dove in each of the parish churches at Pentecost. Shots would then be fired within the building. In May 1581 the chapter renewed its prohibition on firing arms within church, with increased vigour.[119] The bishop repeated injunctions against the opening of taverns during high masses and the use of churches for entertainment and work. The earliest surviving records of the police court at Nantes register a 1574 ordinance forbidding the opening of shops and the import of grains into the town on Sundays and feasts, and the opening of butchers' shops on Fridays. They also list prosecutions of taverners for opening during Sunday mass.[120] These were not new problems but received greater attention in the heightened moral culture of this period.

The ostentatious penitential piety that is associated with the Catholic League after 1588 was not the creation of this movement. Rather, it was the

heightened exercise of practices that had been adopted earlier in the 1580s, in
response to earlier calamities of war, famine and plague. In Nantes, as in many
towns of northern France, the later 1580s saw a growth in barefoot and night-
time processions, oath-swearing and sacramental devotions, often associated
with the Holy Union. There were more events, and they were more theatrical
in their manifestation, as we will see in Chapter 7. But what is striking is not
their novelty but rather their traditional nature, despite the adoption of some
Reformed or Tridentine symbols. Exterior, not interior, communication of
faith and ostentatious, not private, action predominated. The League grew out
of concerns and practices which appeared in Nantes earlier in the 1580s. This
explains its widespread support in the city.

Conclusions: Catholicism in 1589

The religious conflicts after 1560 caused a rapid reinvigoration of Catholicism,
an indigenous movement that predated the influences of Tridentine reformism.
Change did not appear overnight. Already in Nantes in the 1550s there was
evidence for a spiritual awakening. Bishop de Crequi made attempts to reform
the discipline of the lower clergy and he renewed the breviary and liturgy at
Nantes. Evidence from the chaplains of Notre-Dame hints at a growing clerical
piety among some groups at least, based on traditional forms of expression:
confraternity membership, liturgy and especially the eucharist. Sermon foundations in Nantes' churches expanded after 1559. There was thus already a
foundation being laid for the developments of the 1560s.

The 1560s were a vital decade for the renewal of Catholicism in Nantes.
The emergence of Protestantism in the city and in the kingdom at large forced
individuals to reconsider their faith and their position within the wider
community of the faithful. The result was an upsurge of piety and a growth in
militancy. The Catholic Church in Nantes grew in moral authority during this
decade. Certain members of the upper clergy, Vicar-General de Gand, the
archdeacon, the dean of the cathedral and several canons at least, were vocif-
erous in their condemnation of heresy, taking legal action and making representation to city and crown authorities against toleration of Protestantism.
They led public devotions to resacralise and reactivate the urban community.
Clerical influence on municipal government grew, at least in religious affairs,
and the upper clergy were represented on emergency councils and in military–
political debates from this time on. Lay Catholicism also flourished and ritual
participation became an important badge of political and community allegiance. The outward form of much of this piety was intensely traditional,
which may in itself have been an assertive statement of identity. Public rituals

expanded as did confraternity membership, processions and parish devotions, expressions of the traditional urge to collective, intercessory prayer. In addition, there was a greater interest in learning; sermon provision continued to grow and reading expanded. This was a more public, participatory, informed Catholicism, militantly expressed, and it affected all social groups.

A second spiritual revival occurred in the 1580s. Documentary evidence is poor for this decade, but influences seem to have been complex. Tridentine values and ideas were influential on city elites. Bishop du Bec was important here. Frequently resident and a keen preacher, he worked to augment episcopal authority over clerical and lay behaviour, and to inspire morality and devotion. The famine, plagues and wars of the decade also stimulated greater penitentialism, at individual, parish and city level. Prayers, processions and pilgrimages were again part of a public expiation of sin and appeasement of God, and they predated the fervour of the Catholic League. Conversely, traditional devotions declined in the 1570s and 1580s; mortuary foundations of masses and traditional confraternities fell in numbers, while charity and eucharistic piety expanded. There was a move towards good works in all their forms, encouraged by du Bec and by the material circumstances of the times. The religious wars and the process of early Catholic reform were thus inseparable in Nantes. Confessional conflict strengthened the church and the value of Catholic doctrine and culture for many in the city. The religious conflict put the authority of Catholicism and its clergy firmly at the centre of urban life.

The Catholic League grew out of a decade of heightened piety, stimulated by war, material hardship and wider spiritual reform. The religious revival coincided with a national political crisis over the succession to Henry III after 1584. The possibility of a Protestant king forced the issue of heresy and the defence of Catholicism to the forefront of the political agenda, even in Nantes, where the original Protestant movement had been small and was by the 1580s contained. Piety and politics intertwined, and united all social groups. The defence of Catholicism was a major cause of the decision to rebel against King Henry in 1589. We turn to an analysis of the League in the following chapter.

NOTES
1 J.-B. Russon, 'Brève description de la ville de Nantes en 1600 par un Tchèque de passage', *B.S.A.H.N.L.I*, 91 (1952) 139.
2 P. Roberts, *A City in Conflict. Troyes during the French Wars of Religion* (Manchester, 1996), p. 192.
3 A. Galpern, *The Religions of the People in Sixteenth-Century Champagne* (Cambridge, MA, 1976), pp. 95–103.
4 N. Z. Davis, 'City women and religious change', in *Society and Culture in Early Modern France* (Stanford, CA, 1975), p. 74.
5 P. Hoffman, *Church and Community in the Diocese of Lyon 1500–1789* (Ithaca, 1984), pp. 27, 30.
6 B. Chevalier, *Les bonnes villes de France du XIVème au XVIème siècle* (1982), p. 241.

7   A. Pettegree, 'The sixteenth-century religious book project', in A. Pettegree, P. Nelles and
    P. Conner, eds, *The Sixteenth-Century Religious Book* (Aldershot, 2001). p. 1.
8   D. Nicholls, 'Looking for the origins of the French Reformation', in C. Allmand, ed., *Power,
    Culture and Religion in France c.1350–c.1550* (Woodbridge, 1989), p. 134.
9   W. Christian Jnr, *Local Religion in Sixteenth-Century Spain* (Princeton, 1981), p. 147.
10 A. Jarnoux, *Les anciennes paroisses de Nantes*, 2 vols (Nantes, 1982), II, pp. 61–4.
11 The records of mass foundations survived the dissolution of many of Nantes's parishes and
    religious houses after the 1789 Revolution, often alone of all parish records except for regis-
    ters, because they recorded transfers of property from private individuals to the church. This
    property transferred into the hands of the French state after 1791. They were deposited in
    the departmental archives of (modern) Loire-Atlantique before World War II. They come
    from across A.D.L.A. series G and H.
12 Hoffman, *Church and Community*, pp. 28–30.
13 Hoffman, *Church and Community*, p. 29.
14 K. French, G. Gibbs and B. Kümin, eds, *The Parish in English Life 1400–1600* (Manchester,
    1997), p. 19. See Hoffman, *Church and Community*, pp. 18–21.
15 A. Stegmann, 'Transformations administratives et opinion publique en France (1560–
    1580)', *Francia*, 9 (1980) 604–5.
16 R. Mousnier, *The Institutions of France under the Absolute Monarchy 1598–1789*, trans. B. Pierce
    2 vols (Chicago, 1979), I, p. 360.
17 Y. Durand, ed., *Le diocèse de Nantes* (1985), pp. 68–9.
18 A. Jarnoux, *Le diocèse de Nantes au XVIème siècle 1500–1600. Étude historique* (1976), pp. 23–4.
19 M. Dugast-Matifeux, *Nantes ancien et le pays nantais* (Nantes, 1879), pp. 76–9; G. Durville,
    Le chapitre de l'église de Nantes. Aperçu sur son histoire du VIIème siècle au Concordat (Nantes,
    1907), pp. 17–20.
20 A.D.L.A. G482: Paroisse de Saint-Jean.
21 Travers, II, p. 368.
22 Jarnoux, *Les anciennes paroisses*, II, pp. 53–4.
23 A.D.L.A. 4E 2/1389: Notaire Lemoine 1567.
24 M. de Granges de Surgères, 'Fondations pieuses à Nantes 1549–1691', *B.S.A.H.N.L.I*, 24
    (1885) 36.
25 A.D.L.A. G 521: Fabrique de Saint-Vincent; A.D.L.A. 4E II 1390: Notaire Lemoine 1593.
26 Hoffman, *Church and Community*, p. 30.
27 J. Bossy, 'The social history of confession in the age of the Reformation', *Transactions of the
    Royal Historical Society*, Fifth Series, 25 (1975) 35.
28 M. Venard, 'Catholicism and resistance to the Reformation in France 1555–1585', in P.
    Benedict, G. Marnef, H. van Nierop and M. Venard, eds, *Reformation, Revolt and Civil War in
    France and the Netherlands 1555–1585* (Amsterdam, 1999), p. 133.
29 P. Benedict, 'The Catholic response to Protestantism. Church activity and popular piety in
    Rouen 1560–1600', in J. Obelkevitch, ed., *Religion and the People 800–1700* (Chapel Hill,
    1979), p. 170.
30 D. Crouzet, *Les guerriers de Dieu. La violence au temps des troubles de religion (c.1525–c.1610)*, 2
    vols (1990).
31 Benedict, 'The Catholic response to Protestantism', pp. 173–4.
32 Roberts, *A City in Conflict*, p. 165.
33 Benedict, 'The Catholic response to Protestantism', pp. 176–7.
34 A. Tallon, 'Gallicanism and religious pluralism in France in the sixteenth century', in
    K. Cameron, M. Greengrass and P. Roberts, eds, *The Adventure of Religious Pluralism in Early
    Modern France* (Bern, 2000), p. 16.
35 Travers, II, pp. 338–9.
36 Jarnoux, *Le diocèse de Nantes*, pp. 35–7.
37 Durville, *Le chapitre de l'église de Nantes*, pp. 83–4.
38 A.D.L.A. G 314, G 322: Collégiale de Notre-Dame. Fondations.

39 A.D.L.A. G323–326: Collégiale de Notre-Dame. Fondations.
40 A.D.L.A. G 325: Collégiale de Notre-Dame. Fondations.
41 A.D.L.A. G 324, G 313: Collégiale de Notre-Dame. Fondations.
42 A.D.L.A. G 313.
43 Will, 1558–59, A.D.L.A. G 313.
44 A.D.L.A. G 326; A.D.L.A. G 313.
45 Hoffman, *Church and Community*, pp. 35–6.
46 Venard, 'Catholicism and resistance', pp. 134–7.
47 Hoffman, *Church and Community*, p. 34.
48 Travers, II, pp. 347–8.
49 A.M.N. BB 4: Délibérations et assemblées du conseil des bourgeois 1555–62, fo. 331r.
50 Travers, II, p. 383.
51 P. Roberts, 'The most crucial battle of the wars of religion? The conflict over sites for Reformed worship in sixteenth-century France', *Archiv für Reformationgeschichte*, 89 (1998) 257.
52 Travers, II, p. 431.
53 J. R. Major, *From Renaissance Monarchy to Absolute Monarchy. French Kings, Nobles and Estates* (Baltimore, 1994), p. 474.
54 H. Heller, *The Conquest of Poverty. The Calvinist Revolt in Sixteenth-Century France* (Leiden, 1986), p. 49.
55 Travers, II, p. 372.
56 A.M.N. BB 4, fo. 4 359v.
57 A.M.N. BB 4, fo. 4 405r.
58 Travers, II, p. 412.
59 As at Rouen; see Benedict, 'The Catholic response to Protestantism', p. 171.
60 P. Benedict, *Rouen during the Wars of Religion* (Cambridge, 1981), p. 63. See also N. Z. Davis, 'Rites of violence', in *Society and Culture in Early Modern France*, pp. 152–88; Benedict, 'The Catholic response to Protestantism', pp. 171–2.
61 Travers, II, pp. 347–8.
62 Travers, II, pp. 378–9.
63 Travers, II, pp. 399–400.
64 Benedict, 'The Catholic response to Protestantism', p. 178.
65 W. Kaiser sees the decade of the 1560s as vital in religious renovation in Marseille. See Kaiser, *Marseille au temps des troubles 1559–96. Morphologie sociale et luttes de factions* (1992), p. 216.
66 C. Elwood, *The Body Broken*, (Oxford, 1999), pp. 113ff.
67 Galpern, *The Religions of the People*, pp. 158, 199.
68 In Troyes in 1547, a company of the Holy Sacrament was created to combat 'the manifold heresies, sects and blasphemies of impious men'; see Galpern, *The Religions of the People*, pp. 132–3. In Rouen, a general confraternity of the Holy Sacrament was founded in 1561; see Benedict, 'The Catholic response to Protestantism', pp. 172–3.
69 G. Durville, *L'ancienne confrérie de Saint-Sacrement à Nantes* (Nantes, 1909).
70 Durville, *L'ancienne confrérie de Saint-Sacrement*, pp. 35–6.
71 Durand, ed., *Le diocèse de Nantes*, p. 90.
72 Travers, II, p. 403.
73 Galpern, *The Religions of the People*, p. 158.
74 A.M.N. GG 644: Religion réformée.
75 B. Diefendorf, *Beneath the Cross. Catholics and Huguenots in Sixteenth-Century Paris* (Oxford, 1991), p. 36. In Lyon parishes, the laity also increased its influence and there was greater interaction between lay elites, the devout and parish priests; see Hoffman, *Church and Community*, p. 37.
76 Quoted in A. Croix, *Nantes et le pays nantais au XVIème siècle. Étude démographique* (1974), p. 17.

77 Croix, *Nantes et le pays nantais*, p. 94.

78 Jarnoux, *Le diocèse de Nantes*, p. 37.

79 J. du Pré, *Conférences avec les ministres de Nantes en Bretaigne, Cabannes et Bourgonnière, faicte par maistre Jacques du Pré, docteur en théologie à Paris et Prédicateur ordinaire de l'Église Cathédrale de S. Pierre de Nantes en juillet 1562* (1564). Renewed emphasis in sermons was placed on the sacraments after 1560; see L. Taylor, *Soldiers of Christ: Preaching in Late Medieval and Reformation France* (Oxford, 1992), especially pp. 125–7 for baptism.

80 Travers, II, p. 391.

81 Benedict, 'The Catholic response to Protestantism', pp. 173–4.

82 Diefendorf, *Beneath the Cross*, p. 150. In Lyon the mendicants were increasingly active in the city's parish churches; *curés* began to speak on ordinary Sundays, and a reader in theology was appointed to the cathedral. See Hoffman, *Church and Community*, p. 36.

83 Travers, II, p. 387.

84 H. Lapeyre, *Une famille des marchands. Les Ruiz* (1955), p. 566.

85 Travers, II, p. 358.

86 Pettegree, 'The sixteenth-century religious book project', pp. 16–17; L. Racaut, *Hatred in Print. Catholic Propaganda and Protestant Identity during the French Wars of Religion* (Aldershot, 2002).

87 V. Reinburg, 'Books of Hours', in Pettegree et al., eds, *The Sixteenth-Century Religious Book*, pp. 79–81.

88 Jean Christi's will, 1608, reproduced in A. Croix, *La Bretagne aux XVIème et XVIIème siècles. La vie – la mort – la foi, 2 vols (1981)*, II, p. 1,372.

89 M. Giraud-Mangin, 'La bibliothèque de l'archidiacre Le Gallo au XVIème siècle', *B.S.A.H.N.L.I.* 76 (1937) 108.

90 P. Conner, 'A provincial perspective. Protestant print culture in southern France', in Pettegree et al., eds, *The Sixteenth-Century Religious Book*, pp. 288–97.

91 M. de Carné, *Les États de Bretagne et l'administration de ce province jusqu'en 1789*, 2 vols (1868), I, pp. 142, 146.

92. Crouzet, *Les guerriers de Dieu*; Benedict, *Rouen*; R. Schneider, *Public Life in Toulouse 1463–1789. From Municipal Republic to Cosmopolitan City* (Ithaca, 1989); Diefendorf, *Beneath the Cross*.

93 M. Cassan, 'Laïcs, Ligue et réforme catholique à Limoges', *Histoire économie et société*, 10 (1991) 160.

94 *Journal du secrétaire de Philippe du Bec, evêque de Nantes puis archevêque de Reims, 1588–1605*, ed. E. de Barthélemy, (1865).

95 A. Tallon, *La France et le Concile de Trent, 1518–1563* (Rome, 1997) p. 883.

96 Jarnoux, *Le diocèse de Nantes*, p. 47.

97 Travers, II, p. 464.

98 Bishop de Crequi had issued a synodal ruling in 1560 ordering the keeping of marriage registers, but this was poorly observed. See Travers, II, p. 356.

99 L. Grégoire, *La Ligue en Bretagne* (Paris and Nantes, 1856), pp. 24–5.

100 A.M.N. EE 210: Ligue 1577–90.

101 Grégoire, *La Ligue*, p. 25.

102 R. Harding, 'Revolution and reform in the Holy League: Angers, Rennes, Nantes', *J.M.H.*, 53 (1981) 399.

103 A.M.N. BB 21: Délibérations et assemblées municipales 1588–89, fos 217v ff.

104 Benedict, 'The Catholic response to Protestantism', pp. 187–8.

105 S. A. Finley-Croswhite, *Henry IV and the Towns. The Pursuit of Legitimacy in French Urban Society, 1589–1610* (Cambridge, 1999), p. 16.

106 Croix, *La Bretagne*, I, p. 487.

107 A devotion observed in Rouen from 1588. See Benedict, 'The Catholic response to Protestantism', p. 180.

108 Grégoire, *La Ligue*, p. 70.

109 Jarnoux, *Le diocèse de Nantes*, p. 177.

110 Travers, II, p. 470.

111 Galpern, *The Religions of the People*, p. 190.

112 Hoffman, *Church and Community*, p. 24.

113 Durville, *Études sur le vieux Nantes d'après les documents originaux*, 2 vols (Nantes, 1901–15), II, pp. 168–9.

114 A.M.N. GG 692: Aumônerie. Bibliothèque Le Gallo 1582–95.

115 A.D.L.A. G 467: Sainte-Croix Fondations.

116 M. Fardet, 'L'assistance aux pauvres à Nantes à la fin du XVIème siècle (1582–1598)', *Actes du 98ème congrès national des sociétés savantes, Nantes 1972*, Section Philologie et Histoire (1973), p. 392; Croix, *La Bretagne*, I, p. 587.

117 C. Mellinet, *La commune et la milice de Nantes*, 3 vols (Nantes, 1836–44), III, p. 234.

118 A.M.N. GG 743: Secours aux pauvres 1532–80.

119 Travers, II, p. 523.

120 A.M.N. FF 285: Police des cultes.

7

Nantes and the Catholic League rebellion, 1589–98

'The claim of our governor, the Duc de Mercoeur, to the duchy of Brittany is the sole cause and origin of our ills. There cannot be any other because it is well known that there are almost no inhabitants of the so-called Reformed religion in this country, or at least they are so small in number that it is a mockery to claim that they could take up arms.'[1]

In his history of the League in Brittany, published in 1856, Louis Grégoire argued that the causes of rebellion were threefold: religion, Breton separatist tendencies and the ambitions of the Duc de Mercoeur. The Bretons were concerned to defend the ancient traditions of their forefathers and the rights of the province, violated during the feeble yet despotic reigns of the sons of Henry II. The Duc de Mercoeur exploited these sentiments to win the sovereignty of Brittany and detach it once again from the French crown.[2] The League as a separatist movement has since dominated historical interpretations of the 1590s. It has traditionally been seen as a resistance movement against political assimilation into France, exploited by the royal governor, who aspired to reconstruct the ancient duchy of Brittany.[3]

Nantes played a central role in the Bretons' rebellion against the crown. In Charles Laronze's view, the League was above all else an urban movement, where the Breton towns fought in defence of their commercial interests, political privileges and religious beliefs. From 1589 Nantes became Mercoeur's 'capital', the site of the League's provincial administration with a parlement and Chambre des Comptes. The city wanted to become the capital of Brittany, to regain the parlement lost to Rennes in 1560, and to dominate provincial administration and politics. The Duc de Mercoeur exploited the city's ambitions and seduced the Nantais into taking up arms against the crown.[4]

But there are paradoxes in this model, which were shown by Barthélemy Pocquet as early as 1913. The Catholic faith was never in danger in Brittany, where Protestants formed only a tiny minority of the population by 1589. Also, the Duc de Mercoeur never made public any claims to the title or sovereignty of Brittany during nine years of rebellion.[5] Further, in this study it has been argued that the city of Nantes was loyal to the crown and was dependent upon its authority, arbitration and patronage throughout the wars of religion. In addition, the elites' relations with Mercoeur were not always harmonious, with disputes over war costs and soldiery. Yet in 1589 a majority of the bourgeois supported Mercoeur's rebellion against Henry III, and the Catholic League lasted longer here than anywhere else, until March 1598.[6] In this chapter, the aims of the Nantais in their rebellion, the relationship between the city and Mercoeur and the lived experience of the League years will be explored. Finally, the question of why it took so long for Nantes to submit to Henry IV will be considered.

Membership and motives of the Catholic Leaguers in Nantes, 1589–94

In studies of the cities of the French kingdom beyond Brittany, the motivation and membership of the League rebellion have been inextricably linked. In his work on Burgundy, Henri Drouot argued that the League was a social or class conflict between two bourgeoisies, a royalist, upper bourgeoisie who monopolised local political authority and social prestige, and a lesser bourgeoisie blocked from high office by their superiors.[7] Elie Barnavi extended this interpretation for Paris, arguing that the lawyers, small officers and merchants who formed the majority of the League movement were frustrated in their social aspirations by an *officier* oligarchy, a view modified by Denis Richet, who claimed that the League was not a 'class' conflict but a battle for cultural and social dominance between two unequal factions of a single bourgeois group.[8] These studies showed that the chief Leaguers, at least in Paris and Dijon, were minor government officials, merchants and legal professionals and that the movement was a vehicle for urban social revolt. Revisionist studies have increasingly shown, however, that in most towns there was no social revolution. For Paris itself, John Salmon and Robert Descimon have agreed that the League recruited from all the social groups involved in the administration of the capital, from senior officers of justice and finance to city magistrates and merchants.[9] In cities such as Rouen, Aix-en-Provence and Troyes, the Leaguers were drawn almost exclusively from the highest social strata: parlementaires, clerics and city magistrates.[10] While the royal officers of every community were divided in their allegiance to the crown and the League, town councils remained largely unchanged. In Troyes, the League municipality included only two newcomers.[11] The League administration was not the result of a triumph of 'outsiders' against those who held power, but represented the victory of one local faction over another.[12]

Robert Harding has argued that in Nantes, as in other provincial cities, there was no social or professional cleavage between Leaguers and royalists, no anti-aristocratic sentiment, as in Paris, nor any hostility towards royal officers.[13] League activists came from diverse social backgrounds; as in Rouen, they were a faction of the ruling elite 'opposed to the royalist loyalty of another faction, between whom lay an unknown number of neutrals and undecided'.[14] Two groups dominated the city's League administration: the upper clergy and, above all, the mercantile elite, who controlled the municipality. The cathedral chapter of Nantes was strongly Leaguer. Archdeacon Descourants, the *official* Touzelin, the *théologal* Jean Christi and Canon de la Benaste had supported the League at least since 1588.[15] The canons preached in support of the Holy Union, performed militia guard duty in person from 1589 and lent money to League causes. The exception was the bishop, Philippe du Bec. Although he was present at the early meetings of the *conseil de l'Union* in Nantes in April and May 1589, du Bec began to absent himself from proceedings. The chapter accused him of favouring heretics and threatened to imprison him in the château. In September the bishop fled to Tours, to join the royalist party.[16]

Comparison of the municipality of the spring of 1589 and the early League institutions shows great continuity between the two. Harding has argued that city government was not at the heart of the League movement, that it actively resisted the League and that the coup of Madame de Mercoeur amounted to an overthrow of the municipal regime.[17] But of thirty-two participants of the general assembly of 11 February 1589, which resolved to obey the king, twenty-five were present when the League *conseil de l'Union* was formed on 10 April. Of the 'missing' seven, four attended subsequent meetings of the *conseil*.[18] Of the *bureau de ville*, the deputy mayor Fourché de la Courosserie and all six *échevins* supported the League. The fourteen captains of the city militia present in February were still in post in July. The only victim of the purge was the mayor and militia colonel, Charles de Harouys.[19] The majority of Leaguers were merchants, although there was also a significant proportion of royal officers.[20] Guy Saupin's analysis of the *bureau de ville* in 1587–98 shows that the post of mayor was filled by five merchants and three judicial officers; among twenty-three *échevins* elected, there were thirteen merchants, five judicial officers, four legal officers (*avocats*, *procureurs*) and one financial official.[21] Recruitment to the municipality did not change and there was little perceptible shift even in the personnel of the *mairie* during this decade.

In addition, about one-quarter of the royal officers of the courts of Nantes chose to support the League, while the rest fled to Rennes. Harding has argued that the scale of involvement of royal officers in the western League cities is striking: in Brittany, 24 per cent of judges of the parlement opted for the League and nearly 50 per cent of the Chambre des Comptes did likewise.[22] But

Saupin has argued that the principal royal officers of Nantes mostly supported the crown. Charles Harouys, president of the *présidial* court and mayor in 1589, was at the head of suspects rounded up by Madame de Mercoeur and remained imprisoned for two years. The seneschal, Jullien Charette, and his brother Raoul, the *prévôt*, fled to Rennes. Of the sovereign courts, much of the Chambre des Comptes relocated to Rennes along with its *premier président* Jean Avril, while two *généraux des finances* of Brittany, François Miron and Claude de Cornulier, were imprisoned.[23] Of the parlement, only three out of eight *premiers presidents* and sixteen out of sixty *conseillers* came to the League parlement in Nantes. The men of the parlement and the Comptes who supported the League were natives of Nantes or attached to the city: ten of the *conseillers* of the parlement were from Nantes' mercantile or legal families while three had married into such families.[24] For example, Mathurin Drouet was the son of the first mayor of Nantes; Michel Gazet and Guillaume Cousin had relatives who had been *échevins*; while Antoine de Brenezay, *avocat du roi* of the League, had been mayor in 1580. In the Chambre des Comptes, Bernard de Monti, *maître des comptes*, was an *échevin* in 1573–75; Raoul and Pierre Boutin, *maîtres*, were related to the mayor of 1575, while the *auditeurs* Jean Fourché de la Courosserie and Jean de la Tullaye were *échevins* in 1587–89.[25]

Two characteristics of League supporters in Nantes have been identified. James Collins argues that the Spanish origins and links of Nantes' merchants inclined them to support the Catholic League. Of the twenty-three *échevins* elected during the League, seven had links with the association for trading with Spain.[26] But Hispanic Nantais also supported the crown. Jacques de Marques, mayor in 1585, supported Henry III in 1589; André Ruiz the younger was arrested by Mercoeur's troops on the road to Rouen in the same year.[27] He remained a suspected royalist, not least because his brother-in-law, the *parlementaire* Barrin, was considered one of the chief architects of the Rennes counter-coup against Mercoeur. A second characteristic of League supporters was their patronage by the Duc de Mercoeur.[28] The seneschal of Rennes identified the greatest 'traitors' in Nantes as Guillaume du Bot, François Carys and the Pillays family.[29] Carys received a pension from Mercoeur. Saupin has identified the Poullain family as central to the duke's municipal clientage. The patriarch Guillaume Poullain was a wealthy merchant; his nephew Robert was mayor in 1576 and a deputy for Brittany to the Estates General of 1576 and 1588. From 1589, François Poullain was militia captain for Biesse-Vertais, while Étienne and Pierre served as *échevins*.[30] What is clear, overall, is that the League had widespread support among Nantes' municipal elites. The city's institutions continued in membership as they had before. The League was a majority faction in opposition to a smaller, royalist group.[31]

So what did Nantes' notables hope to achieve? Descimon has argued that the aims of the Leaguers differed according to individuals' radicalism or conservatism but that there were essentially three main aims for rebellion.[32] Firstly, the League was a religious movement, its primary objective being the conservation of the Catholic religion. Catholicism would be upheld by combating heresy and eliminating it from the realm. The crown's policy of religious toleration had caused heresy to flourish and would be suppressed.[33] The barring of Henry of Navarre from the throne of France was also a key objective. The League's goal was to secure a Catholic king for France as the only means of securing the Roman religion. A second aim of the Leaguers grew out of their opposition to the fiscal and administrative policies of Henry III.[34] There was to be financial and judicial reform and a reduction in the burden of taxation and a rein was to be put on the actions of the king. At the Estates General of Blois of 1588 the third estate proposed a resumption of all crown lands, and attacks on financial and judicial corruption and venality.[35] Before 1589, Frederick Baumgartner argues, the League was a conservative, monarchist movement, not openly challenging the existing structure of government but wanting to see a reduction in the powers of the central state.[36] Linked with this, a third aim of Leaguers was the reassertion of urban autonomy, to restore the city to an important position within the French state. Historians such as Bernard Chevalier and Descimon have argued that the League was fought to restore the medieval commune, for the defence of municipal privileges and the ending of crown infiltration of urban administrations.[37] For example, the Parisian League was a response by citizens attached to certain traditions of local government originating in the medieval commune and its sociability, against moves by the monarchy to impose its authority.[38] In Amiens, Marie Pelus-Kaplan has argued, the Leaguers sought to maintain the urban oligarchy in its power and uphold the ancient privileges and autonomy of the city with respect to its relations with the crown and high nobility.[39] The *cahiers* of the third estate at Blois in 1588 proposed that the institutions of the kingdom should be reformed, 'in a monarchy that was contractual and controlled in a federal and decentralised kingdom'.[40]

The aims of the Nantes Leaguers were similar to those of other large, provincial cities: the preservation of Catholicism and the reform of monarchical government. The clearest statement of these objectives is found in the published sermons of the Parisian Benedictine Jacques Le Bossu. Harding argues that 'the evidence shows the crucial importance of [preachers] as harbingers and interpreters of the League'.[41] In Nantes, the *théologal* Christi and other canons of the cathedral were important in gathering support for the League in 1588–89, Christi at least preaching for this purpose. In Lent 1589, they were joined by Le Bossu, who was passionately committed to the cause of the Holy

Union. A royalist pamphlet of 1590 considered the preacher to be 'the most mutinous and seditious that there was in France'.[42] But while fiery preaching enthused its listeners for commitment to the League, Le Bossu did not cause the rebellion in Nantes by his sermons. He and others reflected, shaped, influenced and gave words to widespread anxieties and galvanised support for particular causes of action. Sermons were published by the printers Des Maretz and Fauverie, who were present in Nantes from 1589, perhaps brought there by the Duc de Mercoeur, who was also Le Bossu's patron. They provided a clear expression of and justification for the ideological bases of the League. For this reason, Le Bossu's six printed sermons have been used to examine the aims of the Nantais.

In a series of four *devis*, conversations between a Leaguer and a *politique*, and in several funerary orations, the justification and purposes of the rebellion emerge. The League was above all religious in its cause and principally opposed to heresy. 'We have been forced to make a union and confederation between us which is called the Holy League . . . to employ our goods, our life and our blood for the support and defence of our faith . . . to conserve our Catholic religion, for ourselves and our posterity.'[43] The source of all current misery was the royal policy of tolerating the coexistence of Protestantism and Catholicism. The only true source of peace was to have one religion in the kingdom. The League opposed Henry III because he authorised heresy; the king should be forced to uphold the edict of Union, which should become a fundamental and inviolable law of the kingdom.[44] Henry should not be allowed to let the crown pass to a heretic. The League would use all available means to prevent this.[45] Further, Henry had violated the church itself through taxation, imposition, alienation of lands, the imprisonment of clerics such as the Cardinal de Bourbon and the Archbishop of Lyon, and the murder of the Cardinal de Guise.[46] After Henry III's assassination in August 1589, hailed as the will of God, the religious motives of the League were reinforced. The succession of a Protestant king was insupportable and endangered the Catholic Church and faith, physically, for revenge would doubtless be sought for the St Bartholomew's day murders, and morally, for the destruction of Catholicism would cause many souls to be damned.[47]

A second motive for rebellion, emphasised by Harding, was reform in the royal administration. He argues that preachers in the west 'took advantage of a widespread moral revulsion against the state; without grounding their arguments in political theory they undertook to instill a commitment to sweeping reform'.[48] According to Jullien de Moranne, writing in 1588, the problems of the kingdom were the sale of judicial offices, corruption in filling benefices, the abolition of the right of urban citizens to elect mayors and aldermen, excessive taxes, lack of respect for noblemen and an excess of royal officers.[49] To this, Le

Bossu added corruption in the judiciary and usury by merchants.[50] Reform was needed in all the estates of the realm. This was to be a moral reform, within the state and society at large. It was also to be a reform of the royal court and of the relations between crown and provinces. There should be a limited but sovereign monarchy which upheld and respected the ancient laws and privileges of subjects, in which, Le Bossu and the Nantes jurist Pierre Biré argued, the great Catholic nobility would refind its pre-eminent role. The monarch would refound the unity of the kingdom and reform the state to safeguard provincial and city liberties; he would be directly inspired by Catholic morality, which would act as the sole source of law.[51]

There was no separatist agenda in Nantes for the recreation of an independent Brittany. Biré's vision was of Brittany within a Catholic French monarchy.[52] The provincial estates also did not invoke the defence of provincial privilege. In 1592 the estates declared that they wished 'to live and die inviolably devoted to the monarchy from which they remain, regretfully, separated, waiting for when it should please God to give France a Catholic king'.[53] The evidence supports Saupin's conclusions that Nantes' elites favoured the restoration not of a separate Breton state, but of a more contractual monarchy with clear spheres of authority defined for the component social groups and corporations of the province.[54]

All commentators on the League in Nantes are clear about one factor: the city was brought into the rebellion by the Duc de Mercoeur.[55] In Christophe de Rosnyvinen's history of the League, written in the late seventeenth century, he claimed that the aim of the mass party was the conservation of religion, but that of the leaders was pure ambition. Above all, the Duc de Mercoeur wanted to seize Brittany and live as its sovereign.[56] Spanish contemporaries of Mercoeur also considered this to be his principal aim, 'under pretext of an old right claimed by his wife, which he has had published in all the districts'.[57] The Duchesse de Mercoeur presented their infant sons as heirs of the ancient dukes. Louis, born in 1589, was given the title 'Prince and Duke of Brittany' by his mother, and was buried under this inscription before the high altar of the church of the Poor Clares in 1590. In November 1592, baby François was given the ducal title, before his death in the same year.[58] But Mercoeur himself never adopted the Breton ducal title. Even in 1593, at the height of his success, he was referred to in Nantes as 'Monseigneur le duc de Mercoeur, gouverneur de Bretagne'.[59] The court of poets and writers established at the château of Nantes during these years did not promote a ducal image. Pierre Biré, panegyrist and historian to the duke in the early 1590s, wrote that the duke's secular aims were the preservation of his government of Brittany and his honour. He had been a loyal servant of Henry III, driven to rebellion by the king's perfidy, as evidenced by letters found on President Faucon de Ris in March 1589, which showed that the king intended to strip Mercoeur of his governorship and to ruin him.[60] In a later letter to the Duc d'Aumale of July 1599, Mercoeur himself came as close as he ever did to defining his aims in Brittany. He fought, he wrote, 'for the maintenance of my grandeur'; he viewed the governorship of Brittany, lately taken from him by enemies of his house to be rightfully his through his marriage.[61] But Mercoeur's objectives were also the defence of Catholicism and the extirpation of heresy. He was sympathetic to the Catholic League from 1585 and enforced the treaty of Nemours in his province.[62] The duke was genuinely devout. He was a patron of religious orders and made frequent retreats to his hermitage on the island of Indret in the Loire.[63]

The widespread support of Mercoeur by the municipal notables can be explained by a community of interests between the two parties. Of course, Nantes' involvement was related to the realities of power in southern Brittany in 1589. The duke and his army, several companies of which were billeted in the suburbs of Nantes, held effective military authority in the county, and the city faced reprisals if it rejected Mercoeur's tutelage. But both wished to preserve the Catholic faith and to prevent a Protestant regime.[64] Both parties also sought to maintain their local authority through the restoration of a more limited, contractual monarchy. Mercoeur's view was largely feudal in conception: to defend the rights and status of his lineage in Brittany. He chose Nantes as his capital because the financial resources of the city were vital for his campaigns and the town was well fortified. Nantes' notables were monarchist but supported the League aristocracy as the best means of achieving political reform. Mercoeur's forces offered protection against enemy troops, and his good relations with Spain offered to keep trade links open. In the event of a victory of the League, Nantes might even succeed in its ambition to regain the parlement of Brittany and become the principal city of the province, over royalist Rennes.

The League ascendant: administration, warfare and piety 1589–94

In April 1589, the royal administration of Brittany was torn apart. With the exception of Rennes, Vitré and a handful of smaller centres, most towns declared for the League. On 12 April Henry III issued an edict ordering the Chambre des Comptes, *the bureau des finances* and the mint of Nantes to move to Rennes; the membership of these institutions and the Breton parlement divided, royalists occupying Rennes, and Leaguers, Nantes. On 13 April, an *arrêt* of the Rennes parlement declared the Duc de Mercoeur to be an outlaw; several days later he was decreed to be deprived of all his charges in the province and Charles de Bourbon, Comte de Soissons, was appointed royal governor in his place.[65]

In Nantes, the municipal government of *bureau de ville* and general assemblies was effectively suspended on 10 April, with the formation of a *conseil de l'Union*.[66] An assembly of seventy-seven Leaguers, presided over by Bishop du Bec, declared for the Holy Union, for the honour of God and the salvation of the town. The *conseil de l'Union*, which took over urban administration, comprised 'a council of men who are good Catholics, prudent and experienced, and zealous citizens'; like other councils of the League, it included clerical members, in this case Archdeacon Descourants and Canons Touzelin, Christi and de la Benaste.[67] The other members came from the existing *bureau de ville* and the general assembly, including the captains of the city militia. Salmon argues that the *conseils de l'Union* represented a new concept of participatory government created by the revolutionary situation. In theory the old distribution between representatives of central power and ecclesiastical and local urban authorities disappeared, for membership was drawn from all urban estates.[68] In Nantes, the *conseil* was effectively an expansion of normal municipal government, an enlarged committee of public safety, examples of which had been formed during emergencies throughout the wars, with representatives from all three urban estates. This was no revolutionary government. The first acts of the *conseil* were to make contact with other League towns and to garner local support. In late April, Archdeacon Descourants was reimbursed for expenses incurred during journeys secretly made to Orléans and elsewhere, and letters were received from Paris. In May, the *conseil* wrote to the gentlemen and to towns in the diocese, to urge them to join the Holy Union. Relations with non-League towns were severed and their merchants expelled from Nantes, although trade resumed in June.[69]

In June, the Duc de Mercoeur created a *conseil d'état et des finances*, with authority over war, troops and finance. At first, the *conseil d'état* was based firmly in Nantes, comprising three clergy, three judicial and three financial officers of the city, chosen by the duke from a list drawn up by the *conseil de l'Union*. Its interests extended little beyond the city itself.[70] Later, in March 1591, the *conseil d'état* was enlarged to eighteen members, six selected by Mercoeur and twelve by the provincial estates. A. Croix argues that the *conseil d'état* was an attempt to create an autonomous provincial administration that could later govern an independent duchy. It seems, however, that the expanded *conseil d'état* was an attempt to draw the provincial elites more closely to the League cause. Stuart Carroll's study of the Guise affinity has shown the importance of counsel in clienteles; giving advice augmented the status of a client, while seeking counsel assured the participation of subordinates in the decision-making process and bound an affinity together.[71] The *conseil d'état* was used to build networks within the province, to make personal contacts, to ensure a better understanding of the local situation and to gather information. Its authority was limited. Rosnyvinen stated that its power was limited to that which the duke wanted it to do and never extended beyond several rulings on justice, the police of soldiery, the administration of finances, decisions on ransoms and the exchange of prisoners.[72] There is little evidence for activity by late 1591, and Mercoeur seems to have left it to stagnate in inaction. The *procureur-général* complained in 1593 that 'there are several gentlemen who do not attend the *conseil*; some excuse themselves because they are not present in the place, and others are dead, such that only a small number meet'.[73] Little is heard of it from 1594 onwards.

The formation of the *conseil d'état* was followed swiftly by the collapse of the *conseil de l'Union*. In July 1589 the *bureau de ville* began to meet again, under the deputy mayor Fourché de la Courosserie and with all six *échevins* elected for that year. The general assembly of Nantes also met again on 14 July. In August the *conseil de l'Union* met four times, but then seems to have discontinued. There were three reasons for the collapse of the new urban government after only four months. Firstly, the traditional organ of government, whose membership was now proved loyal, was the most efficient for administering the city, with its police powers and regulatory frameworks already in place. Pelus-Kaplan has observed for Amiens that the constitution of municipal government contributed to long-term, widespread support of the League by the majority of the bourgeoisie.[74] The same seems to have been true of Nantes. There was already active participation in government by many of the rich and middling sorts in the city, through the general assembly and the militia. This gave a feeling of consultation and common goals to the majority of the bourgeois. Secondly, Saupin comments that the Mercoeurs preferred to treat with a small administrative and executive structure rather than a large body.[75] Thirdly, and much more importantly, the new organs of government lacked constitutional regularity and had difficulty in raising money. During the first meeting of the *conseil de l'Union* on 10 April, it was recorded in the municipal registers that the *corps de ville* was incomplete because of the absence of the mayor and other notables. There were thus insufficient men present to represent the town and to stand surety for loans to the municipality. The loan voted at the meeting, of 1,800 *écus*, had therefore to be raised under the authority of the preceding assembly of 6 April.[76] When the general assembly met again, on 14 July, it was to validate a request for taxation made by Mercoeur. After July 1589 the municipality was more closely supervised by the governor than in the past – all deliberations or ordinances of the League years begin with 'following the commandment of Madame de Mercoeur'. But the duke and duchess had to respect the process of law and government within Nantes, for these worked best. By the autumn of 1589 traditional forms of authority and governance had reasserted themselves.

In contrast with the continuity found in city government, the judicial institutions of Nantes were more severely disrupted. Early in 1590, in many provinces throughout France, rival royalist and League institutions were set up in different cities. In January a League parlement was formed. There were problems of personnel, however; only three of the eight presidents and eight out of sixty *conseillers* came to Nantes, later being joined by eight more. President Charpentier was made *premier président* and Jacques de Launay promoted to president, but the parlement remained small, with only seven *conseillers* appointed by Mercoeur before 1597.[77] The main preoccupation of the parlement was the condemnation of royalists. *Arrêts* were issued throughout the spring of 1590 against the parlement of Rennes, royalist legal officers and Protestants.[78] For the most part, however, the parlement's declarations were mere propaganda, with little application beyond Nantes itself.[79] By 1593 it was pre-occupied with police matters in Nantes, fixing the price of foodstuffs and regulating the wine trade and artisanal working practices, which brought it into conflict with the municipality.[80] The estates of Brittany also met under the auspices of the League, again in rivalry with estates held at Rennes. The Duc de Mercoeur called estates at Nantes in 1591 and at Vannes each year between 1592 and 1594. Three issues dominated their proceedings: attachment to religious unity, calls for better controls over soldiers in the province, and taxation.[81]

The court of Nantes, *présidial* and *sénéchaussée*, was also reconstructed, for the officers had largely fled. The president of the *présidial* was the only member of his court to remain in the city. Antoine de Brenezay, *avocat du roi* in the League parlement, became seneschal, and Pierre Bidé, the lieutenant-general.[82] Three further *conseiller-juges* were appointed in 1594 and 1596.[83] The two lower courts, the royal *prévôté* and the bishop's *régaires*, were also reconstituted, with Pierre André as *prévôt* and Pierre Charette as bishop's seneschal. The Chambre des Comptes reformed, with some difficulty, following the departure of President Avril and many of the members to Rennes. A new president was created, some of the remaining auditors were promoted to masters, and new auditors were recruited.[84]

Harding has argued that most towns escaped the direct control of the crown to slide deeper under the influence of military governors.[85] There is no doubt that Mercoeur had great prestige as military governor and protector of Catholicism and that he had a strong client base in the institutions of Nantes. Madame de Mercoeur, who acted as governor of Nantes during the frequent absences of her husband, managed the city carefully. The royal governor took over the crown's role in arbitrating disputes between competing city institutions. Pierre André gained the *prévôté* because of her favour, and his authority was upheld in a dispute over police jurisdiction in 1595.[86] In August 1591, a dispute arose between the parlement and municipality over the right to have halberds carried before the mayor and *échevins* in city processions. The *bureau de ville* claimed to be acting in conservation of municipal privileges and appealed to Madame de Mercoeur. She ordered a Te Deum instead of a procession planned for 24 August; but the municipality again appeared with sergeants and halberds, and the parlement had to give way.[87] In 1594, a major dispute arose between parlement and the municipality over urban police. In February, a compromise court was set up, with the mayor, *échevins*, cathedral chapter, seneschal and *prévôt*.[88]

Relations between the municipality and the Duc de Mercoeur were not always harmonious. The city was not always compliant to the governor's wishes. In August 1589 the *conseil d'état* dismissed the militia captain Corvel. Corvel had always been disliked by Mercoeur, who had attempted to demote him in 1583, but was blocked by the municipality. This time Mercoeur succeeded and Corvel was replaced by a loyal auditor of the Chambre des Comptes, Jean de la Tullaie.[89] But the duke did not always get his way. Early in 1591, the Touzelin brothers, both cathedral canons, were expelled from Nantes by Madame de Mercoeur under suspicion of having corresponded with Henry IV and Bishop du Bec. A general assembly was called and lobbied successfully for their return, the chapter and municipality standing surety for the Touzelins' fidelity.[90] In 1595 a dispute arose between the municipality and the duke over the passage of merchants. After a complaint about the imprisonment of a merchant from Orléans, Mercoeur had to explain his actions. He wrote to the municipality that one Godefroy had abused a passport issued to him by coming to Nantes to discuss matters harmful to the Holy League, and had tried there to debauch Mercoeur's followers. The duke asked that the Nantais not interpret his actions as an attack on commerce.[91] Annette Finley-Croswhite argues that League towns initially enjoyed a renewed independence, at least from royal supervision, but that many soon found themselves subject to the orders of powerful magnates, who controlled towns through their urban clientele.[92] There is no doubt that Nantes also found itself with fewer liberties under Mercoeur. But the city and the duke were allied for common purposes, so the municipality's privileges and processes had to be respected, and the city government was not always subservient to Mercoeur.

The main preoccupation of the city between 1589 and 1594 was defence: both external safety against royalist soldiers and internal security.[93] The League wars in Brittany were fought at some distance from Nantes, in the north of the province and on the borders with Normandy and Maine. Vitré, a Protestant stronghold, was besieged in 1589 but did not fall. The Comte de Soissons was defeated and captured at La Guèrche, but escaped shortly afterwards.

Mercoeur's greatest victory came in May 1592, at Craon.[94] The Breton League
wars were like those elsewhere in France, with alternate successes for each
camp and no decisive victories, wars of small actions and sieges of walled towns
and fortified châteaux.[95] The municipality was keen to secure the reduction of
royalist fortresses in the *pays nantais*, which sheltered troops who raided the
countryside and took prisoners for ransom. The city was forced to employ
troops to protect the local harvest and its workers in order to secure provisions
for the town. In June 1589, a commission was issued for a company of 30–40
cuirassiers and 60 mounted arquebusiers, and in May 1590, a company of 50
foot and mounted troops was recruited to combat the raiders from Clisson and
Blain, and was augmented to 100 for three months.[96] For this reason, the
municipality provided provisions, munitions and men for the reduction of local
enemy châteaux. During 1589 militia companies assisted in actions at
Guérande and Le Croisic, and the house of the Chevalier de Goust was attacked
at Cordemais.[97] In 1590 they assisted Spanish troops in capturing the château of
La Bretêche, and in 1591 they supported the siege of Vue.[98] Of greatest
concern was the fortified town of Blain, held by the Protestant Rohan family.
In 1591, the Nantais offered to pay all the expenses of the Duc de Mercoeur if
he reduced the fortress. The sum of 2,000 *écus* was raised to pay Spanish troops,
and in the late autumn the city provided 3,000–4,000 loaves per day, wood and
powder for the army.[99] The fortress finally fell late in 1591.

The defence of Nantes itself was still considered the preserve of its inhabitants, despite the military emergency of the times. Throughout the 1590s,
there was a garrison of about 200 arquebusiers in the château of Nantes under
Captain Gassion, but the city refused to take in further troops under the
command of Mercoeur.[100] From early 1589, two companies of soldiers were
billeted in the suburbs of Saint-Clément and Richebourg; early in 1590 the
bureau de ville asked, unsuccessfully, for their removal from the city.[101] In 1591
the municipality refused to receive soldiers returning from the siege of Blain,
and Madame de Mercoeur was obliged to send them to be quartered on the
parishes of Le Cellier and Oudon.[102] The Nantais maintained that their defence
should be based upon the fortifications of the city and the bourgeois militia.
Both of these exacted heavy demands of the inhabitants. From 1589 there was
almost constant work on fortifications. Mercoeur also revived the royal project
of the fortification of the Marchix suburb, or Villeneuve, to the vulnerable
north of Nantes.[103] There were constant levies for these works. In December
1589, all inhabitants were required to perform fortifications work in person,
carrying hods, or pay 15 *sous* a week. Labour service would continue down to
the end of the League.

The municipality was careful to ensure its continued control of the
militia. The arrest of the mayor in 1589 led to the appointment of a sergeant

major, the Leaguer Michel Loriot, to organise the force, but most of the captains remained in office.[104] After guard duty, a second function of the militia was internal security. There were frequent scares and rumours of conspiracies. In April 1590, the *bureau de ville* received a report that locksmiths had been seen taking impressions of the locks of the city magazines; the manufacture of false keys and seizure of arms were feared, although an investigation revealed nothing.[105] The following July, there was a rumour that royalists were plotting to seize boats on the river Erdre. Captain Lesnaudière asked for reinforcements of 200 arquebusiers from the city militia to be prepared to defend the city in case of attack.[106] There were frequent house-to-house visits and investigations in each quarter for suspects and royalists. On 29 January 1590, a commission was set up of two *conseillers* of the parlement who, with the captains and *cinquantainiers* of each quarter, would investigate and inform against the supporters of Henry IV.[107] Opponents of the League were imprisoned or expelled, their goods confiscated; for example, the master of the Psallette of the cathedral, who refused to take the oath of Union in June 1589, was exiled and deprived of his salary.[108] Vagabonds and prostitutes were periodically ejected. Further, the militia played a part in policing the provisioning and stocking of grain, wine and fodder, through periodic visits to warehouses and granaries. Taxation rolls and forced loans were also allocated with the aid of militia captains. The bourgeois militia, particularly its officers, acted as the eyes, ears and enforcement agency of the League municipality.

Although Nantes' main interests lay in its own security, the chief function of the city within the wider Breton League was to finance its military campaigns. More levies were paid during the years 1589–98 than at any previous time. During the first year or so of the League, the two main forms of imposition were forced loans and rising indirect taxation. The first act of the *conseil de l'Union* was to raise a loan of 1,800 *écus* on the better-off inhabitants of Nantes.[109] In June, the duke demanded a loan of 20,000 *écus* to finance his siege of Vitré, again from the wealthier inhabitants, who were to be imprisoned if they refused.[110] Further loans were contracted on at least two further occasions in 1590 to pay for fortifications. Loans were to be repaid by raising city *octrois*. In June 1589, a tax on merchandise moving upriver from Nantes was granted by Mercoeur, again for fortifications. There were other fiscal expedients. Voluntary collections were taken by the militia captains in their quarters: that raised in April 1589 was used for travel expenses for communications with other League towns, for example. Property belonging to those who fled Nantes for the royalist party was confiscated or sold, such as the merchandise belonging to a Calvinist merchant of Tours stored in a warehouse on the port.[111]

From the summer of 1590, finance seems to have been harder to obtain. In October, the *procureur syndic* stated that the town owed the *miseur* 2,000 *livres* for advances he had made to cover wages, *rentes* and ordinary expenses, while 100,000–120,000 *livres* of debt had been contracted from individuals. The revenue from the farms and receipts of the city were insufficient to pay the *rentes* which had been created, the salaries of officials or other expenses. Fortifications alone were costing 300 *écus* every week.[112] The revenues from *octrois* and taxes on merchandise fell with the war. It become more difficult to constrain the wealthy to lend money, because of their own financial difficulties and despair of ever being reimbursed for previous subventions. A loans crisis seems to have stimulated an attempt to reimburse some of the city's creditors early in 1591. In January, Sieurs Marguez and Guillemot, merchants of La Fosse, were repaid 1,000 *écus* of their loans, and received promises that the rest would be repaid.[113] In April 1590 6,600 *écus* had been loaned to the Duc de Mercoeur by forty-eight individuals, in sums ranging from 30 to 500 *écus*. Six of these creditors were repaid in February and March 1591: the master moneyer of Nantes and the Dame de Breil, the largest creditors, three merchants and the procureur of the *présidial*, all of whom seem to have been clients or supporters of the duke.[114] In April the duke also repaid 5,950 *écus* to the municipality.[115]

The difficulties of obtaining credit led the municipality to impose direct taxation, which avoided the difficulties of borrowing and repaying money: in 1589 and 1590 there were direct impositions on the city and county on at least five occasions, for fortifications work and other military needs. Taxes were imposed on all, 'regardless of estate or quality, noble or non-noble, refugees and those retired to the city including the magistrates and officers of the parlement of Nantes'.[116] There were monthly levies to pay for fortifications work across the summer of 1591, and in November a loan of 4,000 *écus* for the siege of Blain was raised, with the clergy contributing 10 per cent.[117] In January 1592 the general assembly ordered a huge levy of 46,940 *écus* on the city and suburbs, and in 1594 the provincial estates levied 11,500 *écus* on the city and bishopric.[118] Even allowing for differences between the amounts demanded and the sums paid, these were enormous impositions.

The League wars thus saw an appropriation of the royal fiscal machinery in Nantes, as taxes were authorised by the Duc de Mercoeur and collected for the Holy Union. There was also an attack on traditional fiscal privilege. The clergy were constrained to contribute to fortifications work and the maintenance of troops; a number of those holding benefices were forced to alienate part of their temporal possesions to pay the charges imposed upon them.[119] Judicial and financial officers were assessed for tax and constrained to pay.[120] The main burden of League finance fell on the rich. Forced loans were the main form of subsidy in the early League. Thereafter, even when direct taxation was authorised, the wealthy were forced to put up much of the sum in advance, for repayment when the tax was collected. In 1594 the estates levied 11,500 *livres* on the *pays nantais*. To allow for the immediate payment of troops, between 120 and 140 notables of Nantes advanced 15,000 *écus*.[121] Repayment in full was unlikely. In January 1595 12,000 *écus* was granted from the *fouages* of Brittany by the treasurer of the estates to repay Nantes' war expenses. Fourteen creditors received compensation varying from 50 to 200 *écus*.[122] This was a political gesture of goodwill, not a restitution of fortunes.

Legitimacy for impositions of military service and taxation during the League years did not come from the crown. Rather, it was justified by religion. Benedict argues that 'the sacred mission to save the realm for Catholicism . . . gave legitimacy to a form of government unsanctioned by law or precedent and which dared to repudiate the authority of the king, God's anointed'.[123] In particular, the League placed great emphasis on the internal and spiritual renewal of the earthly city, with internalised faith as the principal cleansing and purifying agent.[124] To these ends, in August 1593 the Nantes parlement published the decrees of the Council of Trent.[125] Charles Cardot has shown that the parlement also undertook to enforce canon law prerequisites for appointment to benefices, ordered clerical residence in parishes and took measures against the laity for immorality, blasphemy and sabbath breaking.[126]

Religious zeal and support for the League were expressed in highly ritualised, communal and penitential ceremonies; 'the streets . . . became theatres in which the inhabitants would act out their contrition in a way to avert political calamity'.[127] Public ritual actions were the hallmark of the early League years in Nantes, as elsewhere. The most striking features to contemporaries were expansions in the numbers and types of religious ceremonials. Te Deums were celebrated in the cathedral at every possible opportunity, accompanied by processions and bonfires, after the capture of the Comte de Soissons in June 1589 and for victories of the League in Brittany and elsewhere in the kingdom. But penitence was more the flavour of the movement, to invoke God's pity and pacify his ire. For example, in September 1590 there were three days of processions, involving each of the three houses of friars in turn. The processions were held at night; the city clergy took part clad only in shifts, each carrying a torch in the right hand and a crucifix in the left, chanting the seven penitential psalms.[128] In May 1591 the newly arrived Capuchins, along with other clergy and laity, took part in a barefoot night-time procession, imploring God for mercy, an end to troubles in the state and the victory of the Duc de Mercoeur.[129] Sacramental devotion continued to be important. On 13 May 1592, to plead for success in relieving the siege at Craon, the cathedral chapter organised holy sacrament devotions in all of the city's churches. The municipality supplied bread to be blessed and distributed, and a procession took place. The duke's success at Craon was celebrated with a Te Deum, and the enemy's captured banners were hung in the nave of the cathedral.[130]

The devotions of the League were not entirely novel. In the 1580s plague, famine and the economic sufferings wrought by war had augmented public penitential devotion, which was focused on the holy sacrament. The public, participatory and penitential zeal of the early 1590s was, however, greater than that seen hitherto. It signified assent with the common cause; shared experience of ritual bound together different groups and gave a single purpose to a widely differentiated city population. A hallmark of League piety in Nantes was the extension of parish-based devotions that, as in the 1560s, provided a public setting in which commitment to the cause could be expressed. For example, mortuary foundations in parish churches increased after two decades of decline (see Figure 6.1). One reason for this was the encouragement given to parish-based foundations by the Duc de Mercoeur. Traditionally, the ducal family of Brittany patronised the houses of the religious orders in Nantes, and the Mercoeurs also supported the regulars. In 1589 the Minimes were established at Nantes. The duke supported the order and built part of the convent, despite opposition from the municipality.[131] The Capuchins were established there in 1593, also with the duke's patronage.[132] The existing religious orders received gifts. A mass was founded in the Dominican church; the ducal couple augmented the foundation of the confraternity of the Rosary of the Franciscans, and the cathedral chapter was given gifts of ornaments and velvet for the Corpus Christi processions.[133]

If the duke had been truly aspiring to sovereign ducal status, he might have favoured ducal sites, particularly the Carmelite house where the hearts of the last two duchesses of Brittany, Queens Anne and Claude, were buried. Instead, the Mercoeurs used the parish to demonstrate their piety and to give popular legitimacy to their cause. Baby François, born in 1590, and the twins, born in 1592, were baptised in their parish church of Saint-Vincent. Here the duke founded a mass of Notre-Dame de la Victoire in 1592 to give perpetual thanks for his victory at Craon.[134] A similar foundation of the little office of the Virgin was set up in Notre-Dame church. In 1594, Madame de Martigues founded two weekly masses in Saint-Vincent. The chaplain, whose appointment was reserved to her heirs, was to be one of the serving priests of the church.[135] The parish enabled the Mercoeurs to emphasise the religious basis of their cause in public acts of piety, surrounded by the everyday population of the community. The duke and duchess supported other acts of public devotion as well. Madame de Mercoeur attended the sermons of Le Bossu and took part in nocturnal processions. When her twins were born in 1592, paupers were chosen as godparents and given alms.[136] The duke and duchess promoted an austere, Tridentine-inspired piety, focused on penitence and the eucharist. Righteousness was an important means of legitimising their cause.

The legitimacy of the League was also promoted by the extension of religious or quasi-religious rituals into politics and law. Public oath swearing was an important means of fostering popular support. On 26 June 1589, the inhabitants of Nantes were urged to take the oath to the League, which was similar to that of Paris, Lyon and Toulouse. Le Bossu preached in its favour, and the ceremony was administered by President Carpentier of the parlement. The oath-takers placed their hands on a crucifix which was fixed to a board and carried around the crowd, and the oath was signed by each corporation.[137] On 16 April 1590, another mass oath-swearing, to the Holy Union, Charles X and the Duc de Mercoeur, was held at the *hôtel de ville* before the seneschal.[138] Two days later, the two chapters and the city clergy took the oath and gave 400 *écus* for the upkeep of soldiers.[139]

Judicial sentences, always highly ritualised, added to the theatre of the League. The royalist seneschal of Nantes, Jullien Charette, and his brother Raoul were executed in effigy in March 1590.[140] In November 1591, the judge of Laval and other supporters of Henry IV were hanged in Nantes, in retribution for the execution of Leaguers by the Prince de Dombes.[141] *Arrêts* issued by the parlement of Rennes were publicly burnt and the ashes thrown into the wind. In January 1591, Bishop du Bec wrote to the Nantais to justify his support of the king. The parlement ordered his letter to be lacerated and burnt by the public executioner.[142] On 8 August 1591, a ceremony took place at the cathedral for the public reading of Pope Gregory XIV's bull excommunicating Henry IV. It was followed on 22 August by a general procession to the Place du Bouffay, where the reply from the parlement of Tours, declaring the Pope to be an enemy of the peace, was burnt. Choirboys lit the pyre, recited verses from scripture, and then threw their torches into the flames reciting, 'May their light thus also be extinguished'.[143]

The League in decline, 1594–97

The reconversion of Henry IV to Catholicism in July 1593 and his coronation at Chartres the following February were severe blows to the League cause, for these acts legitimised the king for many subjects.[144] The League split into factions, particularly over the royal succession, while economic crisis and rising taxation caused popular opposition to grow. In March 1594, the submission of Paris served as a catalyst for the return to obedience of other towns. By the end of this year, most of the major cities in northern France had submitted to the king, and in 1595, the Burgundian towns and the Duc de Mayenne did likewise. Governors and nobles were offered pensions in return for their submission, and urban governments were granted generous terms for their capitulation. Calvinist worship was frequently excluded from the town, privileges and franchises were upheld, and League officers were amnestied and allowed to continue in their positions. Great emphasis was placed on reconciliation between formerly hostile parties and on forgetting the past.[145]

In Nantes, the abjuration of King Henry caused a surge of anti-Protestant invective. As in other League centres, preachers claimed that the king was a hypocrite: this was a false conversion and Henry remained a heretic in his heart. The city elites justified their continued opposition to the king because the papal condemnation had not been lifted. Indeed, Clement VIII encouraged the Duc de Mercoeur and the Bretons to continue the struggle against Henry IV.[146] The city remained in opposition to the crown even after papal absolution came in September 1595, and the legate wrote from Paris that Mercoeur would be excommunicated if he did not submit to the king.[147] From early 1596, Mercoeur remained the only League magnate in rebellion against Henry.

But the conversion of Henry IV to Catholicism changed the nature of the League wars in the west. The Estates General held at Paris in 1593 to find a Catholic monarch for France, attended by Jean Christi and other Breton representatives, failed to find a successor to Henry III, and the League in Brittany began to lose its purpose. In August, the Marshal d'Aumont, named commander-in-chief of the royal forces in Brittany, arrived in the province and slowly turned the war to the royalists' advantage. In the campaign of 1594, d'Aumont took the western towns of Morlaix, Quimper and Brest. Saint-Malo submitted and Mercoeur's captains began to capitulate, for example Lézonnet at Concarneau and Talhouet at Redon.[148] Only d'Aumont's death in 1595 prevented further successes. At the same time, much of the countryside in western Brittany descended into anarchy; brigandage and pillage by lords such as la Fontenelle, and peasant insurrection replaced military campaigns. The Duc de Mercoeur's command over the province contracted to southern Brittany. Towards the end of 1593, a truce was negotiated between the League and the royalists which, although badly observed, lasted for more than four years. During this time, Mercoeur took part in long-drawn-out negotiations with the crown about the terms of his submission. He retreated to Nantes and to his Loire island palace of Indret, to play a game of wait and see.

As war retreated from the *pays nantais* the municipality turned away from military concerns to problems within the city. War ruined the economy of Nantes, already weakened by the 1580s subsistence crises and military campaigns. The cloth trade was gravely disrupted. In 1589, royalists occupied Clisson, and merchandise could not be brought to the city from Poitou, while links to Laval and its textiles were also cut. Trade with non-League towns was

initially prohibited, but commerce was so badly affected that Mercoeur negotiated agreements with Rennes and Laval for the exchange of cloth and fish.[149]
Trade across the Bay of Biscay was further reduced by piracy and ship seizures.
There was a shortage of coin for transactions, despite the minting of specie in
the name of Charles X, for this quickly depreciated in value as it was refused
by many outside traders.[150] The city's hinterland was badly cultivated and was
ravaged by enemy troops, so there were shortages of food throughout the
region. The city population shrank in size.[151]

The early years of the League, 1591–93, witnessed three poor harvests,
which were exacerbated by raids on the countryside. Somehow the city
managed to find sufficient grain to avert famine. From early 1595, however,
food shortages became serious. In the spring of this year, there were floods in
the regions and cold weather, which lasted for many weeks, so crops could not
be sown.[152] By May, grain was short. The municipality ordered wealthy inhabitants to find provision for six months and asked the parlement to fix prices.
Mercoeur proposed that several merchants be engaged to furnish the city with
15,000–16,000 *sétiers* of grains, to be stored in public granaries. The *bureau de
ville* refused; it argued that the city lacked funds, and was reluctant to furnish
granaries which could be used for Mercoeur's troops. Instead, in May, a levy of
1,200 *écus* was imposed on the town and suburbs to employ the able-bodied
poor on the eastern fortifications. The cathedral chapter distributed 100 *livres*
in alms and agreed to give their tithe income to the poor.[153]

The harvest of 1596 was again poor. As early as September, an 'overflow'
poor house was constructed in the cemetery of Sainte-Catherine.[154] The main
problems for the municipality were lack of funds and an exhaustion of credit.
In November, Mercoeur repeated his suggestion to create a municipal granary
at an estimated cost of 30,000–40,000 *livres*, or contract provisioning to
twenty to thirty merchants, allowing them a monopoly of trade and an honest
profit. The latter option was preferred for its lower cost, but still failed because
the dealers refused to supply the grain.[155] The spring of 1597 witnessed one of
the worst subsistence crises of the century. At a general assembly of 5 March,
it was agreed to expel all paupers who came from outside the diocese but to
employ all others over the age of twelve on fortifications work. Children under
ten would be allowed to beg, and the sick were to be taken to the hospitals. In
April, commissioners were appointed on a weekly rota to distribute bread at
specific dole points. There were so many needy people that two or three people
from each quarter were delegated to help, and the bread ration was reduced to
half of a rye loaf per day.[156] On 6 May, the mayor reported that there were
2,000 paupers at each gate of the city, or 6,000 a day. Distributions continued
until the end of June. According to the accounts of Jacques Merceron, the city
spent over 28,000 *livres* on bread doles in seventy days, the equivalent of about

275,000 rations of 1 pound, or an average of about 4,000 per day. In addition, 10,500 *livres* was spent on the wages of poor people employed on fortifications work.[157] The municipality was unable to repay loans so a tax of 5,000 *écus* was agreed, and 500 *écus* imposed on the clergy.[158] The city was also greatly indebted to the administrators of the hospital, who used their own means to succour the poor. There were insufficient funds to reimburse them, so they were given *rentes* constituted on city revenues and properties.[159] The subsistence crisis of 1596–97 coincided with a severe visitation of the plague.[160] The height of the epidemic seems to have occurred in June–July 1597, when a new annexe was erected at the Hôtel-Dieu for the sick.[161] In these circumstances, the Nantais could not support a war with the crown.

The end of the League and the victory of Henry IV

The terrible hardships of the years after 1595 pushed many in Nantes to support an end to the League wars and a rapprochement with Henry IV. From December 1594, under the presidency of Henry III's widowed queen Louise, Mercoeur's sister, the duke began negotiations with the king. In 1595 the Duc de Mayenne proposed a joint truce between the remaining League chiefs and the crown, but Mercoeur refused.[162] Discussions took place over the next three years, but with little result. Grégoire commented that 'by talking constantly about peace and treaty, in consenting to truces with royalists [the duke] created hopes among moderate and exhausted men that the passions of the League had subsided'.[163] But Mercoeur, Nantes and southern Brittany persisted in resistance to the crown until March 1598.

It is not easy to explain the prolonged hostility of the Nantes city government to Henry IV. Among the city elites, there were political tensions, difficult to uncover in detail, between die-hard Leaguers and those who supported rapprochement with the king. Ostentatious political gestures in support of the League continued but became much fewer after 1594. In September 1595, a Te Deum with bonfires was celebrated for the defeat of royalist forces at the Mont-Saint-Michel, and the following June, a grand funeral was held for Charles de Gondi, Duc de Retz, who had been killed in another skirmish at the Mont.[164] There were defections to the royalist cause. As early as 26 September 1593, the preacher Mathurin Cornet wrote to Philip II of Spain that 'it is to be feared that the wishes of many turn towards the side of the heretic, being already shaken by the feeble conversion'.[165] The cathedral chapter and city clergy were among those who favoured conciliation, although they were careful in their actions. Several times in 1594, processions were held to ask for peace.[166] In October 1596, the chapter led barefoot, torch-lit procession on three successive evenings, and in the autumn of 1597, during the papal jubilee, prayers were said for peace between princes.[167] Aimer Hennequin and the *conseiller* Jacques de Boderu changed sides in April 1593; in 1595 President Dodieu stood down from parlement, and in December of that year the *conseiller* Alain de Poulpry was arrested.[168] In 1596 several of the bourgeois were associated with a project formed by Philippe Duplessis-Mornay to capture the Duc de Mercoeur, although the plot was discovered and several of the conspirators were executed.[169] The Leaguer Du Bot, elected mayor with Mercoeur's support in 1596, declared neutrality in the struggle with the crown.[170]

Nantes' persistence in rebellion was primarily a result of its domination, politically and militarily, by the Duc de Mercoeur, who resided in the city and whose garrison filled the château. The campaigns of the years 1589–93 strengthened the authority of military commanders. In Rouen, municipal government all but disappeared in these circumstances, and in Amiens the Duc de Mayenne and Duc d'Aumale rode roughshod over the city's liberties and franchises, alienating the general population and the League's supporters alike.[171] In Nantes, city government continued but Mercoeur dominated city politics. He was careful to keep the support of the municipal elites by working with and through existing institutions, controlling them through clientage and common cause, and he kept his troops outside of the city. Municipal elections were influenced to obtain mayors favourable to the duke's position: his clients Du Bot and Fourché de la Courosserie were elected in 1596 and 1597.[172] Clients were carefully cultivated. In February 1596, the son of Sieur Laubier, a former mayor, was baptised in Saint-Nicolas; the duke acted as godfather and gave his name to the baby while the godmother was the wife of his client Captain Gassion of the château.[173] The crown may have attempted to foster its own clients, to aid with the submission of many rebellious communities. Conner has shown that for the Midi, Henry IV's authority was supported by a core of local officials, which he sought to draw into his orbit, developing clientage.[174] But whatever the king's successes, the Mercoeurs were able to keep their own clients in positions of prominence in Nantes down to 1598.

The main reason for the longevity of the revolt of Nantes was the involvement of Spain in Brittany. Until the war between France and Spain was resolved in Henry IV's favour, he was unable to exert his full authority in the west.[175] In 1589, the Duc de Mercoeur appealed to Philip II for aid in men, munitions and money to support the League rebellion, in return for Spanish use of Breton ports. In 1590, Philip's secretary Maldonado made contact with Mercoeur and sent him a subsidy of 20,000 *écus*. Philip II had three aims in his support of Mercoeur. First, the duke's rebellion helped to weaken the French crown. Secondly, Philip had dynastic designs on Brittany. The king hoped to gain the throne of France for his daughter Isabella, the granddaughter of Henry II through her mother, Elizabeth de Valois, but the Salic Law blocked her candidacy. No such stumbling-block existed in Brittany, claimed by Isabella as the direct descendant of its dukes through the duchesses Anne and Claude.[176] Thirdly, there were strategic considerations. A fleet and troops based in Brittany would allow Spain to control the Bay of Biscay and entry into the English Channel, permitting ships to pass more freely between the Low Countries and Iberia. Throughout the war, an ambassador was resident at Nantes to represent Philip's interests.

In October 1590, 5,000 Spanish troops commanded by Juan d'Aquila landed at Saint-Nazaire, at the mouth of the Loire. The fleet sailed on to the mouth of the river Blavet, where a fortified base was established, while the troops marched overland via Nantes to Blain and Hennebont.[177] Spanish soldiers and money assisted Mercoeur's victory at Craon in 1592. But Spanish forces were never put at the duke's disposal; one force stayed at Blavet, and in 1594, Crozon in the far west was fortified, allowing Spanish control over entry into the port of Brest. The Nantais, whether royalist or Leaguer, were opposed to formal attachment to Spain. Pierre Biré was against the idea of a protectorate of Brittany, and at the Estates General of the League in Paris in 1593, the Breton delegation was against the candidature of the Infanta for the throne of France. [178] But good relations were maintained. The Portuguese cleric Emmanuel Lobo Danrado was given an honorary doctorate in canon law by the University of Nantes, naturalised and allowed to practise throughout Brittany.[179]

In 1594, relations between Mercoeur and Spain entered a new phase into which the city of Nantes was closely drawn. To avoid having to come to terms with Henry IV, the duke began complex negotiations with Philip II. What Mercoeur's objectives were it is difficult to say; he justified his actions by stating that Catholics could not, in good conscience, submit to Henry until he gave proof of his sincerity by the extirpation of heresy.[180] Philippe Duplessis-Mornay considered that Mercoeur hoped to secure the duchy of Brittany for himself.[181] Morice and Taillandier saw even grander designs in his actions: to be seen as the final leader to submit to a heretic king, the most zealous protector of the Catholic faith and ultimately, with the death of a childless monarch, his elected successor.[182] Later historians have seen only opportunism tempered with equivocacy. Marc Fardet argues that Mercoeur played a double game with Henry and Philip, to buy time and to find a position most advantageous to himself. This is supported by the view of the secretary of the Spanish ambassador in Nantes, who wrote to Madrid that Mercoeur 'likes to deal with others with artifice, so that he can keep an opportunity and a door open to allow himself to disengage from that which he has promised'.[183] In November, before negotiations began at Ancenis, Mercoeur asked Spain for men and money and offered to restart the war in Brittany, to consider the rights of the Infanta over the duchy and grant the Spanish a fortress in the west.[184] The following May, Mercoeur took an oath in Nantes declaring that he would not come to terms with Henry IV without the consent of Philip II, and that he recognised the rights of Isabella over Brittany. Philip promised to send forces and subsidies; Spanish troops would occupy some Breton fortresses but would uphold the liberties and privileges of the province.[185] During Henry IV's military campaign in north-east France following the Spanish seizure of Amiens, Mercoeur offered to open a second front in Brittany if he were sent 2,000 Walloon troops. Late in 1597 a Spanish fleet anchored in the Loire at Le Pellerin and a Nantes delegation went to greet the commanders.[186] By 1598, the Nantais were afraid that Mercoeur would place Spanish troops in the city, a factor which speeded their submission to Henry IV.[187]

The end of the League in Nantes came with the victory of Henry IV over the Spanish and his recapture of Amiens in 1597. Mercoeur and Brittany were not included in the settlement of Vervins. The severe treatment of Amiens by the king and the slow movement of his army towards Nantes caused panic. In January 1598, Mercoeur moved into the bishop's palace and the city prepared for a siege. Fortifications were strengthened and the *bureau de ville* imposed a tax of 2,000 *écus*. In February, Mercoeur's northern stronghold, the town of Dinan, fell to the king, and in the same month the royal court moved to Angers.[188] Mercoeur and Nantes capitulated. On 4 February a general assembly named deputies to meet with the king. The assembly resolved that His Majesty (the title was used for the first time in Nantes for Henry IV) should be asked in the name of the inhabitants to maintain Mercoeur in his governorship, to allow only the Roman Catholic religion in the city and county and to prohibit the practice of the Reformed religion to people of every status. They also asked that the king confirm the privileges of the clergy, city and Chambre des Comptes.[189]

The conditions of the Duc de Mercoeur's surrender, negotiated largely by Madame, were generous, as was usual with Henry IV. The duke was granted 16,666 *écus* for war expenses from taxation levied in Brittany and 50,000 *écus* to distribute among his captains and supporters. The city of Nantes was to pay his outstanding costs, and he was allowed to keep a company of 100 men at arms.[190] But the duke was deprived of his governorship, which passed to the king's natural son, César, Duc de Vendôme, who was to marry the Mercoeurs' daughter and heir. Mercoeur was to surrender all the towns that he controlled to the king.[191] For Nantes, the terms were also generous. The Reformed religion was not to be exercised within three leagues of the city. Clergy and office holders appointed during the League were to be confirmed in their posts, there was an attempt to amalgamate League and royalist institutions, and judgements made against Leaguers were to be annulled. But all the war debts contracted by Mercoeur would be repaid by the city, a punishment for long-term rebellion. On 4 April the Duc de Retz took possession of the château for the king and administered the oath of obedience to the municipality. On 13 April the king entered the city. The French religious wars ended where they had begun, in Nantes.[192] Royal authority over the city was once more restored.

NOTES

1 *Remonstrances aux habitants de Nantes Par un des Citoyens dicelle: Par où se void les practiques et menées dont a usé le duc de Mercoeur pour usurper le Duché de Bretaigne* (Rennes, 1590), published in *Revue de Bretagne et du Vendée*, 27 (1883) 472.

2 L. Grégoire, *La Ligue en Bretagne* (Paris and Nantes, 1856), pp. ix–xvi.

3 Travers, III, p. 22; C. Laronze, *Essai sur le régime municipale en Bretagne pendant les guerres de religion* (1890), p. 6; B. Pocquet, *Histoire de Bretagne*, V: *1515–1715* (Rennes, 1913; reprint Mayenne 1975); H. Le Goff, *La Ligue en Basse-Bretagne 1588–98* (Ploufragan, 1994), p. 258.

4 Laronze, *Essai sur le régime municipale*, pp. 200, 253.

5 Pocquet, *Histoire de Bretagne*, V, pp. 106, 118–19.

6 Work on Grenoble also shows the hesitation of the bourgeoisie before opting to join the Catholic League. See, for example, S. Gal, 'Peurs urbaines et engagements politico-religieux au XVIème siècle. L'exemple de la ligue grenobloise', *Histoire économie et société*, 20 (2001) 3–21.

7 H. Drouot, *Mayenne et la Bourgogne. Étude sur la Ligue (1587–96), 2 vols (Dijon, 1937). An issue of *French History* has been devoted to discussion of the League and the *bourgeoisie seconde*. See *French History*, 17/4 (2004).

8 E. Barnavi, *Le parti de Dieu. Étude sociale et politique des chefs de la Ligue parisienne. 1585–1594* (Louvain, 1980); D. Richet, 'Aspects socio-culturels des conflits religieux à Paris dans la seconde moitié du XVIème siècle', *A.E.S.C.*, 32 (1977) 764–89.

9 J. Salmon, 'The Paris Sixteen, 1584–1594. The social analysis of a revolutionary movement', *J.M.H.,* 44 (1972) 540–76; R. Descimon, *Qui étaient les Seize? Mythes et réalités de la ligue parisienne (1585–94)* (1983).

10 P. Benedict, *Rouen during the Wars of Religion* (Cambridge, 1981), chapters 7–9; S. Kettering, 'Political parties at Aix-en-Provence in 1589', *European History Quarterly*, 24 (1994) 181–211; P. Roberts, *A City in Conflict. Troyes during the French Wars of Religion* (Manchester, 1996), chapter 8.

11 Roberts, *A City in Conflict*, p. 176.

12 Benedict, *Rouen*, p. 182.

13 P. Ascoli, 'A radical pamphlet of late sixteenth-century France. Le Dialogue D'Entre Le Maheustre et Le Manant', *S.C.J*, 5 (1974) 3–22; R. Harding, 'Revolution and reform in the Holy League. Angers, Rennes, Nantes', *J.M.H.*, 53 (1981) 414–16.

14 G. Saupin, *Nantes au temps de l'édit* (La Crèche, 1998), p. 200.

15 Saupin, *Nantes au temps de l'édit*, p. 160.

16 A.M.N. BB 21: Délibérations et assemblées de la municipalité 1588–89, fo. 217r–v; Grégoire, *La Ligue*, pp. 60–1.

17 Harding, 'Revolution and reform', p. 395.

18 A.M.N. BB 21, fos 177r–178v, 217r–218r.

19 E. Tingle, 'Nantes and the causes of the Catholic League 1580–89', *S.C.J.*, 33, (2002) 109–28.

20 F. Joüon des Longrais, ed., 'Information du sénéchal de Rennes contre les ligueurs 1589', *B.S.A.I.V.*, 41/1 (1911) 148; 41/2 (1912) 216–18.

21 Saupin, *Nantes au temps de l'Édit*, pp. 170–71; G. Saupin, *Nantes au XVIIème siècle. Vie politique et société urbaine* (Rennes, 1996), p. 256.

22 Harding, 'Revolution and reform', pp. 386–8.

23 Details of officers come from Saupin, *Nantes au temps de l'édit*, pp. 175–9.

24 J. Collins, *Classes, Estates and Order in Early Modern Brittany* (Cambridge, 1994), p. 129.

25 Prosopographical details on Nantes families are from Saupin, *Nantes au temps de l'édit*, p. 179.

26 Collins, *Classes, Estates and Order*, p. 129; Saupin, *Nantes au XVIIème siècle*, p. 256.

27 H. Lapeyre, *Une famille des marchands. Les Ruiz* (1955), p. 89.

28 See Bibliothèque Nationale, Paris, Nouvelles acquisitions françaises 21,878: Account of Duc de Mercoeur's treasurer, 1585.

29 Longrais, ed., 'Information du sénéchal de Rennes', p. 149.

30 Saupin, *Nantes au temps de l'édit*, p. 173.

31 Harding, 'Revolution and reform', p. 397.

32 Descimon, *Qui étaient les Seize?*, p. 89; supported by D. Crouzet, *Les guerriers de Dieu. La violence au temps des troubles de religion (c.1525–1610)*, 2 vols (1990).

33 M. Holt, *The French Wars of Religion 1562–1629* (Cambridge, 1995), p. 150.

34 Descimon, *Qui étaient les Seize?*, p. 68.

35 R. Bonney, *The King's Debts, Finance and Politics in France 1589–1661* (Oxford, 1981), p. 40.

36 F. Baumgartner, *Radical Reactionaries. The Political Thought of the French Catholic League* (Geneva, 1975), p. 79.

37 B. Chevalier, *Les bonnes villes de France du XIVème au XVIème siècle* (1982); Descimon, *Qui étaient les Seize?*

38 Descimon, *Qui étaient les Seize?*, pp. 281, 296.

39 M.-L. Pelus-Kaplan, 'Amiens, ville ligueuse. Le sens d'une rébellion', *Revue du Nord*, 78 (1996) 296.

40 Pelus-Kaplan, 'Amiens, ville ligueuse', p. 299.

41 Harding, 'Revolution and reform', p. 399.

42 *Remonstrances aux habitants de Nantes Par un des Citoyens dicelle*, 473–4.

43 J. Le Bossu, *Sermon funèbre pour l'anniversaire des Très-Illustres, Très-Magnanimes & très-Catholiques Princes feus Messeigneurs Henry & Loys de Lorraine, celuy-là le duc de Guyse et cestuy-ci Cardinal de Guyse* (Nantes, 1590).

44 J. Le Bossu, *Deux Devis d'un Catholique et d'un Politique sur l'exhortation faicte au peuple de Nantes, en la grande église de Sainct-Pierre, pour jurer l'Union des catholiques, le 8e jour de juin 1589* (Nantes, 1589), p. 22.

45 Le Bossu, *Deux Devis*, p. 131.

46 Le Bossu, *Deux Devis*, p. 81.

47 J. Le Bossu, *Troisième devis du Catholique et du Politique qui a esté réuny sur la mort de Henry de Valois, selon ce qu'en a esté presché à diverses fois en la grande église de Nantes* (Nantes, 1589), pp. 48, 66; J. Le Bossu, *Quatrième devis du Catholique et du Politique réuny, sur l'exemple de Nabu-chodonosor, rapporté en l'église de Nantes, en un sermon, le dimanche 18e jour de novembre 1590* (Nantes, 1590), p. 41; J. Le Bossu, *Sermon Funèbre pour la mémoire de dévote & religieuse personne F. Edmond Bourgoing qui fut cruellement martyrisé à Tours par le supplice de quatre chevaux le 23 de février 1590* (Nantes, 1590).

48 Harding, 'Revolution and reform', p. 382.

49 J. de Moranne, *Les causes qui ont contrainct les Catholiques à prendre les armes* (no publication details, 1589), pp. 4–5, 10–14.

50 Le Bossu, *Deux Devis*, pp. 131–2.

51 P. Biré, *Alliances Généalogicques de la Maison de Lorraine illustrées des faites et gestes des princes d'icelles* (Nantes, 1593).

52 Adherence to Catholicism in Burgundy was an important element of provincial identity and a cause of League rebellion against the crown. Rather than a separatist agenda, the re-Catholicisation of the French state as a whole was one of the objectives of revolt. See M. Holt, 'Burgundians into Frenchmen. Catholic identity in sixteenth-century Burgundy', in M. Wolfe, ed., *Changing Identities in Early Modern France* (Durham, NC, 1997), pp. 345–70.

53 Quoted in A. Croix, *L'âge d'or de la Bretagne 1532–1675* (Rennes, 1993), p. 60.

54 Saupin, *Nantes au temps de l'édit*, p. 205.

55 A comparison of aristocratic involvement in a city League is S. Carroll, 'The Revolt of Paris 1588. Aristocratic insurgency and the mobilisation of popular support', *F.H.S.*, 23 (2000) 301–38; see also J.-M. Le Gall, 'Les Guises et Paris sous la Ligue 1588–90', *F.H.S.*, 24 (2001) 157–84.

56 C. de Rosnyvinen, 'Histoire particulière de la Ligue en Bretagne', in Abbé Guyot-Desfontaines, ed., *Histoire des Ducs de Bretagne*, III (1739), pp. i-ii, 98.

57 Quoted in Le Goff, *La Ligue en Basse-Bretagne*, p. 234.

58 Grégoire, *La Ligue*, p. 202.

59 Travers, III, p. 72.

60 Biré, *Alliances Généalocgiques*, pp. 246, 273.

61 F. Joüon des Longrais, 'Le Duc de Mercoeur, d'après des documents inédits', *B.A.A.B.* 13 (1895), 289.

62 Grégoire, *La Ligue*, pp. 56–7.

63 B.N.F.F. 18,704: Conduite de Mercoeur pendant la Ligue; Saupin, *Nantes au temps de l'édit*, p. 194.

64 M. Fardet, 'La vie municipale à Nantes sous le gouvernement du duc de Mercoeur. Le rôle militaire joué par cette ville (1582–1598)' Thèse, École des Chartres, Paris, 1965, p. 193.

65 Travers, III, p. 21; Morice & Taillandier, II, p. 369. See also, for a general history of the League, B.N.F.F. 23295–6: Histoire de la Ligue.

66 A.M.N. BB 21, fos 217r–218r and passim.

67 Travers, III, p. 22.

68 J. Salmon, *Society in Crisis. France in the Sixteenth Century* (London, 1976, pbk 1979), pp. 252–3; The *conseil de l'Union* of Nantes was similar to that of Lyon, where the *conseil* also originated as a partisan alternative to the traditional municipal government. In Lyon the *conseil de l'Union* seems to have merged into the governor's *conseil d'état*, whereas the two institutions remained separate in Nantes. See R. Harding, *Anatomy of a Power Elite. The Provincial Governors of Early Modern France* (New Haven and London, 1978), p. 92.

69 Travers, III, p. 23.

70 Travers, III, p. 22–4.

71 S. Carroll, 'The Guise affinity and popular protest during the wars of religion', *F.H.*, 9 (1995) 128–9.

72 Rosnyvinen, 'Histoire particulière de la Ligue', p. 135.

73 Joüon des Longrais, 'Le duc de Mercoeur', p. 256.

74 Pelus-Kaplan, 'Amiens, ville ligueuse', p. 297.

75 Saupin, *Nantes au temps de l'édit*, p. 141.

76 A.M.N. CC 132: Compte d'un emprunt fait pour l'entretien des gens de guerre 1589–90.

77 Saupin, *Nantes au temps de l'édit*, p. 179.

78 Travers, III, p. 35.

79 Joüon des Longrais, 'Le duc de Mercoeur', 254–5; see also C.-A. Cardot, 'Le parlement de la Ligue en Bretagne, 1589–98', 3 vols, Thèse de Droit, University of Rennes, 1964, a detailed study of the parlement during these years.

80 Pocquet, *Histoire de Bretagne V*, p. 238.

81 Pocquet, *Histoire de Bretagne V*, p. 187.

82 Croix, *L'âge d'or*, p. 53.

83 Saupin, *Nantes au temps de l'édit*, p. 181.

84 Travers, III, p. 37.

85 Harding, *Anatomy of a Power Elite*, p. 98.

86 Saupin, *Nantes au temps de l'édit*, p. 196.

87 Travers, III, pp. 57–8.

88 Travers, III, p. 77.

89 Travers, III, p. 29.

90 Travers, III, pp. 61–2.

91 A.M.N. EE 214: Ligue 1586–1606.

92 S. A. Finley-Croswhite, *Henry IV and the Towns. The Pursuit of Legitimacy in French Urban Society, 1589–1610* (Cambridge, 1999), p. 1.

93 Roberts notes for Troyes that the role of the League council was predominantly military. See Roberts, *A City in Conflict*, p. 177.

94 Morice & Taillandier, II, p. 378.

95 Croix, *L'âge d'or*, p. 53.

96 Travers, III, pp. 26, 41.

97 Grégoire, *La Ligue*, p. 118.

98 Travers, III, p. 53.

99 A.M.N. CC 138: Dépense pour le compte de Mercoeur du siege de Blain 1591–95; Fardet, 'La vie municipale', p. 223.

100 V. Audren de Kerdrel, 'Documents inédits relatifs à l'histoire de la Ligue en Bretagne', B.S.A.I.V., 2 (1861) 236.

101 Travers, III, p. 34.

102 Fardet, 'La vie municipale', p. 212,

103 Saupin, *Nantes au temps de l'édit*, p. 150.

104 Saupin, *Nantes au temps de l'édit*, p. 143.

105 Travers, III, p. 40.

106 Travers, III, p. 43.

107 Travers, III, p. 35.

108 Travers, III, p. 25.

109 A.M.N. CC 132; Grégoire, *La Ligue*, p. 37.

110 A.M.N. EE 211: Ligue 1585–89.

111 A.M.N. BB 21, fos 234r–235v; Travers, III, p. 27; Fardet, 'La vie municipale', p. 81.

112 Travers, III, p. 43; Fardet, 'La vie municipale', p. 95.

113 A.M.N. EE 211.

114 A.M.N. EE 212: Ligue 1590–91.

115 A.M.N. EE 211.

116 A.M.N. CC 137: Compte de Maître Guillaume Rousseau 1589–93.

117 Fardet, 'La vie municipale', p. 96; Travers, III, p. 64.

118 A.M.N. CC 138: Dépense pour le compte de Mercoeur du siege de Blain 1591–95.

119 Grégoire, *La Ligue*, p. 276.

120 A.M.N. CC 86: Impôts 1592–1600.

121 M. Fardet, 'Nantes au temps de la Ligue. La lutte contre les Protestants au sud de la Loire sous le governement du duc de Mercoeur (1582–1598)', *Revue du Bas Poitou et des provinces de l'Ouest*, 1–2 (1969) 125.

122 A.M.N. EE 213: Ligue 1595.

123 Benedict, *Rouen*, p. 187.

124 Holt, *French Wars of Religion*, p. 150.

125 Travers, III, pp. 74–5.

126 Cardot, 'Le parlement de la ligue', I, pp 614–20; Travers, III, pp. 74–5.

127 Benedict, *Rouen*, pp. 189–91.

128 Travers, III, pp. 38, 46.

129 Travers, III, p. 53.

130 Travers, III, p. 68.

131 Travers, III, p. 33.

132 Fardet, 'La vie municipale', p. 182.

133 Travers, III, p. 54.

134 Biré, *Alliances Généalogicques*, p. 247.

135 A.D.L.A. G 521: Fabrique de Saint-Vincent.

136 Grégoire, *La Ligue*, p. 201.

137 A.M.N. BB 21, fo. 301v; Travers, III, pp. 24, 27.

138 Fardet, 'La vie municipale', pp. 190–91.

139 Travers, III, p. 39.
140 Travers, III, p. 35.
141 Travers, III, p. 64.
142 Travers, III, pp. 49–50.
143 Grégoire, *La Ligue*, pp. 93–4.
144 A detailed study of Henry's conversion and its political aftermath is found in M. Wolfe, *The Conversion of Henri IV* (Cambridge, MA, 1993).
145 Finley-Croswhite, *Henry IV and the Towns*, p. 22.
146 Joüon des Longrais, 'Le Duc de Mercoeur', p. 277.
147 Travers, III, p. 88.
148 Saupin, *Nantes au temps de l'édit*, pp. 153–54.
149 Lapeyre, *Une famille des marchands*, p. 432.
150 Grégoire, *La Ligue*, p. 285; Chevalier, *Les bonnes villes*, 111.
151 Benedict, *Rouen*, pp. 223–5; the militia survey of 1592 revealed that many properties of the city were empty, their residents having fled or simply left town. See A.M.N. EE 30.
152 Travers, III, p. 79.
153 Travers, III, pp. 81, 85.
154 Travers, III, p. 87.
155 A.M.N. BB 22 Délibérations et assemblées de la municipalité 1596–98, fos 55v–57v, 60r–61v; A. Croix, *La Bretagne aux XVIème et XVIIème siècles. La vie – la mort – la foi*, 2 vols (1981), I, p. 416.
156 Fardet, 'L'assistance aux pauvres à Nantes à la fin du XVIème siècle (1582–1598)', *Actes du 98ème congrès national des sociétes savants, Nantes 1972*, Section Philologie et Histoire (1973)', pp. 404, 408.
157 Croix, *La Bretagne*, I, pp. 442, 447.
158 Travers, III, p. 90.
159 Fardet, 'L'assistance aux pauvres', pp. 424–5.
160 Croix, *La Bretagne*, I, p. 271.
161 Fardet, 'L'assistance aux pauvres', p. 408.
162 Morice & Taillandier, II, p. 451.
163 Grégoire, *La Ligue*, p. 339.
164 Travers, III, pp. 79, 86.
165 Saupin, *Nantes au temps de l'Édit*, p. 155.
166 Jouan des Longrais, 'Le Duc de Mercoeur', p. 281.
167 Travers, III, pp. 93–4.
168 Grégoire, *La Ligue*, p. 275; Saupin, *Nantes au temps de l'Édit*, p. 179.
169 Grégoire, *La Ligue*, p. 306.
170 Saupin, *Nantes au temps de l'Édit*, p. 196.
171 Benedict, *Rouen*, pp. 215, 217; Finley-Croswhite, *Henry IV and the Towns*, p. 37.
172 Grégoire, *La Ligue*, p. 306.
173 Travers, III, pp. 82–3.
174 P. Conner, 'Huguenot Heartland. Montauban during the Wars of Religion', PhD thesis, University of St Andrews, 2000, pp. 192, 197.
175 Saupin, *Nantes au temps de l'édit*, p. 156.
176 G. de Carné, *Correspondance du duc de Mercoeur et des ligueurs Bretons avec l'Espagne*, 2 vols (Rennes, 1890), I, p. vii.
177 Grégoire, *La Ligue*, p. 315.
178 Saupin, *Nantes au temps de l'édit*, p. 156.
179 Travers, III, p. 52.
180 Morice & Taillandier, II, p. 455.
181 Grégoire, *La Ligue*, p. 355.
182 Morice & Taillandier, II, p. 451.
183 De Carné, *Correspondance du duc de Mercoeur*, I, p. xxxii.

184 De Carné, *Correspondance du duc de Mercoeur*, I, p. xxxi; Travers, III, p. 77.
185 De Carné, *Correspondance du duc de Mercoeur*, I, pp. xxxvi–xxxvii.
186 Saupin, *Nantes au temps de l'édit*, pp. 156, 159.
187 Grégoire, *La Ligue*, p. 302.
188 Pocquet, *Histoire de Bretagne*, V, p. 323.
189 A.M.N. BB 22: fo. 7r–v.
190 Grégoire, *La Ligue*, p. 359.
191 Morice & Taillandier, II, pp. 476–8.
192 Eudes de Mezeray, quoted in J. H. M. Salmon, 'Opposition to the Edict of Nantes', in R. Goodbar, ed., *The Edict of Nantes. Five Essays and a New Translation* (Bloomington, MN, 1998), p. 19.

8

Conclusions: authority and society in Nantes during the religious wars

On 30 April 1598 the last edict of pacification of the wars of religion was issued in the château of Nantes.[1] The municipality had little part in its creation.[2] Of greater concern to the city's elite was Henry IV's order for new elections to the *bureau de ville*, to take place on 1 May. The king dissolved the privilege that allowed Nantes to elect its own mayor and *échevins*. Instead, three candidates for mayor and eighteen for the *échevinage* were to be presented to the king, who would choose the officers for the posts. In 1598 Henry chose Charles de Harouys, president of the *présidial* court and the mayor who had been deposed by Madame de Mercoeur in 1589. Nine out of twelve militia captains were replaced and new porters were appointed to the city's gates, in spite of protests. In 1600 the king selected as mayor Gabriel Hus, who was treasurer of the estates of Brittany and another enemy of the Catholic League, in spite of the general assembly's lack of support for his candidacy.[3]

During the first half of the twentieth century, historians interpreted Henry IV's actions as part of a policy of rebuilding royal authority over the French state in a more 'absolute' monarchy. He aimed to destroy municipal privileges as a punishment for rebellion against the crown, and to weaken the authority of the towns. More recently, a view has emerged that Henry's interference was sporadic and that much local autonomy remained.[4] As Robert Knecht has commented, the wars revealed the weakness of a monarchy which depended for its authority on the person of the ruler and the degree of support he had from the more powerful subjects.[5] This remained true after 1598. Even after capitulation to Henry, towns resisted 'any blatant move towards more authoritative rule [on the part of Henry IV] while . . . depending on him to act as a problem solver'.[6] Annette Finley-Croswhite argues that the king's actions in Nantes, and other cities, were rather to restore stability after years of conflict and war. In exchange for peace, Henry confirmed town charters and extended patronage to their elites. This underscored his policy of conciliation, reopened the dialogue between crown and the towns and enhanced royal authority in the process.[7]

But the wars of religion were not simply a time when central authority weakened and failed, to be rebuilt by the Bourbon monarchy. This was a period when the relationship between crown and local authorities underwent dynamic change, as both parties sought practical solutions for difficult problems.[8] This study of Nantes has shown the inter-dependency of royal and local authority for effective government at the city level. Authority was not the sole preserve of the crown. It was shared, ideologically and on the ground, by a wide range of institutions and social groups. During the 1550s the crown increased its authority within Nantes with a reform of justice, increased supervision of the city's military affairs, appointment of greater numbers of officers and more taxation. But the extent of control should not be exaggerated, for city governance remained the preserve of local institutions, regulated by law, custom and privilege. Nor should local resistance be over-estimated. City administration was heavily dependent upon royal authority to legitimise and support its actions. The crown gave the lead in policy, particularly where religious, military and judicial affairs, areas of the king's prerogative, were concerned. When sedition and heresy appeared publicly in Nantes from 1560, the municipal elites looked to the crown for guidance and assistance. These were not forthcoming. Protestantism was never a large movement in Nantes, but it did comprise perhaps 7 per cent of the urban population at its height. Adherents were visible, provoked sectarian passions and thus posed a challenge to urban government. The royal policy of conciliation and toleration of Protestantism did not solve the problems of governance in Nantes. Rather, it jeopardised the crown's legitimacy, for the contract that bound king to subjects required that he eliminate heresy and uphold the Catholic Church. Royal vacillation and indecision also made practical governance in the city more difficult. The result was irresolute government and outbursts of religious passions that went unpunished. A vacuum of authority appeared at city level. France descended into civil war as rival confessions attempted to resolve the religious issue by force.

The first civil war can be seen as a watershed in crown–city relations. It had an immediate and important impact upon conceptions and exercise of authority. Both the crown and the *conseil des bourgeois* of Nantes were determined to rebuild practical authority and good governance. The crown pursued two principal courses of action with regard to urban communities. Conflict was directed away from violence into the arena of law and justice. A second policy was to improve security in the cities of the kingdom and to prevent disorder on the streets through enhanced police. The edict of Amboise of 1563, enforced carefully by the royal government and its commissioners, and the reforming edict of Moulins of 1566 are examples of attempts to augment crown authority through the exercise of its traditional prerogatives of law and justice. In Nantes itself, conflict and war had shown the bourgeois just how vulnerable the town was to disorder and to the orders of military commanders, who usurped urban privileges. The *conseil des bourgeois* sought urgently to augment its powers to prevent such events from happening again. The result of the coincidence of interest between crown and city was the creation of a municipality in 1565, with its own police authority over defence, social policy and economic affairs. Almost immediately, police in the city was reinforced and expanded with the creation of a permanent bourgeois militia, reform of poor relief and closer supervision of provisioning and economic production. The crown supported the municipality's authority by providing sovereign legitimacy for its actions, and asserted its authority over city institutions by arbitrating disputes between them. In return for this devolution of authority, or at least a rearrangement of responsibilities between jurisdictions, the city was better administered. The wars of 1567–70 and of the early 1570s disturbed the relationship of city and crown and made practical city governance more difficult, but there was little disorder in Nantes. The city remained firmly loyal to the crown to the end of Charles IX's reign.

Royal authority had to be exercised within the agreed constitutional constraints of law and contract, mediated through the upholding of the privileges of cities and provinces. After 1574, the crown began to undermine its own position in Nantes though frequent intervention in fiscal affairs, in contravention of contemporary views of the just extent of royal power. Until 1584 the authority of the crown did not undergo any demise. The crown remained the source of municipal authority. The king arbitrated authoritatively in internal city disputes and passed edicts for the better ordering of urban government, particularly with regard to municipal police jurisdiction and the city's military affairs. But in the mid-1570s a serious dispute arose between Henry III, the city and the Breton estates, over taxation and the sale of offices. The main cause of this was seen to be the crown's over-assertion of its authority, the overstepping of traditional limits of power, at the expense of the legal privileges of town and province, enshrined in the contract of Union of 1532. The same constitutional dispute arose again in the mid-1580s. This time, the issues were compounded by war, economic dislocation and growing concerns over religion. Discontent with the monarchy grew, and in April 1589 Nantes rebelled against Henry, to force him to return to the traditional governance of shared authority based on custom and contract.

Throughout the religious wars, the stability of urban governance in Nantes is striking. This arose from the shared nature of authority, which was widely disseminated among many different groups in the city. Urban government was not simply a system of regulation imposed from above. While participation in the municipality itself was the preserve of the wealthy elite, this was a relatively open group. Further, all householders could take part in the general assemblies of the city, as witnesses to communal decision-making, giving a wide sense of involvement in urban affairs. Parishes, through their churchwardens and other officers, had long been responsible for the collection of taxes, poor rates and distribution of alms; after 1569, parish officers played an enhanced role in identifying, registering, supervising and relieving the domiciled poor among their community. The day-to-day administration of the city's hospitals was largely in the hands of men of the middling sort. The bourgeois militia was another important vehicle through which authority was disseminated downwards through the community. In the 1560s and particularly the 1580s, the militia's captains and especially its officers, who were drawn from artisans and small traders, played an enhanced role in surveillance of the population and the maintenance of order. Finally, the period after 1565 saw the creation of several craft guilds, the most important of which were those of the bakers and the butchers. Police of these trades was devolved down to the masters themselves; in return for greater control of their trade they gained heavier responsibility for its good order, for which they were accountable to the municipality. The result of a wide diffusion of authority among the artisans and middling men of Nantes was greater integration of these groups into civic governance. Large numbers of ordinary citizens had experience of practical authority. A wide participatory public gave greater numbers of residents a stake in the commonwealth of the city and in the maintenance of order, stability and hierarchy. Thus the community was able to weather the vicissitudes of civil war.

Further, the social welfare policies of the city government legitimised its actions and enhanced its authority over the labouring population. Above all, there was a strong moral underpinning to the relationship between elites and ordinary citizens. A rhetoric of obedience and common values of Christian charity and civic responsibility created bonds of interest between municipal leaders and all social groups. This increased with the growth of Catholic reformism in the later sixteenth century, with its strong emphasis on moral discipline and the spiritual value of good works. Thus adequate provisioning of foodstuffs, relief of the poor and care of the sick were essential in forging bonds between the city's governors and popular groups.[9] The measures taken were regulatory and disciplinary; they 'enhanced [the] municipal authority's knowledge about, access to and control over a large amount of the urban population . . . [and] hampered mobilisation prompted by deprivation'.[10] But public acts of regulating food supply and assisting the poor and hungry were also important legitimising acts of paternalist authority. Robert Duplessis and Martha Howell have argued that city governments subscribed to an ethic which judged matters by their effects on the entire republic regardless even of the interests of the dominant class, where restrictions on the ambitions of some individuals were justified in terms of the benefits accruing to the greater community.[11] This was not just the action of a self-interested elite but was shared by all groups. Social welfare 'curbed the potentially destabilising influence of either a polarised class structure or intractable material griev-ances', but it also reflected a dominant discourse of the 'commonweal'.[12] The League coup of April 1589 occurred in a context of immiseration, a decade of famine, disease, war and poverty, increasingly attributed to the religious and secular ills of royal government. Widespread support for the League rebellion must also be seen in a context of increased municipal authority within the city and a heightened popular conscience of collective necessity, forged in the years of adversity after 1580.

Bernard Chevalier and Robert Descimon have argued that in the later wars of religion there was a resurgence of independence in the cities of France, an attempt to remake the semi-autonomous medieval commune. Breton histo-rians have argued this case particularly strongly, seeing the Catholic League in particular as a last-ditch attempt to recreate ducal sovereignty in the region, with Nantes as the duchy's capital. But there is little evidence for this from the municipality itself. There was enduring respect for royal authority, which was the essential prop for urban government. Disputes with the crown, including the League revolt, were about the just limits of power on both sides, not about the reduction of royal authority or the assertion of regional or urban rule. Michael Wolfe argues that the crises of the 1580s and 1590s were not the result of a desire for greater independence from the crown, but rather 'reconfirmed the integral relationship between king and community', for autonomy meant 'anarchy, not civic renewal'.[13] The aim of the city's elites was to return consti-tutional relations to their traditional order, where the rights and privileges of each group were respected. As a result of the wars, after 1598, as Guy Saupin comments, Nantes' municipal elites were only too aware that they had imper-iled their urban privileges in rebellion and that the best way of safeguarding the city's franchises was to tie its fate to that of the restored monarchy.[14] The result was 'the forging of a new sense of identity and purpose among Catholic elites, which made possible the later growth of Bourbon absolutism'.[15] In Nantes, a Catholicism 'pur et dur' and an ostentatious loyalty to the crown were the best means of safeguarding the city's future and the pre-eminence of the elites within it. This was less of a defeat of the city than a restitution of traditional ideologies and practices. The authority of crown and city together was restored.

NOTES
1   Travers, III, p. 111. There is dispute over whether the date of the edict was 13 or 30 April. Travers opted for 30 April, as Henry only entered the city on 13 April.

2   Brittany was one of the last provinces to accept the edict, which was formally registered in
     the Rennes parlement only in August 1600. Royal commissioners visited Nantes in 1601 to
     enforce the statute, securing a site for worship at Sucé-sur-Erdre and a cemetery for the
     Huguenots in the suburb of Saint-Clément. See R. Joxe, *Les protestants du comté de Nantes
     XVIème–XVIIème siècles* (Marseille, 1982), pp. 234–6.

3   Travers, III, pp. 106–7, 111; also discussed in S. A. Finley-Croswhite, *Henry IV and the
     Towns. The Pursuit of Legitimacy in French Urban Society, 1589–1610* (Cambridge, 1999),
     pp. 6–7.

4   See Finley-Croswhite, *Henry IV and the Towns*, p. 6.

5   R. Knecht, *The French Civil Wars* (London, 2000), p. 295.

6   Finley-Croswhite, *Henry IV and the Towns*, p. 182.

7   Finley-Croswhite, *Henry IV and the Towns*, pp. 63, 183, 185.

8   L. Bourquin, *Les nobles, la ville et le roi. L'autorité nobiliaire en Anjou pendant les guerres de
     religion (1560–1598)* (2001), p. 236.

9   M. Prak, 'The carrot and the stick. Social control and poor relief in the Dutch Republic,
     sixteenth to eighteenth centuries', in H. Schilling, ed., *Institutions, Instruments and Agents of
     Social Control and Discipline in Early Modern Europe* (Frankfurt am Main, 1999), p. 165.

10 R. Duplessis, *Lille and the Dutch Revolt. Urban Stability in an Era of Revolution 1500–1582*
     (Cambridge, 1991), p. 156.

11 R. Duplessis and M. Howell, 'Reconsidering the early modern urban economy. The cases
     of Leiden and Lille', *Past & Present*, 94 (1982) 80.

12 Duplessis, *Lille*, p. 309.

13 M. Wolfe, *The Conversion of Henri IV* (Cambridge, MA, 1993), p. 188.

14 G. Saupin, *Nantes au XVIIème siècle. Vie politique et société urbaine* (Rennes, 1996), pp. 255–6.

15 Wolfe, *The Conversion of Henri IV*, p. 189.

Select bibliography

Manuscript sources

Paris: Bibliothèque Nationale

Cinq Cents Colbert. MSS 41, 491.
Fonds français. MSS 1,4399, 1,8704.
Manuscripts Dupuy. MSS 233, 848.
Nouvelles acquisitions françaises. MS 2,1878.

Nantes: Archives Départementales de la Loire-Atlantique

Series E: 4E, notaires, 1/46 (Le Moyne); 2/90 (Le Feigneux); 2/300 (J. Bodin); 2/487 (Charier); 2/1389 (Lemoine); 2/1390 (Th. Lemoine); 2/1684 (Quenille).
Series G: 94 (cathedral chapter); 144–169, 171–184 (obit foundations, cathedral); 309–332 (parish of Notre-Dame); 421–479 (parish of Sainte-Croix); 480 (parish of Saint-Denis); 482 (parish of Saint-Jean); 483–485 (parish of Saint-Laurent); 486 (parish of Saint-Léonard); 487–488 (parish of Saint-Nicolas); 491–492 (parish of Sainte-Radegonde); 493–497 (parish of Saint-Saturnin); 498–499, 500–501, 506–511, 516 (parish of Saint-Saturnin); 517 (parish of Saint-Similien); 521–522, 526–527 (parish of Saint-Vincent).
Series H: 223–226, 233–238, 240–243, 246–249 (Carmelites); 250–256, 264–265, 269–273 (Carthusians); 283–285, 289 (Franciscans); 299–309 (Dominicans); 332–333 (Capuchins); 425 (Clares); 472 (confraternity of Saint-John); 482 (Saint-Lazare); 493–495 (Aumônerie de Toussaint); 496 (Hôtel-Dieu).

Nantes: Archives Municipales

Series AA: 3 (Mandements du roi et privilèges de la ville 1560); 4–5 (royal letters); 6 (Duc de Mercoeur 1593); 21, 23 (taxation 1553–81); 24 (royal correspondence); 33–34 (royal entries); 42, 45 (entries of royal governors); 60–68 (correspondence with deputies at court); 77 (remonstrances).

Series BB: 4–22 (deliberations of the town council 1555–98).

Series CC: 71–76, 86 (taxation); 77–80 (reclamations and remonstrances); 84–86 (military taxation); 119–131 (accounts of the *miseurs* of Nantes); 132–148 (league war expenditure); 341–345 (fortifications of Marchix/Villeneuve); 346 (entry of Henry IV).

Series DD: 61 (militia); 324 (repurgation).

Series EE: 23, 198 (château garrison); 29 (watch and guard); 30–34 (militia surveys and company rolls); 36–38, 60 (militia and guard duty); 150 (fortifications of Marchix/Villeneuve); 193–207, 265 (religious wars); 210–214 (Catholic League); 217 (piracy); 221 (outfitting ships).

Series FF: 50, 52–56, 110 (police); 148, 150, 152, 154 (police of bread and bakery); 174, 176, 180 (police of grain commerce); 186–187 (provisioning during the religious wars); 280 (expulsion of poor); 285 (police of religion).

Series GG: 1 (parish register of Notre-Dame); 13–16 (parish register of Saint-Clément); 44–47 (parish register of Saint-Denis); 137–138 (parish register of Saint-Laurent); 151 (parish register of Saint-Léonard); 172–178 (parish register of Saint-Nicolas); 295–299 (parish register of Saint-Saturnin); 330–333 (parish register of Saint-Similien); 395–396 (parish register of Saint-Vincent); 416–418 (parish register of Sainte-Croix); 594 (processions); 613–615 (confraternities); 463 (religion); 642–645 (Reformed religion); 682 (*aumônerie* of Saint-Clément); 688 (*aumônerie* of Toussaints); 691–703, 722 (Hôtel-Dieu); 726 (alms, collections and taxes); 731 (lists of paupers at Hôtel-Dieu); 743–744 (poor relief); 768–770 (epidemics).

Series HH: 1 (grain prices); 17 (police regulations); 153 (guild of plumbers and glaziers); 188 (commerce with Spain); 493, 495 (*aumônerie* of Toussaints).

Series II: 5–6 (translation of the parlement to Rennes); 7 (League parlement).

Bibliothèque Municipale de Nantes

Collection générale:

MS 119 Entrée du duc de Mercoeur dans la ville de Nantes.

MS 366 Registre des fondations faites dans la communauté des Carmes de Nantes 1318–1767.

MS 1579 'Cayer concernant le consulat de Nantes 1565 – fin XVIIIè siècle'.

Collection Dugast-Matifeux:

MS 160 Ville et municipalité 1400–1787.

MS 164 Compte de Jean Caris receveur des devoirs de la prévôté de Nantes 1589–90.

Printed primary sources

Arrest de la Court de Parlement de Bretaigne contre ceulx qui faulsement usurpent le nom et le tiltre de Parlement en la ville de Nantes (Rennes, 1590).

Arrest de la Court de Parlement de Bretaigne, séant à Nantes, donné contre les hérétiques, fauteurs d'hérétiques, apriures, perfides, proditeurs de la patrie et perturbateurs du repos public (Nantes, 1590).

Articles accordez pour la Trêve générale du pays et duché de Bretagne, Anjou et Touraine (Paris, 1597).

Audren de Kerdrel, V., 'Documents inédits relatifs à l'histoire de la Ligue en Bretagne', *B.S.A.I.V.*, 2 (1861) 235–60.

Barthélemy, A. de, ed., *Choix de documents inédits sur l'histoire de la Ligue en Bretagne*, 2 vols (Nantes, 1880).

Biré, P., *Alliances Généalogicques de la Maison de Lorraine illustrées des faites et gestes des princes d'icelles* (Nantes, 1593).

Bodin, J., *Les Six Livres de la République*, trans. R. Knolles as *The Six Bookes of a Commonweale* (London, 1606).

Bruslé de Montpleinchamp, *L'histoire de Philippe-Emmanuel de Lorraine, duc de Mercoeur* (Cologne, 1689).

Carné, G. de, *Correspondance du duc de Mercoeur et des ligueurs Bretons avec l'Espagne*, 2 vols (Rennes, 1890).

Champion, P. and François, M., eds, *Lettres de Henri III, roi de France* (1959–).

Cimber, L. and Danjou, F. eds, 'L'Histoire du Tumulte d'Amboise (1560)', *Archives curieuses de l'Histoire de la France* (1835), IV, pp. 25–32.

Crespin, J., *Histoire des Martyrs Persecutez et mis à mort pour la verité de l'Évangile*, 3 vols, ed. D. Beniot (Toulouse, 1885–89).

De la Mare, N., *Traité de la Police*, 4 vols (1705).

'Documents pour servir à l'histoire de la cathédrale de Nantes', *B.S.A.H.N.L.I.*, 27 (1888) 1–364.

Dubuisson-Aubenay, 'Itinéraire de Bretagne en 1636', *Archives de Bretagne*, 10 (1902) 1–314.

Du Pré, J., *Conférences avec les ministres de Nantes en Bretaigne, Cabannes et Bourgonnière, faicte par maistre Jacques du Pré, docteur en théologie à Paris et Predicateur ordinaire de l'Église Cathédrale de S. Pierre de Nantes en juillet 1562* (1564).

Du Preau, G., *Harangue sur les causes de la guerre entreprise contre les rebelles, & séditieux, qui enforme d'hostilité ont pris les armes contre le Roy en son Royaume: & mesme des causes d'où proviennent toutes autres calamitez & misères qui journellement nous surviennent* (1562).

Du Val, A., *Mirouer des Calvinistes et armure des Chrestiens, pour rembarrser les Luthériens et nouveaux Évangelistes de Genève: Renouvellé et augmenté de la plus part, à tel signe* (1562).

Gassion, H. de, *Original des Troubles de ce Temps* (Nantes, 1592).

Geisendorf, P.-F., ed., *Livre des habitants de Genève*, 2 vols (Geneva 1957).

Isambert, F.-A., ed, *Recueil général des anciennes lois françaises depuis l'an 420 jusqu'à la Révolution de 1789*, XIV (1829).

Jouan, A., Recueil et discours du Voyage du Roy Charles IX en Bretaigne par un de ses serviteurs, 1566, ed. in Marquis d'Aubais, *Pièces fugitives pour servir à l'Histoire de France*, I (1759).

Joüon des Longrais, F. ed., 'Information du sénéchal de Rennes contre les ligueurs 1589', *B.S.A.I.V.*, 41/1 (1911) 1–90; 41/2 (1912) 191–347.

Journal du secrétaire de Philippe du Bec, evêque de Nantes puis archevêque de Reims, 1588–1605, ed. E. de Barthélemy (1865).

Le Bossu, J., *Deux Devis d'un Catholique et d'un Politique sur l'exhortation faicte au peuple de Nantes, en la grande église de Sainct-Pierre, pour jurer l'Union des catholiques, le 8e jour de juin 1589* (Nantes, 1589).

Le Bossu, J., *Troisième devis du Catholique et du Politique qui a esté réuny sur la mort de Henry de Valois, selon ce qu'en a esté presché à diverses fois en la grande église de Nantes* (Nantes, 1589).

Le Bossu, J., *Quatrième devis du Catholique et du Politique réuny, sur l'exemple de Nabuchodonosor, rapporté en l'église de Nantes, en un sermon, le dimanche 18e jour de novembre 1590* (Nantes, 1590).

Le Bossu, J., *Sermon funèbre pour l'anniversaire des Très-Illustres, Très-Magnanimes & très-Catholiques Princes feus Messeigneurs Henry & Loys de Lorraine, celuy-là duc de Guyse et cestuy-ci Cardinal de Guyse* (Nantes, 1590).

Le Bossu, J., *Sermon Funèbre pour la mémoire de dévote & religieuse personne F. Edmond Bourgoing qui fut cruellement martyrisé à Tours par le supplice de quatre chevaux le 23 de février 1590* (Nantes, 1590).

Le Maistre, R., *Original des troubles de ce temps Discourant breifvement des Princes plus Illustres de la très-ancienne et très-illustre famille de Luxembourg* (Nantes, 1592).

Le Noir, P., *Histoire ecclésiastique de Bretagne depuis la Réformation jusqu'à l'édit de Nantes*, ed. B. Varigaud (Nantes, 1851).

Lettres de Catherine de Médicis, ed. H. de la Ferrière and B. de Puchesse, 11 vols (1880–1943).

'L'Histoire du tumulte d'Amboise advenu au mois de mars 1560. Ensemble un avertissement et une complainte au peuple françois', (1560), in F.-J. Verger, ed., *Archives curieuses de la ville de Nantes et des départements de l'Ouest*, 5 vols (Nantes, 1837–41), IV, pp. 25–32.

Moranne, J. de, *Les causes qui ont contrainct les Catholiques à prendre les armes* (no publication details, 1589).

Moreau, J., *Histoire de ce qui s'est passé en Bretagne durant les guerres de la ligue* (Saint-Brieuc, 1857).

Morice, H., *Mémoires pour servir des preuves à l'histoire ecclésiastique et civile de Bretagne*, 3 vols (1742–46).

Narration sommaire de ce qui est advenu en la ville de Nantes par ceulx que l'on a prétendu conspirateurs contre la majesté du roy (1560), ed. E. Gautier (Nantes, 1860).

Ordonnance du Roy sur le faict de la Police générale de son Royaume, contentant les Articles et Reiglements que sa Majesté veult estre inviolablement gardez, suyvis & observez, tant en la ville de Paris, qu'en toutes les autres de sondict Royaume (1578).

Potter, D., ed, *The French Wars of Religion. Selected Documents* (Basingstoke, 1997).

'Privilèges de la ville de Nantes', *Archives de Bretagne*, 1 (1883) 1–207.

Remonstrance faict par Monsieur Carpentier, conseiller du roi et président en sa Cour de

Parlement de Bretagne, à l'ouverture du Parlement de la Sainct Martin 12 jour de novembre 1596 (Nantes, 1597).

Remonstrances aux habitants de Nantes Par un des Citoyens dicelle: Par où se void les practiques et menées dont a usé le duc de Mercoeur pour usurper le Duché de Bretaigne (Rennes, 1590), published in *Revue de Bretagne et du Vendée*, 27 (1883) 470–80.

Remonstrances faictes en la Court de Parlement et assemblées des Estats de Bretaigne par Monsieur Carpentier, président en ladicte court (Nantes, 1596).

Rosnyvinen, C. de, 'Histoire particulière de la Ligue en Bretagne', in Abbé Guyot-Desfontaines, ed., *Histoire des Ducs de Bretagne*, III (1739).

Russon, J., 'Brève description de la ville de Nantes en 1600 par un Tchèque de passage', *B.S.A.H.N.L.I*, 91 (1952) 136–41.

Seyssel, C. de, *La monarchie de France*, ed J. Pujol (1961).

Stegmann, A., ed., *Édits des guerres de religion* (1979).

Travers, l'Abbé, *Histoire civile, politique et réligieuse de la ville de Nantes (c.1750)*, 3 vols (Nantes, 1837).

Verger, F.-J., ed., *Archives curieuses de la ville de Nantes et des départements de l'Ouest*, 5 vols (Nantes, 1837–41).

Selected secondary works

Abad, R., *Le grand marché. L'approvisionnement alimentaire de Paris sous l'Ancien Régime* (2002).

Ascoli, P., 'A radical pamphlet of late sixteenth-century France. Le Dialogue D'Entre Le Maheustre et Le Manant', *S.C.J.*, 5 (1974) 3–22.

Barnavi, E., *Le parti de Dieu. Étude sociale et politique des chefs de la Ligue parisienne. 1585–1594* (Louvain, 1980).

Baumgartner, F., *Radical Reactionaries. The Political Thought of the French Catholic League* (Geneva, 1975).

Benedict, P., 'The Catholic response to Protestantism. Church activity and popular piety in Rouen 1560–1600', in J. Obelkevitch ed., *Religion and the People 800–1700* (Chapel Hill, 1979), pp. 169–90.

Benedict, P., *Rouen during the Wars of Religion* (Cambridge, 1981).

Benedict, P., 'Les vicissitudes des églises réformées de France jusqu'en 1598', *B.S.H.P.F.*, 144 (1998) 53–73.

Benedict, P., 'La chouette de Minerve au crépuscule. Philippe Le Noir de Crevain, pasteur sous Louis XIV, historien des églises réformées du XVIème siècle', *B.S.H.P.F.*, 146 (2000) 335–66.

Benedict, P., Marnef, G., van Nierop, H., and Venard, M., eds, *Reformation, Revolt and Civil War in France and the Netherlands 1555–1585* (Amsterdam, 1999).

Blau, P., *Exchange and Power in Social Life* (New York, 1964).

Bohanan, D., *Crown and Nobility in Early Modern France* (Basingstoke, 2001).

Bois, P., ed., *Histoire de Nantes* (Toulouse, 1977).

Bonney, R., *The King's Debts. Finance and Politics in France 1589–1661* (Oxford, 1981).

Bossy, J., 'The social history of confession in the age of the Reformation', *Transactions of the Royal Historical Society*, Fifth Series, 25 (1975) 21–38.

Bourdeaut, A., 'Le culte et les arts à Saint-Nicolas de Nantes avant le Concile de Trente', *B.S.A.H.N.L.I.*, 62 (1922) 101–43.

Bourdeaut, A., 'Le clergé paroissial dans le diocèse de Nantes avant le Concile de Trente. Les infiltrations protestantes', *B.S.A.H.N.L.I.*, 24 (1940) 90–9.

Bourquin, L., *Les nobles, la ville et le roi. L'autorité nobiliaire en Anjou pendant les guerres de religion (1560–1598)* (2001).

Braddick, M. and Walter, J., eds, *Negotiating Power in Early Modern Society* (Cambridge, 2001).

Brault, F., 'Le couvent des Cordeliers de Nantes. Étude historique (1250–1791)', *B.S.A.H.N.L.I.*, 65 (1925) 165–92.

Brunelle, G., 'Contractual kin. Servants and their mistresses in sixteenth-century Nantes', *Journal of Early Modern History*, 2 (1998) 374–94.

Cameron, K., Greengrass, M., and Roberts, P., eds, *The Adventure of Religious Pluralism in Early Modern France* (Bern, 2000).

Cardot, C.-A., 'Le parlement de la Ligue en Bretagne, 1589–98', 3 vols, Thèse de Droit, Rennes, 1964.

Carluer, J.-Y., 'Deux synodes provinciaux bretons au XVIème siècle', *B.S.H.P.F.*, 135 (1989) 329–51.

Carroll, S., *Noble Power during the French Wars of Religion. The Guise Affinity and the Catholic Cause in Normandy* (Cambridge, 1998).

Cassan, M., 'Laïcs, Ligue et réforme catholique à Limoges', *Histoire économie et société*, 10 (1991) 159–75.

Cassan, M., *Le temps des guerres de religion. Le cas du Limousin (vers 1530–vers 1630)* (1996).

Chevalier, B., *Les bonnes villes de France du XIVème au XVIème siècle* (1982).

Chevallier, P., *Henri III, roi shakespearien* (1985).

Christin, O., *Le paix de religion. L'autonomisation de la raison politique au XVIème siècle* (1997).

Church, W., *Constitutional Thought in Sixteenth-Century France. A Study in the Evolution of Ideas* (Cambridge, MA, 1941).

Collins, J., *Classes, Estates and Order in Early Modern Brittany* (Cambridge, 1994).

Conner, P., 'Huguenot Heartland. Montauban during the Wars of Religion', PhD thesis, University of St Andrews, 2000.

Constant, J.-M., *Les français pendant les guerres de religion* (2002).

Cornette, J., ed., *La monarchie entre Renaissance et Révolution 1515–1792* (2000).

Croix, A., 'Deux notes sur Nantes', *Annales de démographie historique*, (1970) 143–9.

Croix, A., *Nantes et le pays nantais au XVIème siècle. Étude démographique* (1974).

Croix, A., *La Bretagne aux XVIème et XVIIème siècles. La vie – la mort – la foi*, 2 vols (1981).

Croix, A., *L'âge d'or de la Bretagne 1532–1675* (Rennes, 1993).

Crouzet, D., *Les guerriers de Dieu. La violence au temps des troubles de religion (c.1525–c.1610)*, 2 vols (1990).

Davis, B., 'Reconstructing the poor in early sixteenth-century Toulouse', *F.H.*, 7 (1993) 249–85.

Davis, N. Z., *Society and Culture in Early Modern France* (Stanford, CA, 1975).

De Carné, M., *Les états de Bretagne et l'administration de ce province jusqu'en 1789*, 2 vols (1868).

Delumeau, J., *Le catholicisme entre Luther et Voltaire* (1971).

Descimon, R., *Qui étaient les Seize? Mythes et réalités de la Ligue parisienne (1585–94)* (1983).

Descimon, R., 'Paris on the eve of St. Bartholomew. Taxation, privilege and social geography', in P. Benedict, ed., *Cities and Social Change in Early Modern France* (London, 1989), pp. 69–104.

Descimon, R., 'Milice bourgeoise et identité citadine à Paris au temps de la Ligue', *A.E.S.C.*, 48 (1993) 885–906.

Deyon, P., *L'état face au pouvoir local* (1996).

Diefendorf, B., 'Simon Vigor. A radical preacher in sixteenth-century Paris', *S.C.J.*, 18 (1987) 399–410.

Diefendorf, B., *Beneath the Cross. Catholics and Huguenots in Sixteenth-Century Paris* (Oxford, 1991).

Drouot, H., *Mayenne et la Bourgogne. Étude sur la Ligue (1587–96)*, 2 vols (Dijon, 1937).

Duby, G., ed, *L'histoire de la France urbaine*, 5 vols (1980–85).

Dugast-Matifeux, M., *Nantes ancien et le pays nantais* (Nantes, 1879).

Duplessis, R., *Lille and the Dutch Revolt. Urban Stability in an Era of Revolution 1500–1582* (Cambridge, 1991).

Duplessis, R., and Howell, M., 'Reconsidering the early modern urban economy. The cases of Leiden and Lille', *Past & Present*, 94 (1982) 44–84.

Durand, Y.. ed., *Le diocèse de Nantes* (1985).

Durville, G., *Études sur le vieux Nantes, d'après les documents originaux*, 2 vols (Nantes, 1901–15).

Durville, G., *Le chapitre de l'église de Nantes. Aperçu sur son histoire du VIIème siècle au Concordat* (Nantes, 1907).

Durville, G., *L'ancienne confrérie de Saint-Sacrement à Nantes* (Nantes, 1909).

Elwood, C., *The Body Broken* (Oxford, 1999).

Fardet, M., 'La vie municipale à Nantes sous le gouvernement du duc de Mercoeur. Le rôle militaire joué par cette ville (1582–1598)', Thèse, École des Chartres, Paris, 1965.

Fardet, M., 'L'assistance aux pauvres à Nantes à la fin du XVIème siècle (1582–1598)', *Actes du 98ème congrès national des sociétés savantes, Nantes 1972*, Section Philologie et Histoire (1973), pp. 383–425.

Farr, J., 'Popular religious solidarity in sixteenth-century Dijon', *F.H.S.*, 14 (1985) 192–214.

Farr, J., *Authority and Sexuality in Early Modern Burgundy 1550–1730* (Oxford, 1995).

Febvre, L., 'Une question mal posée. Les origines de la Réforme française et le problème général des causes de la Réforme', *R.H.*, 141 (1929) 1–73.

Finley-Croswhite, S. A., *Henry IV and the Towns. The Pursuit of Legitimacy in French Urban Society, 1589–1610* (Cambridge, 1999).

Foucault, M., *Discipline and Punish* (Harmondsworth, 1977).

Friedrichs, C., *Urban Politics in Early Modern Europe* (London, 2000).

Galpern, A., *The Religions of the People in Sixteenth-Century Champagne* (Cambridge, MA, 1976).

Gascon, R., *Grand commerce et vie urbaine au XVIème siècle: Lyon et ses marchands (environ 1520 – environ 1580)*, 2 vols (1971).

Giesey, R., 'Models of rulership in French royal ceremonial', in S. Wilentz, ed., *Rites of Power* (Philadelphia, 1985), pp. 41–64.

Giraud-Mangin, M., 'La bibliothèque de l'archidiacre Le Gallo au XVIème siècle', *B.S.A.H.N.L.I.* 76 (1937) 105–20.

Goodbar, R., ed., *The Edict of Nantes. Five Essays and a New Translation* (Bloomington, MN, 1998).

Granges de Surgères, M. de, 'Fondations pieuses à Nantes 1549–1691', *B.S.A.H.N.L.I.*, 24 (1885) 29–69.

Greengrass, M., *The French Reformation* (Oxford, 1987).

Greengrass, M., *France in the Age of Henri IV* (London, 2nd ed., 1995).

Grégoire, L., *La Ligue en Bretagne* (Paris and Nantes, 1856).

Grell, O., 'The religious duty of care and the social need for control in early modern Europe', *The Historical Journal*, 39 (1996) 257–63.

Grell, O. and Scribner, B., eds, *Tolerance and Intolerance in the European Reformation* (Cambridge, 1996).

Harding, R., *Anatomy of a Power Elite. The Provincial Governors of Early Modern France* (New Haven, 1978).

Harding, R., 'Revolution and reform in the Holy League. Angers, Rennes, Nantes', *J.M.H.*, 53 (1981) 379–416.

Hardwick, J., *The Practice of Patriarchy. Gender and the Politics of Household Authority in Early Modern France* (University Park, Pennsylvania, 1998).

Hauser, H., *Études sur la Réforme française* (1909).

Heller, H., *The Conquest of Poverty. The Calvinist Revolt in Sixteenth-Century France* (Leiden, 1986).

Henshall, N., *The Myth of Abolutism* (London, 1992).

Hickey, D., *The Coming of French Absolutism. The Struggle for Tax Reform in the Province of Dauphiné 1540–1640* (Toronto, 1986).

Hoffman, P., *Church and Community in the Diocese of Lyon 1500–1789* (Ithaca, 1984).

Hoffman, P., 'Early modern France, 1450–1700', in P. Hoffman and K. Norberg, eds, *Fiscal Crises, Liberty and Representative Government 1450–1789* (Stanford, 1994), pp. 226–52.

Holt, M., 'Putting religion back into the wars of religion', *F.H.S.*, 18 (1993) 524–51.

Holt, M., 'Burgundians into Frenchmen. Catholic identity in sixteenth-century Burgundy', in M. Wolfe, ed., *Changing Identities in Early Modern France* (Durham NC, 1997), pp. 345–70.

Holt, M., 'Wine, community and Reformation in sixteenth-century Burgundy', *Past & Present*, 138 (1993) 58–93.

Holt, M., *The French Wars of Religion 1562–1629* (Cambridge, 1995).

Höpfl, H. and Thompson, M., 'The history of contract as a motif in political thought', *A.H.R.*, 84 (1979) 919–44.

Jarnoux, A., *Le diocèse de Nantes au XVIème siècle 1500–1600. Étude historique* (1976).

Jarnoux, A., *Les anciennes paroisses de Nantes*, 2 vols (Nantes, 1982).

Jeulin, P., *L'évolution du port de Nantes. Organisation et trafic depuis les origines* (1929).

Jeulin, P., 'Aperçus sur la Contractation de Nantes 1530 environ – 1733', *A.B.*, 40 (1932–33) 284–331, 457–505.

Joüon des Longrais, F., 'Le duc de Mercoeur, d'après des documents inédits', *B.A.A.B.*, 13 (1895) 214–93.

Jouanna, A., *La France du XVIème siècle* (1996).

Joxe, R., *Les protestants du comté de Nantes XVIème–XVIIème siècles* (Marseille, 1982).

Kaiser, W., *Marseille au temps des troubles 1559–96. Morphologie sociale et luttes de factions* (1992).

Kaplan, S., *Provisioning Paris. Merchants and Millers in the Grain and Flour Trade during the Eighteenth Century* (Ithaca, 1984).

Kettering, S., 'Clientage during the wars of religion', *S.C.J.*, 20 (1989) 221–39.

Kettering, S., 'Patronage in early modern France', *F.H.S.*, 17 (1992) 839–62.

Kettering, S., 'Political parties at Aix-en-Provence in 1589', *European History Quarterly*, 24 (1994) 181–211.

Kettering, S., *Patronage in Sixteenth- and Seventeenth-Century France* (Aldershot, 2002).

Kingdon, R., *Geneva and the Coming of the Wars of Religion in France, 1555–1563* (Geneva, 1956).

Knecht, R., *Catherine de' Medici* (London, 1998).

Knecht, R., *The French Civil Wars* (London, 2000).

Konnert, M., 'Urban values versus religious passions. Châlons-sur-Marne during the wars of religion', *S.C.J.*, 20 (1989) 387–405.

Lapeyre, H., *Une famille des marchands. Les Ruiz* (1955).

Laronze, C., *Essai sur le régime municipale en Bretagne pendant les guerres de religion* (1890).

Leboucq, K., 'L'administration provinciale à l'époque des guerres de religion. Henri III, François d'O et le gouvernement de Basse-Normandie (1579–1588)', *R.H*, 298/2 (1998) 345–408.

Le Gall, J.-M., 'Les Guises et Paris sous la Ligue 1588–90', *F.H.S.*, 24 (2001) 157–84.

Le Méné, M., 'L'hospitalisation à l'Hôtel-Dieu à Nantes (décembre 1537 – juillet 1539)', *Université de Nantes. Enquêts et documents*, 4 (1978) 11–21.

Lukes, S., ed., *Power* (Oxford, 1986).

Maitre, L., *L'assistance publique dans la Loire-Inférieure avant 1789. Étude sur les leproseries, aumôneries, hôpitaux-généraux et bureaux de charité* (Nantes, 1879).

Maitre, L., *L'instruction publique dans les villes et les campagnes du pays nantais avant 1789* (Nantes, 1882).

Major, J. R., *The Monarchy, the Estates and the Aristocracy in Renaissance France* (London, 1988).

Major, J. R., *From Renaissance Monarchy to Absolute Monarchy. French Kings, Nobles and Estates* (Baltimore, 1994).

Maréjol, H.-J., *La Réforme et la Ligue. L'édit de Nantes (1559–1598)* (1904).

Mellinet, C., *La commune et la milice de Nantes*, 3 vols (Nantes, 1836–44).

Mentzer, R. and Spicer, A., eds, *Society and Culture in the Huguenot World* (Cambridge, 2002).

Meyer, J., 'Le commerce nantais au XVIème siècle. Tentative de mise en situation', in P. Masson and M. Vergé-Franceschi, eds, *La France et la mer au siècle des grandes découvertes* (1993), pp. 91–125.

Miller, J., 'Politics and urban provisioning crises. Bakers, police and parlements in France, 1750–1793', *J.M.H.*, 64 (1992) 227–62.

Morice, H. and Taillandier, C., *Histoire ecclésiastique et civile de Bretagne*, 3 vols (1756; reprinted 1974).

Muchembled, R., *L'invention de la France moderne. Monarchie, culture et société (1500–1660)* (2002).

Nassiet, M., 'Brittany and the French monarchy in the sixteenth century. The evidence of the letters of remission', *F.H.*, 17 (2003) 425–39.

Nicholls, D., 'The social history of the French Reformation. Ideology, confession and culture', *Social History*, 9 (1984) 25–43.

Nicholls, D., 'Looking for the origins of the French Reformation', in C. Allmand, ed., *Power, Culture and Religion in France c.1350–c.1550* (Woodbridge, 1989), pp. 131–44.

Nicholls, D., 'Protestants, Catholics and magistrates in Tours, 1562–72. The making of a Catholic city during the religious wars', *F.H.*, 8 (1994) 14–33.

Parsons, J., 'Governing sixteenth-century France. The monetary reforms of 1577', *F.H.S.*, 26 (2003) 1–30.

Pelus, M.-L., 'Marchands et échevins d'Amiens dans la seconde moitié du XVIème siècle. Crise de subsistances, commerce et profits en 1586–1587', *Revue du Nord*, 64 (1982) 51–71.

Pelus-Kaplan, M.-L., 'Amiens, ville ligueuse. Le sens d'une rébellion', *Revue du Nord*, 78 315 (1996) 289–303.

Pettegree, A., Nelles, P. and Conner, P., eds, *The Sixteenth-Century Religious Book* (Aldershot, 2001).

Pied, E., *Les anciens corps d'arts et métiers de Nantes*, 3 vols (Nantes, 1903).

Planiol, M., *Histoire des institutions de la Bretagne*, V: *Le XVIème siecle* (1895; reprinted Mayenne, 1984).

Pocquet, B., *Histoire de Bretagne*, V: 1515–1715 (Rennes, 1913; reprinted Mayenne, 1975).

Potter, D., *War and Government in the French Provinces. Picardy 1470–1560* (Cambridge, 1993).

Prak, M., 'The carrot and the stick. Social control and poor relief in the Dutch Republic, sixteenth to eighteenth centuries', in H. Schilling, ed., *Institutions, Instruments and Agents of Social Control and Discipline in Early Modern Europe* (Frankfurt am Main, 1999), pp. 149–66.

Racaut, L., *Hatred in Print. Catholic Propaganda and Protestant Identity during the French Wars of Religion* (Aldershot, 2002).

Randall, A. and Charlesworth, A. eds, *Moral Economy and Popular Protest. Crowds, Conflict and Authority* (Basingstoke, 2000).

Richet, D., 'Aspects socio-culturels des conflits religieux à Paris dans la seconde moitié du XVIème siècle', *A.E.S.C.*, 32 (1977) 764–89.

Richet, D., *De la Réforme à la Révolution. Études sur la France moderne* (1991).

Robbins, K., *City on the Ocean Sea. La Rochelle 1530–1650* (Leiden, 1997).

Roberts, P., *A City in Conflict. Troyes During the French Wars of Religion* (Manchester, 1996).

Roberts, P., 'The most crucial battle of the wars of religion? The conflict over sites for Reformed worship in sixteenth-century France', *Archiv für Reformationgeschichte*, 89 (1998) 247–66.

Roelker, N., *One King, One Faith. The Parlement of Paris and the Religious Reformations of the Sixteenth Century* (Berkeley, 1996).

Romier, L., *Les origines politiques des guerres de religion*, 2 vols (Paris, 1913–14).

Rubin, M., *Corpus Christi. The Eucharist in Late Medieval Culture* (Cambridge, 1991).

Salmon, J., 'The Paris Sixteen, 1584–1594. The social analysis of a revolutionary movement', *J.M.H.*, 46 (1972) 540–76.

Salmon, J., *Society in Crisis. France in the Sixteenth Century* (London, 1976; pbk 1979).

Saupin, G., *Nantes au XVIIème siècle. Vie politique et société urbaine* (Rennes, 1996).

Saupin, G., *Nantes au temps de l'édit* (La Crèche, 1998).

Sauzet, R., ed., *Henri III et son temps* (1992).

Schneider, R., *Public Life in Toulouse 1463–1789. From Municipal Republic to Cosmopolitan City* (Ithaca, 1989).

Sée, H., 'Les états de Bretagne au XVIème siècle', *A.B*, 10 (1894) 3–38, 189–207, 365–93.

Skinner, Q., *The Foundations of Modern Political Thought*, II: *The Reformation* (Cambridge, 1978).

Souriac, R., *Décentralisation administrative dans l'Ancienne France. Autonomie commingeoise et pouvoir d'état 1540–1640*, 2 vols (Toulouse, 1992).

Stegmann, A., 'Transformations administratives et opinion publique en France (1560–1580)', *Francia*, 9 (1980) 594–612.

Sutherland, N., *The Huguenot Struggle for Recognition* (New Haven, 1980).

Tallon, A., *La France et le Concile de Trent, 1518–1563* (Rome, 1997).

Tanguy, J., *Le commerce du port de Nantes au milieu du XVIème siècle* (1956).

Taylor, L., *Soldiers of Christ. Preaching in Late Medieval and Reformation France* (Oxford, 1992).

Travers, L'Abbé, *Histoire civile, politique et réligieuse de la ville de Nantes*, 3 vols (written c.1750; Nantes, 1837).

Thompson, E. P., *Customs in Common*, (London, 1991), pp. 187–258.

Vailhen, J., 'Le conseil des bourgeois de Nantes', 3 vols, Thèse du Doctorat, University of Rennes, 1965.

Varigaud, B., *Essai sur l'histoire des églises réformées de Bretagne (1535–1808)*, 3 vols (1870–71).

Venard, M. ed., *Le temps des confessions 1530–1620/3* (1992).

Venard, M., *Le catholicisme à l'épreuve dans la France du XVIème siècle* (2000).

Watson, T., 'The Lyon City Council c.1525–1575. Politics, Culture, Religion', D.Phil. thesis, University of Oxford, 1999.

Watson, T., 'Friends at court. The correspondence of the Lyon city council c. 1525–1575', *F.H*, 13 (1999) 280–302.

Wolfe, M., *The Fiscal System of Renaissance France* (New Haven, 1972).

Wolfe, M., *The Conversion of Henri IV* (Cambridge, MA, 1993).

Wrong, D., *Power. Its Forms and Uses* (Oxford, 1979).

Zeller, O., *Les recensements lyonnais de 1597 et 1637. Démographie historique et géographie sociale* (Lyon, 1983).

Index